Poland, A Unique Country & Its People

by

Alicja Deck-Partyka

Bloomington, IN

authorHOUSE™

Milton Keynes, UK

AuthorHouse™
1663 Liberty Drive, Suite 200
Bloomington, IN 47403
www.authorhouse.com
Phone: 1-800-839-8640

AuthorHouse™ UK Ltd.
500 Avebury Boulevard
Central Milton Keynes, MK9 2BE
www.authorhouse.co.uk
Phone: 08001974150

First published by AuthorHouse 6/8/2006

ISBN: 1-4259-1838-7 (sc)
ISBN: 1-4259-1839-5 (hc)

Library of Congress Control Number: 2006901605

Printed in the United States of America
Bloomington, Indiana

This book is printed on acid-free paper.

Jadwiga, King of Poland, a black & white photo of painting of Polish painter, Jan Matejko (1838-1893). This picture is in public domain.

Hussar ("Winged Horsemen") photo compliments of Chevalier Rik Sulima-Suligowski Fox, Guildmaster of the Polish Nobility Commonwealth Guild.

Black Madonna photo compliments of Mr. Darrell L. Peck, http://www.darrellpeck.com/travel/1998-east-europe/images/043-madonna.jpg

Salt Statue of John Paul II in Wieliczka Salt Mine photo compliments of Donna M. Kocinski from New Berlin, WI at website http://www.exchangezones.com/page258.htm

This book is dedicated to my Grandmother,
Katherina Partyka; my Mother,
Sophia M. Deck and my favorite aunt,
Mary Partyka
for their love and encouragement
to be proud of my Polish heritage.

Table of Contents

ECONOMY

CULTURE

APPENDIX

INTRODUCTION

Poland, because of its location and geography, has been an area of conflict throughout its long and turbulent history. It has had periods of greatness, independence and prosperity alternated with phases of foreign domination and disaster during which its boundaries and people have been divided by conquering nations. Despite this, culture flourished within the country and Poland was one of the most active countries during the Renaissance with some religious and social laws many countries today still do not have. The Sejm voted the monarchs of Poland into power beginning in 1572, which became an important step for political progress in Europe. On May 3, 1791, Poland adopted Europe's first democratic constitution -- the world's second after the American Constitution.

As a country that has fought to survive and fend off a succession of occupiers since its formation in 966 AD, Poland has become a nation that values pride, tenacity and perseverance. It is unique because it is the only country to cease to exist on the maps of the world because of foreign domination and occupation and successfully come back as a free, democratic country. The Polish people are unique because of their ability to persevere through adversity and still maintain their love of freedom and strong feeling of nationalism.

The Catholic Church has been significant part of Polish national identity since the country's conversion to Christianity in 966 AD. During the period of the partitions, the church symbolized and defended this national identity. The church, together with underground resistance, once again represented Poland's national identity during World War II. After the consolidation of a Soviet-dominated communist system in 1948, the church was the only independent institution in Poland. It enjoyed massive support not only from the intelligentsia but also from the bulk of the population because it was part of Polish national identity and opposed communism.

Prior to 1989, Poland was struggling to keep a democratic spirit alive under the yoke of the Soviet Union. Today, as the oldest of Eastern Europe's new democracies, it's nurturing a growing economy. Poland submitted its application for acceptance into the European Union to the European Commission in 1994. In 1999 Poland joined NATO and joined the EU in May 2004.

HISTORY

SETTLEMENT OF THE SLAVS

The ancient aboriginal Slavs were an obscure group of farmers and herders living in the marshes and woodlands of what is now eastern Poland. The earliest traces of man from 180,000 BC was found in the Ojcow Caves near Kracow. From the end of the Neolithic Age (about 2,000 BC) the Slavs occupied all of the Vistula River basin as well as most of the Oder River basin in addition to their eastern settlements between the Pripet Marshes and the Black Sea.

Polish archaeologists uncovered the remains of a Bronze Age fort at Biskupin in Wielkopolska (greater Poland). This fortress was built on a peninsula that went into Lake Biskupin. The settlement was about 5 acres in size and surrounded by a wooden, box-type fence about 20 feet high by 10 feet wide. There was a breakwater on the lakeside about 23 feet wide with a 26-foot gateway (causeway) that allowed main access from the landside. The structure was built to protect the community from enemy raids and wild animals. The village contained approximately 100 homes with thatched roofs of longhouse form.

The people of Biskupin were from the Wingfield culture (an ancient Slavonic people) and were both agricultural and industrial. They raised pigs, cattle, oxen, sheep and goats, hunted deer and wild boar and grew crops of wheat, barley, millet and pulses. The inhabitants of Biskupin were the first, on Polish land, to use oxen for ploughing the land and harvested crops with scythes made of bronze and later iron. When citizens of Biskupin died, they were cremated and their bones buried in urns across the lake. Archaeological evidence suggests that the inhabitants were clothworkers and leatherworkers. Glass and amber beads from the Baltic Sea were discovered suggesting trade routes. Pottery, stone, metal and wood found helped date the site to around 700 BC. Evidence of metalworking on some of the buildings was also found. The settlement was abandoned at the beginning of the 5th Century.

In the first Century of Christ, the Carpathians and the Vistula became the cradle of the Slavs from where they spread in all directions. From about 150 AD, the Slavic tribes expanded north along the rivers of Russia and occupied territory populated by Finnish and Baltic people many of which they absorbed. To the west, they encountered Germanic and Celtic tribes.

Three main geographical and linguistic divisions that had evolved by 800 AD were:

1. The East Slavs who inhabited a large part of European Russia;
2. The South Slavs who settled in the Balkan Peninsula; and
3. The West Slavs who settled in what is now Poland, Czechoslavakia and East Germany.

The West Slavs suffered different fates; the Lusatians and Veleti were absorbed by German expansion, the Czechs and Moravians merged to form the Czech Kingdom and the Slovaks became part of the kingdom of Hungary. The Polanie, Wislanie, Pomorzanie and the Mazovians tribes, joined together (in time) to form the Polish State.

The Teutons who pushed the Slavs to the east very early annihilated the westernmost outposts of the Slavs. The Slavic tribes called the Polanie who lived along the Warthe, Oder, and Netze Rivers halted this early German invasion. They were a strong sturdy race; predominately agricultural whose extensive and fertile lands reclaimed from primitive forests stretched along a great chain of lakes and rivers which made possible interchange among the tribes. As a result, they attained a high economic and social structure and it was in this region that the nucleus of the Polish Nation was formed.

Though somewhat differing in civilization, the tribes of the Polish Nation were alike in their social, moral and religious ideas. They were scattered in large clans with the lands belonging to a clan held in common. However, there existed private belongings especially in tools. From their early history, the Polish Slavs exhibited strong individualistic characteristics. A popular assembly called "Wiec" to which all male adults of the community belonged decided important matters. The dowry system was very important to the Slavs. They were especially energetic in agriculture and traded on land and sea to the Ruthenians and to Constantinople.

The pre-Christian Slavs were not literate and left no written records about their culture and religion. Like all primitive peoples, they deified the forces and phenomena of nature. One feature of the Slavic religion was the calmness and serenity of the Slavic gods that emphasized the peaceful character of the Slavs. They believed in the immortality of soul and in an afterworld with punishment and reward. The dead were objects of care and funerals were very elaborate.

When the migratory movements had ended, there appeared among the Slavs the first rudiments of state organizations; each headed by a prince with a treasury and defense force, and the beginning of class differentiation. Due to frequent raids of the Norsemen, the people of this region organized an effective military force of defense. Under the protection of the military bands, the fields could be cultivated safely and the little, fortified towns became places where:

- Intertribal business and barter could be transacted;
- Common worship;
- Storage of goods during a foreign invasion could be defended;
- Wrongs of the people could be redressed.

The military bands and their leaders became the unifying force and the fortified towns became centers of a larger political organization.

The first historical town of this nature was Kruszwica on Lake Goplo. The change in the political organization of the primitive Polanie tribe is attributed to the influence of foreign commerce centered on Lake Goplo. In the jungles of the Vistula lived the most savage of the Polish tribes, the Mazurs. This tribe was the last to come under the sovereignty of the principality that began its political existence on the bank of Goplo Lake under the leadership of the wheelwright Piast, whose dynasty ruled the country until 1370.

EARLY HISTORY

National custom identifies the starting date of Polish history as 966 AD when Prince Mieszko accepted Christianity. This strategy inaugurated the intimate connection between the Polish national identity and the Roman Catholic Church that became a prominent theme in the history of Poland. The adoption of Christianity in Poland was important in several ways:

- Diplomatic - Poland was recognized as an independent state in Europe.
- Political - Church administration was an example to follow by the newly established state administration.
- Economical - Clergymen brought new technologies and new ideas in agriculture and handcrafting from western countries. Polish culture, economy and technology developed independently.

In the first centuries of its existence, Poland was led by a series of strong rulers who created a strong Central European country and integrated Poland into European culture.

During the period of Federative State (1138-1306), Poland was divided into regions ruled by princes from the royal family. One of them, usually the prince residing in Krakow, was formally a supreme prince with little executive power over the others. In 1226, Konrad Mazowiecki brought the Teutonic Order to Poland to Christianize and fight against the Prussians. The Teutonic Order took Gdansk and Central Pomerania in 1308 and the war continued until peace treaty with the Teutonic Order at Kalisz in 1343.

At the beginning of the 14th Century, formidable foreign enemies had much of Poland under foreign occupation. As a result of the Union between Poland and Lithuania which was concluded at Krewo in 1385, the Poland-Lithuania alliance was ranked as one of the leading powers of the continent for the next 400 years and exerted a major influence on the history of Eastern Europe. Various ethnic groups and religions inhabited the land, which compelled the rulers to be completely tolerant and guarantee rights to all inhabitants irrespective of their descent or religion. It was an era of stability, affluence and cultural advancement unmatched Poland's history and regarded by Poles as their country's "Golden Era".

When the Polish Republic was founded, Poland was the world's only major country that was a republic until the founding of the United States. It had a larger number of voting citizens than the United States did 200 years later at the time of the Declaration of Independence in 1776. During the First Republic of Poland, noblemen elected the kings and usually the elections were for life-long term of office. Several of the kings elected during this period had goals of the Swedish crown and involved Poland in war with Sweden, Russia and the Turks.

After Sweden invaded Poland in 1655, the cruelty of the Swedish soldiers caused a strong reaction by Poles of all classes. The peasants, armed with scythes, sickles and flails, began guerilla warfare. The local armed attempts evolved into provincial armies that became united by an act of confederation. The devastation caused by the Swedish soldiers and their desecration of Catholic churches, the successful defense of Czestochowa and the final defeat of the Swedish forces, all contributed to the rise of religious fervor and fanaticism in Poland and the identification of Catholicism with patriotism. The future history of Poland further realized the combination of these two conceptions.

POLISH NOBILITY

The nobility of Poland was particularly unique both in its structure and privileges. From ancient times until the Third Partition in 1795, with the exception of those families who held the title of Prince, there was only one class of nobility in Poland - *szlachta*. The Polish system of nobility was based on the principles of equality among an exclusive group of peers who had earned their spurs in battle. Poland's ancient code of chivalry forbade the bearing of titles and the formation of chivalric orders was looked upon with contempt. Both were regarded as a means of creating division among a group of equals.

The Polish Nobility began when the Poles were in an early stage of social development and the clan was the basic unit of social structure. Each clan had its own mark that later evolved into the symbols found on Polish coats of arms. With the introduction of tokens of office, whole clans were admitted to nobility. Although possession of land was not a prerequisite to a title of nobility, those of the nobility who were landowners enjoyed special privileges. These privileges included exemption from taxation, exemption from confiscation without due process of law and access to the highest-ranking civil and spiritual offices. Of great importance is the fact that, although polish society had originally evolved from clan structures and the later introduction of Christianity, the feudal system was <u>never</u> introduced in Poland.

Even though the szlachta (nobility) inherited both status and land, they were required to perform military service for the king and to submit to his tribunals. Polish nobles initially divided their estates equally to their sons and unmarried daughters but when this resulted in loss of wealth in later generations, the system changed to the eldest male inheriting who was obligated to serve in the military. Nobles were unique because there was no strong feelings about intermarriage, bastardy or miscegenation - only that the children of these irregular unions could not claim nobility.

In early Poland, the Church was the most influential social institution and a measure of the actual progress and unity of Poland's development. It exercised considerable control over the administration of the state, created schools, encouraged the fine arts and was a close friend of the King. However, by the 12th and 13th Century, the nobility began to monopolize Poland's cultural development.

By the 12th Century, a new style of clans emerged which was based on patronage called *rod klientarny* (clan of clients). The role of patron was played by the king or by prominent knights (landowners). The emergence of szlachta as a distinct class was well advanced by the reign of Kazimierz, the Great (1333-1370) but the process of strengthening and codifying its legal privileges continued until the 16th Century when the nobility became a closed society.

The noble pedigree and the coat of arms have always been regarded, as much more valuable than land estates because becoming a member of the hereditary szlachta with all its privileges was very difficult. The following is a list of some of the more important privileges of the szlachta that were the backbone of the concept of Nobel Democracy:

- <u>Statute of Czerwinsk (1422)</u> - An act was passed which protected a nobleman's land and property from the Crown's seizure unless a sentence is passed against him in a court of law.
- <u>Statute of Jedlino (1430)</u> - A law was passed protecting noblemen from arrest unless sentence is passed against him in a court of law, known in Latin as *Neminem captivabimus nisi iure vicum* (no one who has not been convicted can be imprisoned). This is similar in principle to *Habeas Corpus*.
- <u>Statute of Niexzawa (1454)</u> - The King concedes that

no new tax will be levied nor army raised without the consent of the new noble seymik (a meeting, at which all nobles of the district could join in discussion, vote and choose delegates to the noble assembly called Sejm). The principle of government by consensus derives its origin from the times of early Polish Kings. By the 13th Century, the Sejm played a major role in governing the provinces and later of the entire country.

- Nihil Novi Constitution of Radom (1505) - The Sejm passes a constitution of *nibil novi nisi commune consensu* that proclaims that no new laws can be introduced without consent of both the Sejm and the Senate.

The Nihil Novi Constitution marked an end to the evolution of the clan system and szlachta became a separate, closed, hereditary class that jealously guarded its rights, privileges and the means of access. In addition to being very powerful, Polish nobility also was quite numerous. By the 16th Century, there were approximately 2,500 noble families including at least half a million people.

On the basis of significant differences in wealth, the socioeconomic structure of szlachta was divided into several groups:

1. Magnates - Very wealthy and influential families who controlled the key offices of the state and were strongly represented in the senate. This group, as a whole, exercised power and influence disproportionate to its numbers.
2. Wealthy Nobles (owners of both land and serfs) - Even though the size of wealth varied, the nobleman owned his living to no-one if he held two or three properties as well as serfs to work on them. This middle nobility made up about 40% of all Polish nobility.
3. Noble small-holders - Nobles families of this group owned land but not serfs and had to work the land

themselves.

4. Rent-paying Nobles - These Nobles were tenants or leaseholders of their more prosperous countrymen. This group was the most numerous.
5. Nobles performing menial duties - Nobles in this group held positions of responsibility at estates belonging to magnates or wealthy nobles.

The position of szlachta within the above groups was not constant. Fortunes increased and decreased according to individual situations and abilities of the families. In addition, szlachta had its own culture and its own value system. Since szlachta was so large, its prevailing culture and etiquette influenced many areas of life and was accepted by other social classes. Some aspects of this influence can be seen among present-day Poles.

Knighthood:

Although brotherhoods of knights existed in Poland during its earliest formative years, these brotherhoods existed to pursue very specific and limited goals and, when the objectives were achieved, the brotherhoods were disbanded. During and after the crusades, foreign crusading orders were introduced in Poland but they never achieved popularity and eventually disappeared shortly after the partitions.

There were several attempts by Polish Kings to establish orders of knighthood such as the Order of the White Eagle instituted by King Wladyslaw V in 1325. But formal orders of knighthood were extremely unpopular among the Polish nobility and prohibited by law from the mid-17th Century since such orders were perceived as a corruption of the ancient principles of equality among all members of the szlachia class. As a result of open hostility of the nobility, the Order slowly disappeared.

When August II reinstated the Order of the White Eagle in 1704 in an effort to unify the nobility against foreign powers, the Polish nobility accepted it. In 1765, King Stanislaw Augustus created the Order of Saint Stanislaw and in 1792 established the Order of Virtuti Civili and the Order of Virtuti Militari, which today is the best known and most coveted of all Polish decorations. In fact, by 1790 orders of knighthood became so sought after that young nobles had to secure an Order of Chivalry before they could hope to rise through the socio-political hierarchy. The partitions signaled the decline of this distinction of noble status as many of the Polish orders were abolished for political reasons.

POLISH KINGS & RULING PRINCES

Although Monarchs and Kings ruled Poland as early as 550 AD , the political history of Poland beginning with the introduction of Christianity to the end of the 17th Century revolved around the relationship of the Polish Kings to the German Emperors. The rulers of Poland recognized the German Emperor only when the Germans were able to force them to do so. As soon as events broke-down the power of the German Empire, Poland immediately tried to secure emancipation.

Early Monarchy - Piast Dynasty

Mieczyslaw I (922-992)
The first historic ruler of Poland and founder of the Piast dynasty, he united several western Slavonic tribes under his rule in 963 and consolidated his power by marrying the Bohemian princess, Dobrava. His major achievement was the adoption of Christianity in 966, which shaped Poland's history through the 20th Century. As a result, Poland was brought into the European political system and established relations with the greatest powers of that period. He died in 992 and was buried in Poznan.

Boleslaw Chroby I (967-1025)
The first king of Poland, he was crowned in 992 and reunited the country after his father's death. After declaring Poland independent of the Holy Roman Empire, he embarked on a vigorous program of expansion. In 1003, he conquered Lusatia and Meissen in the west and in 1018 invaded the East Slavic state of Kievan Rus. Boleslav continued his father's support of Christianity and made the Polish church independent and established Gniezno as an archbishopric. He was also instrumental in having Bishop Adalbert canonized in 999, the patron saint of Poland. In 1138, his Will shattered the precarious unity of Poland by dividing the country among his sons. This was the start of 150 years of dynastic struggle in which the

Church played a vital role in maintaining some appearance of national unity.

Mieczyslaw II Lambert (990-1034)
He became king in 1038 under the will of his father but his brothers opposed his father's decision and in their struggle against Mieczyslaw solicited support from a German-Rus coalition. During his reign, Bohemia captured Moravia, Germany occupied Lusatie, Denmark entered Pomerania and Rus recovered Grody Czerwienskie. Poland was collapsing. Meanwhile, his wife Richeza left Poland clandestinely and took the royal insignia with her to Germany. In 1033, Mieszko resigned from the crown and his death a year later was followed by a civil war.

Kazimierz I Odnowiciel (1016-1058)
When he failed to take control of the country, he was exiled in 1037. Shortly after, Bohemia invaded Poland, sacked Poznan and Gniezno, stole the relics of Adalbert (the patron saint of Poland) and captured Silesia. Kazimierz returned and was crowned King in 1041. He then proceeded to reconstruct the country by subjecting the Polish tribes to his rule and driving the Czechs from Silesia, incorporating Mazovia and restoring the country's economy and civilization. He also moved the capital of Poland to Krakow.

Boleslaw II Szczodry (1039-1082)
During his reign (1058-1079), he conducted many wars and got involved in dynastic conflicts in Hungary and Rus. His strong-arm rule provoked discord among the nobles including the Bishop of Krakow, St. Stanislaus of Szezepanow, who was put to death for treason. As a result of the Bishop's death, the nobles revolted and Boleslaw was excommunicated and had to abandon the throne in 1079 and seek refuge in Hungary where he died.

Wladyslaw I Herman (1079-1102)
Although he was titled Grand Duke, he was a weak ruler who based his policies on alliances with the Germans and Bohemians, recognized Bohemia's claim to Silesia and let the power slip into the hands of the voivode Sieciech.

Boleslaw III Krzywousty (1085-1138)
In 1109, he successfully defended Silesia against an invasion by Henry V who was defeated at the battle of Psie Pole near Wroclaw. However, his most lasting achievement was the capture of Gdansk Pomerania on the Baltic coast and the Christianization of its people. Although he established the institution of the sovereign prince, he undid his great successes when he divided Poland among his three adult sons. This was beginning of the period of a federative state that lasted from 1138 to 1306.

Wladyslaw II Wygnamiec (1105-1159)
The first sovereign prince, he was the first of the Silesian Piast rulers but only ruled for 7 years (1138-1146). In addition to his hereditary province of Silesia, he took over the sovereign's province as well as Krakow and Gniezno and sought allies in his efforts to reunite the country. In 1146, he turned against his brothers but was defeated and exiled.

Boleslaw IV Kedzierzawy (1125-1173)
He ascended the Krakow throne in 1146 after the banishment of his brother and had to fight to keep this position since his brother attempted to win back the throne with the support of the church and the German States. Under his rule, Poland lost Pomerania.

Mieczyslaw III Stary (1126-1202)
He became sovereign prince and ascended the Krakow throne in 1173 after the death of his brother. His attempts at increasing his authority provoked discontentment among the nobles and

then an open revolt. He only ruled for 4 years and was exiled in 1177.

Kazimierz II Sprawiedliwy (1138-1194)
After a revolt by the nobles in 1177, he became sovereign prince in Krakow and took over the principalities of Mazovia and Kujawia. He sought Church support and at the Congress at Leczyca in 1180, the Polish nobility and Church granted sovereignty over Poland to him and his descendants.

Leszek Bialy (1186-1227)
The prince of Sandomierz, he reigned from 1194-1199 and from 1207-1227. During his reign, he attempted to capture Halich Rus, also claimed by Hungary, but failed. In 1227, during a diet of Polish barons at Gasawa in Pomerania, he was assassinated.

Wladyslaw III Laskonogi (1165-1231)
Prince of Gniezno and Poznan, he ascended the throne after the death of his father and reigned from 1203-1207. Because the majority of the nobles supported the prince of Sandomierz, he was exiled and sought refuge in Silesia.

Boleslaw V Wstydliwy (1226-1279)
He reigned from 1227-1234 and from 1243-1279. When he assumed the throne in Krakow in 1243, he failed to attain his objectives since Sandomierz and Krakow provinces were invaded by the Mongols and attacked by Rus. In his foreign policy, he relied on alliance with Hungary.

Henyk I Brodaty (1163-1238)
The first representative of the Silesian Piasts on the Krakow throne, he reigned from 1232-1238. During this time, he focused on the country's economic expansion, supported the foundation of new towns and villages, the development of mining and monetary reform. Although he worked toward reunification of Poland, he never succeeded. His son was

killed in 1241 in the battle of Legnica during the first Mongol invasion, which threatened the West.

Leszek III Czarny (1241-1288)
He inherited the Krakow throne in 1279 and took power peacefully with no opposition. In his efforts to reunite the country, he looked to the towns for support and quelled a revolt by the nobles. In 1287, the Mongols invaded Poland for the third time, approached the walls of Krakow but failed to capture the city. Leszek's death in 1288 began a long struggle for the Krakow throne.

Przemyslaw I (1257-1296)
As prince of Poznan, his effort to unify Poland was supported by an outstanding politician, the archbishop of Gniezno, Jakub Swinka. In 1294, he incorporated Gdansk Pomerania and was crowned King of Poland in 1295 in Gniezno. This first coronation after almost 200 years was a significant event for the unification of Poland. Przemyslaw was murdered a year later.

Waclaw I (1271-1305)
He was crowned King of Bohemia in 1283, became prince of Krakow in 1291, crowned himself King of Poland in Gniezno in 1300 and took the Hungarian crown in 1301. He introduced the office of starost (governor) with large powers and attempted to strengthen royal power, which was a difficult task after the long period of feudal disintegration and unrest.

Reunited Kingdom

Wladyslaw IV Lokietek (1260-1333)
He inherited the province of Kuyavia and had plans to unite the Poland. In 1300, he captured Sandomierz. Although he lost Gdansk Pomerania to the Order of the Teutonic Knights, the Hungarians helped him to conquer Little Poland. After suppressing a rebellion of the Krakow townspeople in 1311,

he captured Great Poland and crowned himself in Krakow in 1320. This date is acknowledged as the end of the feudal disintegration of Poland.

Kazimierz III Wielki (1310-1370)
He was Poland's only king with the sobriquet "Great". He began his reign in 1333 by making peace with the Teutonic Knights and King John of Bohemia and made Poland a major power in Eastern Europe. In foreign policy, he was in favor of compromise because he felt that Poland needed internal stability and peace. Under a 1339 Treaty of Visegrad with Hungary, it was agreed that the throne would pass to the Angevins in the event of his childless death. He attached great importance to economic development and it is said that he found Poland built in wood and left it built in stone. His civil projects included the first stone bridge in Poland. He developed commerce, encouraged Jewish immigration to Poland and so improved the condition of the peasants that he became known as the Peasants' King. In 1347, he codified the laws of the kingdom, carried out monetary reform and established the Krakow Academy in 1364, the first Polish university. He was the last ruler from the great Piast dynasty.

Beginning in 1370, the nobility elected kings in general elections for life-long term of office. This democratic feature was unknown in other European countries.

Ludwik I Wegierski (1326-1386)
He became King of Poland in 1370 under the 1339 Treaty of Visegrad. After his coronation, he gave the nobles extensive privileges known as the Kosice Pact, which became the foundation of the freedom and political power of the gentry in Poland. He left Poland united.

Queen Jadwiga (1374-1399)
The Polish lords recognized her rights to the throne and she was crowned *Hedwig Rex Poloni* (King of Poland) in 1384. The

masculine gender in her title meant that she was a monarch in her own right, not a Queen consort. She became the only woman ruler in Poland's history and the only head of state in Poland declared saint by the Catholic Church. Under the 1385 Treaty of Krevo, Jagiello, the Grand Duke of Lithuania, converted to Christianity, married Queen Jadwiga in 1386 at age 13 and was crowned King of Poland. She enjoyed great popularity and the nobles looked to her as their true king as long as she lived. Queen Jadwiga ruled jointly with the king, traveled on diplomatic missions, negotiated with German, Muscovite and Italian princes of the Church and helped to establish the church in Lithuania and a college in Prague. She also renovated the Krakow Academy, the oldest in Eastern Europe and renamed it Jagielonian University. It became a beacon of learning in law and theology. The Church remembers her efforts in the founding of the bishopric of Wilno.

Jagiellonian Dynasty

<u>Wladyslaw II Jagiello</u> (1348-1434)
Grand Dukeof Lithuania, great statesman and founder of the Jagielonian dynasty, he was crowned King of Poland in 1386 and opened a new era in the history of Poland. Through him, Poland entered into union with Lithuania, a country covering a vast territory between the Baltic and Black Sea. The union was not an annexation as Lithuania retained its identity but the King of Poland was also Grand Duke of Lithuania. This union resulted in Poland becoming the largest power in Europe, which remained in force for centuries. On July 15, 1410, King Jagiello with combined armies of Poland, Lithuania, Tartars, et al, defeated the whole of the Teutonic Knights at the Battle Grumwald. In 1413, he concluded a new union at Horodio that increased Poland's links with Lithuania and issued new privileges for the nobles.

Wladyslaw III Warnenczyk (1424-1444)
He was crowned King of Poland in 1434 at age 10 and King of Hungary in 1440. In 1444, he was in a war with the Turks and killed in battle at Varna where the anti-Turkish forces were defeated. One of the best known rulers of medieval Poland, his defeat on the battlefield of Varna was the basis of a legend about a young king who died in a war between two different civilizations.

Kazimierz IV Jagiellonczyk (1427-1492)
After being crowned King of Poland in 1447, he attempted to strengthen royal authority by seeking supporters among the knights and limited the influence of the nobles. Under the 1466 Treaty of Torun that ended the war with the Teutonic Knights, he incorporated Royal Prussia. Under his long reign Poland became a European power and continued economic and cultural development.

Jan I Olbracht (1459-1501)
Crowned King of Poland in 1492, he carried out reforms which strengthened the gentry. The 1496 Statute of Piotrkow reserved church positions for the gentry exclusively, barred the townspeople from buying land and restricted the peasant's freedom of movement.

Aleksander Jagiellonczyk (1461-1506)
When crowned King of Poland in 1501, he issued the Mielnik privileges which provided that the Monarch's chairmanship of the Senate was granted the exclusive right to make decisions on state matters. This generated strong protests by the gentry who were in favor of the participation of the lower chamber in government. The Constitution Nihil Novi, adopted by the Sejm in Radom in 1505, determined that no new law could be established without consent of both chambers of government. This was the beginning of the system called gentry' democracy in Polish history.

Zygmunt I Stary (1467-1548)
King of Poland from 1506, he opposed the rising power of the gentry and allied himself with the higher nobles. Under his rule, the level of education among the nobles and gentry grew, Latin was replaced by Polish and a national literature was born, townspeople became more active in literature and the Polish language began to prevail in literature and diplomacy. A patron of the arts, he embellished the cathedral and royal palace of Krakow in the Italian Renaissance style. While discussion on the Reformation developed freely and the gentry continued its struggle against the nobles, the golden age of the Renaissance began. In 1529, Zygmunt incorporated Masovia to Poland, the last province that remained outside Poland.

Zygmunt II August (1520-1572)
Although crowned King of Poland in 1529, he assumed power in 1548. He supported the reformatory movement of the gentry resulting in the re-seizure of royal lands and establishment of a standing army. A supporter of tolerance, he prevented persecution and religious wars by halting the spread of Protestantism by peaceful means and by encouraging Catholic reform. In 1539 a royal ordinance established the liberty of the press and in 1543, the Diet of Krakow granted the freedom of studying at foreign universities to all Polish subjects. He was also a well-educated protector of science and learning which flourished during his reign. An enthusiastic book collector, his library of books collected from the mid-1540s included many treatises on the theory of art and architecture. In 1559, he annexed Livonia to his domains and formally joined Poland and Lithuania by the Union of Lublin of 1569. When he died childless, the Jagiellonian dynasty ended.

In 1561, the King Zygmunt II August of Poland protested to Queen Elizabeth of England against the illicit trade in arms which English sailors were carrying on with Russia. In this document, Poland sounded the following remarkable and prophetic warning:

> *"The Muscovite (Russia), who is not only our opponent of today but the eternal enemy of all free nations, should not be allowed to supply himself with cannons, bullets and munitions or with artisans who manufacture arms, hitherto unknown to those barbarians."*

The Diet of 1562 passed a law whereby all land grants after 1504 were declared void and lands ordered returned to the Crown. The revenues from the returned lands were to be used:

- ¾ of the revenues to be used for maintenance of the king and all the Crown offices and officials, and
- ¼ of the revenues to be devoted to the maintenance of a regular army for defense of the country.

The Diet also enacted legislation regarding the economic life of the country. It abolished all restrictions on the free export of raw products and the free import of manufactured goods and prohibited free export of domestic manufactures. The Polish cities that were already impoverished rapidly declined.

THE NOBLE REPUBLIC

Beginning in 1572, changes were made in the constitutional system and the lower nobility were now included in the selection process. The power of the monarch was further reduced in favor of the expanded noble class. During this period, the king was effectively a partner with the nobility and was constantly supervised by the Sejm.

In the periodic opportunities to fill the throne, the szlachta exhibited a preference for foreign candidates who would not found another strong dynasty. This policy produced monarchs who were either totally ineffective, in conflict with the nobility or inclined to subordinate the interests of Poland to those of their own country. Foreign princes were elected because of their neutrality to the Polish-Lithuanian Union.

Henryk III Walezjusz (1551-1589)
Son of King Henry II of France, he was the first King of Poland to be elected in free elections by all the gentry in 1573 and ruled until 1574. At this time the Henrician Articles were formulated which contained a statement of the rights and privileges of the Polish gentry that all elected kings of Poland had to confirm and that severely limited the authority of the Polish monarchy. The articles listed the most important principles fundamental to the state system including the superior role of the Sejm. The Sejm had the right to choose the king's successor and restricted the king's power over the army and legislation. The king was also required to confirm the 1573 Compact of Warsaw that guaranteed religious freedom in Poland. The Henrician Articles remained the fundamental laws of Poland until 1795.

Stefan Batory (1533-1586)
Duke of Transylvania, he was elected King of Poland in 1575 and crowned in 1576. He opposed the license of the gentry and the nobles and continued the policy of religious tolerance that the Convocation of Sejm of 1573 made one of the principles

of the political system of Poland. He introduced important reforms in the army including the creation of the first regular Polish infantry and the system of taxes. Although in favor of strong government, he relinquished his judicial powers and appointed separate tribunals for Poland and Lithuania. In 1579, he created the University at Vilno, the capital of Lithuania and the easternmost outpost of Western European culture. A great military leader, he defeated Ivan IV, the Terrible of Russia in a war called the First Northern War 1579-82 and recovered Livonia.

Zygmunt III Waza (1566-1632)
Son of King John III of Sweden, he was elected King of Poland in 1587 and King of Sweden in 1592-98. Patron, collector and amateur painter, goldsmith and wood carver, he was a learned man and spoke several languages. The arts and artists he promoted reflected his profound religious devotion and were symbolic of the Baroque style and of Catholic ideology. He considered the art of painting, along with poetry and historiography, to be a noble vocation. In 1596, he moved the capital of Poland from Krakow to Warsaw. His claims to the Swedish crown involved Poland and Lithuania in many conflicts and wars that resulted in the loss of Livonia in 1629. He conducted wars with Muscovy (Russia) and also fought several wars with the Turks in the 1620s.

Wladyslaw IV Waza (1596-1648)
He became King of Poland following the election of 1632 and unlike most of the gentry, he was in favor of armed moves. He made several unsuccessful attempts to claim the Swedish crown as well as the crown of Muscovy, which had been offered him in 1610. Polish troops even occupied the Kremlin for a short time in 1612. Poland's military expeditions created great Russian resentment and left bitter memories in Russian minds. During his reign, the Cossacks in the Ukraine started open rebellion against Poland and their army defeated the Polish knights more than once.

Jan II Kazimierz Waza (1609-1672)
He became a Roman Catholic cardinal in 1640 and was elected King of Poland in 1648. His reign was marked by invasions of the Tartars and Cossacks in 1649, a disastrous 13-year war with Muscovy from 1654-67 and a war with Sweden known as the Swedish deluge from 1655-1660. The Swedish army captured most of Poland and the king had to leave the country. According to the king, the reason for the disasters that befell Poland was weak royal power and the gentry's license. His attempts at reforms provoked a civil war, called Lubomirski's rebellion in 1665. He brought the Sisters of the Visitation of Our Lady to Poland and in 1654 founded a convent in Warsaw. He abdicated in 1668 and became Abbot of St Germain-des-Pres in Nevers, France.

Michal Korybut Wisniowiecki (1640-1673)
A native Pole and Piast, he was elected King of Poland in 1669. Unfortunately, he was unable to cope with his responsibilities and with tensions among the various political fractions. He lost a war against Turkey in 1673 and under the peace treaty Turkey occupied Podolia with Kamenets Podolsk, a stronghold once built for the defense of the southeastern borders of the country.

Jan III Sobieski (1629-1696)
A native Pole of noble blood, he was elected King of Poland in 1674. An outstanding military commander and strategist, he was one of the leaders in the fight to expel the Swedes and defeated the Tartars and the Cossacks near Podhajce in 1667. At the request of the Pope, he lead the army that sent the Hussaria into their last great charge and defeated the Turks in Vienna in 1683, one of the most decisive battles of European history. It made the Polish King a hero to all of Christian Europe. He was unsuccessful in his attempts to regain Moldavia and Walachia from Turkey.

Of all the Polish rulers of the 17th Century, he was the best educated and took the greatest interest in literature and cultural life. His letters to his wife are masterpieces of Polish late 17th Century literary language. Unfortunately, in domestic policy, he was unable to strengthen the position of the crown or stabilize the army. Rebellion and dissention among his subjects finally led to Poland's downfall in the 18th Century as it fell increasingly under Russian influence.

<u>August II Mocny</u> (1670-1733)
Son of John George of Saxony, he was elected King of Poland in 1697 and reigned from 1697-1704 and from 1711-1733. He attempted to introduce absolute monarchy in Poland, which provoked many conflicts and involved Poland in the Northern War, originally fought by Sweden and Russia. When Sweden invaded Poland, he was forced to abdicate but regained the crown in 1711. Under his reign, Poland ceased playing any major role in international relations.

<u>Stanislaw Leszczynski</u> (1677-1766)
After serving as governor of Poznan, he was elected King of Poland in 1704 under pressure from the Swedish forces of King Charles, but subsequently went into exile in 1709. In 1733, he was again elected King of Poland but abdicated in 1736 in exchange for the Duchy of Lorraine because of Russian and Saxon intervention. He fled to France where he wrote political works advocating freedom for the peasants and attacking the Liberum Veto which allowed any deputy to prevent legislation since all resolutions had to be carried unanimously. An intellectual and protector of arts and sciences, he had an excellent reputation as a ruler but was not a politician. During his prolonged rule in Lorraine, he introduced a broad economic, social and cultural program including founding schools and hospitals as well as establishing the first public library in the Duchy. He also began a number of extensive architectural projects especially the Place Royale, which is one of the most important examples of European urban planning.

August III Wettin (1696-1763)
He was brought to the throne in 1735 following an armed intervention by Russian and Saxon forces and the deposition of the elected king. Poland completely lost her international standing under his reign as well as the greatest period of instability within the country. Most significant was the fact that Russia, Prussia and Austria entered into a secret alliance known as the Alliance of the Three Black Eagles to maintain the paralysis of law and order within Poland in 1227. The Saxon period in Polish history became synonymous with backwardness and apathy that drove the country into decline. Fortunately, during these times, the enlightenment ideas reached Poland and the first projects for the reform of the country were prepared without the participation of the king.

Stanislaw August Poniatowski (1732-1798)
The last King of Poland, he became king in 1764 as a protégé and lover of Catherine II of Russia. He did a lot to improve the level of the Polish elite, modernized the country and hoped that Poland would preserve its independence thanks to the generosity of Catherine the Great. An enlightened, well-educated and sensitive man, he was a knowledgeable protector of the arts and culture. Although his three attempts to found an academy of fine arts failed, the painting, sculptural and architectural studios at his court became a focal point for the education of young Polish artists. The Royal Library under his reign included collections of artistic albums, illustrations and drawings, manuscripts, maps, mathematical instruments, coins, antiques, precious stones, minerals, statues, busts and other sculptures in marble and bronze.

As part of a public education program, he saw the arts as a way to prepare the nation for political reform and produce citizens capable of administering a modern state and of defining and developing a sense of Polish national consciousness. Because he wanted inexpensive decorative items accessible to the average nobleman or commoner, he established factories to manufacture belts, ornamental fabrics, carpets, marble vases and obelisks that were distributed throughout Poland. He wanted to reform the Polish system of government and helped establish government commissions for the Army and the Finances that worked by majority rule. One of his greatest achievements was his active participation in the drafting of Constitution of May 3rd 1791. His abdication in 1795 forecast the end of the independent Polish-Lithuanian State.

POLAND's WARS

The Teutonic Order - In 1226, Duke Konrad of Mazovia invited the Teutonic Order to combat pagan Prussian tribes from the base of the Chelmno. In time, the Order turned on the Poles and began to grab large chunks of Polish territory, finally invading Gdansk in 1308 and massacring its Polish inhabitants. At the Battle of Grunwald in 1401, the Teutonic Order was crushed. A subsequent victory in 1466, led to the Peace of Torun by which the Order was humiliated and Prussia partitioned.

The Hordes of Genghis Khan - In 1241, the fierce Mongols overran, burned and killed the Rus, then divided and ravaged Poland and Hungary. The Mongols sacked Krakow and burned it down on Easter Day, then rode on to Silesia. These raids depopulated the eastern and southern areas of Poland.

The Cossack Wars - Cossacks were runaway serfs from central Muscovy and Polish estates in Ukraine and formed military communities of free men. Polish Kings used "registered" Cossacks to fight the Tartars. Unfortunately, the Kings did not have enough money to employ all the Cossacks willing to serve, to provide regular pay to the "registered" Cossacks in Polish service nor to recognize their land titles which angered them.

Cossack revolts against Poland began in 1591, but the great revolt came in 1648 with a brutal massacre of Jews and Polish nobles in Kiev. When the Cossack Commander-in-Chief Bohdan Khmelnitsky (1595-1657) suffered at the hand of a Polish neighbor and failed to obtain justice in Warsaw, he decided to use the Cossack masses and establish his own kingdom. The Cossacks defeated the Polish armies in two major battles and penetrated deep into Poland.

The Polish nobles tried to win over the Cossacks and offered them autonomy in union with Poland under the 1658 Union of Hadiach. But the peasant Cossack masses opposed the union and their revolt led to a Polish-Russian War over Ukraine in which Poland lost east Ukraine to Russia by the Treaty of Andrusovo in 1667. The division of Ukraine between Poland and Russia interrupted the natural development of Ukraine statehood. This treaty marked the emergence of Russian as the pre-eminent power in Eastern Europe, replacing Poland.

<u>The Swedish Wars</u> - The first of these wars broke out over Livonia in 1626 because Sweden was trying to extend its rule to the southern Baltic shores. After some Polish victories, an armistice was signed at Nowy Targin 1629.

When Sweden invaded Poland in 1655, it broke the armistice and began a war known as “The Deluge” because of the multiple evils it brought on the country. The war devastated much of Poland especially the towns and was accompanied by a flare up of the Black Death. Between war damage, famine and the plague, Poland-Lithuania lost between one-third and one-half of its population.

The turning point of this war was the successful Polish defense of the fortified monastery of Jasna Gora at Czestochowa in 1655. The victory, due to a combination of good defense and the exhaustion of the Swedish armies, was attributed to the miracle-working picture of the Virgin Mary in the monastery church. King Kazimierz proclaimed the Virgin Mary as “Queen of Poland” and Poles have prayed to her by that name ever since. The monastery is the chief religious shrine in Poland today.

<u>Polish-Swedish-Brandenburg Prussian War</u> - While Poland was fighting Sweden, Prussia threatened them in the north. By the terms of the 1660 Treaty of Oliva, Poland gave up her claim to Livonia - a region which had been under Polish sovereignty since the last Grand Master of the Teutonic Knights swore

loyalty to Poland in 1525. Only Royal Prussia remained with Poland together with the port city of Gdansk.

The treaty marked the first step in Prussian expansion to the East, this time at Poland's expense. After acquiring sovereignty over East Prussia, Prussian leaders desired to unite the two Prussias at Poland's expense. Only a small part of East Prussia called "Royal Prussia" as well as the port city of Gdansk remained with Poland. Because the Swedes and Prussians were Lutherans and the Russians and Ukrainians were orthodox, religious toleration declined in Poland during the 17th Century wars.

The Turkish Wars - Polish wars with the Ottoman Turks lasted off and on for about two centuries. However, after the 1523 Battle of Mohacs, most of the fighting was with the Tatars. In 1674 the Polish army marched to the relief of Vienna besieged by the Turks and Polish winged hussars played a major role in defeating the Turkish army in 1683.

Great Northern War (1700-1721) - During the Great Northern War, Swedish and Russian armies devastated Poland again. The outbreak of the war was preceded by the 1699 alliance between Peter I of Russia, Frederick IV of Denmark and Augustus II of Poland (who was also elector of Saxony) against Charles XII of Sweden. At this time, Russia was a huge power territorially but with no access to the Black Sea or to the Baltic Sea and winning such an outlet became the main goal of Peter I.

Late in 1700, Sweden defeated a much superior Russian force at Narva. Instead of destroying the Russian army, Sweden invaded Poland in order to expel the Saxons and to insure the election of a friendly Polish king. Sweden took Warsaw and Krakow in 1702, secured the election of Stanislaus I as King of Poland in 1704, followed Augustus into Saxony and forced him to break his alliance with Russian and to recognize Stanislaus as king by the Treaty of Altranstadt in 1706.

In 1709 a superior Russian army utterly defeated the Swedes and King Charles XII of Sweden retired on Turkish territory where his intrigues induced the sultan to declare war on Russia in 1710. Meanwhile, Augustus II took advantage of King Charles' absence and invaded Poland in 1709 and expelled Stanislaus I.

PARTITIONS of POLAND

The era of the Three Partitions began during the reign of Empress Catherine the Great (1762-1796) of Russia, and Poland-Lithuania was wiped from the map of Europe.

Proposals to reform the Polish political system were made as early as the 16th Century. Andrzej Frycz-Modrzewski advocated equal citizenship for all Poles, the democratization of the state and the church and a centralized though not absolute monarchy. Unfortunately, these ideas were greatly ahead of the time not only in Poland but also in all of Europe.

In the mid-1700s, the Czartoryski family proposed explicit proposals to reform the Polish political system. Specifically, their goal was to abolish the Liberum Veto in favor of majority rule in parliament. The Czartoryskis looked to Russia, assuming its rulers would wish to have a strong Poland as an ally. Unknown to the Poles, Russian rulers preferred to have a weak Poland that they could control.

Although the proposals to reform the political system in Poland and their failure to do so were a contributing factor in the decline of Poland, the primary reasons were:

1. The bankruptcy of the Polish crown due to wars;
2. The narrow-mindedness of a large part of the gentry and their reluctance to agree to material and political sacrifices; and
3. The rise of absolutist military powers to the East, West and South of Poland, who took advantage of Polish weakness.

<u>The First Partition</u> - 1772

King Stanislaw Augustus (1764-1795) pressed for reform of the government in order to strengthen Poland and preserve its independence. The first years of his rule were devoted to military and financial reforms. He founded the Knights School and put the municipal economy in order and established modern workshops. Russia, however, did not appreciate the reforms and using military pressure forced the Sejm of 1768 to pass the so-called Cardinal Rights which amounted to free election, liberum veto, the right to mutiny against the king and a monopoly on political activity by the gentry.

The brutality of the Russian intervention provoked an armed resistance by the noblemen who established the Confederation of the Bar. Guerrilla-type fighting ensued for 4 years but the Confederation (the first Polish uprising) was defeated and thousands of Poles were sent to Siberia.

Russia faced a dilemma -- either maintain its domination over the entire country of Poland to accept the repeated propositions by Prussia to partition Poland. By a secret partition treaty in 1772, Frederick II of Prussia, Catherine II of Russia and Empress Maria Theresa of Austria seized about 28% of Polish territory. Russia took Livonia and lands east of Dvina and Dnieper Rivers, Austria took Galicia-Lodomeria and Prussia took Royal Prussia. The First Partition was the result of three factors:

a) The territorial ambitions of Frederick II of Prussia and Catherine II of Russia;
b) Empress Maria Theresa of Austria's decision to seize part of Poland to balance the expansion of Russia and Prussia; and
c) Polish military weakness.

<u>Era of Revival & Reform</u> - 1772-1793

The trauma of the first partition and the processes of economic and demographic development shook Polish society out of its lethargy. Reforms began with the establishment of the National Commission of Education in 1773. As the first ministry of Education in Europe, it followed the educational reform established by Konarski in his Collegium Nobilium founded in Warsaw in 1740. The first results of the educational programs and political journalism resulted in the appearance of a better-educated generation of Poles capable of making sacrifices. The Commission introduced modern school textbooks and subordinated schools to universities, which were also reformed. Ideas of Enlightenment, together with patriotic and reform-minded programs were promoted by the press, literature, theater, music, painting and historical geography.

Ideas were discussed and reforms to the Polish political system worked out in the "Great Sejm" which sat during 1788-1792. The deputies' work culminated in the Constitution of May 3, 1791, which was drafted by the King himself. It was the first written constitution in Europe to be passed by a parliament. Key features of the Constitution of May 3, 1791 include:

1. The Elective Monarchy was abolished and was replaced by Hereditary Monarchy.
2. The Liberum Veto was abolished and replaced by majority rule.
3. A Constitutional Monarchy was established on the English model. Thus, the King was to rule with a Council whose members were answerable to Parliament and there was a constitutional separation of powers.
4. There was to be a standing army with appropriate funding and the King as commander-in-chief.
5. Royal cities were granted their own municipal governments and could send deputies to parliament.
6. The peasants were promised protection by the law. This meant they could appeal their landlords' judgment to the royal courts.
7. The Catholic religion was proclaimed the state religion. However, all religions had the right to exist, provided they did not call for the overthrow of the monarchy.

The government, based on the Constitution, stood every chance of pulling the country out of its political crises but the Constitution evoked fierce opposition from Russia. Incited by Russia, the Confederation of Targowica was established to defend the old system. Despite strong Polish resistance the war of 1792 ended in defeat, abolishment of the Constitution and the second partition was made by Russia, Prussia and Austria. However, the Constitution of May 3, 1791 continued to inspire generations of Poles.

The Kociuszko Uprising of 1794

When Tadeusz Kociuszko returned to Poland in 1784, he was much influenced by his experiences in American and American democratic ideas. Like many Poles, he refused to accept the abolition of the May 3 Constitution and the second partition of Poland. In 1789, he was appointed a Major General in the Polish army and fought in the war against Russia in 1792.

After taking an oath "To the Polish Nation" in 1794, he issued the Polaniec Manifesto calling on all Poles to fight for their country and promised land and freedom to peasants who joined the Polish army. There were peasant infantry units in his army who were armed with scythes attached to pikes. They were quite effective in some battles especially at Raclawics where they overran Russian artillery positions. However, dissension among the Polish high command, overwhelming numerical superiority of the Russians and intervention by Prussia and Austria, made the Polish cause hopeless. After winning a decisive victory at Maciejowice, Russian forces entered Praga, a suburb of Warsaw, and massacred much of the population.

The Second Partition - 1793

Russia and Prussia were alarmed by the May 3 Constitution and feared that if a strong Polish government emerged, it would try to regain the territories lost in 1772. They formed a confederation with some Polish nobles in the town of Targowica. (Ever since, Poles have called any Russian-supported Polish movement "Targowica".)

As a result of the Kociuszko Uprising, the Polish Sejm was forced by the Russians ratify the Second Partition. Russia seized a very large portion of eastern Poland, most of Lithuania, western Belorussia, Volhynia and most of the left-bank except for Eastern Galicia. Meanwhile, Prussia besieged Gdansk, took the city or Torun and annexed Wielkopolska.

But the Poland partitioned in 1794 was not the country it had been in 1772. It had a modern constitution supported by most of the noble class that provided a good central government, a standing army and an excellent educational system. It was partitioned purposely because these reforms would make Poland a strong country which Russia and Prussia wanted to prevent and succeeded in doing.

The Third Partition - 1795

Although the three partitioning powers, Russia, Austria and Prussia in St. Petersburg, signed the final treaty in 1797, the Third Partition of Poland was instituted in 1795. In the aftermath of the rebellion, the constitution, the Sejm and the Polish army was abolished. The Poles were deprived of civil liberties and their country was robbed of literary and art treasures.

After the Third Partition of Poland in 1795, the Poles formed the 1st Polish Legion in the French army at Lombardy, Italy to begin their fight to regain their independence. Other unsuccessful insurrections and nationalist demonstrations occurred in various parts of Poland in 1846, 1848, 1861 and 1863.

> Russian Poland - The Russian Empire instituted a program for the Russification of the Polish lands under its rule. It introduced the Russian language in the schools, restricted the use of the Polish language and interfered with the activities of the Roman Catholic Church. Culturally, politically and economically, the

parts of Poland under Russian rule lost almost all signs of its former autonomy.

Prussian Poland - The Poles in Prussian Poland were subjected to a policy of Germanization, although not as severe as in the Russian zone.

Austrian Poland - Poles in Austrian Poland were treated more liberally and developed their own leaders and political life.

The significance of this Third Partition of Poland was:

- It marked the disappearance of independent Poland from the map of Europe for 125 years until 1918.
- It marked the beginning of the rise of Prussia as the strongest of the German states.
- Russia gained a firm foothold in Europe and became a European power. After Napoleon's invasion of 1812, Russians felt that holding on to the Polish lands was vital for the defense of the Russian Empire.
- Austria added some territory in central Poland to Galicia that had been taken in 1772.
- The Third Partition cemented the alliance of the three partitioning powers that were bound together by their interest in keeping the Polish lands they had taken.
- The Poles refused to accept the loss of their independence and immediately began the fight to regain it along with the lands of old Poland. Since any kind of independent Poland would mean losses by the partitioning powers, the issue of Polish independence became known as "The Polish Question".

The three partitioning countries were absolute monarchies and their political systems stood in complete contradiction to the Polish tradition of democracy, self-government and civil freedoms of the gentry. During the 123 years of partition, successive generations of Poles launched attempts to regain independence but it was impossible to defeat the three countries at the same time.

Continual violations of the Constitution and setbacks suffered by opposition led Polish youth to join conspiratorial organizations and prepare for an uprising that broke out in Warsaw in 1830. The well-trained and armed Polish army held out until 1930 but was not able to win the Polish-Russian war because of the enormous human and economic resources of Russia. The Polish Democratic Society discussed the causes of the uprising's defeat while preparing for further armed struggle. The main part of those discussions focused on the situation of the Polish peasantry.

Emancipation and the granting of land to peasants were regarded as essential conditions for modernizing the economic structure and attracting the peasant masses to the Polish independence movement. The first to free peasants was Prussia, which became the foundation for economic development of that part of Poland annexed by Prussia. Austria freed peasants during the Spring of Nations. In 1864, Russia issued a decree to emancipate peasants. Its goal was to attract the peasantry to Russia but instead the peasants gradually became members of the Polish national community.

1846 Krakow Revolution

The Krakow Revolution was a military uprising against Austria in the Krakow Republic (Rzeczpospolita Krakowska) as part of an all-Polish uprising prepared by the Polish Democratic Society and other secret revolutionary organizations in partitioned Poland. But on February 26th a revolutionary detachment was defeated by Austrian troops and by November 6th the Krakow Republic was incorporated into Austria. Polish institutions were replaced with Austrian, with German-speaking civil servants; German was introduced as the language of instruction at Jagiellonian University and numerous plagues caused a sudden economic crisis which resulted in an increase of the cost of living and poverty.

Although the collapse of the Krakow revolution hampered the conspiracies in partitioned, the 19th Century uprisings were not in futile. By the turn of the Century, the desire for independence and the willingness to make sacrifices became universal among Poles.

Meanwhile, during the years of the Third Partition of Poland (1795-1918) when Poland lost its independence, the family became the stronghold of national identity. Women played an important role in society during this period because their personal achievements as well as their work in educating children contributed to the cultural survival of their country. As a result "Matka Polka" (mother) became a heroic figure in Polish national mythology.

WORLD WAR I

During World War I, almost all of the fighting on the Eastern Front took place on Polish soil. The Second Polish Republic was established in 1918 and although it did not survive, many economic advances were made, Polish education and culture were revived and Polish nationhood reaffirmed.

During the years of partition, Poland had been united by its culture, language and religion and maintained its distinct identity despite attempts at Germanization and Russification. The great seer Mickiewicz prayed that a great cataclysm like World War I, in which the three powers that tore Poland apart were arrayed on opposite sides, would liberate the nation from its political bondage. If the anticipated war should occur, what should be the attitude of the Polish people?

In 1912, the representatives of all the independence parties of the Kingdom of Poland formed a Temporary Committee of the Confederated Independence Parties, known as KSSN. The committee was mandated with the task of preparing a detailed plan of procedure in case of a world war and of making military preparations for such a contingency. Since Russian oppression extended over 80% of the ancient Polish Empire and because in the event of a confrontation between the Central Powers and Russia, it was believed that Russian would be defeated, Poland was to take an active part against Russia. This course was indicated by sound reasoning and by all the past experiences and traditions of the Polish nation. Since Poles without exception had nothing but the most bitter feeling toward the Prussians because of the brutal and unjust treatment accorded by them to the Polish people throughout history, sympathy for Prussia was not a factor in this decision. The decision was founded on intimate knowledge of political and military conditions and an opportunity to deal successfully with one of the formidable despoilers of their national heritage and a chance of redeeming the lost sovereignty over a major part of the ancient Polish lands.

Although Poland had no part in starting World War I, she became one of the greatest theatres of the war by reason of her geographic position. As the Eastern Front rolled across Poland it left devastation and the tragedy of fratricidal warfare since about 2 million Poles of military age were drafted into the three foreign armies - Russia, Germany and Austria.

Two political camps emerged with different ideas as to how this could be accomplished. Roman Dmowski advocated siding with Russia believing in the ultimate liberalization of Russian rule after an Allied victory. His hopes perished when Russia withdrew from the war in 1917 as a result of the Bolshevik Revolution.

Jozef Pilsudski took a different route to Polish autonomy. He organized the "Polish Riflemen's League" and sided with the Austro-Hungarian Empire. Following the command of the Revolutionary National Government, he established headquarters at Kielce in Russian Poland where his small army swelled to considerable proportions in a few days. There he issued a manifesto that marked the beginning of a new era for Poland. The manifesto stated in part:

> *"In this hour of bloody transformation of Europe, we may regain a great deal but we must also sacrifice much... In this hour the nation must prove that it lives and wants to live; and that it desires and knows how to retain the place assigned to it by God and to defend it before the enemy... Under Polish command and in close connection with the chief direction of the Austro-Hungarian army, the Polish Legion will enter the struggle in order that they may also, throw upon the scales of the greatest war a deed worthy of the Polish nation, as a condition and beginning of a brighter future."*

The chief objective in creating the Polish army was to guarantee that the Polish Question would come up for solution at the Peace Congress. By its existence, Poland wanted to emphasize that it was a distinct national entity with a will to live and to shape its own destiny. Recognizing the righteousness of the Polish cause, US President Woodrow Wilson strongly advocated the restoration of a free and independent Poland with access to the Baltic Sea as one of the 14 Points for Peace. Liberation Day, November 11, 1918, is celebrated as a national holiday.

INTERWAR PERIOD - Rebirth of Poland

During the course of World War I, Joseph Pilsudski distinguished himself as a general and strategist and acquired wide popularity among the people as the country's redeemer. A born leader of men, he was distinguished for his patriotism, esteemed for his high principles and admired for his conception of duty, bravery and modesty.

Pilsudski's popularity and resignation from active service in the army in 1916 together with the resignation of the powerful Socialist deputy from the Polish Parliamentary Club in Vienna were responsible for the recognition of Poland's independence by the Central Powers. It was a dramatic way of serving notice on the governments of the Central Powers that the Polish people had ceased to believe in the sincerity of the indefinite promises made on various occasions and that they did not propose to be deceived any longer. The Rector of the Warsaw University, in the name of the Polish delegation, laid down the following conditions:

First. A Regent must be nominated.

Second. The frontier zones of military occupation must be abolished.

Third. A Polish State Council must be formed at once to elaborate a constitution and to regulate the administration of the State.

Fourth. A military department must be brought into being to organize a Polish army.

As a result of the negotiations came the manifesto of November 5th, 1916, which declared Poland's independence. Pilsudski's first task was to reunite the Polish regions that had assumed various economic and political identities since the partitions of Poland in the late 18th Century and especially since the development of political parties. He took immediate steps to consolidate the Polish regions under a single government with its own currency and army.

Waclaw Niemoyowski was appointed Polish Provisional Regent and known as Marshal of the Crown. Pending the convening of the Sejm, a Council of State was organized, composed of 25 representatives from all parts of the country. All political parties, religious creeds and social classes were represented. The State Council was presided over by the Marshal of the Crown and constituted the provisional government of the country. On January 15, 1917, the Council met for the first time and adopted rules and by-laws, appointed a number of committees and created 8 executive departments.

Meanwhile as a result of the Bolshevik Revolution in 1917, Russia was unable to maintain control over its lands in Poland and was driven out by Polish nationals. When Austria collapsed in 1918 another portion of Poland was freed. Finally, Germany withdrew from Warsaw leading the way for a new autonomous Poland. Josef Pilsudski established the Second Republic on November 11, 1918.

The Second Polish Republic struggled to secure and maintain its existence with difficulty and the unusual complications of defining its frontiers preoccupied the state. The 1919 Treaty of Versailles gave Poland access to the Baltic Sea via the Polish Corridor and forced Germany to return Prussian Poland to Poland. Gdansk became a free city and parts of Silesia were awarded to Poland. These terms were an incentive for the German aggression that ignited World War II. The new communist government of Russia saw Poland as a bridge over which communism would pass into the labor class of a disorganized postwar Germany. As a result, war broke out between Poland and Russia regarding the Polish-Russian border. In 1920, the Poles drove the Russians back from Warsaw and the 1921 Treat of Riga split the disputed territory between Poland and Soviet Russia.

Reborn Poland faced a host of daunting challenges:

- Extensive war damage
- A ravaged economy
- One-third of its population composed of wary national minorities
- The necessity to reintegrate the 3 zones forcibly kept apart during the partitions

The postwar parliamentary system proved unstable and erratic. As occurring elsewhere in Europe, the attempt to implant democracy did not succeed. In 1926, the parliamentary government was suspended by a military coup by Pilsudski following 4 years of ineffectual government. For the next decade, he dominated Polish affairs as strongman of a generally popular regime that was military in character. The government of Pilsudski mixed democratic and dictatorial elements while pursuing sanacja or national cleansing. After his death in 1935, his successors drifted toward open authoritarianism.

Poland achieved significant economic growth despite world economic crisis between 1921 and 1939. A republican constitution was adopted in 1921. Financial and agricultural reforms were undertaken and industrialization progressed. It was during this period of time that Poland developed and manufactured its own automobiles. Unfortunately, the landowning aristocracy retained most of its wealth while the condition of the peasantry remained poor.

However, the biggest threat to Poland's longevity came from abroad, not from internal weaknesses. The center of Poland's postwar foreign policy was a political and military alliance with France who guaranteed Poland's independence and territorial integrity. In addition, Poland's inability to establish planned alliances in Eastern Europe meant greater dependence on France, whose enthusiasm for intervention in the region diminished considerably after World War I. Over the next 10 years, substantial discord arose between Poland and France over Poland's refusal to compromise with the Germans and France's refusal to resist Hitler's rise to power.

The military expansion of Russia and Germany made the situation more threatening for Poland. In a desperate attempt to maintain peace, Poland entered into non-aggression treaties with Germany and the Soviet Union in the early 1930s. At the beginning of 1939, Germany proposed that Poland accede to the Anti-Soviet Pact but it was assumed in Poland that agreement would lead to loss of independence. Meanwhile, Russia was negotiating with Germany, England and France at the same time, promising assistance against Germany if Poland would consent to the entry of Russia's Army onto Polish territory. The fate of Lithuania, Latvia and Estonia in 1940 later demonstrated what the result of allowing Russia's army onto Polish soil would have meant.

In 1939, Russia and Germany signed their own treaty, which allowed Germany to invade Poland without worrying about being attacked by Russian. Later, Hitler decided to ignore the Soviet-German non-aggression treaty and attacked Soviet troops in Eastern Poland in 1941. The Germans chased the Soviet Union out of Poland and into Russia itself.

Poland's independence lasted only 20 years but the statehood regained as a result of the struggle of several generations was of great value to Poles. The greatest success was the consolidation of the areas and economies of the three former partitions into a uniform state. The slow implementation of agricultural reform and poverty in the rural areas were significant failures. However, there were remarkable developments in literature, architecture, film, science, history, and archaeology. Nonetheless, one of the most enlightened, courageous and patriotic generations in Polish history flourished despite all the economic difficulties.

WORLD WAR II

Polish Armed Forces fought the enemy from the very first day of the war to the very last day of World War II in Europe -- **they never surrendered**. Many Poles fought with great bravery, courage and honor in almost every major battle of World War II. Polish intelligence made a major contributions to the Allied side. The Home Army became one of the largest and most effective underground movements of the war. By the end of the war, 6 million Poles perished and much of the country was in ruins.

World War II began with Hitler invading Poland in 1939. On August 22, 1939, a few days before the official start of World War II, Hitler authorized his commanders to kill "*without pity or mercy, all men, women and children of Polish descent or language. Only in this way can we obtain the living space we need*". Heinrich Himmler echoed Hitler's decree: "*All Poles will disappear from the world... It is essential that the great German people should consider it as its major task to destroy all Poles.*"[1] It was his goal to obliterate all traces of Polish history and culture. Nazi contempt for the Slavs originated with an ancient German-Slav hostility as the conflict between Germans and Slavs was a 1,000 years old. German nationalists believed that the Slavs were biologically inferior peoples destined to become a caste of slaves; they also occupied valuable space that was needed by the Germans who, by virtue of their superiority, had every right to take it.

On August 31, 1939, Nazi soldiers dressed in Polish uniforms attacked, captured the German Radio Station in Gliwice and transmitted a message in Polish. This incident became the pretense for the outbreak of World War II. On September 1, 1939, Germany invaded Poland on three fronts:

---

[1] Cited from the WWW page http://www.holocaustforgotten.com.

East Prussia in the north, Germany in the west and Slovakia in the south. They had 2600 tanks against Poland's 180 and over 2000 aircraft against Poland's 420. Germany began bombing all major Polish cities and saturated the main communication centers in an attempt to disrupt and prevent the mobilization and deployment of Polish air and ground forces.

The simultaneous attack by several German divisions surprised Polish defenders with its synchronized military action. The new and powerful tactic of the modern war forced Polish fighting units to retreat toward central Poland in a vain hope to stabilize their defenses around the city of Warsaw. Though outnumbered 10 to 1, the Polish Air Force and ground forces made desperate attempts to hold back the enemy during the entire campaign. The recently designed light tank, the first in the world to be designed with a diesel engine, proved to be superior to German tanks and inflicted serious damage to the German forces.

At the same time, on the eastern border of Poland, the Soviet Union invaded and quickly conquered. Just like the Nazis, the Soviets also reigned terror in Poland. They took over Polish businesses and factories, destroyed churches and religious buildings and closed all Polish banks. The Polish people were given Soviet citizenship and all young Polish men were subject to being drafted into the Soviet army. Also, the Soviets sent almost 1,700,000 Polish non-Jews to Siberia.

Soon only Warsaw, the capital of Poland, continued to fight the Nazi troops and the defenders of Warsaw repelled every attempt of the Nazi units to enter the city for thirty days. After thirty days of fighting, often without food and water, with weapons and ammunition running out, the mayor of the city, Stefan Starzynski surrendered the ruined city to the dreaded enemy. Radio Warsaw was silenced.

The Poles had held on for twice as long as expected and had done serious damage to the German forces. The Germans lost 50,000 men, 697 aircraft (almost a third of their aircraft) and 993 tanks and armored cars. Though defeated and temporarily out of the fight, all that was left for the Polish people was the sad legacy of the struggle for freedom and the inspiration in the words of the National Anthem of Poland -- "Poland is not lost as long as we live".

In accordance with the so-called "Unternehmen Tannenberg', mass execution of Poles were carried out beginning in 1939. There has been no research as to the level of awareness, if any, within the closed ghetto communities of the real intensity of German terror against the Poles, and especially of the carefully planned campaign to exterminate the Polish intelligentsia. The brutal extermination of the Polish nation by both its German and Russian occupants over the next six years resulted in the death of more than 12 million Polish natives. Whole families and villages were executed. Poland's educated class was purposely targeted because the Nazis knew that this would make it easier to control the country. The survivors of the war were also victims frequently dying of dreadful diseases resulting from inhumane conditions in the concentration camps. More than 90% of the pre-war industrial installations ceased to exist and the Warsaw, the capital, had to be totally rebuilt. Even today, Poland still suffers from the consequences of those crimes.

The government left to represent Poland's interests on the Allied side and direct the activities of the extensive, well-coordinated resistance organization in occupied Poland which was the largest of all national resistance movements in Europe.

The Polish Underground State

The division of Poland into two occupied zones, German and Soviet, did not break the will of the Polish people to continue its fight for freedom. Throughout the history of European resistance movements, the Polish Underground State, which functioned under the German occupation in World War II, was unique. In September 1939, the Sluzba Zwyciestwu Polski (SZP) [Polish Victory Service] was formed as an underground political military organization and was the beginning of the underground state. Based on the organizational network of the SZP, the new Polish Government created Zqiazek Walki Zbrojinef (ZWZ) [Union for Armed Struggle] in December 1939 with the goal of creating centers of national resistance and rebuilding the Polish nation through armed struggle. Decrees of the Polish Government stated that ZWZ is universal, national, non-party and non-class and would include all Poles wishing to fight against the occupying forces.

- **Zqiazek Walki Zbrojinef (ZWZ)** [Union for Armed Struggle] - During 1939-1941, the main efforts of the ZWZ were focused on organizational work preparing for later military action. At the same time, ZWZ was fighting the occupying forces on three fronts: propaganda, reconnaissance and sabotage. Propaganda activity consisted of printing secret bulletins, periodicals and news sheets that were widely distributed among the population. The intelligence activities of the ZWZ were done in occupied Poland as well as in Germany. It obtained and sent important information to London including information about a German attack against the Soviet Union in June 1941. Sabotage activities were directed primarily against economic targets that contributed to the German war effort, industry and transportation.
- **Bureau of Information and Propaganda (BIP) -** Although it was part of ZWZ and later Home Army Headquarters, it had no equivalent in the Polish Army before the war. BIP played a vital role in raising morale and influencing attitudes among the soldiers of the underground movement as well as members of the Polish Community. Between 1943-1944, it published over

400,000 copies of brochures, leaflets and other forms of printed literature. Another function of the BIP was to gather political information and its Information Department was a large underground research institute dealing with about 100 issues concerning social, economic, cultural and ethnic issues as well as special subjects. It produced extensive reports covering all aspects of life that kept the Government in Exile informed on the general situation in occupied Poland. Although the actual influence of the BIP is unknown, it did have a fundamental impact on the Polish population's attitude towards the invaders during the war, especially the Germans, as well as provide united support of the Polish Republic's lawful authorities.

- **Polish Armia Krajowa (Home Army)** - Before the last shots of the Polish 1939 campaign were fired, the nucleus of the future resistance organization, the Polish Armia Krajowa (AK) [Home Army], was created in Warsaw and became the backbone in Poland's struggle with occupying forces. It was the largest in Europe with 400,000 men and women on the home front and there were no Polish collaborators as in other occupied countries. The Home Army under the command of General Stefan Roweki and after his capture by General Tadeusz Komorowski, fought a very varied war. They managed to free many trains carrying Jews to concentration camps and frequently

Sabotage/Diversionary Actions	Totals
Damaged locomotives	6,930
Damage to railway wagons	19,058
Army vehicles damaged or destroyed	4,328
Fuel tanks destroyed	1,167
Fuel destroyed in tons	4,674
Built-in faults in parts for aircraft engines	4,710
Built-in faults into artillery missiles	92,000
Built-in faults into condensers	70,000
Damage to important factory machinery	2,872
Acts of sabotage	25,145
Planned assassinations of Germans	5,733

halted weapon deliveries to the eastern front. Also, they terrorized and harassed the Nazi occupation forces and also engaged in sabotage and intelligence gathering for the Allies. A very important contribution of Poles to the victory over Germans was the uncovering of German plans with V2 missiles and delivery of a whole V2 rocket to the British military. In 1944 the Polish Armia Krajowa staged the tragic Warsaw uprising which though unsuccessful tied down large numbers of Nazi troops for 63 days and helped the Allies to defeat the German armies in western Europe.

- **The Home Army Intelligence Service** - One of the major tasks of the Home Army Intelligence Service was to organize an efficient intelligence gathering service both for its own needs and that of the allied war effort. Built on the pre-war structure of Polish intelligence, the Home Army Intelligence Service became the chief source of information for the allies about the eastern front. It supplied the allies with regular and continuous information about the order of battle of German forces on the eastern front; troop transports between the eastern and western fronts; identification and battle order of Luftwaffe units and morale of German troops and civilian population. Polish Intelligence performed industrial espionage in its widest sense including production of synthetic fuels, U-boat, tank and armored vehicle construction and supplied the allies with complete instructions, analysis and full rocket parts of the V2 which enabled them to prepare an adequate defense of the British Isles.
- **Home Army Air Force Department** - The idea of a clandestine resistance army operating in occupied territory having an air force department was unusual. The Air Section was created in 1940 and upgraded into the Air Force Department in 1942. It was divided into the organizational, intelligence and communications sections. The organizational section organized the evacuation of air force personnel and was responsible for arranging safe

covers for those who remained in Poland. The intelligence section arranged for continuous observation of enemy airfields, prepared detailed plans and took photographs that were passed on to the Allies. Meanwhile, local Home Army detachments were responsible for stockpiling fuel near the airfields targeted for capture and cement to repair damaged runways. The Communications section's task was to prepare for direct air communications and, when this idea became difficult to accomplish, studies turned to the feasibility of airdrops. This section was directly responsible for organizing airdrop reception parties, sabotage of enemy airfields and organizing the landing operations of Dakota aircraft.

- **Women's Military Service** - Polish women participated in the national uprisings of the 19th Century and the struggles for independence during World War I. The Sejm granted women the right to serve in auxiliary detachments in 1938, including anti-aircraft, sentry and communications units as well as other services necessary for defense purposes. In 1942, the Organizacja Przysposobienia Wojskowego Kobiet (OPWK) [Women's Auxiliary Army Service] was created and was officially raised to the rank of Women's Military Service in 1942. The Polish President issued a decree in 1943 stating that female soldiers have the same rights and obligations as male soldiers which provided legal grounds for resolving various issues including granting ranks.

The day-to-day operations of underground resistance would have been impossible without women. They organized liaison operations, served as messengers and couriers and played a considerable role in the distribution of illegal newspapers and other AK publications. There was special women's diversion and sabotage detachment and women's mine laying patrols that blew up railway lines around Warsaw. In partisan detachments, women played a vital role as field nurses, organizing first aid posts and field hospitals. During the Warsaw Uprising over 60% of a special platoon running a courier network in the sewers of the Polish Capital were women. After the uprising, Germans granted over 2,000 Polish women soldiers prisoner-of-war status, a fact unprecedented in European history. Many women soldiers of the AK received decorations and, in a few exceptional cases, women were decorated with the Order Virtuti Militari (class V).

Katyn Forest

On September 17, 1939, Russian troops moved across the eastern border of Poland on the pretext that they would protect the Polish people. As a result, more than 15,000 Polish Officers were sent to NKVD (Soviet Secret Police) prison camps at Kozielsk, Starobielska and Ostashkov in the Soviet Union where they were interrogated for several months about their political beliefs, family backgrounds and education. In 1940 a secret communication was made that all three camps would be liquidated. The prisoners of the camps were evacuated, brutally murdered and systematically buried in mass graves in the Katyn Forest. Since the Polish Officers were all educated, professional people including physicians, attorneys, accountants, engineers, priests, university professors, journalist and the Chief Rabbi of Warsaw, the Soviet Secret Police was able to obliterate the intellectual elite of Poland.

Many people suspected the truth and worked hard to reveal the lies and perfidy of the Soviet Union. Despite the growing body of evidence, the Soviet Union still continued to deny any involvement in the inhumane torture and murder of the prisoners. Finally, after the collapse of the Soviet Union, Gorbachev broadly admitted Soviet guilt in 1991. The next year, Yeltsin turned over to Poland secret documents including the death sentences signed by Stalin. The world at last knew the truth:

"The Soviet Union had annihilated the Polish Officers in Katyn Forest to get rid of potential political opposition to their plans to occupy Poland and establish a puppet government after the war".

Catholic Church in Poland

The Catholic Church in Poland was the subject of particular hatred from the Germany. More than 90% of all Catholic priests were killed. Churches and crosses were deliberately destroyed. Even under these conditions, the Church made tremendous efforts to safe the lives of oppressed people, especially Jews. By attending Church, the Polish people found the spiritual strength to survive psychologically during that awful time.

Polish Jews

Jews actively participated in the national uprisings that took place on Polish lands during the Fourth Partition. The Jewish population made up about one-third of the population of the cities in central Poland. Over 3-million Jews died in the Nazi death camps on Polish soil. Poland was the only country where death at the hands of the Nazis was the punishment for aiding Jews. Even so, thousands were saved by their fellow citizens - Poles who risked their lives.

- <u>Warsaw</u> - In 1939, about 380,000 Jews lived in Warsaw. The Germans deported 300,000 to the Treblinka in 1942. Many died in the Warsaw Ghetto from hunger and disease. At the time of the Warsaw Ghetto Uprising in 1943, only around 60,000 people still lived in the Ghetto. After the uprising, 56,065 captured Jews were deported to Treblinka.
- <u>Lodz</u> - The city of Lodz was one of the largest Jewish centers at the outbreak of World War II. In 1931, the Jewish population of Lodz was 202,497; of these, 870 survived the war.
- <u>Krakow</u> - Of the 68,000 Jews interred in the Krakow Ghetto, few survived.

Nazi Death Camps in Poland

The Nazis located the largest extermination camp a few dozen miles outside of Warsaw at Treblinka. It was designated exclusively for the murdering of Jews from the Warsaw Ghetto and the ghettos of other Polish cities as well as for thousands of Jews from nine other European countries. Of the 800,000 Jews who lost their life here, only 10% were citizens of other countries. This extermination was not documented and the Nazis concealed evidence of their crimes.

Auschwitz-Brzezinka was the largest factory of death in the history of humanity. Many millions of people lost their lives there including Jews from all over Europe. The Oswiecim State Museum displays exhibits and documents concerning Nazi crimes.

Other Nazi death camps include Majdanek (300,000 Jews murdered there), Belzec (half million Jews murdered there) and Sobibor (250,000 Jews from many countries were killed there).

POLISH MILITARY IN EXILE

POLAND NEVER SURRENDERED! A short time after the fall of Poland, the government in exile was formed first in France and later England. Polish men and women who escaped Nazi occupied Poland arrived to form new fighting units.

<u>Polish Air Force</u> - Following mobilization on August 30, 1939, Polish squadrons were sent to reserve airfields and played an active role in the campaign until Russia invaded Poland.

When the Polish pilots reached Britain, their skills were mostly unknown but because of the small size of the pre-war Polish Air Force, they were the best-trained pilots in the world. The training program at the Aviation Cadets School in Deblin and the Advanced Flying School in Grudziadz-Ulez was very demanding both regard to flying and shooting skills. At the outbreak of World War II, Polish pilots were the best-trained pilots in the world. With their homeland in enemy hands and news of Nazi atrocities in the occupied Poland, they took their hate into the air and became ferocious fighters.

In 1940, Polish fighter pilots distinguished themselves by bringing down 15% of the Nazi planes that attacked London during the Battle of Britain. Polish pilots defended Britain against German air raids and took part in operations all over the continent -- fighter pilots sweeping the skies clean and support ground units during and after D-Day, bomber crews flying night missions deep into Germany.

The Polish Air Force was the fourth largest Allied air force numerically and the equipment used was leased by Britain to Poland. After the war, a bill for over 68 million was paid from the Polish gold reserves deposited in Canada.

<u>Polish Navy</u> - Due to the hopeless position in light of the overwhelming superiority of the German forces both on the sea and in the air, the core of the Polish Navy, three destroyers, were evacuated to Britain and where they took part in Allied naval operations. The units of the Polish Navy patrolled German submarine-infested waters, protecting convoys that brought vital supplies to England from the US and Canada. In 1945, the Polish Navy had 1 cruiser, 6 destroyers and convoy escort vessels, 3 submarines and 5 motor gunboats.

<u>Polish Army</u> - The Independent Carpatian Brigade took part in the defense of Tobruk in Africa where their military exploits earned them glory. These forces became the 2nd Polish Corps in 1943 and were sent to Italy in 1944. The Corps gained fame by capturing the Nazi-fortified monastery of Monte Cassino, thus opening the road for the Allied forces to pursue retreating German forces.

1st Polish Armored Division - This division was organized in 1944 as part of 1st Canadian Army and fought in most of the major battles in the France and lead the drive to surround the Nazi troops in the area of Caen-Falaise. During the operations to trap several German units, the Polish troops deployed near the French village of Chamboix stood their ground for seven days and prevented the enemy units from rejoining the retreating German forces. The Poles prevented all desperate attempts of the enemy to break out of the encirclement and in fierce battles took large numbers of prisoners and war material. The Canadians called the area of Chamboix "The Polish Battlefield".

Polish Intelligence Service

The Polish Intelligence Service operated not only in Poland but also in Germany, Scandinavia and the Middle East. It had more than 3,000 agents. During the war years, reports on the Germany Army, the war industry, the economy of the Third Reich, the sociopolitical situation at the time and public feeling in occupied countries were submitted. Reports on the effectiveness of Allied air raids were particularly important. In addition, Polish intelligence contributed to the seizure of the original V-2 rocket made by the Germans.

In an October 1940 alliance agreement, the Polish government-in-exile gave the British all Polish intelligence records. These files from World War II constitute an invaluable depository of historical documents as well as providing clear evidence of the great contribution made by occupied Poland to defeat Nazi Germany.

Enigma

One of the most impressive successes of Polish intelligence was the breaking of the German code and the reconstruction of the Enigma - the original German coding machine. The Enigma resembled a tremendous typewriter. The keyboard activated three rotating drums, which contained the 26 letters of the alphabet. An electrical current ran from one to the other and back creating 100,391,791,500 variations.

In 1932, Marian Rejewski, Jerzy Rozycki and Henryk Zygalski, Cryptoanalysts in the Cipher Bureau of the Polish Intelligence Service, constructed a decoding machine that could translate Enigma's messages automatically. The decoder, called La Bomba, traced Nazi naval, air and land movements for the Polish high command. Britain and France were given replicas of the Enigma encoding machine and the decoder along with all the work Polish mathematicians had done on it. The Allies could not have broken the Enigma military encoding system without Poland's contribution.

Poland honored Marian Rejewski for his work on the Enigma code by awarding him the Order of Merit in 1977 and the Commanders Cross in 1978. In 2000, the Duke of York presented Poland with a model of the Enigma machine in a symbolic gesture recognizing Poland's role in help to break the top-secret system. Poland asked that the Encyclopedia Britannica entry on the Enigma be changed to credit the Poles for their role in breaking the code.

COMMUNISM ERA

At the end of World War II, Poland was severely weakened by the war and economically devastated. Russia entered Poland with a provisional government promising free elections but the first post-war elections were rigged by Polish communists who had previously sought refuge in Russia. With the suppression of all opposition, Poland was once again controlled by a foreign power. The only positive accomplishment during this period was the patriotic effort to rebuild the devastated country especially Warsaw that had been 88% destroyed. By 1948, the communists had eliminated the private sector and instituted a central economy focused on industrial enterprises that primarily favored heavy industry. However, the Soviet occupation was never economically successful and was plagued by petty dictators and rebellions from discontented workers.

Poland, the most uncontrollable and rebellious of the Soviet satellites, was the first to provoke a change in party leadership. Dissatisfaction with economic conditions expressed itself in strikes and open protest in Pozman in 1956 that was suppressed with armed force. However, this revolt did result in the election of Wladyslaw Gomulka as First Secretary. After World War II, the call for workers in Poland to rebel against the state and to establish free trade unions in Poland were discussed in the Polish language broadcasts of Radio Free Europe which could be heard in Poland in 1965. Economic stagnation and the denial of student demands to end censorship in 1968 ended the hope that communism could be reformed.

Realizing that some economic reform was necessary and desiring to eliminate other budget deficits, Secretary Gomulka decided to cancel the Christmas bonus and raise prices for food, fuel and other basic goods in December 1970. This announcement led to demonstrations by shipyard workers -- the elite of the working class -- in Gdansk, Gdynia and Szczecin. Gomulka was so out of touch with the workers that he saw the demonstrations as a “counter-revolution” and decided to crush it with troops and special riot police. Three notable facts of these demonstrations are:

1. The badly beaten or death of many workers.
2. In Gdansk and Szczecin, the workers’ demands included the establishment of free trade union that had existed in Poland even before the rebirth of Poland in 1918.
3. The three strike leaders in Szczecin were reserve officers of the Polish army, which meant they were members of the intelligentsia. In Gdansk, one of the strike leaders was an electrician by the name of Lech Walesa.

Gomulka resigned for “health reasons” and Edward Gierek became Poland’s new leader. The change in leadership calmed the workers for a while but the threat of more strikes remained until Gierek restored the old prices in 1971. He granted more freedom to the media and also sanctioned the restoration of the Royal Castle in Warsaw, which was very popular with the Polish people. The castle, now a museum of Polish history, is one of the most impressive examples of historic restoration in Europe. His government tried to improve economic conditions in Poland by taking out loans to improve Polish industry and infrastructure and make Poland competitive on world markets. His plan failed because of bad management, corruption and waste.

Opposition to Soviet domination and communism fused with support for the church, which became the preeminent moral authority in the country. Cardinal Stefan Wyszynski, Primate of Poland from 1951 to 1980, personified this authority. In 1970, he appealed not only for hard work and forgiveness, but also in defense of workers’ rights and demanded freedom of conscience as well as freedom of religious belief. In addition, he spoke of the nation’s right to free cultural activity and demanded freedom of speech and recognition of the right to truth. Later, in 1976, Cardinal Wyszynski demanded independent judiciary and civil service as well as free elections to the Parliament. Regarding the draft of the new Polish Constitution, he demanded respect for the fundamental civil rights of all Poles. Lastly, he said that the Constitution should not contain anything that could limit the sovereignty of the Polish nation and state. As a result of his outspokenness, Cardinal Wyszynski was seen by most Poles as the spokesman of the nation.

Faced with a budget deficit caused by large subsidies for basic products especially food, Gierek raised prices again in June 1976. This action again provoked worker protests that were brutally put down. This repression brought the workers and the intelligentsia together and as a result, Polish society began to develop a united opposition to the communist state. Later that year, a group of intellectuals organized the Komitet Obrony Robotnikow (KOR) whose original goal was to assist workers. It was the first intelligentsia organization to establish direct contact with the workers. KOR adopted the policy of open activism.

Another organization was Ruch Obrony Praw Czlowieka I Obywatela (ROPCIO) which was not limited to defending workers' rights. It represented the moderately reformist and right-wing intelligentsia. A third organization was Konfederacja Polski Niepodleglej (KPN) whose primary goal was to regain Polish independence. In 1978, Towarzystwo Kursow Naukowych (TKN) was formed as an underground educational organization. They organized seminars for university students on subjects such as recent Polish history, literature, philosophy, sociology, law and economics. Finally, a large underground press and all kinds of publications came into existence in 1976 and kept on growing. In these organizations, the Poles learned the techniques of organization and non-violent demonstrations.

KOR, ROPCIO, and KPN inspired and helped organize annual celebrations on May 3rd in honor of the Polish Constitution of 1791. A national holiday in Poland, it was a symbol of Polish rights. Since the government could not simply abolish these organizations because of the bad economic situation and the open support by the church, it rarely went beyond harassing the opposition.

The next pivotal event occurred in 1978 when Cardinal Karol Wojityla was elected Pope. He took the name John Paul II and became the first Polish Pope. The Pope's visit to Poland the following year had a tremendous impact on the country. When millions of people gathered to cheer their Pope, 34 years of communism seemed to vanish overnight and the people broke the barrier of fear when they realized that they had strength in numbers. This mass demonstration of Polish national feelings and Catholicism in 1979 was a prelude to the birth of Solidarity in 1980.

By 1979 the visible decline in the standard of living was a clear sign of the economic crisis facing Poland. While Poland was then the 5th largest coal producer in the world, power cuts idled the factories and mines for several hours a day. Why? Because not enough large power plants and power lines had been built by the government to keep up with the growth of industry and because government had contracted to export electric power. Expensive machinery stood idle and rusted while the construction of factories where the electricity was to be used was delayed -- or not built at all because party leaders had changed investment priorities. Purchased computers were received without manuals thus delaying production in factories and increasing costs while workers learned how to operate them by trial and error.

Although a series of poor harvests due to bad weather was partly to blame for food production to be down, governmental discrimination against the private farmers who owned about 78% of the land was the major cause. Furthermore, at least 25% of all perishable food was spoiled regularly due to a constant shortage of refrigerated rail and road cars and storage facilities. Despite increased housing construction, there was a permanent housing shortage and young married couples had to wait 15 years or more for government subsidized housing. Lastly, hospitals were severely overcrowded and in disrepair, doctors and nurses shockingly underpaid causing the free medical service to deteriorate to the point of disaster. In addition, people were dying for lack of foreign medications, which the government had stopped importing to save foreign currency.

Government and party officials, the military, politicians, and industrial managers had good housing, plentiful food, superior medical care and special vacation resorts. Due to the disparity between what was available to the government officials and what the people had to stand in line for, Unrest was growing.

No other country in Eastern Europe had such an organized resistance to communist authority, as did Poland. Because of a unique cooperation between workers, intellectuals and the Church during the years 1982-89, an underground society developed in Poland. When communism and Soviet domination collapsed in 1989, Poland was the only country which had a small "civic" society, i.e., one proficient with the ideas of democracy and civic/human rights, with a group of leaders ready to take power.

SOLIDARITY

On July 1, 1980, Premier Babiuch announced new price increases for meat and other basic food products which was followed by strikes all over Poland. The strikes were uncoordinated permitting government officials to settle one after another by agreeing to wage increases.

Then, Komitet Obrony Robotnikow (KOR) began to act as an information exchange within the country. While KOR did not organize the strikes of August 1980, it played an important role in these events because:

1. It had prepared the workers' awareness for these strikes through its paper, Rubotnik (The Worker).
2. It distributed information about the strikes - by telephone where possible and by courier where it was not.
3. Assumed the role of advisers to Solidarity in its negotiations with the government.

The two precipitating causes for the strike at the Lenin Shipyard in Gdansk in mid-August led by Lech Walesa were:

a) The dismissal of a popular woman crane operator, Anna Walentynowicz.
b) The price hikes that led the workers to demand pay raises.

When the shipyard manager promised the workers pay raises, agreed to the return of Anna Walentynowicz and agreed that the shipyard workers were to have their own union, the workers began to go home. But just then, delegates from other striking factories and from Gdansk city transport arrived and appealed to the workers not to give up because then the other strikers would have to go back to work without obtaining their demands. The workers agreed and began an occupation strike.

A regional Interfactory Strike Committee (Miedzyzakladowy Komitet Strajkowy (MKS)) was formed. The MKS gathered more and more enterprises, not only from the Baltic port cities but also from other parts of the country. Thus, workers and intellectuals cooperated on a new level - negotiations with the government. The meetings between the government delegation and the strikers' representatives were broadcast over the shipyard loudspeaker system and taped on recorders. The cassettes were then carried to the other striking enterprises and played there. (This was called "the cassette revolution").

The Gdansk agreement known as the 21 Points was signed on August 31st and marked the birth of Solidarity. Most of the 21 Points dealt with economic matters such as wages, working conditions, health insurance, etc., the core was political and included:

1. The right to form free trade unions.
2. The right to strike.
3. The demand for the legal definition of censorship (i.e., the passing of a law to this effect).
4. The demand that the Government free all political prisoners.
5. The demands for free access to the media for both the church and the free trade unions.

Solidarity was not just a labor movement; it was also a national movement. It had the support of the vast majority of Poles. Solidarity chapters and free unions of every kind sprang up everywhere and soon its membership rose to 10 million, out of a labor force of 18 million, including peasant farmers who wanted their own union. By this time, self-government was the demand voiced by all strata of Polish society.

Meanwhile Solidarity leaders cooperated closely with Polish intellectuals and drew up a list of Solidarity-national goals. These goals included the realization of basic Polish values such as Christian ethics and toleration as well as social justice, civil liberties and Polish patriotism. The proposed economic reforms included independence for socialized enterprises, various forms of ownership and also the right to work. Various legal reforms envisioned included guarantees for legality and a demand for openness in public life and for self-government in the shape of freely elected people's councils.

Solidarity was a unique Polish combination of socialism, democracy, nationalism and Catholicism. It opposed any use of force, a policy that was advocated by the church. Nor did Solidarity want to take power; its leaders and members knew that this could provoke a Soviet invasion.

- Socialism - Solidarity was socialist because it accepted the nationalization of heavy industry, transport and banking; it also supported full employment, free medical care and free education.
- Democracy - Solidarity also demanded democracy and self-government at all levels of public life; it was also a program to build democracy up from the grass roots.
- Nationalism - Solidarity was national because it represented the desires of the vast majority of Poles.
- Catholicism - Solidarity was Catholic because it reflected three key factors:
    1. 98% of the Polish population was Catholic
    2. The Catholic Church was a key part of the Polish national identity.
    3. The Catholic Church demanded respect for human and civil rights.

Thus, in 1980-81 Solidarity represented the desires and hopes of the vast majority of Poles and today is seen as the forerunner of the fall of the communist system and Soviet domination both in Poland and elsewhere. Outside Poland, Solidarity aroused great interest and support in Western Europe and in the US and the subsequent suppression of the movement aroused widespread indignation. Furthermore,

Western governments particularly the US exerted pressure on the Polish authorities to restore Solidarity which provided moral support for those Poles who continued their resistance in the underground.

Since 1990, Solidarity has placed greater emphasis on traditional union matters but the political group Solidarity Electoral Action, an outgrowth of the union founded in 1996, is a significant force in Polish politics. In the late 1990s, Solidarity had a total of 1.3 million members.

MARTIAL LAW

Meanwhile the Soviet leadership constantly pressured the Polish leaders to crush Solidarity because they wanted to avoid Soviet military intervention. Two factors in the Soviet decision not to invade Poland in 1980 were:

- US warning against invading Poland
- The Pope's warning that, if an invasion took place, he would go to Poland and face the Soviet troops at the head of his own people.

In September 1981, the Polish party leadership received a Soviet ultimatum that if the situation in Poland did not change by January 1982, the Soviets would drastically reduce supplies of basic raw materials, especially oil and gas.

In December 1981, Wojciech Jaruzelski, acting as Premier, Head of the Council of Ministers and Minister of Defense, arrested Solidarity leaders all over the Poland to prevent any further union activity and effectively seized control of the country by military coup. The official justification for martial law was the charge that Solidarity leaders were preparing to overthrow the government and party. The unspoken justification was that if Jaruzelski had not acted, there would have been a Soviet military intervention, resistance and a terrible bloodbath. In fact, his decision to impose martial law is still the subject of great controversy in Poland.

By the new year, Poland was once again under the firm grip of a conventional communist regime. Under martial law, severe restrictions were imposed on civil liberties, universities were closed and thousands of Solidarity activists, including Lech Walesa, were imprisoned. The government believed that initiating martial law effectively extinguished the challenge posed by Solidarity. Time, however, proved that Jaruzelski's tactics had staggered Solidarity but not killed it. Members of the union operated underground or from jail cells, advocating a waiting game to preserve the principles of the Gdansk

Agreement. Resistance took the form of an underground press and unsanctioned lecture circuits that became the training ground for a new generation of activists.

The Pope's visit to Poland in June 1983 probably assisted in ending martial law for it was lifted the next month. When Lech Walesa was awarded the Nobel Peace Prize in December 1983, the prize became a symbol of world recognition both for him as the leader of Solidarity and for the Polish people for their peaceful struggle for freedom and human rights.

Poland was shocked in 1984 by the abduction and murder of Father Jerzy Popieluszko, a priest who had gained recognition as the spiritual adviser of the repressed Solidarity. His funeral was attended by thousands of people, including foreign statesmen visiting Poland, and his grave became the site of pilgrimages.

In 1985, Mikhail S. Gorbachev became the First Secretary of the Communist Party of the Soviet Union and began calling for restructuring of the economy. Two years later, the Polish government announced it would carry out extensive economic reforms following the lines of Gorbachev's reforms. The Polish plan was to reduce bureaucracy, close down deficit industrial plants and raise prices. The economic reforms brought no improvement and the combination of a weakening economy and runaway inflation had lowered Polish living standards and deepened the anger and frustration of society. The situation continued to deteriorate and spontaneous strikes broke out in several parts of the country during 1988. The demands in each strike were for higher wages and also the re-establishment of Solidarity.

The head of the government-controlled trade unions challenged Walesa to a TV debate in November 1988 in an effort to discredit him but Walesa came out the clear winner.

Even more important, some 25 million Polish viewers saw the debate - many of whom saw Walesa for the first time and liked what they saw.

INDEPENDENT & DEMOCRATIC POLAND

Surrounded by widespread predictions of a social explosion, Jaruzelski took the eventful step of beginning round table talks with Solidarity and other opposition groups. The government believed that the Polish people would be satisfied with a limited democratization and assumed that the party had the money and organization facilities to win a majority of seats in the Lower House. Even more important, such an arrangement had the blessings of Gorbachev.

Round table talks began in 1989 with government-party representatives on one hand, and Solidarity representatives led Walesa on the other. After months of haggling, the talks yielded a historic compromise:

- Solidarity would regain legal status and the right to post candidates in parliamentary elections (with the outcome guaranteed to leave the communists a majority of seats).
- Solidarity agreed that the Diet would elect General Jaruzelski as President for 6 years with extensive powers.
- Solidarity agreed that the communists were to control the Ministries of Foreign Affairs, the Interior (Police) and the Army.

In the time available before elections, Solidarity organized local citizens' committees to canvass the voters, while Walesa personally confirmed Solidarity candidates and was photographed with them. (This was crucial for voters because the election rules, prepared by the communists, did not allow the printed ballots to contain information about the candidates' political affiliations.) On Election Day, June 4th, most Polish voters crossed off all communist candidates on their ballots, showing their true feelings. Thus, not one of the communists was elected - for none obtained the required 50% of the vote.

However, Solidarity honored the April Round Table Agreement and the communists were allowed to win seats in a second round of voting. Solidarity used its superior position to broker a coalition with various small parties that until then had been silent satellites of the communists. As a result, the communists were unable to secure the “guaranteed” 65% of the seats in the Diet because puppet peasant and democratic parties combined with Solidarity producing a non-communist majority. In the Sejm, 99 of the 100 seats went to Solidarity.

Again per the agreement, General Jaruzelski was elected by Parliament to be President for six years; he got the requisite number of votes plus one. He had great powers on paper (mostly in defense and foreign policy) but he could hardly exercise them without the support of Parliament where the decisive power belonged to the Civic Parliamentary Club, an umbrella alliance that included all supporters of Solidarity.

After two communists Premiers in succession failed to form a coalition government dominated by communists, General Jaruzelski consulted with Walesa on selecting a new Premier. Walesa favored Tadeusz Mazowiecki, a Solidarity journalist and devout Catholic, who had been one of his leading advisers since 1980. He was duly nominated and confirmed as Premier by the Parliament. A new government emerged in September 1989 - the first government in a former communist state in which communists were a minority. The new government was committed to dismantling the communist system and replacing it with a Western-style democracy and free market system.

In 1990, Lech Walesa was elected President of Poland and resigned his union post. Poland stabilized its economy as a result of the ‘shock therapy’ program and other reforms instituted in the early 1990s. Termination of the commitment to heavy industry that had been subsidized by the government resulted in unemployment - a new development in Poland. Reorganizing the economy and speeding up privatization placed over half of the economy in private hands and attracted foreign capital.

Poland is becoming a strong economic force in Eastern Europe with much foreign investment and a health GDP. The political scene within the country has been stabilizing and in 1997 a new constitution was ratified. In 1999 Poland joined NATO, the ultimate step in ensuring Poland's protection from any Russian plans to reestablish domination over the country.

GEOGRAPHY

GEOGRAPHY

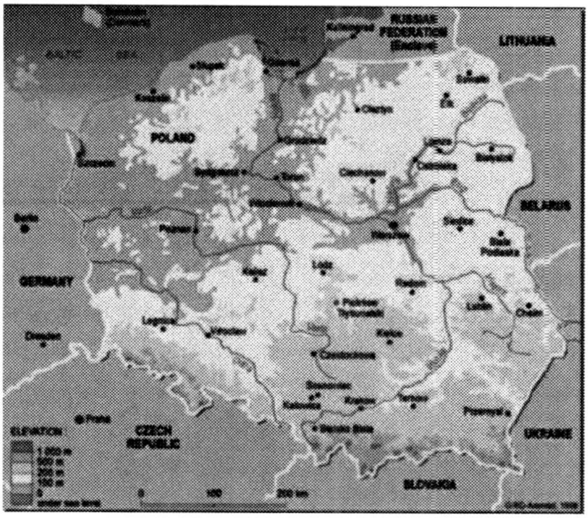

Slightlysmaller than New Mexico, Poland is the 69th largest country in the world and the 8th largest country in Europe. Poland's shape is roughly square, measuring 400-440 miles across.

Poland is located at the center of the European continent with geographical coordinates of 52°N, 20°E. Poland has an area of 120,727 square miles and a frontier of 3,582 km including 528 km of coastline. The Baltic Sea and Russia border Poland to the north. Its northern frontier on the Baltic Sea gives Poland access to Scandinavian and North Sea ports. To the west, the Poland/German border runs along the Oder and Neissee rivers. The Sudeten and Carpathian Mountains separate Poland from the Czech Republic and Slovakia to the south while its eastern neighbors include Lithuania, Belarus and Ukraine

Historically, Poland has been an area of conflict because of its flat terrain and the lack of natural barriers. The country lies almost entirely on the North European Plain and is a land of gentle relief, rarely rising above 350 feet except along the southern border with the Sudeten and Carpathian mountain ranges. Poland's highest peak, Rysy is located in the Tatra Mountains and rises 2,499 meters above sea level.

The surface of Poland is 91% lowlands and 6% highlands. Mountains located in southern Poland cover about 3% of the land. Land use includes 46% arable land, 13% meadows and pasture, 28% forests and woodland. As a result of glacier activities, even the lowlands are hilly. One of the characteristic features of Poland is that belts of hills and lowlands occur repeatedly in the same direction as the parallels of latitude.

The countryside is nevertheless varied: with lake regions, forests and mountains. The longest rivers, which cross the country northward are: the Vistula which flows 675 miles in the center from the Western Carpathians to the Baltic Sea and the Oder, which flows along Poland's western border. Both rivers are used as transport routes.

Poland's seven regions are:

1) The Coastal Lowlands - extend in a narrow strip along the Baltic Coast of northwestern Poland and sandy beaches form much of the predominantly smooth coastline. The coast forms natural harbors at Gdansk, Gdynia and Szezecin and these three ports are the only major cities located in the region.
2) The Baltic Lakes Region - is a scenic, hilly area with thousands of small lakes that covers most of northern Poland. Parts of the area are covered with forests and peat bogs and most of the land is not good for farming although some farmers raise potatoes and rye. Because it is sparsely populated, it is a popular vacation site where many Poles enjoy camping, hiking and fishing. The major industry in this region is lumbering.
3) The Central Plains - are low-lying plains that stretch across the entire width of Poland and make up Poland's major agricultural area. Farmers grow potatoes, rye, sugar beets and other crops. Several of Poland's most important cities including Poznan, Warsaw and Wroclaw are located in this region.
4) The Polish Uplands - are located south of the plains

region and consist of hills, low mountains and plateaus which contain most of Poland's mineral wealth including coal, copper, lead and zinc. Much of its richest farmland is located here and corn, potatoes and wheat are the major crops. Coal-mining and metal-processing industries have made this area the most highly industrialized regions in Poland.

5) <u>The Carpathian Forelands</u> - are located within the branches of the Vistula and San rivers in southeastern Poland. The majority of the area is densely populated and crops flourish in the fertile soil that covers the gently rolling hills. The region's most important manufacturing center is Krakow where iron and steel industries have developed.
6) <u>The Sudeten Mountains</u> - border southwestern Poland and its peaks are covered with forests. The valleys and foothills are used for crops and pastureland and textile industries operate in many of the small cities and towns.
7) <u>The Western Carpathian Mountains</u> - are steep, scenic mountains that form the southernmost region of Poland and bears, wildcats and other animals live in the thickly forested mountains. Rural towns and villages are scattered throughout the region and the region has several national parks.

Due to the relatively low level of change in the landscape, Poland's level of biological diversity is high compared to Europe. Poland is located in a zone containing a large diversity of rich flora and fauna. Maintaining traditional forms of individual agriculture in large areas of the country has enabled the survival of many primitive species of crop plants and farm animals. Since 1990, the number of protected nature areas has almost doubled and the surface area increased by 50%.

The Pustynia Bledowska located midway between Krakow and Czestochowa is central Europe's only true desert. It consists of 20 square miles of shifting sands, oasis-like vegetation along the River Biala Przemsza that cuts through the desert and even mirages on hot summer days.

Germany, Czech Republic, Slovakia, Ukraine, Belarus, Lithuania and Russia are Poland's neighbors as a result of post-communist geographic changes. Poland's border with Russia in the north is at the Kaliningrad enclave, the headquarters of Russia's main Baltic naval installations.

CLIMATE

Poland's climate is temperate with cold, cloudy, moderately severe winters with frequent precipitation and mild summers with frequent showers and thundershowers.

The climate in Poland is greatly influenced by oceanic air currents from the west, cold polar air from Scandinavia and Russia as well as warmer, sub-tropical air from the south. In winter, polar-continental fronts dominate bringing crisp, frosty weather. The late summer and autumn months enjoy plenty of warm days as a result of the dry, sub-tropical, continental air mass. The greatest amount of sunshine in the summer is found on the Baltic coast while in winter this is true of the Carpathian Mountains. In the mountains the climate is dependent on the altitude.

The westerly wind belt that sweeps across Poland gives it variable weather. Moist, cloudy and warm days commonly alternate with cold, clear and dry days. Although these changes tend to be lost in the average climatic figures for the country, they are an essential element in Poland's climate. All seasons enter Poland not from the south or north but from the west (spring) and from the east (winter) due to the transitional nature of the climate. Only summer enters the country from the south.

In Warsaw temperatures average from 68-77°F in July and winters are cold with average January temperatures ranging from 32-23°F. Snow may lie on the ground up to three months. The average yearly rainfall varies from 450mm in the northeast to 1000mm in the mountains.

Drought

One of the negative characteristics of the climate in Poland is the frequent occurrence of droughts. They occur periodically in different seasons of the year and can cause serious economic losses. Droughts cause a change in the natural water balance which leads to excessive soil over-drying, lowering of the underground water table and reduction of the volume of water flowing in rivers. Since Poland has relatively poor natural water resources in relation to its economic requirements, it is faced with serious negative effects during drought periods.

Regions with the longest duration of drought are located in a zone stretching from Podlasie Lowland in the northeast through central Poland to the Silesian Lowland in the southwest. These threatened regions are where the majority of Polish farming potential is situated. Such a vast distribution of drought is detrimental to the Polish economy, particularly agriculture. Investigations are being undertaken to determine the results of the occurrence of drought. There is a lack of resources available for preventive measures against droughts and no regional cooperation with respect to droughts in Poland.

On average, droughts occur in Poland once every three years. During the last 50 years, droughts with the largest territorial range occurred in 1959, 1969, 1982 and 1992. As a result of a disastrous flood in the southern and western parts of Poland in 1997, action plans for flood control and drought fighting programs are under review as well as plans to improve monitoring and early warning systems.

ABUNDANCE OF NATURAL RESOURCES

The geological diversity of the country has resulted in the existence of a wide variety of mineral resources. Next to France, Poland has one of the richest assortments of minerals of all European countries.

Soils

Soil is one of the more essential components of the natural environment and its quality has a significant affect on the development and geographical distribution of a country's population. Surface geological deposits of different ages are the parent rock of Polish soils. Soils are directly dependent on the climate, mineral content of the mother rock, hydrological conditions and plant cover. The development of soils on the territory of Poland dates back to the retreat of the last ice sheet about 12,000 years ago. Over 75% of the territory of the country are occupied by Pleistocene formations, mostly boulders, clay and sand.

Poland is located in the humid climate zone where precipitation is larger than evaporation. As a result of the constant soil washing and movement of mineral components from the surface, which took place mainly in coniferous forests, podsolization of the soil has occurred. These soils are very acidic, lack minerals and humus, contain poor buff properties and are easily devastated. They occupy over 30% of the farmland in Poland. Brown soils are good forest habitats and when farmed can become average or even high quality farmland.

The value and usefulness of soils for agriculture and forests in many Western European countries is about 25% higher than the quality of Polish soils with more favorable climatic conditions for farming. Poland is one of the few countries which has prepared a detailed plan of their soils and studies of soil conditions and the changes of their properties are done systematically.

Water

The hydrological phenomena are shaped by geological build, climate, and surface features. 99% of the territory of Poland lies in the catchment of the Baltic Sea, mainly in the basins of the Vistula and Oder Rivers. Their characteristic feature is an irregular build with a better-developed eastern side and low watershed that influences the high hydrographical conformity of the territory of country. Poland also has a large number of lakes the majority of which are of glacial origin.

Surface waters are the third largest form of land use in Poland and occupy 2.65% of the area of Poland. This area increased recently due to the construction of several new reservoirs. There are many lakes in Poland but most of them are shallow. All of the lakes are slowly waning as a result of silting-up, overgrowth, erosion processes and reclamation. The water accumulated in the lakes has a moderating influence on the environment and, through increased evaporation, affects the amount of precipitation.

Poland's inland water resources of both surface and groundwater are small and, in most cases, are derived from the territory of Poland. The water resources of Poland result from the yearly water input, 97% of which is shaped by atmospheric precipitation. Evaporation constitutes the main outputs and represents nearly 70% of water loss. Compared to other European countries, Poland has the least favorable water system. Errors in water resource management during the 1970s contributed to this situation and included extensive deforestation, excessive straightening and deepening of the river channels and the drainage of marshes, moors and wet farmlands.

The protection of water resources must include the storage of as much water as possible from the spring thaw and during periods of heavy rainfall. Measures that reduce or slow down water runoff and allow for utilization of water resources according to the needs of agriculture include:

- Protection of marshes, meadows and rushes.
- Preservation of streams and reservoirs.
- Utilization of natural depressions for periodic retention of surplus drainage water.

Prior to 1990, water was a resource that was freely accessible or available for a token fee. The implementation of operational tariffs and fees since the early 90s has resulted in significant decrease in water use especially for commercial purposes.

Wetlands, marshes and peat bogs play an important role in shaping the water resources of Poland. The largest wetland, Bagna Biebrzanskie, was recognized as a natural retention reservoir and became a National Park in 1993. Due to improper water drainage and a several year drought, the surface area of the wetlands, marshes and peat bogs are deteriorating constantly and permanently.

Poland's priorities for freshwater are:

- Ensuring healthy and safe drinking water;
- Limiting industrial water use and protecting underground waters against pollution;
- Protection of lakes, inland water reservoirs, estuaries, and Baltic water bays against pollution;
- Limiting the impact of salt water from mining on the purity of water;
- Increasing reservoir retention of surface waters;
- Use of water for energy production; and
- Meeting the commitments resulting from the international conventions signed by Poland.

Farmland

The location of Poland in the belt of the European plains has significantly influenced the way land is utilized. Plains and large hilly country areas are suitable for farming even though the soil quality is poor. Grains clearly dominate agricultural land use. Although arable land is spread uniformly throughout Poland, it is the only form of land use, which is systematically decreasing.

Poland is one of the poorest European countries in regard to permanent grassland. The distribution of permanent grassland depends on the existence of favorable habitat conditions for grassy ecosystems, namely sufficient water. Large meadows exist in the lowland part of Poland as a result of such favorable habitats, such as wide river valleys in which the level of ground water is maintained at a fairly high level throughout a majority of the year. However, the northeast region of Poland has the greatest concentration of grassland. This region has the shortest vegetation period, the lowest yearly temperatures and an average precipitation of 600-700 mm annually.

Meadows in Poland are mainly unnatural and formed as a result of riverside forest clear-cutting or by turning former tillable fields into meadows and pastures. Very few of the meadows are cultivated and as a result are either too dry because of poor reclamation or too wet. Few of the meadows produce high yields of hay and pastures are overgrazed and not very productive.

Forests

The second largest form of land use in Poland is forests. The distribution of forests in Poland is very uneven with the greatest number of forests existing in the northwestern and western part of the country. Central Poland lacks a major forest. The last of all forest complexes exist in the mountains, particularly in the Carpathian Mountains where natural spruce coniferous forests are preserved.

Satellite photographs reveal that many areas in great forest complexes are totally devastated because of huge military training grounds located there. A lot of effort is required to reforest these areas. The satellite photographs also reveal that some forest complexes were too intensively exploited. In some cases, the acreage of the logged area is almost equal to the area occupied by trees.

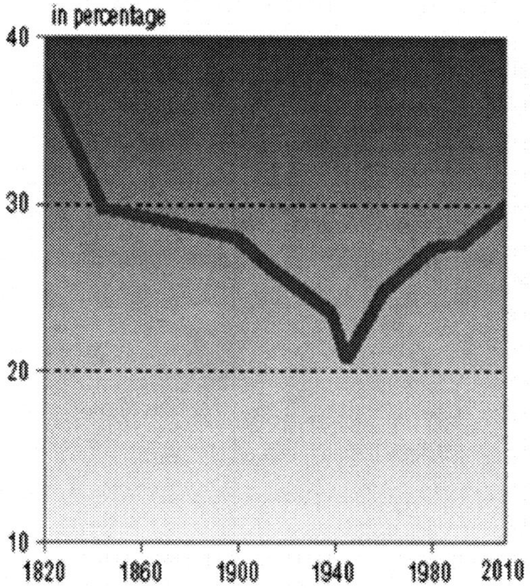

The change in woodiness of Poland between 1820 and 1992 and the forecast to year 2010 (according to data from Forestry Research Institute)

Forests have grown since the end of World War II because of the reforestation of the weakest farmland. Postwar reforestation increased the woodiness of Poland and as a result, many forests in Poland are younger than 40 years. The majority of forests in Poland occupy poor forest habitats and sandy soils on which pine tree stands are dominant.

Harvesting of timber stock between 1967-1989 was on the average 17% greater than the cutting plan. These breaches of the cutting limit were mostly immature cuttings that were cut in order to clean the forest and to make clearances for sanitary reasons. The most difficult period for Polish forestry was during years 1982-83 because cuttings of immature trees were twice the limit. Cuts were necessary for the following reasons:

- Natural disasters (blowdown of trees);
- Climatic catastrophes (droughts); and
- Pest damages (Lymantria monacha).

A historical turning point in forest utilization was reached in 1990 when the amount of timber harvested was below the cutting limit.

Bialowieza Forest in northeast Poland was the favorite hunting grounds of Polish royalty and is the last remaining primeval forest in Europe. The majority of this lowland park is covered with dense forests, meadows, peat bogs, thickets and water vegetation along the Orlowka River. It is home to 11,000 animal species, including 8,500 kinds of insects, and is best known as the last natural habitat of European bison and tarpan, a unique small Polish wild horse. Today, Bialowieza is dedicated to conservation and environmental preservation and in 1992 was the first Polish national part to join the UNESCO list of World Human Heritage.

In 1992 there were three times more forest fires than in the preceding years and they burned an area that was 12 times larger. A new category of fire hazard explains the fire dynamics of 1992 that were extraordinary in many forest regions of Poland. This new category is the result of coexistence of at least three reinforcing phenomena:

- prolonged drought possibly the result of global climate changes,
- the effects of air pollution which caused dieback of trees, thinning of tree stands, rampant growth of grasses and accumulation of large amounts of combustible material, and
- the increased flow of transportation and tourist traffic going through the forests.

The condition of Polish forests are being physically affected by phenomena occurring outside of forestry and these new threats are industrial pollution of air and soil, water deficit and pollution, global climatic changes, damage to the ozone layer and radiation contamination. These phenomena are reshaping the healthy condition of forests and their limits, effects and character are unknown.

Observations of the condition of forests since the late 1970s show:

- an increase in the activity of insect pests and fungal diseases;
- a disappearance of certain symbiotic fungi that existed in the environment;
- structural changes of plant tissues, including anatomical changes of the wood;
- an increase in the quantity of deadwood, thinning of tree stands and pathological deforestation;
- the worsening of health conditions of deciduous species of trees, especially oak and beech;
- chemical damages to the soil and root systems, especially the increase in acidity and contamination by heavy metals, which speeds up and worsens the degradation of habitats.

Mountains

Mountains in Poland are defined as areas higher than 350 m above sea level. This area covers about 8% of the country, and includes the Sudeten and Carpathian Mountains in the South, and the Saint Cross Mountains in central Poland. It is estimated that the mountains in Poland are the source of about 30% of all water resources. Forests cover about 40% of the mountain area. Mountains constitute the area for mineral and rock exploitation. The main hazards to mountain forests are the following:

a) Acid rains and industrial dust, which have caused forest dieback and an increase of erosion and water flow in the famous Black Triangle on the border area of the Czech Republic, Poland, and Germany;
b) Excessive development of settlements and recreational

areas in the West region of Karpaty at the foot of the Tatra Mountains, the highest mountain in Poland; and

c) Mineral resource mines primarily in the Sudeten Mountains.

Currently, many programs preserve and protect the mountains and forests of Poland as soil and water protection forests and recreational forests. There is no danger of excessive deforestation of the mountain areas at this time.

Mineral Resources

Poland, next to France, has one of the richest assortments of minerals among European countries. Mineral resources in Poland include:

- Anthracite - The only identified deposits of anthracite in Poland named Wabrzych-Gaj lie in the Lower Silesian Coal Basin. It occurs in 22 beds with an average thickness of 1.9m. In 1995, 276 thousand tons were extracted of which 74 thousand tons were exported to United Kingdom, Czech Republic, Germany and Ukraine.
- Hard Coal - The adaptation of coal mining to market economy has produced changes in the magnitudes of resources and output. More than 23.5% of excavated coal is designated for export. Hard coal deposits occur in three basins in Poland:
    1. Lower Silesian Coal Basin - A considerable thickness variability and small horizontal and vertical extent of coal-bearing formations characterize the Lower Silesian Coal Basin. The difficult geological mining conditions and unprofitable exploitation result in the closing of mines in this basin.
    2. Upper Silesian Coal Basin - Exploited deposits cover 30% of the Upper Silesian Coal Basin and reserve deposits cover 23% of the whole area. Over 80% of coal deposits in Poland in this

basin.

3. Lublin Coal Basin - The Lublin Coal Basin is in the early stage of management and exploration of its borders is relatively poor. The intrinsically economic reserves constitute a little more than 14% of the total Polish coal resources.

- <u>Crude Oil</u> - Oil fields occur in the Carpathians, the Carpathian Foredeep, the Polish Lowland and on the Baltic Sea. In the considered regions, besides oil fields, there are also oil condensate fields. In 1995, the recoverable resources of the Carpathian fields amounted to 25.5% of the country's resources, the Carpathian Foredeep to 25.6% and Polish Lowland fields to 48.9%.
    1. Carpathian Oil Fields - The Carpathian oil is of methane type and the reserves are small and depend on the quantity and type of structures in which they occur. Over many years, the exploitation has caused exhaustion of the reserves in this region.
    2. Carpathian Foredeep Oil Fields - They are mainly bedded fields that lie mostly under impermeable Miocene clay sediments.
    3. Polish Lowland Oil Fields - Oil from these fields occur in Permian, carboniferous and Cambrian rocks and yields medium paraffin oil with sulfur content exceeding 1%.
    4. Poland also has rather rich oil beds under the Baltic Sea and Przedsiebiorstwo Poszeukiwan Ropy and Gaz Petrobaltic has been extracting oil and gas for several years.

In 1996, huge oil and gas deposits were found in western Poland. Reserves at Poland's largest oil field are estimate at more than 64 million tons of oil and 29 billion cubic meters of natural gas which more than justifies its billing as the "Polish Kuwait".

- <u>Natural Gas</u> - Natural gas fields occur in the Carpathians,

Carpathian Foredeep, the Polish Lowland and in the Western Pomerania. Gas occurs in separate fields or together with oil or oil condensate. In 1995, 53% of the proven resources occurred in lowland fields. The gas output for this year covered 48% of the country's demand and the deficit was balanced by imports mainly from Russia.

1. Carpathians - Gas of the Carpathian fields is exploited in gas-pressure conditions. The gas has a high methane and low nitrogen content (usually over 80% of methane).
2. Carpathian Foredeep - Gas fields in this region occur in Jurassic, Cretaceous and Miocene sediments. The gas has a high methane and low nitrogen content (usually 70-98.8% of methane).
3. Poland Lowland - The gas in these fields usually have high nitrogen content up to 80%.
4. The Baltic also yields natural gas. It is not yet being extracted from the four fields discovered because the possibility is being considered of sending it through a pipeline straight to the gas power station in Zarnowiec.

- <u>Helium</u> - The main source of helium are in fields of natural gas with high nitrogen content. Helium occurs in almost every gas field in the Polish Lowlands. It is extracted from gas in the Nitrogen Separation Plant in Odolanow. Extraction began in Poland in 1971 and reached its maximum state in the mid-80s. All helium extraction is intended for export mainly to the United States.
- <u>Copper Ores</u> - Copper ores of industrial value occur in Lower Silesia and in the pre-Sudetic monocline. The main deposits in production lie in the monocline near Lublin. Over 75% of the total resources occur in deposits in exploitation and a considerable part of the copper production from domestic deposits is destined

for export.

- Silver - In Poland silver occurs mainly in copper ores of the Zechstein formation in Lower Silesia. Silver extraction from copper ores is the most important in Polish economy and over 93% are exported.
- Gold - Gold occurs in Zechstein copper ores in the pre-Sudetic monocline and is extracted during the processing of these ores. Resources of gold have not been explored as yet although preliminary prospecting indicates that several tons are located here.
- Tin - Tin occurs in the Sudetes in two deposits in Gierczyn and Krobica, which are classified as potentially economic ones.
- Zinc & Lead Ores - Deposits in Poland occur in the Silesia-Krakow region, which constitutes the northern and northeastern area surrounding the Upper Silesian Coal Basin. They lie in several deposit regions: Bytom, Chrzanow, Olkusz and Zawiercie. The Bytom region has historical meaning since exploitation was conducted there since the Middle Ages and now only potentially economic ones are left. The deposits of the Zawiercie region have not been exploited as yet.
- Rock Salt - Poland has numerous and rich rock salt deposits. The explored rock salt resources make possible a great salt mining development, mainly regarding the unexploited salt dome deposits in central Poland and bed desposits of the pre-Sudetic monocline. Some deposits in the southern salt region have been exploited since the Middle Ages -- Wieliczka-Bochnia were exploited since the 12th Century, but others were explored after World War II. Currently, six salt mines are in operation including K'odawa which is the only shaft mine exploiting dry salt suitable for dietary purposes.
- Sulfur - In Poland, the content of native sulfur in the rock can reach 70% and is important for the country's economy. The deposits occur in the northern part of the Carpathian Foredeep and were formed during

the formative rebuilding of the gorge at the end of Badetian.

- Amber - The Baltic amber ranges in color from pale yellow to reddish brown and is found in Poland in tertiary and quaternary formations.
    a) Large accumulations of amber in tertiary sediments occur in the northern and southern marginal zone of the Eocene Sea of which the area lying in the Gdansk Gulf has the greatest concentration of amber.
    b) The biggest quaternary sediments of amber have been accumulated due to the glacier and postglacial rivers transport from tertiary sediments of the Chapowska-Sambijska delta. Huge concentrations of amber are found in Kurpie and the northern part of Bydgoszcz where it occurs in the outwash fan measures.
    c) Extensive amber concentrations are also encountered on the Baltic beaches from Koobrzeg to the eastern border of Poland where this raw material occurs in the fossil measures of Holocene beaches.
- Barite - Barite deposits occur in Lower Silesia and the Holy Cross Mountains.
    a) Lower Silesia - four deposits have been explored with two of them exploited. Deposits occur in veins in fissures of varying length and thickness. The average $BaSO_4$ content is 80%.
    b) Holy Cross Mountains - occurs in carbonate rocks in the form of irregular nests and bands. This deposit is not exploited because of its small size and the low $BaSO_4$ content of about 30%.
- Fluorspar - Fluorspar resources are explored in two deposits in Lower Silesia. It forms irregular bands and its content usually increases with depth. Fluorspar is not exploited because it occurs predominantly in deeper parts of the deposit.

- Gypsum - The Nida valley is one of the richest gypsum bearing regions in Poland and is of importance to the Polish economy. Gypsum in this area occurs just under the ground surface and its content amounts to 85-95%.
- Limestones & Marls - Limestones and marls are used in the production of cement and lime and in the metallurgy and food industry. These materials are located in the following regions: Lower Silesia, Silesiani-Kracow area, Holy Cross Mountains, Carpathians, Lublin area and the Kujawy-Pomeranian area. The resources of limestones and marls cover the total country's demand and allow substantial exports of limestone processed products.
- Chalk - There are two types of chalk deposits that occur in Poland: Cretaceous chalk and lacustrine chalk. The Cretaceous chalk is utilized in the rubber, paper, chemical, pigment and cement industries. It occurs in 16 deposits in eastern and northeastern Poland. Lacustrine chalk is utilized as calcareous fertilizer in agriculture and is found in northern and central Poland.
- Dolomites - Dolomites are used in the metallurgical industry as fluxes, in agriculture as fertilizer, in the ceramic industry and also as building and road materials. The deposits are located:
    a) Katowice - Deposits in this area are suitable for the metallurgical industry.
    b) Lower Silesia - Dolomites for the ceramic industry are located here where they form lentil deposits in metamorphic shales.
    c) Holy Cross Mountain - The numerous bedded Devonian dolomites that are found in this region cannot be exploited because they occur in ecologically protected areas.
- Mineral Pigments - Mineral pigments are the main materials for the production of mineral paints and are also used for oil paints, varnishes, enamels, putties, etc. In Poland, two deposits of ochre, argils and ochre

claystones have been explored in the Kielce region.

Gold mining has a long history in Polish and was mined as early as the 12th Century in Lower Silesia. Geologists estimate that between the end of the 15th Century and the mid-18th Century, the Zloty Stok gold mine along yielded almost 9 tons of gold. After World War II, gold mining in Poland ceased. Geologists today believe that Polish soil may still hide considerable gold deposits.

NUMEROUS NATIONAL PARKS

One of Poland's strengths is its system for nature protection. Protected areas cover nearly ¼ of Poland's area and encompass varied ecosystems: mountains, swamps, forests and river valley. Poland is unique in Europe because of its large areas unaffected by humans. About ⅔ of Poland's area are relatively intact environments. Major assets are its biological diversity, including the presence of reintroduced mammals such as the bison and beaver.

Poland's National Parks constitute the biggest form of nature protection and are exceptional in Europe for their range of wildlife, their size and varying geographical interest. There are 22 national parks in Poland, which cover approximately 1% of the country's area. Bialowieza National Park is a rarity of primeval mixed lowland forest while Narwia Park covers the part of the Narwia river valley called the Polish Amazon area. A national park protects the entire nature and specific landscape features within its borders. The main task of a national park, which has priority over all other activities, is to study and preserve the unity of natural systems of the area as well as to restore the disturbed or extinct elements of a native nature.

Besides accomplishing its main goal - nature conservation, the parks carry out scientific, academic and tourist activities. The later enables all interested people to experience the direct contact with unique nature. This privilege requires that visitors to the parks conform all rules within a national park. Educational and academic activities are carried out through preparation of "educational trails". New forms of environmental education and related activities are being developed and tested as well.

In addition to national parks, Poland has landscape parks, areas of protected landscape and natural reserves. Landscape parks are areas that include examples of outstanding landscape boasting aesthetic, historical and cultural values.

Today, science and technology provide endless opportunities of altering the Polish natural environment and are threatening it with destruction. The national parks, which protect the most precious and invaluable areas of the country with their vast richness of flora and fauna, provide an opportunity to preserve this wonderful nature for future generations.

Biebrzanski National Park

Biebrzanski National Park was established on September 9, 1993 and is the largest of Poland's National Parks. It covers a large part of the Biebrza proglacial valley and protects most of the valley's peatland. The main task of the Park is to protect the variety of species of fauna and flora within the existing ecosystem, including various kinds of peats and peatbogs. The Biebrza River Valley is the largest and the best-preserved area of low bogs and forest raised bogs in the temperate biogeographical zone.

The ecological characteristics of the Biebrza Marshes as well as their vastness contribute to the survival of the fauna, typical of natural swamp and water ecosystems, which is nearly extinct elsewhere. They also serve as a highly valuable object of natural and ecological research, which is quite rare nowadays. The Biebrza Marshes provide a good living environment for elk (North American - moose), beaver, wolf, crane, black grouse, double snipe, dunlin, jack snipe, whooper, swan, widgeon, and many other species.

The breeding birds of the Biebrza River Valley includes as many as 185 species and is characterized by the exceptional biodiversity in comparison to both Polish and Central European communities of birds. This high number is related primarily to the great diversity of landscapes in the Biebrza Valley and the good preservation of all types of pristine wetland and marshland habitats. The marshes are also an important resting-place for birds that migrate from Northern and Central Europe to Africa and Asia. The number of water and mud birds that stop here is many times higher than in other river valleys of Poland and the whole Europe.

In the spring and summer, the air swarms with butterflies and insects that have not yet been classified and may include some rare species of butterfly. Many fish species live in the Biebrza waters and numerous old river bends. Five types of the aquatic environment, differing both in the prevailing species and quantities of fish have been identified in the Biebrza River basin.

43 plant communities were identified in the Biebrza Marshes and, of particular interest, are those that shape the features of the Valley and those that are rarely found in other regions. The pristine character of these marshes allowed the species typical of glacial flora and of the boreal zone to survive and some extremely rare species of plants have found suitable living conditions in the Biebrza Marshes.

Kampinoski National Park

Kampinoski National Park, located northwest of Warsaw, occupies part of the Vistula proglacial valley in the Warsaw basin with a large forest complex - Kampinos Primeval Forests. It was founded in 1959 and is not only the sole national park that borders on a capital with over a million inhabitants but is one of the largest national parks of the European lowland, which stretches from the Atlantic Ocean to the Bug River.

The landscape of the Park was formed over 12,000 years ago when rivers flowing from the south met the receding ice-front of the Scandinavian glacier and turned along its edge to the west. Towards the end of the glacier period, windborne processes created sand dunes that reach a height of 30m above the horizon and reveal different morphologic forms closely resembling mountain ranges. About 12,500 years ago these sand dunes were stabilized with vegetation, spread over a vast Park area and form one of the largest midland dune complexes in Europe. The abundance of plant life is due to the Park's location at a conglomeration of river valleys, as well as to the morphological variety of its soil and variable water conditions. The flora of the Kampinos Forest includes species typical of many geographic environments including glacial, Atlantic or mountainous. There are altogether 1,100 species of plants including 27 species of trees and 40 species of shrubs growing in Poland. Some of the trees are of immense size, especially oak and small-leafed linden. In the protection zone, some imposing cottonwood and black poplar trees may be found. Yew has been reintroduced into the Park.

The emblem of the Kampinoski National Park is the elk (North American - moose), which lives here again after 150 years of its absence from the Park. The European beaver was reintroduced in 1980, after several hundred years of absence, while the lynx returned to the park in 1992. Red deer, the roe deer, wild boar, badger and fox also inhabit the forest. In addition, the fauna in the park consists of an amazing number of rare species.

Since it is located on a bird migration route, many birds live in the Park. Nearly 20 bird-of-prey species nest in the Kampinos Forest, including the lesser spotted eagle, the honey buzzard, as well as great numbers of buzzards, and goshawks. With the inclusion of amphibians, reptiles and insects, over 4,000 species of fauna live in the Kampinoski National Park. The territory of the Kampinoski National Park has close ties with history and was the site of many battles, including those fought in September 1939. The Park and its surroundings contain many graves of Polish insurgents of 1831, 1863 and soldiers and partisans of WW II, killed in the Kampinos Forest. There are also cemeteries of Nazi victims like the one at the Palmiry village, where a number of Poles and Jews were shot and then buried in mass graves.

In the Park's protection zone there are some historic and architectural monuments of great value. Thousands of tourists visit the museum located in the small mansion at Zelazowa Wola, where Frederic Chopin was born in 1810. He was baptized at the nearby Brochow defensive church, built in the 16th Century of red brick. A narrow-gauge train from the Museum of Narrow-Gauge Railways at Sochaczew takes tourists to the western edge of the Park. The neatly designed Museum and Educational Center at Granica, near the village of Kampinos, has been named after the initiators of this national park.

A Memorandum was signed in 1998 designating Kampinoski National Park in Poland and Indiana Dunes National Lakeshore Park in Chicago, IL to be "sister parks". The plant communities and soils of each are similar, both are dominated by upland dunes intermixed with marshes and other wetlands and both are located near major urban cities and face many common threats including air and water pollution, ecosystem fragmentation and growing urban encroachment. The "sister parks" plan to increase efforts toward environmental education so that their country's people can become committed partners in conservation and will seek to enrich the experience and training of the personnel of both parks through projects of international cooperation including:

- Exchange of technical and professional knowledge.
- Scientific research and data collection.
- Sharing resource management methods and techniques.
- Electronic communication and technical information exchange.
- Environmental education techniques, programs and facilites.

Pieninski National Park

The Pieninski National Park was founded in January 1955. A truly unique natural feature of the Pieninski National Park is the Dunajec River Gorge, which is one of the most beautiful in

Europe. For the last 150 years, rafting down the Dunajec River, through the Gorge, has been a major tourist attraction. On the Park's border there are two famous castles, in Czorsztyn and in Niedzica, both clearly visible from many spots in the Park. Adjacent to this park is the Pieniny National Park on a territory of the Slovak Republic.

The Park contains unique landscape and natural features and is unusual in many respects. A narrow strip of rocks, which has developed into relatively low but picturesque Pieniny Mountains range, extends as a belt along the boundary line between the Outer and the Central Western Carpathians. The limestone rocks of this belt, throughout millennia, have been weathered into round shapes from the north and the dramatic, high cliffs on the southern side all towering over the Dunajec River. The Dunajec River, which is a tributary of the Vistula River, has incised a narrow and sharply winding gorge in rocks. This is the most glorious part of the Pieniny Mountains. The Dunajec River and most of its tributaries rise in the Tatra Mountains. Two dams have recently been constructed - at Niedzica Castle and at Sromowce Wyznie - as a protective measure against the danger of severe floods, which have occurred in this region in past, as well as to generate power.

Plants in the Park are represented by a abundance of species including some which are rare in Poland, as for example *Carlina acaulis* and the mountain arnica (*Arnica montana*). The forests contain fir, beech, larch, and spruce trees, offering a dazzling display of colors in the fall.

The animal kingdom of the Park is also rich. This Park is home to the lynx, wildcat, wolf, stag and many other animals. There are numerous colonies of bats (14 species), of which the most interesting is *Miniopterus schreibersi* - the only animal common to both Poland and Australia. They find convenient winter quarters in the limestone caves. The Pieniny Mountains are a paradise for any entomologist. The most fascinating among numerous butterflies here is the *Parnassius apollo* with its white wings, decorated by black lines and red spots.

Swietokrzyski National Park

The Swietokrzyski National Park was established in l950 and covers the central, best-preserved part of the Swietokrzyskie Mountains (The Holy Cross Mountains). At 650 million years old, the mountains are among the oldest in Europe and take their name from an old Benedictine Abbey that is located on the Lysa Mountain. These mountains are the oldest Polish mountain formations, and are built from Paleozoic rocks. The rich geological history of this area involved successive inundations by sea, transformations of sediments into rocks, and their folding. The main mountain-building movements, the Variscian movements, occurred here some 300 million years ago. In the Quaternary period the Swietokrzyskie Mountains were temporarily covered by glaciers, which formed the boulder fields known in the Polish language as goloborza, on the slopes of the highest peaks in the range.

The flora and fauna of the Park include some protected species, for example, fir-club moss, tropical fern, gentian *Acontinum variegatum*, Siberian iris, as well as beaver, black stork, smooth snake, and other animals. The goloborza, vast fields of rock scree, are especially imposing on the northern slopes of Lysa Gora and Lysica, and are a local peculiarity. The Cambrian quartzite in the Lysa Gora region contains the traces of organic life hundreds of millions years old, including the Cambrian *Corallicyathida*, and fossilized algae.

Human activities in this area started before the Iron Age. Visible evidence of copper ore mining, red sandstone cutting, and iron smelting, have been discovered at Rudki near Chelmowa Gora hill, and at Nowa Slupia, a village that now hosts the museum of ancient iron smelting. Archaeologists have confirmed, Lysa Gora (Bare Mountain) was a site of a pagan religious worship dedicated to the Slavic Gods in early medieval times. After the Baptism of Poland, the monks of the Benedictine order from Hungary built a church and a monastery here in the l2th Century.

The Swietokrzyski National Park is one of the few national parks in Poland that contains many architectural monuments in addition to its beautiful nature and landscapes. Among the most valuable is the complex of the former Benedictine abbey on Lysa Gora, called Swiety Krzyz (Holy Cross). It includes the Baroque-Neo-classical church built in 1781-1789, the Gothic cloister from the l5th Century with a fragment from the 12th Century, the Romanesque wall, and the Olesnicki Chapel (early l7th Century), which contains the Holy Cross relic. Today, the west wing of the monastery houses the Research Laboratory and the Park's Museum. The oldest preserved piece of Polish religious prose from the 13th/l4th Century, known as The Swietokrzyskie Sermons, is associated with the monastery. The remnants of the 14th Century bishops' castle at Bodzentyn are an interesting example of lay architecture. An old, l9th Century farmhouse, preserved in the same village represents the rural style of building in the Swietokrzyski region.

The first attempts to protect the area's environment date back to the year 1909. As a result, the Chelmowa Gora reserve was established in l920 and the Lysa Gora (Swiety Krzyz) and Lysica became reserves in 1922. The Park serves a protective, scientific, educational, and recreational role but pollution and the excessive penetration by the local population are threatening its environment. It is one of the most endangered national parks in Poland and has already witnessed the disappearance of 25% of the lichen species and many species of symbiotic fungi. In recent years fir trees have begun to die out, while many other living organisms have become weaker.

Karkonoski National Park

Karkonoski National Park was created in 1959 to protect the unique environment of the higher parts of the Karkonosze Mountains, including Mount Sniezka, the highest peak of Sudeten Mountains and interesting geomorphological forms and rich fauna and flora. The Park protects many rare species facing extinction, and is among the World Biosphere Reserves in Poland. The topography of the Park is exceptionally diverse and entails lakes in post-glacial depressions, steep cliffs, and lively streams forming numerous cascades and waterfalls, and sub-crown plateau. The most characteristic features of Karkonosze landscape are flattened bare tops with a large plateau below postglacial cirques, and picturesque groups of rocks.

The character of the flora is dependent on the elevation. The lower mountain forests are made up of beech while the upper portions consist of spruce, with dwarf pine appearing at the higher elevations. The uppermost reaches, which belong to the alpine zone, are enriched with a large variety of moss and lichen species. The flora of the Polish Karkonosze entails about 900 species of vascular plants, 452 mosses, about 400 lichens, and about 80 myxophyta. The Karkonosze flora includes many protected relict species, which underscores the uniqueness of this region's wildlife.

At the foot of the mountains, the Eurosiberian species, typical of deciduous forests, dominate the local fauna. At higher altitudes mountain species are found. The Park is home to about 100 bird species and about 40 mammal species including Corsican muflon, which is the most interesting among the park's inhabitants, since its introduction 80 years ago.

Despite the extensive human exploitation of the Karkonosze wildlife and forests since the 15th Century, many ecosystems, especially those mountainous ones, have retained their natural character. However, the easily accessible lower parts of the mountains have been significantly changed. The main threats for the Karkonosze wildlife are air pollution and tourism. The Krkonose National Park in the Czech Republic is Adjacent to this park.

Ojcowski National Park

The Ojcowski National Park, established in 1956, is the second smallest among the Polish National Parks. It is situated in the Jura Krakowsko-Czestochowska, just north of Krakow and encompasses the most beautiful fragments of the Krakow-Wielun Upland. The Park embraces rich plant and animal life, an unusual landscape made up of canyons and white limestone cliffs containing innumerable caves formed by the eroding action of water. The Park's Museum houses a rich collection exemplifying the region's flora, fauna, geological samples and archeological discoveries.

The view of the Pradnik Valley as it is seen from both the high vantage points such as the Okopy Hill, and from some points at the bottom of valleys, is truly unforgettable. Another picturesque place is the karst form, known as Krakowska Gate, carved by geological processes through millennia in the limestone. The Ciemna Cave is a long system of corridors and chambers where traces of human settlement from 120,000 to 115,000 BC have been found. The Lokietek Cave is reputed to be a shelter used by the Polish King Wladyslaw Lokietek in 14th Century.

The richness of this small Park embraces luxurious plant and animal life. Beautiful mixed forests cover most of the Park area, especially around Zloty Potok. Rare species of plants, including plants typical of mountainous regions and those of a much warmer climate are easily found in the Park. Fauna is represented by small mammals typical of a climatic zone (for example badger, marten, fox etc.), bird species that include owl and black woodpecker in addition to more common ones, reptiles, rare snails, and numerous insects. The caves are inhabited by 17 out of the total of 21 species of bats living in Poland because they like the calm winter quarters in the caves of Ojcow. This Park is also home to many species of butterflies and boasts over 600 species including the royal page.

DIVERSITY OF WILDLIFE

Aurochs (*bos taurus primigenius*)

The aurochs were no longer common in Poland before the 13th Century but did not become extinct until the beginning of the 17th Century. They were found only in the Mazowsze region, the most forested and least populated part of the country and were also known as "forest oxen". The long survival of the original species of aurochs in Poland was due:

- Favorable natural conditions, such as the abundance of forests, and a favorable climate, and
- An equally important cultural factor, namely the legal protection of this animal that had its origin in the early medieval period.

In Poland these animals were always regarded as being strictly covered by the regaleducale law that meant that only the king could hunt them which was done in moderation. The exclusion of the auroch from the hunting law and extension of the "sacred privilege of immunity" which, according to old custom, only the king was not obliged to obey, were the major factors which contributed to the long period of survival of this species.

Bats

The increase of the bat population in Poland bodes well for the ecosystem and is proof that Poland's environment is getting cleaner. According to chiropterologists (bat specialists), bats are sensitive indicators because they need an exceptionally clean habitat for survival. Bats get the urge to hibernate when the temperature drops to 10°C. About 90% of all bats hibernating in Poland do so at a bat reserve made of World War II underground bunkers in Gorzow province.

Scientists held their first bat count in 1988 which was organized by the Chiropterological Information Center of the Polish Academy of Sciences Animal Taxonomy and

Evolution Institute in Kracow. More than 100 scientists and amateurs spend the first two weeks of February performing the annual winter bat census designed to keep a check on the bat population. The results of the census is published in Wszechswiat Nietoperzy (Bat Universe), a supplement to the nature magazine Wszechswiat (Universe).

Bison

Before the 13th Century, bison were common all over Poland. They had once roamed throughout much of Europe and were wiped out in England in the 12th Century, in France in the 14th Century and in Germany in the 18th Century. The rich, flat lowlands were first declared a hunting reserve for the protection of European bison in 1541. Today, the rare European bison live on the border between Poland and Belarus in two herds in an area that is part of the Bialowieza National Park on the Polish side and the Belovezhskaya Pushcha National Park on the Belaurus side. Conservationists' hope that these two parks will become an international peace park uniting mutually distrustful neighbors in common conservation projects.

Horses

Tarpans, wild horses that once inhabited Polish wilderness, originally lived where forests and plains met. They ate brushwood and survived in the forests until the late 18th Century and early 19th Century. In the early 19th Century, wild tarpans interbred with domestic horses resulting in the local breed of small Bilgoraj horses, some of which have similar hair color to their wild ancestors.

Poland's oldest breeding center for koniki polskie (small Polish horses which are descendants of the tarpan) operates in the Roztocze National Park in eastern Poland with traditions dating back to the 19th Century. The Polish horse is naturally peaceful, easy to groom, relatively strong, not choosy regarding food and excellent for equestrian therapy.

Wolves

After World War II, wolves became persona non grata in Poland as the number of deer and other large animals was dramaticaly low. In 1955, the Council of Ministers passed a law to exterminate wolves and a bounty equivalent to the average monthly salary was paid for each dead wolf. Wolves were put on the game list in 1975 and killing was limited to hunters.

In 1996 some ecologists believe that the wolf should be placed on the list of endangered species because of its usefulness in controlling the deer population which helps reduce the destruction of forests. But hunters and foresters think that the Polish wolf population is in good shape.

Poland enjoys the status of wolf nursery for Central Europe. Wolves born in Poland migrate to Germany and the Czech Republic where they have been almost totally exterminated.

ENVIRONMENTAL CONDITIONS & CRISIS

Poland is characterized by large environmental contrasts. Some natural areas are relatively well preserved in comparison with Europe while, at the same time, other regions are the most devastated in Europe. As a result, Poland has 27 ecologically endangered areas including Karkonosze National Park with its forest dying due to acid rain where indicators of environmental pollution exceed the norms allowable for the life of nature and the human health. The basic threats are:

- Excessive emission of chemical pollutants, poisons and fertilizing elements.
- Changes in land use that damages the structure of nature.
- Decrease of bio-diversity on ecosystems.
- Decrease of environment-generating functions of biologically active areas especially in urban and industrial areas.

The threat to the environment is part of the grim legacy of communism and part of newly transplanted capitalism. Also, some of Poland's environmental problems have their source outside the country's borders. Its proximity to Russia as well as its practices after World War II until the end of the Cold War has resulted in Poland becoming one of the most polluted countries in the world. Researchers of Bialystok Medical Academy in southeast Poland discovered thyroid changes in every second woman and in 10% of all young people as a result of fallout from the 1986 Chernobyl nuclear reactor disaster.

Increased environmental concern by the post-communist government has improved the environmental situation since 1989. Key current environmental issues in Poland include:

- Air pollution from sulfur dioxide emissions from coal-fired power plants.
- Water pollution from industrial and municipal sources
- Disposal of hazardous wastes.

- Forest damage from acid rain.
- Deforestation.

The situation is additionally complicated by pollution concentrated in small areas. Half of Poland's emissions are concentrated in six of its 49 provinces. The worst example is Upper Silesia.

Industrial Waste

Among European countries, Poland is leading in the amount of produced and accumulated industrial waste. Almost half of the overall amount is mining waste. Furthermore, there are floatation failings, fly ash, slugs from heat and power stations, blast-furnace slugs, and phosphogypsium. Ongoing research work is being done to reduce the impact of chemical degradation of soil and on plant contamination by means of immobilization of heavy metals in soils. Efforts to restructure industry include the introduction of low-waste technologies and higher use of waste as recyclable material.

The low level of economic reuse of solid waste causes increases in the volume of solid waste accumulated in the environment. There are ongoing activities on comprehensive recovery systems for waste paper, rubber waste, plastics, glass, and aluminum cans. Efforts are being made to introduce selective waste collection and recycling. The reclamation of degraded areas of former military bases of the Russian Federation is in progress.

Mining Sites

Specific to the Upper-Silesia Industrial Area is the existence of old underground mining sites which cause buildings to crumble, forests to dehydrate and dry areas to unexpectedly become damp -- all resulting from the settling of the delicate system of underground water and layers of rock off balance.

Air Pollution

The pollution situation in Poland has improved since 1989 due to decline of heavy industry and increased environmental concern by the post-communist government. Air pollution remains serious because of sulfur dioxide emissions from coal-fired power plants and the resulting acid rain that has caused forest damage. Water pollution from industrial and municipal sources is also a problem as is disposal of hazardous waste.

Rationalization of manufacturing processes and energy consumption, together with the vigorous controlling activities of environmental protection agencies have brought about some positive results in reductions of water and atmosphere contaminating emissions and decrease in industrial waste volume. The total emission of air pollutants in Poland is one of the highest among European countries.

Waste Water

Increased volume of accumulated waste, both industrial and municipal are a serious threat for the public and the environment. The Waste Management Act of 1998 has provided the new legal basis for waste management and control. By 1999, waste treatment plants serviced only 52% of the population as opposed to more than 90% in western European countries. Modern waste treatment plants treat and discharge 24% of the waste through urban and rural sewage systems. This ratio varies between 50-90% in countries of Western Europe.

Clean Water

Although the pollution of the water in Poland has decreased from 87% in 1995 to 78% in 1998, Warsaw has the indisputable distinction of being one of the few European cities that still lacks drinkable tap water.

Energy

The largest quantities and most toxic air pollutants are created in the generation and distribution of utilities (electricity, steam and hot water) and in production of metals and chemicals. In Poland 60-70% of total emission originates from these sources and the efficiency of reducing these pollutants is low due to about 86% of these plants lacking gas filtering equipment and systems.

Specific environmental needs relating to the energy sector include:

- Improving coal quality through desulfurization of coal dust.
- Modernization of combustion technologies in power plants.
- Improvement of heating system efficiencies.
- Use of alternative energy sources (i.e., hydroelectric, wind, nuclear, geothermal).

In 1998, new emission standards for existing plants went into effect, which are in line with EU standards. Under these standards, all new coal and lignite plants require flue gas desulfurization and all plants require low NOx burners and improved fly ash particulate removal.

Environmental Conditions & Crises:

In 1991, Poland designated five official ecological disaster areas. Of these, the densely concentrated heavy industry belt of Upper Silesia had suffered the most acute pollution. As a result of industrial waste deposits, 12,000 hectares of agricultural land had been declared permanently unfit for cultivation and, between 1921 and 1990, the average number of cloudy days per year increased from 10 to 183. Nearly two-thirds of Poland's forests had sustained some damage from air pollution and half of Poland's lakes had been damaged by acid rain.

Water and air pollution affects all of Poland. A 1990 report indicated that 65% of Poland's river water was so contaminated that it corroded equipment when used in industry. River water could not be used for irrigation, half of Poland's lakes had been damaged by acid rain and 95% of Poland's river water was considered undrinkable. Special environmental problems were discovered in Poland in 1990 when Polish authorities began inspecting Soviet military bases. Among the most serious conditions observed were uncontrolled fuel leakage, untreated sewage release, noise pollution from air bases and widespread destruction of vegetation by heavy equipment.

In 1989, Polish experts estimated total economic losses from environmental damage at over US$3.4 billion including soil erosion, damage to resources and equipment from air and water pollution and public health costs. Despite heavy spending in 1989 to reverse the communist legacy of industrial pollution, the EU named Poland in 1999 for lagging behind in environmental reform. Poland is especially having problems in providing clean water to homes, treating wastewater, removing garbage and dealing with contaminated soil. The EU advised Poland that it was going to have work harder and raise its ecological standards or risk a delay in admission to the EU.

CITIES & VOIVODSHIPS

Biskupin

Biskupin is a large, partly reconstructed settlement dating from the 7th Century BC that was discovered in 1933. The settlement is the leading center for experimental archaeology in Poland. Once a year in mid-September, The Archeological Festival is held in Biskupin. During this time, thousands of visitors from all around the country, especially children can see professions, techniques and crafts that no longer exist or are vanishing.

Gdansk

Gdansk (also known as Danzig) is located at the mouth of the Vistula River on the Baltic Sea in northern Poland. It was founded in 997 and is one of Poland's oldest cities. In the 12th Century, Gdansk was a center of political and economic life. The town was full of many languages and it absorbed cultural novelties from around the world.

Merchants from Lubeck arrived bringing the greatest achievements of civilization in 1224, including the "Lubeck Law," which codified all matters to do with trade. In 1361, Gdansk became a full member of Hansa, a mercantile organization. The Hanseatic League whose aim was economic co-operation attempted to standardize laws, regulations and currencies, to introduce mutual reductions in payments and to act together to eliminate competitors. It covered an area that included the Baltic Sea, the North Sea, Portugal, Spain, Russia, Finland and Iceland.

The Teutonic Knights took over Gdansk in 1308, renamed it Danzig and redeveloped the city into a major trading hub. After the battle of Grunwald in 1454 when the Knights were thrown out, Danzig remained an independent city and grew into the greatest port in central Europe. Part of its strength depended on its being a multi-cultural and multi-ethnic melting pot as well as tolerant of religious differences. The Swedish wars of the 17th Century halted the city's economic growth and began its decline. In 1772, Gdansk was seized by Prussia and in 1793 it became part of that country. The city remained in German hands until after World War I.

Following the partitions of the 18th Century, Danzig regained its independent status in 1918 and was called "Free City of Danzig. It did not remain free long as World War II began there in 1939. After the war during which 90% of Danzig was destroyed, the city was returned to Poland and renamed Gdansk. After years rebuilding the city and its shipping industry, in 1980 Gdansk was again in the news when the Lenin Shipyard strike made Lech Walesa and the labor union Solidarity world headlines.

Gdansk is the center of the metallurgical, chemical, brewing/ distilling and saw milling industries. Located in Gdansk is the Gothic Church of St. Mary built in 1343 and one of the largest Protestant churches in the world. In 1997, Gdansk celebrated its 1000th anniversary. An event of great significance during the celebration was the 17th International New Hansa Conference under the slogan "Hansa invests in Hansa". People from 12 countries and 108 cities came to the conference. New Hansa is an association of over 100 European towns including Gdansk that wishes to continue economic and cultural cooperation. Its first conference was in 1980 in the Dutch city of Zwolie.

Gniezno

It was the first capital of Poland and the place where unification of Polish lands began. Two important sites in Gniezno are:

1. Gothic Cathedral which was built in the 15th Century and contains the unique door from 1170 which contains the history of Saint Wojciech, the patron and martyr of Poland.
2. Museum of the Beginnings of the Polish State which

contains information about the oldest history of Poland.

Jawor

Settlement of the town dates from 1242 at the old Piast settlement at the crossroads of the important commercial routes. The town was an important commercial center of agricultural items, animals and wool. The Piast castle dates from 1292. In 1367, the town received the so-called law of the mile. It was also a main center of the weaving and flax industries until the Thirty Years War. The Peace Church, built in 1645 entirely of wood is one of only three churches of this type in Lower Silesia. After a large fire in 1646, the town's position deteriorated until the second half of the 19th Century when the founding of industrial companies accelerated its growth. During World War II, Jawor was heavily damaged but after 1945, rapid development in building construction and industry occurred especially with regards to machinery and agriculture. In 1992, Jawor celebrated its 750th anniversary.

Karpacz

The Karkonosze Mountains are strangely shaped, unique rock formations, post glacial lakes called Maly Staw and Duzy Staw, mountain bogs at the foot of Sniezka Mount, the highest peak of the Karkonosze Range and steep pot-holes. A great part of the Karkonsze on both sides of the Polish-Czech border has been turned into Karkonosze National Park. At the foot of Sniezka lies Karpacz, one of the most popular holiday resorts in the Karkonosze. Attractions of Karpacz include St. Laurentius Chapel on the tope of Snieczka built in the 15th Century and the 13th Century timber temple brought from Norway. There are numerous chair lifts, ski lifts and ski runs in Karpacz and adjacent areas where snow remains until late spring.

Katowice

Katowice is a product of industry and owes its size to the Industrial Revolution. Industry took hold here securely because this region sits atop a lot of coal -- some claim 1/10th of known global supplies. That coal as well as other metals attracted the Prussian overlords who developed the area under the Partitions. Under communism, miners fared well but the land and the people's health did not.

Today, the region and Katowice suffer from serious pollution. Cleanups are in progress, the area is updating its antiquated equipment and this developing industrial base of Poland is expected to expand.

Klodzko

Klodzko, a town situated on the Nysa Klodzka River, is in the center of Kotlina Klodzka and surrounded by the Srodkowe and Wschodnie Sudety mountain ranges. The earliest historical records about the town go back to 981. The town center has Old Town architecture going back to the 13th Century and almost 400 historical buildings recorded in the State Historical Monuments Register.

The district has a thorough inventory of mineral deposits and mining is one of its dominant industries. Large-scale industry and small-scale enterprises produce industrial and construction fittings and fixtures, construction materials, food products, clothing, underwear, hosiery, furniture, fishing equipment, gold and silver jewelry.

Kolobrzeg

The sea resort of Kolobrzeg may look new but it was initially settled in the 7th Century when salt was discovered in nearby springs. The town fell to the Russians in the 1700s and the French in the following Century. The ruins that accompanied both invasions altered the town's purpose away from the industrial and as a result, Kolberg became a spa. The town was totally devastated at the end of World War II.

In a symbolic gesture, Kolobrzeg was married with the sea by ceremonially throwing a ring into the ocean thereby reclaiming the city for the long-gone Piasts, Poland's first dynasty.

Krakow

Krakow, one of the oldest cities in Poland, was founded over 1,000 years ago. It is situated on a rocky point overlooking the Vistula River. Archeological findings provide evidence that Wawel Hill was settled in the early Stone Age era. The Mounds of Krakus and Wanda, legendary rulers of the Slavonic tribe of Wislanie, probably date back to the 7th Century. According to folklore, Krakow was named in the 7th Century when Krak (the hero) poisoned the dragon that was terrorizing the people and the liberated town took his name. The story was immortalized by the fire-belching dragon, which stands to one side of Wawel Castle.

In the 11th Century, Krakow was the main seat of the first Polish kings of the Piast dynasty. In 1241, after a Tartar raid, the settlements located around the Wawel Hill were substantially destroyed. The first crowning of Ladislaus the Short in the Wawel Cathedral strengthened the rank of the capital city of Krakow in 1320. In the 1300's it was one of the most beautiful and cosmopolitan European cities. King Kazimierz established Jagiellonian University, Poland's first university, in Krakow in 1364, created a second town where the newly welcomed Jews settled, and straightened out the legal system.

Wawel Castle where Polish kings ruled

After Poland united with Lithuania, the city gradually lost its political importance in favor of the centrally located Warsaw. Krakow was captured for the first time and plundered by the Swedes in 1655. The Black Plague and the Swedish invasions wiped out a fair portion of the population and the city itself.

After the fall of Poland in 1795, Krakow became part of the Austrian Empire. Initially, it retained pseudo-independence as a free city from 1815-1846 and even afterward, its Austrian masters were lenient. Krakow nurtured the Polish culture and its rebellious adherents until Poland regained independence.

When Poland regained its independence in 1918, the city slowly began to be restored. World War II interrupted the restoration when the city became a place of martyrology of the Jewish nation. Jews were first confined to the Krakow ghetto, later taken to the Plaszow camp from where they were taken to Auschwitz. After the war, significant sociological changes took place in Krakow primarily related to the uncontrolled development of industry.

Krakow is now considered Poland's intellectual capital. Because of the many historical and cultural treasures, it has been placed on UNESCO's World Heritage List. Krakow is also a major tourist site in Poland. One of the main attractions is Wawel Castle, where Polish kings were crowned and buried.

Wieliczka Salt Mine - On the outskirts of Krakow is the Wieliczka Salt Mine. Although the mine has been worked for 900 years, it is not known exactly how or when this deposit was discovered. The first reference to the mining of salt in Wieliczka was made in 1044. As early as the 14th Century, the mine was shown to privileged visitors of the royal court and by the end of the 15th Century tourist activity began in the Mine. Today Wieliczka Salt Mine receives up to a million visitors yearly, most of them during the warmer summer months. Its museum is one of the biggest mining museums in Europe and *the original excavations of the mine illustrate all the stages of the development of the mining technology over time*

Over the centuries, miners established a tradition of carving sculptures out of the native rock salt. Wieliczka's managers also encouraged crews and, later, outside artists to decorate the mine's dark interior. As a result, the mine contains entire underground churches, altars, bas-reliefs, and dozens of life-size or larger statues. Over the centuries, these freestanding statues, bas-relief carvings, and immense chandeliers--all carved from salt--have gained worldwide artistic and cultural renown. (See picture of salt statue of John Paul II on cover.) As a testament to its historical and artistic importance, UNESCO included the Wieliczka Salt Mine on its First International List of the World Cultural and Natural Heritage sites in 1978 and designated it as having "outstanding universal value to mankind."

Kudowa Zdroj

Kudowa Zdroj is a health resort with spa traditions going back to the 16th Century. Therapies and treatment are based on the mineral water deposits, specialist medical consultation and laboratory diagnosis. Located on a flat plain surrounded by the Stotwe Mountains on the north, the Lewinskie Hills on the East and the Orlickie Mountain ranges, its picturesque landscapes, numerous mineral water springs and abundance of the mountain shapes, rock forms, flora and fauna make Kudowa Zdroj a real beauty spot. The town's goal is to make Kudowa a clean and pre-ecological town.

Lublin

The city was founded in the late 9th Century, grew around a 12th Century castle and was chartered in 1317. When the Union of Lublin was signed in 1569 between the Kingdom of Poland and the Grand Duchy of Lithuania, it was already a prosperous commercial center. Under Austrian rule from 1795, Lublin was passed to Russian Poland in 1815 and to the Polish republic in 1918. The Germans established the Majdanek concentration camp on the outskirts of the city in 1941.

Today, it is an industrial and commercial city located about 100 miles southeast of Warsaw and its industries include the manufacturing of motor vehicles, farming equipment and food products. The Lublin region is the most important hop production area in Poland, producing many locally made beers. The people of the area are renowned as being one of the most hospitable in Poland. If a visitor wishes to meet local people in their homes, the local Information Center can arrange social events and even the opportunity to have their evening meal with a local family! Lublin has several colleges, a Roman Catholic University and many museums including the former Majdanek concentration camp.

Malbork

A city at the intersection of European commercial routes, Malbork was the headquarters of the Grand Master and the highest Teutonic authorities for nearly 150 years. Archaeologists are interested in the area just south of the town where there are traces of a settlement dating back to the New Stone Age (Neolithic period). In the second quarter of the 13th Century the Teutonic Knights, who established their state on the right bank of the Vistula, conquered this territory. Malbork, along with part of the Order's land, came into possession of the Polish Crown in 1466 for 316 years pursuant to the 2nd Treaty of Thorn. The city and castle retained their exceptional significance because they were the capital of the ¯u³awy region and the royal residence. Its location in ¯u³awy by a navigable waterway enabled intensive trading in grain and timber from inland Poland and was the basis for economic development of the city. Malbork suffered extensive damage during the warfare of 1945 when nearly 80% of the buildings in the Old Town were destroyed. Today, Malbork is home to the biggest armoury of the Republic of Poland.

In 1276 The first building work in the oldest part of the Malbork Castle, a former residence of Poland's kings and German emperors, was built by the monastery of Zantyr. Together with a system of multiple defense walls with gates and towers, covering over 80 acres, Malbork Castle is one of the largest such strongholds in the world. The castle itself contains three major parts; the oldest section is the rectangular High Castle with arcaded courtyard containing among others refectory, chapterhouse, St. Mary's chapel and treasury. (See picture of Malbork Castle on cover.) A UNESCO heritage site, Malbork Castle is a classical example of a medieval fortress, one of the best of its kind in entire Europe.

Olsztyn

Like most other towns in this region, the formerly titled Allenstein began as a fort on the river Lyna. In 1353, the Teutonic Knights controlled the area but after the battle of Grunwald in 1410, Allenstein reverted to Poland in 1466. Fortunately, for town its regional administrator, Mikolaj Kopernik returned to plan the successful defense of the town against the Knights attacks in the 1520s. As a result of the Partition of 1772, Allenstein remained in Prussian hands until 1945. After World War II, the Soviet Army attacked and burned 40% of the town. The now-named Olsztyn rebuilt and is a mix of old and new. Some of the new buildings incorporate some aspects of the old but are not reproductions. The town has developed into an industrial center with a large and growing population.

Poznan

More than 1,000 years old, Poznan is Poland's 5th largest city but trails Warsaw in importance as a business and commerce center. Beginning as a fortified village in the 10th Century, it was capitol of Poland between 968-1039 and the residence of the first two Polish kings. Poland's first cathedral was built here in 968. The town flourished as a trade center during the 15th and 16th centuries but later declined due to fires and wars. It prospered again during the two world wars but a 1945 siege left the city in ruins.

Poznan has been a center of trade for centuries and today is known around the world for its trade fairs. It is a major cultural and literary center with several colleges, scientific organizations and many interesting museums including the Museum of Musical Instruments. The Poznan University of Economics founded in 1926 is the only school having a Faculty of Commodity Science with full academic rights. It is also home to Poland's largest botanical garden. One of Poland's largest industrial and commercial centers, its industries includes metallurgical works, chemical and furniture factories, textile mills and food-processing plants.

Szczecin

Ptolemy first mentioned Szczecin in the 1st Century. It is located at the mouth of the Odra River and used its strategic location to grow into a maritime and industrial center rivaling Gdansk. King Mieszko I incorporated the city and the surrounding regions into his kingdom near the end of the 10th Century. The Danes come to town in the 12th Century and controlled Szczecin for about 40 years. In 1630, the Swedes invaded and stayed for 100 years. The town was sold to Prussia in 1720, who added more to Szczecin than many of its former occupiers. After World War I, Szczecin suffered greatly because the land-compromise isolated it from its natural market. The city was finally returned to Poland after World War II and has rebuilt and redeveloped into a strong maritime center.

With the Goleniowska Forest, Wkrzanska Forest and Bukowa Forest encroaching upon the town limits, Szczecin is very rich in greenery. The city has a university, medical academy, engineering college, agricultural academy, maritime school and a philharmonic orchestra. Industries like shipbuilding, food production, chemical works, machine-building, electrical plants and clothing manufacturing have developed to make Szczecin very important to the Polish economy.

Torun

Torun is located along side the Vistula River. As a result of trade, the city grew wealthy over the centuries and built to display that wealth. For hundreds of years, Torun was known as "the queen of the Vistual" or "the inland port of the Polish Baltic areas". The first written document concerning Torun is dated 1233 and is called the "Chelmno Charter". It grants Chelmno city status and is named for the place where the ceremony of bestowing the privilege was held. In 1280, Torun became a member of the Hanseatic League.

In the 15th Century, the Teutonic Knight Castle fell to the angered citizens whose revolt ignited a regional uprising against the Knights. The ruins of the castle still remains as a reminder to all who might hope to conquer them. In 1966, Torun celebrated the 500th anniversary of the signing of the Second Torun Peace Agreement and completed the archaeological and conservation project in the Teutonic Order's castle.

Across the river from Torun is an island called Kepa Bazarowa and its forest is home to many rare species of birds and other small animals. In order to protect them, a part of the island which has been least affected by human presence has been designated a nature preserve. A fortified bridgehead located on the island was fiercely defended during the two Swedish invasions and the Napoleonic War. The primeval forest on the island has destroyed all traces of human presence and almost totally hidden the outline of fortifications dating back to the 1600 and 1700s.

Books were always an important part of Torun intellectual life. In the Middle Ages, richly ornamented manuscripsts of the monastery collection were located in SS Johns' Church. In

1402, the Council decided to discontinue the practice of loaning its volumes because some were not returned. In 1568 a print shop was established in Torun which printed the first edition of Adam Mickiewicz's "Pan Tadeusz" printed on Polish soil. A 20th Century contribution to the printed word was the development and popularization of a new typeface called "Torun Roman".

The 18th Century saw a decline of Torun's splendor. During the 1703 siege by Charles XII of Sweden, the city was seriously devastated. The second partition of Poland in 1793 was a severe shock to Torun and marked the beginning of over 100 years of Prussian rule. The former trade routes lost all significance as the city's strategic role was as a major fortress and garrison.

The Nazi occupation in Torun was a time of terror and extermination of the Polish people. Several thousand of the most active participants of the political, social and cultural life of the city were executed in nearby Barbarka. The city was incorporated into the Third Reich and all forms of Polish cultural life were prohibited. Speaking Polish was a crime punishable by concentration camp. Since there was no direct fighting in the city, Torun survived World War II essentially intact.

Some important dates in Torun's history:

1. Construction of Dybow Castle which served as residence for Polish monarchs. It was serious damaged during the 1st Swedish war and never restored.
2. The Church of SS Johns receives the "Tuba Dei" bell in 1500, cast in Torun and the largest in Poland at the time.
3. The royal mint opens in 1528.
4. Torun Scientific Society formed in 1875.

Also, the Pomeranian Factory of Low Voltage Equipment was constructed in 1948. During 1964-70, other large factories were constructed including Elana Plastics Factory, Worsted

Wool Spinning Factory and Torun branch of the Gdansk Towimor Shipyard. The 500th anniversary of Nicolaus Copernicus birth was celebrated in 1973.

Walbrzych

Numerous historical monuments illustrate the 700 years of history of Walbrzych. The capital of the Province, it is located in a mountainous valley surrounded by the Walbrzyskie Mountains and the eastern part of the Walbrzyskie Foreland. Parks and forested hills divide the town into districts in a natural way. The Ksiaz castle, the third largest in Poland, is one of the largest in Europe. The industries in Walbrzych are currently undergoing a process of intensive restructurization and development in compliance with the demands of the market economy.

Warsaw

The first settlements in Warsaw stretch back to the 10th Century and the first records to the 11th. According to legend, a beautiful mermaid asked the fisherman Wars and his wife Sawa to build a city on the River Vistula and thus was born the city of Warsaw. It remained a political backwater until Poland and Lithuania united in 1569. By 1573, the kings were being elected there and in 1596 King Zygmunt III moved the capital from Krakow to Warsaw.

Between 1655 and 1658, Warsaw was besieged and entirely plundered three times by the Swedish and Siedmiogradzkie forces. Warsaw remained destabilized for most of the 18th Century. Before the Century ended, King Stanislaw August Poniatowski led efforts to transform the city into a modern city. This period was later called Warsaw's second "golden era". Surpassing these architectural achievements, the first European democratic constitution was declared on May 3, 1791. At the same time, Poland's on-going partitions limited the freedom of the city.

Warsaw is located in central Poland, is the largest Polish city and is divided in two by the Vistula River. The right bank is modern Warsaw, home to Polish industry and countless housing projects. The left bank is Warsaw's "Old Town" which dates back to the 13th Century. Warsaw is the country's scientific and cultural center. When Poland regained its independence in 1918, the people of Warsaw worked energetically to revamp and expand the city and its infrastructure. The invasion of Poland by Germany in 1939 ended their efforts. In World War II, 90% of the city's buildings were destroyed. After the war, the people of Warsaw recreated an exact replica of the city as it had been before the war.

HISTORIC SEA PORTS & MODERN CHANGE

Gdansk

As early as the 9th and 10th Centuries, luxury goods were arriving in Gdansk from the Arabian states and by the 12th Century, Gdansk was an important seaport. In 1224, the "Lubeck Law" was enacted which set in order and codified all matters to do with trade. Gdansk shipyards launched their first warship in 1572. The length of the port quays was greater than in London and the Gdansk crane was, until the 19th Century, the largest port crane in Europe.

Today, Gdansk is Poland's most important port on the Baltic Sea and has some of the largest shipyards in the world. In 1998, EuroPort Poland initiated plans to install state-of-the-art-loading equipment on an uncompleted pier in Gdansk. When completed, it will be the most technologically advanced pier in Central Europe. The impact of a modern, ice-free, deep-water port in the Baltic is far-reaching. Feasibility studies indicate that the pier's completion has the potential to dramatically change European cargo routes and many believe the terminal will revive the historic role of Gdansk as a grain gateway to Europe and the Commonwealth of Independent States.

Port Kolobrzeg

The port (and city) is situated at the mouth of the river Parseta that flows into the Baltic Sea and is almost 1000 years old. It was famous for rich layers of salt, fishing, trade and agriculture for centuries.

Kolobrzeg is the 6th largest commercial seaport in Poland and is one of the leading trade ports. It is also an important fishing and fish processing center and many yachts under different flags visit the extended and modernized port. In addition, it is the homeport of Polska Zegluga Baltycka -- one of the busiest ferry operators in the Baltic area.

Port of Gdynia

In 1922, the Sejm agreed to build the seaport Gdynia in the Pomeranian region and in 1926 city municipal rights were granted to Gdynia by the Polish government. The Polish navy base was moved to Gdynia and the first crane started its service in 1926.

"Polonia" was the first Polish passenger ship that flew the Polish flag and the first Polish regular passenger shipping line started operation in 1930. By 1933, Gdynia handled more cargo than the port of Gdansk. Port of Gdynia was nearly totally destroyed during World War II. The SS Krakow came back to its mother port, Gdynia, in 1945 -- the first Polish vessel to return after the war.

In 1963, the large US merchant vessel, "Manhattan", visited the Port of Gdynia. The tanker "Kasprowy Wierch", owned by Polish Steamship Company was, in 1974, the largest vessel served by the port in its history. Gdynia's waterfront serves as a mooring for "tall ships" visiting Gdansk Bay. Also, the three-masted frigate, Dar Pomorza, and the World War II destroyer, Blyskawica, lie at anchor here and have been converted into nautical museums.

The Port of Gdynia constructed container terminal in 1976 and modernization of the grain elevator was undertaken in 1992. In 2000, Gdynia was a universal port, handling various types of cargo including general and bulk cargo, grain, fuels, fertilizers and cement. It is also the Polish leader in reloading containers and cars as the port handles 90% of all cargo transported in containers and 95% of all motor vehicles. The port has a permanent ferry connection with Sweden and connections with ocean ports such as Hamburg, Bremerhaven, Antwerp, and Rotterdam.

Port of Swinoujscie

The town of Swinoujscie is located in Poland's northwestern corner at the mouth of the Swina River to the Baltic Sea. The port was established in 1729 as a busy seaworthy port. In the 19th Century, it became a fashionable spa and bathing resort.

The Port of Swinoujscie provides port services: handling of dry bulk and general cargo (especially coal, ore and chemical materials) as well as towage and moorage of ships. The ferry terminal operated by Polska Zegluga Baltycka provides ferry berths and facilities for passenger services. Other important contributions to the port's economic development are deep-sea fishing and fish processing as well as ship repair services.

Port Szczecin

The existence of Port Szczecin is established by virtue of a shipwreck of a Slovian boat from the end of the 9th Century. Its favorable location at Odra estuary was instrumental in the port becoming one of the biggest Baltic ports in the Middle Ages. One of the first trade houses was established in the middle of the 13th Century and served general purposes. Since the 14th Century there have been bridges cut far into the river to facilitate unloading of goods without using smaller boats.

During the 18th and 19th centuries, numerous repairs were made, wharves were expanded, and the warehouses and port facilities were improved. At the end of the 18th Century, the Bydgoski Channel was constructed which allows Port Szczecin to handle cargo transported by the Vistula River waterway. The 19th Century brought expansion of transport connections via hardened roads to several cities including the town of Pomerania and establishment of railway connections to Berlin, Poznan and Wroclaw.

During World War II, the port was incorporated into the totalitarian war machine of Hitler. At the end of the war, because of military industry there, Port Szczecin became the target of allies' air raids. Significant damages were caused by the attacks particularly to port facilities including cranes demolished and warehouses ruined. The damages were so severe that the first ships entering Port Szczecin after the war had to be handled manually. In addition, numerous shipwrecks, harbor slime and mines in water basins restricted normal operation of the port.

Port Szczecin is one of three principal seaports of Poland and is located at the estuary of the Odra River into the Szczecin Firth. The port is equipped with over 130 portal bridges and overhead cranes with lifting capacities of 2T to 50T, floating hook crane of 200T for moving heavy lifts as well as floating grab cranes with 16T capacity. Several hundred pieces of other handing equipment such as forklift trucks, mobile cranes and container handlers ensure fast and safe transfer of cargo.

Port Ustka

The first visitors arrived at Ustka as early as the 9th Century. It developed from a fishing settlement with the original name of Ujsc. From 1335, it was the port of Slupsk. Noteworthy buildings include:

- 9th Century lighthouse with small astronomical observatory;
- old port granary from the 18th Century which presently serves as Baltic Gallery of Art; and
- Neogothic church from 1882 with old organs and valuable paintings.

Two concrete breakwaters form the entrance to Port Ustka which is located at the mouth of the Slupia to the Baltic Sea and. It is a commercial port, fishing harbor visited by many yachts, center for shipbuilding and fish processing industries. Also, because of the wide beaches, walking promenade and breakwaters going far out to sea, Ustka has become popular as a leading seaside resort and recreation center.

GOVERNMENT

POLAND's COAT OF ARMS

The majestic, high-flying white-tailed sea eagle that often nested in Polish woods is the prototype for the Polish National Emblem and a proud and regal symbol of independence. One of the oldest State Coats of Arms, the Crowned White Eagle has been the Coat of Arms of Poland for seven centuries. The Eagle is linked to Gniezno, Poland's first capital, where Lech the legendary ancestor of the Piast dynasty found an eagle's nest and assumed the Eagle as his personal coat of arms. Traditions and legends, however, refer to the origin of the White Eagle prior to the establishment of Poland as a country (see Folklore).

Polish coins between 922-1146 depict the oldest known images of birds while coins of the 14th Century show an eagle with a slender silhouette, raised beak and widespread wings. This style, which introduced the eagle wearing a crown, remained unchanged until the end of the 15th Century. The eagle changed its style over time when various geometric shapes became popular. During the Renaissance, the eagle adopted a shape that could be placed in a circle or on a coin while during the Baroque period, the eagle took on a more spindle-shape when the oval shape was popular. From the period of the last Polish king, the eagle remained unchanged until the 1920s.

As a result of the partition of Poland in 1795, the White Eagle lost its significance as Poland's Coat of Arms. During this time, the black eagles of occupying forces replaced the white eagle on official flags and seals. Since it was impossible to use the eagle after the partitioning powers abolished autonomous Polish institutions, the symbolic "white eagle" reappeared in every national uprising and other efforts to restore independence. It became traditional in daily life as the main visual symbol of the struggle for national independence and represented patriotism and everything that was Polish.

After the restoration of Poland's independence in 1918, the crowned White Eagle became the Coat of Arms of the Republic of Poland and was used as the state emblem. During the German and Soviet occupation, the White Eagle, as Poland's coat of arms, was strictly forbidden. It became the symbol of Poland's fight to be free and was used by the underground army at home and by the regular Polish army abroad. During the communist period, authorities deprived the eagle of its crown. In 1955, a degree was passed establishing Poland's emblem to be the image of the white eagle; its head turned to the right with outspread wings, golden beak and claws on a red shield.

In 1989, the Polish Sejm brought back the White Eagle's crown and its official design was defined close to that of 1927. The traditional emblems of the Polish Army were restored including the Crowned White Eagle. The 700th anniversary of the White Eagle's coronation as the Coat of Arms of Poland was celebrated in 1995.

ORDERS & DECORATIONS

The nobility of Poland vehemently resisted the introduction of chivalric orders until the twilight of the Commonwealth. The acceptance of Chivalric orders as part of the Polish nobility status occurred in the late 18th Century. At that time, the Electors of Saxony ascended to the Polish throne which resulted in an influx of Western European ideals, attitudes and customs, a number of which were to the detriment of the clan and caste system of the old nobility.

Today, Poland has over 50 different awards and decorations that are awarded to military, civilian and foreigners for service to the country. The following is a brief description of a few of the oldest and most prestigious orders and decorations:

Order of the White Eagle

Although King Wladyslaw created this order in 1325, King Augustus II did not officially institute it until 1705. It is considered the highest Polish decoration and few have been awarded. The Order of the White Eagle came in a single class and was awarded for exceptional merit to the Polish Commonwealth. Foreigners could receive this Order and one such recipient was the Duke of Wellington.

After the partitions of Poland, the Order was absorbed into the Imperial Russian honors system. In 1921, the Polish Republic once again restored the Order as the highest Order of the Republic. Between 1921-1945, the Order was bestowed only 30 times. From 1939-1990, the Government (in Exile) awarded this decoration but ceded its authority to the democratically elected government under President Lech Walesa. The President of Poland is always the Grand Master of this order and it is conferred on both Polish citizens and foreigners for exceptional merit to Poland.

Order Virtuti Militari

King Augustus instituted this order in 1792 after the victorious battle of Zielence during the Polish-Russian War. It is the best known and most coveted of all Polish decorations equivalent to British *Victoria Cross* or American *Medal of Honor*. The order comes in five classes. The Polish Republic revived the Order of Military Virtue in 1919 not as an order of chivalry but as the nation's highest award. It is the most senior decoration for war bravery and is conferred on soldiers of the Polish Armed Forces, irrespective of their rank, solely for deeds of exceptional bravery and valor at the risk of their lives before an armed enemy, above and beyond the call of duty. It can also be conferred on allied soldiers, civilians, military units, cities and other communities.

Order of Saint Stanislas

In 1765, King Stanislaus II Augustus Poniatowski founded the Order of the Knights of Saint Stanislaus, Bishop and Martyr to honor his patron saint and to give visible recognition to knights who served the monarch. It was awarded in three classes. The number of knights in the Order of Saint Stanislaus was limited to 100 excluding the king and members of the Order of the White Eagle who were automatically admitted into the Order. All Poles and Lithuanians admitted into this Order had to prove nobility for a minimum of four generations via both paternal and maternal lines.

After the partitions of Poland, this Order was also taken over by Imperial Russia. Later in history, the Order fell into abeyance and was not revived by the Polish Republic. In 1979, the Polish Government (in Exile) re-established the Order of Saint Stanislaus, which was used as a distinctive reward for those who had served against the might of communism. Many very well known members of the western world and senior military officers were awarded this decoration. By 1990, the Order of Saint Stanislaus had become a powerful lobby group in the fight against communism and had established a network of trustworthy contacts throughout Eastern Europe. The Order was then given an independent character as a charitable order of chivalry and is now established worldwide.

Order of Polonia Restituta

This order was instituted by act of Parliament in 1921 and is conferred on Polish and foreign citizens for merit to Poland in the field of art and science, industry, agriculture, politics as well as for acts of civilian bravery and self-sacrifice.

Independence Cross and Medal

Established in 1930, it is formally a decoration not an order. It was awarded to those individuals who took active part in the struggle of Poland before and during World War I. Recipients of both the cross and medal enjoyed numerous privileges.

Cross of Valor

One of only two awards of the Second Republic for acts of valor in the field, it was first awarded in 1920 for the participants in the insurrections of 1863-64. It was also awarded to Polish soldiers who fought in World War I. In 1992, it was revived and can be awarded for acts of valor while serving with UN peacekeeping missions. The cross is equivalent to the American *Silver Star*, French *Croix de Guerre* or German *Iron Cross*. It is awarded for acts of valor in the battlement and in exceptional cases can be granted to allied soldiers and civilians.

Cross of Merit

Established in 1923, the Cross of Merit is the most common of all Polish decorations and is awarded to civilians or military for merit to the country or its citizens beyond their normal duty. It has been awarded for merit in almost all areas of human activity -- professional or non-professional work, charity, art and science, sports, life saving, long marital life as well as for mothers of many children.

The Cross of Merit for Bravery was established in 1928 and reintroduced in 1992 for members of the Police, Customs Service and Frontier Corps for acts of bravery in defense of law, state frontier or human life. Recipients were entitled to a pension.

Academy Laurel

In 1934, the Minister of Public Enlightenment established this award for merit for Polish culture and Polish literature. The first grade is awarded to writers, poets, journalists and public persons who distinguish themselves by using beautiful language in word and script. The second class is awarded to individuals for popularizing literature.

Boleslaw Chomica Medal

This medal was established in 1995 on the occasion of the 75th anniversary of the Voluntary Fire Brigades' Association of the Republic of Poland. Named in honor of Boleslaw Chomica, a pioneer of Polish firefighting and former President of the Association, it is awarded to the most outstanding member for long and exceptional meritorious service.

Medal of St. Hubertus and Medal of Hunting Merit

Both of these medals are awarded by the Polish Hunting Society. The goals of the organization is to cherish and popularize the traditions of Polish hunting, develop friendly relations between Polish hunters, protect forest animals and guard principles of the hunting code. The Medal of St. Hubertus was established in 1992 and is awarded every 5 years to members or non-members for merit in cherishing and popularizing hunting traditions in Poland. The Medal of Hunting Merit was established in 1929 and is awarded for merit in organization of Polish hunting, animal breeding, supporting of hunting culture and care of wild animals especially endangered species.

THE SEJM & POLAND'S POLITICAL SYSTEM

The Republic of Poland is a parliamentary democracy with a division of powers between the legislature, executive and judicial bodies.

The head of the executive body is the President who is elected directly by the people for a 5-year term. The President is the head of state and commander of the armed forces. His executive powers include the ability to declare a state of emergency, to veto legislation (which may be overturned by the Sejm) and to dissolve the National Assembly. He also designates the Prime Minister who leads the cabinet and has the right to dissolve Parliament if it fails to pass a budget within 3 months of submission.

Poland's parliament called the National Assembly, is the national law making body and is composed of two houses. Its members are elected for 4-year terms. The lower house, called the Sejm, has 460 members and the upper house, called Senate, has 100 members. The members of Parliament are elected by Polish citizens' 18 years and older. The Sejm appoints Council of Ministers, including Prime Minister, which head government departments and carry out the operations of the government

The judiciary is an independent body of the government. All courts are presided over by judges who are appointed by the President on recommendation of the National Council of Judiciary for an indefinite period. The Sejm chooses Constitutional Tribunal judges for 9-year terms. The Supreme Court is the highest court of Poland. The Council of State appoints Supreme Court judges to 5-year terms. The Minister of Justice exercises the powers of the Attorney General and governs the Public Prosecution Office, which is a nationwide organization.

The entire country is divided into 49 administrative regions called voivodships. Each region is governed by the voivod, who is appointed by the central government. Local self-government is the commune, which has legal status and is subject to property rights.

FOREIGN POLICY

Poland's principal foreign policy goal is full integration into Western economic and security structures, principally the European Union (EU) and NATO.

European Union (EU)

Poland has forged ahead on its economic integration when it became an associate member of the EU and its defensive arm, the Western European Union (WEU) in 1994. After full membership in the Office of Economic Cooperation and Development was achieved in 1996, Poland submitted its preliminary documentation for full EU membership. Poland formally joined the EU in June, 2004.

NATO

Poland has promoted its NATO candidacy through energetic participation in the Partnership for Peace (PFP) program and through intensified individual dialogue between Poland and NATO.

Lack of fluency in Western languages, particularly English, among Poland's military was a hurdle on its path to joining NATO. Poland faced an urgent task of reaching "the minimum standard of interoperability" with the Alliance's forces. The linguistic fluency was essential to fulfill that requirement. Other key tasks included integrating the Polish command system with NATO, achieving compatibility with NATO telecommunications and linking Polish air-traffic and data processing systems with NATO. There was also a need to "re-train" the Polish officer corps so it could develop full understanding of behavioral patterns and values maintained in the Western military. Most Polish officers were trained in a different, Eastern environment.

A member of NATO's Partnership for Peace program since 1994, Poland has actively participated in the peacekeeping operations in Bosnia. It has developed close ties to the French, the German and the Danish military establishments, three important members of the Alliance. Poland has taken part in, has hosted numerous NATO military maneuvers and has set up military exercise bases on its territory for NATO troops. It has also been actively involved in the Alliance's work at NATO military headquarters in Belgium.

At the same time, Poland has been active in developing cooperative relations with its eastern and southern neighbors, securing their support in its efforts to enter NATO. During recent months alone Poland has reached agreements with Lithuania and Ukraine on setting up joint military battalions to be used in peacekeeping and humanitarian operations sponsored by either NATO or the United Nations. It has maintained close links with the Czech Republic and Hungary, the two other Central European candidates for an early entry into the Alliance.

Poland was widely regarded as the leading Central European candidate for an early entry into NATO and was formally accepted into the Alliance in April 1999, NATO's 50th anniversary. Poland has worked long and hard to gain the invitation to NATO and will also bring a significant military potential to the alliance. It has seen the membership in the Alliance as both a guarantee of its security and a proof of international acceptance into the world of Western democracies. During recent years, Poland's role in the coalition that invaded Irag in 2003 has increased its international standing.

Foreign Relations

Poland is increasingly regarded by countries both inside and outside the current round of NATO and EU enlargement to be a crucial regional power with influence in European and Euro-Atlantic affairs. Since the mutual recognition of borders in 1990, a normalization of relations with Germany has been underway.

When the Soviet Union disintegrated, attention turned to potential ethnic and border conflicts among the newly independent countries. Poland has actively pursued good relations with all its neighbors. In 1992, Poland initiated a policy called "European standards" which was designed to smooth the way for Poland's return to Europe. The aim was to persuade the country's eastern neighbors that certain norms of international law were binding in Europe, and that their acceptance would help post-communist countries to join Western institutions.

Poland has developed close partnerships with the Czech Republic and Hungary and has forged special relationships with Lithuania and Ukraine. Poland and Ukraine have formed a joint peace-keeping battalion meant to serve in future missions of the UN or of the Organization for Security and Cooperation in Europe (OSCE). In 1998 Poland chaired the OSCE, actively participating in addressing security problems in Europe and particularly in Kosovo.

Since shortly after the parliamentary elections in 1989 signaled the rebirth of Polish democracy, the United States and Poland have enjoyed warm bilateral relations. Poland has been a strong supporter of continued American military and economic presence in Europe and has been a major ally for the United States in the region.

At the same time, Poland's relations with Australia are based on growing commercial links and talks on subject of mutual interest such as international security and political, financial and social issues. The active Polish community in Australia is also an important catalyst in the overall relationship.

HISTORY of POLAND's ARMED FORCES

Poland's armed forces are divided into army, navy, air and air defense forces and territorial defense forces. The draft for Army is for 18 months while navy and air force is for two years.

ARMY:

The Polish army during its early years had to operate in all types of terrain and climates and frequently the fighting was far from home. As a result, Polish military thinking was based on the ideas of mobility, adaptability and self-sufficiency.

Husaria - "Polish Winged Cavalry"

The cavalry was the backbone of Poland's military power and the pride and glory of its cavalry was the Husaria, the winged cavalry. In the 14th Century the name "hussar" denoted a mounted knight in southern Slavic languages and by the end of the 15th Century the first hussar troops were created and served as a light cavalry. They were a unique, highly trained, maneuverable hard-hitting cavalry who used tactics of maneuverability and speed, especially in the charge which was carried out at a full gallop in tight, knee-to-knee formations. In a few generations, they evolved into armored assault cavalry, which was unique in all of Europe. There is no English equivalent for "husaria" - the Polish armored cavalry of the 16th and 17th Centuries. An elite force, the husaria began a new martial aristocracy and became the largest and most acclaimed horse army that Europe had ever known. They seldom lost a battle and frequently won against superior forces.

Hussars were volunteers, who fought for personal glory and duty, were recruited almost exclusively from among Poland's nobility who owed military service to the nation. During this period, the horse and chivalric culture in Poland were ingrained in Poland's society and stood at an incredibly high level. Although knightly ideals were lost in the West, they were very durable and were adhered to in Poland for centuries longer. Noblemen's children were fostered early to be future soldiers trained and disciplined in the use of all weapons and language but most important in riding and military horsemanship. Acceptance into the hussars was based upon experience, training and exceptional horsemanship as well as expertise with the lance, saber and firearms. The hussars, who came from the most affluent of Polish nobility, was also the most elaborate and most decorative unit of the army and had a reputation for lavish and extravagant finery, armor and dress.

Husaria units were organized in pulks (regiments), led by a Rotmistrz (Captain of Horse) who was responsible for training the troops as well as the provision of great sturdy horses, weaponry and equipment. The Captain was issued a commission to raise a fixed number of men under a single flag and appointed his own porucznik (lieutenant) as his second in command, an ensign-bearer to carry the unit's flag and a handful of drummers and musicians. Each regiment consisted of 150-200 hussars and their horses plus the men they brought with them. To encourage enlistment the troops were offered 1/3 higher pay than any other unit within the army along with great privileges and great opportunities such as the promise of offices, land and much more. Under King Stefan Balory, the second elected Polish king, the husaria made up about 85% of the Polish cavalry forces and, unlike the other divisions of the armed forces, consisted exclusively of volunteers.

The Polish hussar's horse was their most valuable item and cost five to ten times as much as the rider's salary. Polish horses were breed for speed and endurance and were among the finest in Europe. They could not be sold outside of Poland.

The armor of the husaria was comprised of small geometric steel plates shaped for strength, linked over a lightweight flaxen vest that permitted ventilation and unimpaired movement. It was quite simple, covering only the most vulnerable parts of the body and not hindering the wearers' movement in melee. The total weight of the armor was about 15kg, which permitted the horses to charge at full gallop. Other components of the armor included:

1. Zischagge (helmet) - featured a semi-circular shape with a nose guard, two side protectors and a long neck guard attached to the back.
2. Cuirass (front and back plate) - was essentially the main piece that protected the upper body and the area just below the midriff of the hussar. It was the most important part of the armor because it protected the hussar against bullets and saber slashes. The breastplate usually had 3-5 "lames" or bands that allowed the wearer to bend forward somewhat while the back-plate did not flex.
3. Pauldrons - were made in the lamellar style and attached to a gorget worn around the neck and were protection for the shoulders and upper arms.
4. Karvash - were arm protection for the lower arms and consisted of either mail sleeves or were based on the Eastern style of the Turk's armor.
5. Clothing - there was no regulation for uniformity of their clothing which varied from unit to unit but red was the most popular and recognizable color. Also worn were tight fitting trousers, mustard colored knee-boots that were the precursor to today's western cowboy boots and large spurs.

Since the main task of husaria during battle was that of a "shock force", the hussars were sent in at a decisive moment to breach enemy formation. Beginning at a walk, then a trot, to a cantor and finally a gallop, the hussar's would charge in a formation of open space varying to a 'knee-to-knee' formation and like a tidal wave smash into their enemy and shattering their formation.

In battle, the primary weapon of the hussar (and only weapon supplied by the king) was a long hollow lance, "Kopia", up to 16-20 feet in length. The lance was made from two halves of hollowed out Aspen wood, re-glued and reinforced with an iron or steel tip followed by a long swallow-tailed pennant of the unit's livery colors. Once breaching the enemy's lines and piercing the ground troop's armor and bodies, the lance would snap off and shatter into the enemy. This snapping of the pennant was the reason that the enemy's horses became terrified. If the hussars were experiencing difficulty in breaking the enemy's formation, they would charge in waves giving the impression of more numbers than they actually possessed. After the lances were discarded, the hussar could choose from a lethal cocktail of weapons including:

- Palasz (Broadsword) - It was a heavy slashing sword used during the early period and was strapped to the hussar's saddle under his right leg. This sword had a sabre grip and a straight, edgeless blade between 4-6' long. The cross-section of the blade was square like a fireplace poker and was used to pierce armor once the hussar had broken his lance.
- Estoc - a 5-6 foot piercing rapier for punching through chainmail, which was strapped to his saddle under his left leg.
- Koncerz - It originated from a medieval sword and appeared at the end of the 15th Century. The Koncerz was a stabbing sword with a sharp pointed end and no cutting edge. It was also carried below the saddle.
- Szabla (or Sabre) - It was the favorite weapon of the hussars and was worn by all noblemen. In the 17th Century a special hussar sabre was developed that was very versatile with 82cm long blade and double-edged towards the point that provided a very efficient ratio of effort to cutting ability.

- Batorowka - A particularly lethal version of the sabre that was designed heavier toward the tip allowing the user to put more power and lethality into its swing and produced devastating wounds.
- Czekan - The most lethal of their weapons was the czekan, a long steel hammer that could go through heads and helmets like butter!
- Nadziak - A war hammer weighing about 6 pounds with a long tether, it could be thrown with deadly skill and, if not 'stuck' in the head of the enemy, could be retrieved.
- Buzdygan - A medium-sized hand mace that could crack armor and break bones in a melee.

In addition, each rider carried four primed pistols in protective, decorative saddle holsters, a wheel-lock musket and grenade launcher, and a laminated bow with 100 42-inch arrows in a decorative quiver. This variety of weapons gave the hussars the ability to attack infantry, light Tartar cavalry or other armored riders.

The most famous accessory in the hussar's arsenal was the 'wings' worn singly or in pairs. Originally, the wings were attached to the back of the saddle or the shoulders. They were long wooden carved 'hockey-stick' shaped frames, covered in decorative red velvet and trimmed in a scalloped brass edging. Diagonally lining the center of each wing was a row of bristling eagle (or other bird of prey) feathers. The wings were only employed during a major engagement to exaggerate and amplify height stature and noise. The strange sound emitting from the wings during high-speed charges frightened enemy horses and contributed to the unnerving of an enemy. The combination of wings projecting an illusion of greater size, animal skin capes, fluttering lance pennants gave the husaria a spectacular, awesome, frightful and terrifying appearance and created an early version of psychological warfare. Also, the Tartars' lasso was difficult to use against soldiers with wings protruding above their heads. Today, husaria wings are present in emblems of the Polish Air Force and Armored Division.

Light Artillery

Light artillery in Poland had to adapt to a cavalry-dominated army's operational and tactical conditions. It had to be mobile enough to keep up with the cavalry and had to provide concentrated firepower when needed to disrupt the enemy. The Poles invested heavily in artillery and mastered the tactics of bombardment in concentration with mobility ahead of their enemies. When faced with the need to keep up with the cavalry, the Poles were particularly advanced in carriage design and the tactical aspects of handling horse artillery.

King Stefan Batory made important reforms in the army and, for the first time, introduced recruitment among Polish peasants. They were known as 'Wybraniecka' infantry because one man was to be 'selected' from every 20 farms on royal land. As a result, the Polish army received its first 2-3,000 peasant soldiers who played a vital role in the Livonian War. The infantry did not wear helmets or armor and were armed with muskets and other types of early flintlocks, pistols, sabers, short swords and hatchets. They also did most of the routine work of scouting, picket duty and finding provisions as well as providing critical support in the highly mobile battles the Poles favored. Although the cavalry continued to remain in the spotlight, the infantry continued to play a vital role throughout Poland's military history.

The Poles set great importance on artillery and were years ahead of their enemies until the 18th Century. In the 1500's artillery was typically placed on top of a hill before the battle but the Poles developed the use of light artillery that was integrated with the battle line. In the 1550's, a Polish regiment possessed 10 times greater firepower on a man-to-man basis than standard European infantries. Although the term 'horse artillery' is associated with the 18th Century, the concept was well established some two hundred years earlier in Poland. Horse artillery worked closely with mounted infantry to form skirmishing screens in front and some security to the battery line itself. The horse artillery with the Polish army was a factor in the cavalry battle of Lopusza in 1512. Although not a dedicated and specialized horse artillery, it was a joint effort by cavalry and highly mobile artillery. In addition, Poland also used rocketry including the first multi-stage rocket to great effect during this period. Kazimierz Siemienowicz, as Lieutenant General of the Crown Artillery, directed it's technical and tactical refinement in the mid-17th Century. (He published a treatise on multi-stage rocketry in 1650![2]).

During Germany's invasion of Poland in 1939, it had vastly under-rated Polish anti-tank capabilities. The Polish anti-tank gun was one of the best in the world at that time. Also the recently-designed 7TP "czolg lekki (light tank), the first to be designed with a diesel engine, were superior to German tanks and inflicted serious damage to the German forces.

In 1996, the development of TRD-1211, a surveillance radar system, disproves opinions that Polish military technology is obsolete. The state-of-the-art aircraft tracking system is one of the latest pieces of military equipment developed at the Industrial Telecommunications Institute (PIT) in Warsaw. It has a remarkable range, is able to locate and track targets flying anywhere between ground level and 40 km high, can withstand seismic shock and can operate in all conditions including snow, humidity, hurricanes, and thunderstorms.

Today, Poland's army is the largest in Europe after Russia's. There are also large paramilitary units and border guards. A 15-year program to modernize the armed forces was introduced by the government in 1997. Due to the need for modernization,

---

[2] For more information about Kazimierz Siemienowicz, see Appendix "A".

it will be an attractive market for defense industries in supplying armaments and military technology.

NAVY:

During Poland's war with Sweden, King Zygmunt III Wasa formed a naval fleet to challenge Swedish supremacy on the Baltic. In 1627, Poland's fledging navy of 10 vessels won its greatest victory. Not only did the Poles capture the Swedish flagship, they also sank a second vessel and forced the remaining Swedish ships to flee. Poland's naval experiment ended in 1629 when the ships were loaned to the German Imperial Fleet and lost in 1632.

The Polish Navy was re-established in 1918, 17 days after Polish independence was declared. Its goals were to support Polish claims for the Pomeranian coast and to secure inland waterways in the newly emerged Polish state. The Polish river flotillas, created in 1919 proved themselves during the Polish-Soviet War of 1919-1920 (the only war lost by the USSR).

The early 1920s spelt the end of the ambitious Polish naval programs because of budget cuts and for the next decade, the Polish Navy consisted of 6 torpedo boats, 2 gunboats, 4 minesweepers and 6 river monitors. A naval base was built at Gdynia to house and supply the Polish ships. After the economic situation in Poland improved, the KMW (Kierownictwo Marynarki Wojennej - Directorate of the Navy) ordered 4 replacement minesweepers in 1933 from Polish shipyards. The Polish shipbuilding industry produced quite satisfactory boats in a reasonable time - a notable achievement that proved its ability to produce warships. In 1936, a 6-year rearmament program was authorized which promised a thorough modernization of the Polish armed forces, based mainly on the country's own industrial capability.

When Germany invaded Poland in 1939, the Polish Navy consisted of 4 destroyers, 5 submarines, 2 gunboats,

1 minelayer, 6 minesweepers and several old or auxiliary vessels. Hours before the war started, the core of the Polish Navy, 3 destroyers were sent to the British Isles under Operation "Peking". They took part in Allied naval operations, i.e. Norway 1940, evacuation at Dunquerque, the Battle of Atlantic, escorting convoys in the Mediterranean and in landing operations in Sicily, Anzio and Normandy. The Polish submarines had no targets for their torpedoes and had to use neutral harbors. Only 1 escaped and after a lone patrol in the Baltic, she sailed for Britain. Nonetheless, the Polish Navy sank the first German ship in the World War II!

After the disintegration of the Soviet Union in 1991, Poland needed a healthy military for two reasons:

1. Historically, the army had represented Polish self-esteem and the survival of the Polish State. National leaders wanted to recapture that tradition to boost domestic morale.
2. Also, a capable military establishment would help Poland present itself to the world as a viable, independent state.

To achieve these goals, Polish leaders sought a complete restructuring of the defense establishment. The reform program was to streamline the Ministry of National Defense, include civilians in the process of defense decision making and extricate the Polish Army from the constraints of the Soviet military doctrine and training standards. Finally, reform leaders wanted to reestablish the prestige of the armed forces as a national organization separate from and above politics.

Today, the Polish Navy consists of 157 vessels organized in four major subdivisions:

- 3-warship flotilla based at Oksywie (part of Gdynia) harbor.
- 8 coastal defense flotilla based at Swinoujscie harbor.
- 9 coastal defense flotilla based at Hel peninsula.

- Naval Air Brigade based at Gdynia, Darlowo and Siemirowice.

When Poland joined NATO in 1999, the Polish Navy received new tasks from NATO headquarters and the Polish Naval Command created a new development plan. The main task of the Polish Navy is protection of the Baltic Sea and guarding teams of NATO ships. Meanwhile the basic task of the Polish Navy Command is to introduce information and communication systems of NATO into PMW (Polska Marynarka Wojenna) and fitting their ships with systems compatible to NATO's systems.

In 2000, the Polish Navy's fleet was increased by one guided-missile frigate given free of charge by the US Navy to Poland to upgrade its naval forces to NATO standards. The frigate was renamed "Pulaski" and will be the second largest ship in the fleet.

Polish Naval Academy

In 1918, Jozef Pilduski issued an order establishing a Polish navy. The end of the Polish-Russian war and initial efforts to organize the Polish Navy resulted in an increased demand for officers (called maritime specialists). The demand for ensigns resulted from the necessity for Poland to build its own national officers' corps who did not have the trait of service in the invader countries. The first courses called Provisional Instruction Courses for Naval Officers (PIC) lasted 18 months and the trainees were cadets and junior officers from all branches of the Army who wished to focus their careers to service at sea.

The first recruitment for Maritime Division of Naval Officers' School (NOS) was in 1923 and the course of study lasted 2 years. The term of study was changed to 3 years by 1924 and in 1925 the school held its first promotion ceremony to the rank of first officer.

As a result of restructuring of the Polish Armed Forces in 1928, the Midshipmen's School (MS) was established. The school modernized its cadet-education program and the period of study became 3 years and 3 months including boot camp. The training and education was split into periods of theoretical education and shipboard or combatant training onboard ships of the fleet or the riverine flotilla. The demand for technical officers (mechanics and electricians) led to the establishment of the Technical Division in 1931. As a result of the continued growth of the fleet, an Administration Division was established in 1935 that trained administration officers and commissaries (quartermasters) for the Navy. After World War II began in 1939, the school was dissolved.

Prior to 1939, the main mission of NOS and MS was to establish Poland's own, national system of training officers for the needs of the Polish Navy. It was also necessary to develop original Polish naval concepts, free of the negative influence of the patterns of the invaders' and allied fleets.

During World War II, a wartime training system for officers was established within the general training program of naval personnel of the Polish Navy in Great Britain. The reactivated Midshipmen School included both theoretical education and shipboard training on both Polish and British combatant ships. Due to the specific wartime conditions, periods of theoretical education and practical training varied for individual midshipmen depending on the missions carried out by ships aboard which they were having their shipboard training. During this period, the Midshipmen School trained 156 officers for the needs of the Polish Navy.

In 1945, efforts were once again undertaken by MS to organize a constant supply of maritime, land and air specialists required by the navy. As a result of the growth of the educational base in the early 1950s, the Naval Midshipmen School (NMS) was increasingly used to upgrade the existing skills and knowledge of the professional personnel. A new stage in the development of naval officer training began in 1955, when NMS was changed into Higher Naval College (HNC)- a higher military school with university accreditation.

Between 1957-1975, HNC underwent internal restructuring and curriculum changes. Of major importance were officer improvement courses and courses designed to prepare officers to discharge duties at new posts or become familiar on the new equipment introduced to the Polish Navy. Also, in 1963, the Minister of National Defense authorized HNC to supervise doctoral studies in the area of military sciences. In 1987, by act of the Sejm on military education, HNC was renamed Naval University.

The Naval University cooperates with maritime schools from other countries and maintains especially tight ties with the Royal Netherlands Naval College, the Royal Danish Naval Academy and the US Naval Academy. The cooperation consists of the following:

- Exchange of academic experience
- Visits and return visits by training ships
- Academic teachers exchange
- Midshipmen exchange during practical training periods
- Attendance at international conferences and symposia
- Scientific consultations on research projects
- Mutual exchange of publications and scientific papers

MERCHANT MARINE:

Poland's merchant marine consisted of 61 ships broken down by type as follows:

- 53 bulk
- 3 cargo
- 2 chemical tanker
- 1 roll-on/roll-off cargo
- 2 short-sea passenger

By 1997, the merchant marine was comprised of 154 ships. The principal ports are Gdynia, Gdansk and Szczecin. Ocean-going services consist of Polish Ocean Lines in Gdynia which operates regular liner services and Polish Shipping Company in Szczecin which operates cargo services. Poland also has a share in the Gdynia America Line.

Gdynia Maritime Academy:

Poland's first civil maritime college, Gdynia Maritime Academy was established in 1918. The sailing ship *Lwow* began its first ocean training voyage to Brazil in 1923. The school also had a coastal steamship, the *SS Kopernik*, which served as a training vessel for students of the Engineering Department. In 1927, the flag was raised on the first Polish merchant vessel, the *SS Wilno*, which belonged to the newly created Polish Shipping Company. Its crew consisted of graduates of the first Polish maritime college. The fully rigged frigate *Dar Pomorza* was a symbol of the school's 10th anniversary.

Prior to World War II, the school not only educated future officers but also extended maritime education to the Polish society. A number of professional courses were offered such as Navigation course for seagoing fishermen, coastal shipping masters, skippers and machine operators and a Fisheries course. In 1937, a free 2-year Seaman School provided practical training for future professional seaman.

During the defense of Gdynia at the beginning of World War II, the school's graduates were killed on shore and many cadets were injured and taken to prisoner-of-war camps. The school building was transformed into a hospital. Many important school documents were destroyed but the school's banner was saved and sent abroad for safe storage. London gave shelter to the Polish Maritime School and subsequent courses took place in Southampton, England. Almost all graduates and students participated in the war at sea onboard Polish and allied vessels and warships.

The Maritime School always adjusted the educational process to meet the demands of ship-owners. In 1945 courses (including radar operations) were offered to shippers and machine operators because such training was essential to rebuild the coastal and fishing fleet. The Maritime Education Center was established in 1946 to design a multi-step program of study. The first step included a course in seamanship, the second a one-year cadet training, then onboard training and finally a two-year course for officers as well as courses for masters and chief engineers.

In the early 1950s, the Maritime School was reorganized and in 1958, obtained university level status and offered training in three departments: Navigation, Marine Engineering and Marine Radio Engineering. In 1967, the newly established Department of Administration and Economics started training pursers and chief stewards. A year later, the Maritime School incorporated the School of Fisheries and also acquired the training ship *m/s Jan Turlejski.*

AIR FORCE

The Polish Air Force (Polskie Sily Poweietrzne) was founded at the end of the Great War and was supported by a substantial aviation industry during the 1920s and 1930s. It was the first air force in the world to equip its front-line fighter force entirely with all-metal monoplanes and many international aviation records were established.

During World War II, the Polish Air Force was an autonomous part of the sovereign forces of the Republic of Poland that served <u>with</u> the RAF but was not part of it. At its peak strength, the Polish Air Force was the largest allied air force after the RAF and USAF. It flew day fighter, night fighter, bomber, coastal, army cooperation and transport aircraft. The Polish Airforce remained in Britain and disbanded in 1947.

The Air Force Academy continues the time-honored traditions of the Polish Air Force. The Officers' Aviation School was founded in 1925 in Grudziadz and moved to Deblin in 1927. It was the only place in Poland where the members of flying personnel of the Polish Air Force were educated and trained. Prior to 1939, 270 pilots and 700 navigators were trained in Deblin and they made Polish aviation famous al over the world.

The Polish Air Force currently has 7 air defense regiments with supersonic interceptors and 4 tactical regiments operating close-support fighters. There are also reconnaissance, ECM, transport, helicopter, surface-to-air missiles and training units.

AADF

Wojska Lotnicze I Obrony Powietrznej (Air Force and Air Defense Force) was formed in 1990 by combining the Air Force and Country Air Defense Force. It is a branch of the Polish Armed Forces and its duty is the defense of the country against aerial strikes and reconnaissance as well as protection and support of the ground forces and navy. The tactical air squadrons are responsible for protecting Polish air space, reconnaissance and the destruction of enemy air, ground and surface targets. The transport service is grouped into squadrons which:

- Carry out tactical transport, airdrop, supply transport and similar missions.
- Special tasks, i.e. passenger and VIP transport.
- Air search and rescue.

Finally, the radar service is equipped with radar stations and C31 systems to provide for the collection, processing and transmission of radar intelligence data about the air situation and command and control of active combat forces.

LEGAL RIGHTS & THE JUDICIAL SYSTEM

In 1346, the first Polish Legal Code was created under Casimir the Great (Kazimierz Wielki). In 1430 the law "Niemineum Captivabimus" (the Polish Habeas Corpus) was enacted. Parliament was established in 1493 with two houses; the Senate (officers, dignitaries and archbishops of the country) and the Sejm (elected representatives). The Statute of Nihil Novi was enacted in 1505, which stated that nothing new could be decided without Parliament's consent. During Jagiellon era, legal rights were enacted which were the prototype of rights generally granted to citizens of modern democracies and the memory of the "golden freedoms" of Poland-Lithuania is an important part of the Poles' present-day sense of their tradition of liberty.

Since 1989 Poland is in a transition period from a centrally planned economy (the communist system) to a market-oriented and democratic system. Political changes and law reforms have been initiated with the amendment of the Polish Constitution by the parliament in December 1989. It was set forth in Article I of the Constitution that the Republic of Poland is a "democratic state based on the rule of law".

The legal system in Poland is based on statutes enacted by the Parliament and is a mixture of Continental (Napoleonic) civil law and holdover communist legal theory. In 1999 The Constitutional Tribunal became final, which rules on the constitutionality of legislation and only an absolute majority in the Sejm may overrule its decisions. Poland's contemporary penal legislation is comprised of three basic laws: the Penal Code (adopted in 1969), the Code of Criminal Procedure and the Code for the Execution of Penalties. Court decisions can be appealed to the European Court of Justice in Strasbourg.

The administration of the judicial system is vested in the hands of the Minister of Justice. The hierarchy of the courts of Poland consists of four levels:

- Lowest – Regional Court
- Second level – District Court
- Third level – Courts of Appeal
- Highest – Supreme Court in Warsaw

All courts exercise both criminal and civil jurisdiction. Special courts include Family Court (which deal with offenses by juveniles) and Military Courts (which handles cases involving offenses by military defense staff).

Felonies, which include homicide, rape and robbery, are punishable with deprivation of liberty, life imprisonment or the death penalty. Most other crimes are misdemeanor offenses. For minor crimes there is provision for probation sentences and fines. A separate category of punishable acts is transgressions, which include petty theft and traffic tickets.

Presently, there are eight offenses punishable with death penalty as stated in the Penal Code. They include:

- Homicide
- High Treason
- Attack on independence of the State
- Espionage
- Terrorist attempts
- Sabotage

Recent public opinion polls show that more than 70% of Poles favor the death penalty but most parliamentary groups want to see it abolished. In 1995, the death penalty was suspended for 5 years and a new penal code abolishing the death penalty was adopted in 1997.

In 1977 family consultative centers were established for cases involving divorce and domestic relations but divorce suits were transferred to ordinary courts in 1990. The minimum age of criminal responsibility is 17 years. A person under 17 is a juvenile who is liable to educational and corrective measures. Criminal responsibility is restricted only to individuals; corporations may not be held criminally liable.

Crime Statistics

Since 1985, Poland has experienced a considerable growth of crime. The data in this chart was taken from official criminal statistics known by the police. The figures represent rates per 100,000 of the total population.

Serious Crime in Poland
(1970-1995)

Year	Homicide	Rape	Robbery	Burglary
1970	1.5	5.9	18.3	166.8
1975	1.8	5.7	15.9	183.8
1980	1.6	4.4	14.4	198.2
1985	1.8	5.6	22.8	370.6
1990	1.9	4.8	42.5	1128.9
1995	2.9	5.9	69.6	789.7

An international crime survey conducted in 1992, which included Poland, indicated that Poland had the highest scores for theft of personal property, second highest for robbery and theft from cars and fifth highest for assaults/threats. At the same time, the survey data indicate that Poland had the lowest overall crime reporting rates.

With need for legalization of new independent economic entities, the government turned to the pre-war Commercial Code (Kodeks Handlowy). The Commercial Code sets the legal requirements for various forms of business organizations and their operations. In 1990, the Privatization Act was passed which regulates the manner of ownership transfer from the state to the private sector. The Foreign Investment Act, passed in 1991, permits foreign investment in Poland and grants the foreign companies the same basic rights and obligations possessed by domestic companies. A representative office of a foreign company is permitted to operate in Poland, but may only engage in foreign trade. After the Anti-Monopoly Act was passed, the Anti-Monopoly Office, a government agency, was created to prevent monopolies. The office may restrict certain acquisitions and mergers if they would create enterprises with a predominant market position.

Police

The border guard provides the regular defense of Poland's frontiers. The Office of the Protection of the Constitution (UOP), established in 1989, is responsible for the country's intelligence services. The police force is centrally organized under the authority of the Main Commander of Police who is subject to the Minister of the Interior. As stipulated by the Police Act of 1990, the formal organization of the regular police forces are divided into six basic departments: criminal police, traffic police, prevention and anti-terrorists squads, special police, local police and other police agencies. A territorial division of the police service in Poland corresponds basically to the administrative division of the country. In 1990, Poland rejoined Interpol and the Polish Interpol Office is located at Police Headquarters in Warsaw.

In 1992, the police employed 105,000 persons of which women comprised 11% of the police staff. Police officers are required to undergo three years of training and can become officers only after graduating from the Police Academy in Szczytno, the only police officer's school in Poland. Police forces vary on the types of weapons carried by their personnel. An out-dated telecommunication system and insufficient police vehicles currently impede police efficiency. Computerization of the territorial police headquarters is underway.

The European Police Bureau (Europol) was established by agreement based on the Treaty of Maastricht in 1996. Its task was to improve cooperation between the police forces of EU member countries in preventing and fighting all forms of international crime posing a threat to two or more member countries and requiring joint action. In 2001, an association agreement was approved whereby Poland's police force and border guards became the only uniformed services in the group of European Union candidate countries to be associated with Europol. Although according to the agreement, Poland will not have full membership in Europol, it will be given access to 99% of the information stored in Europol's electronic databases.

Polish FBI

The Ministry of Internal Affairs and Administration established the Central Bureau of Investigation (CBS) in 2000. The new Bureau will include the following departments:

- Narcotics - two narcotics departments combating drug production and trafficking.
- Criminal - to fight against extortion and the arms and explosives trade.
- Economic - to combat corruption, money laundering, business rackets and stock market scams.
- Analytical
- Operational techniques - to bring order to the database.
- Witness Protection - includes anti-terrorist and special operations such as undercover operations and police provocation.

To become a CBS officer, all the officers have completed at least several years of exemplary service in the ranks of the regular police. Surprisingly, there's no shortage of candidates, even though each has to go through a multi-stage procedure, involving examinations by the special services, including lie-detector tests.

In 2001, another department was organized within the CBS, for combating economic crime. Pyramid schemes, money laundering, taking out bank loans on the basis of forged documents and forging credit cards were hardly known in Poland until recently. Effectively fighting them requires police officers to acquire completely new skills. It is also necessary to give the police new rights, including the right to check private bank and insurance accounts. An amendment to the police law is currently being prepared, which includes a regulation on extending police prerogatives in combating "electronic crime."

Institute of Forensic Research

The Institute of Forensic Research was formally established in 1929 by decree issued by the Minister of Justice although the institute had begun its activities long before this date. The institute consisted of three departments: Department 1 of Physical and Chemical Research, Department II of Chemical and Toxicological Research and Department III of Biological Research.

When Warsaw was occupied by Germany during World War II, the property of the institute including the most up-to-date equipment, laboratory aids and the library were stolen and sent to the Security Police in Berlin. During the Nazi occupation, the Chemical Department of the National Institute of Forensic Medicine and Criminalistics remained open at the underground Jagiellonian University in Krakow. This department became a secret refuge for conspirators and activist in the Polish underground movement. As Director of this Department, Dr. Jan Zygmunt Robel organized covert studies of medicine and managed to acquire the remaining property of the Institute of Forensic Research including documentation and archives.

The outstanding achievement of the underground department during the occupation period was the research it undertook on documents and depositions found on or near Polish victims of the Soviet massacres at Katlyn. The Institute was reorganized in 1952 and was relocated to its current location. In 1992, the Institute of Forensic Research was completely renovated, acquired modern equipment and has developed relations with similar organizations around the world.

Prison

There are 210 prisons in Poland. The Ministry of Justice and Central Prison Administration is responsible for prison administration. Prisons are no longer as overcrowded as they were in the mid-80's but the imprisonment rate is still one of the highest in Europe. Prisoners are housed in old buildings, of which 70% were built prior to World War I. The living conditions are generally inadequate and most cells house at least four people. Prisoners serving sentences are required to work. Prison leave may be granted either for an important reason or as an award for good behavior. In less than 5% of the cases where leaves were granted did the prisoners not return to prison on time or not return at all.

Extradition and Treaties

Poland is a party to 45 bilateral extradition agreements and treaties that have priority over domestic law. Extradition law provisions are contained in the Polish Constitution, the Penal Code and the Code of Criminal Procedure. Since 1993, Poland has been a party to the European Convention on Extradition. Poland is currently a party to bilateral agreements on legal assistance in criminal matters with 45 countries. These agreements provide grounds for mutual assistance with regard to taking evidence from witnesses, carrying out searches and seizures, serving and supplying documents and records. In 1996, Poland ratified the 1959 European Convention on Mutual Assistance in Criminal Matters.

Traffic Code

A new Traffic Law went into force in 1998, which created order on Polish roads. The objectives of the new law was:

1. Introduce stricter rules to decrease danger and accident rates on crowded roads.
2. Adapt the regulations to new conditions, such as cellular phones or bicycles.
3. Bring regulations into accordance with those of EU.

One of the strictest innovations is a ban on registration of cars assembled outside official factories. The regulation may help fight the terrible pollution levels on Polish roads. Under the new regulations, drivers are forbidden to use cellular phones unless using a hand-free apparatus.

All drivers are required to carry their driver's license, vehicle registration certificate and insurance policy. A driver may lose his license if he/she does not carry a valid insurance policy or if a police officer has any doubts concerning vehicle inspection approval. The penalty point limit has been tightened and drivers can lose their license if they collect 20 points. The decision to replace the black license plate with white characters with EU-like white plates with black writing is an attempt to adjust to EU standards. Lawmakers showed some patriotism by allowing the long-standing Polish tradition of drivers flashing their high beams to warn other drivers that police radar is nearby.

TAX SYSTEM IN POLAND

Corporate Income Tax

Companies whose headquarters are located in Poland are liable to have their entire earnings taxed at the rate of 40%. If the company is based abroad, only that income generated in Poland is subject to taxation.

Investment Tax Relief

According to a new investment relief system introduced in 1994, companies whose pre-tax profits are equal to 8% of their earnings and which have no tax arrears or other liabilities are able to deduct from the tax base any sum invested up to 25% of profits earned. If at least 60% of receipts come from exports, the tax relief rises to 50% of earnings.

Sales Tax (VAT)

The basic characteristic of this tax is the fact that it is calculated from the net value of every transaction, which in practice results in the tax liability falling wholly on the final purchaser of a product. Taxpayers who pay income tax by means of tax cards are exempt from VAT liability. The VAT Law provides for three levels of taxation:

1. The basic rate of 22% - The basic rate is applicable to goods and services to which the lower rates do not apply.
2. The lower rate of 7% - Categories of goods and services to which this applies subject to change; consult current regulations.
3. The 0% rate – The 0% VAT rate is applicable to leasing of stalls at exhibitions and trade fairs, international transport and transfer of electrical energy across Polish territory.

The following commodities are free of VAT: meat products, poultry and egg products, fish and seafood products, raw dairy products, horticultural products, game and forestry products and basic medicines. Tax reform is maintaining momentum with passage of the value-added tax (VAT) bill in 2000.

Personal Income Tax

Three tax rates apply with just a few people exempt from taxation (see chart for rates). When tax rates rise, the accepted practice is that those with the highest incomes are the most affected particularly in cases where incomes are spent on consumption rather than investment. The tax is levied on all individuals residing permanently in Poland and those who remain in the country for more than 6 months.

TAXATION RATES
(Per Million Zlotys)

Tax Rate	Income
21%	Less than 90.8
33%	Between 90.8 & 181.6
45%	More than 181.6

When income tax was introduced in Poland in 1992, taxpayers were allowed to deduct a portion of their taxable income on the education of their children in independent schools. Since 1997, these deductions cannot be made from taxable income but from the tax itself but cannot exceed 19% of the amount of tax.

Property Tax

There are three different types of property tax in Poland: property, agriculture and forestry. The difference between these taxes is important, as the rate of property tax is higher than the other two. If not protected by Law provisions covering agriculture or forestry, the land is taxed at property levels. Commune councils have the authority to reduce these rates or to grant tax concessions in legally recognized situations.

Agricultural tax is calculated on the basis of the “convertible hectare” units held, that is, the tax takes into account diverse classes of arable land as well as the different economic and climatic conditions. Exemptions include:

- Land given to non-agricultural economic use.
- Land containing poor quality soils.
- Unproductive land

Farmers also have the right to a temporary suspension of tax from 1 to 15 years or a reduction in the tax rate in hilly or mountainous areas.

Social Security

The new social security system addresses the problems of the high and distorted payroll taxes, sector-specific privileges, large expenditures in survivor and disability benefits, generous benefits for old-age retirees, liberal early retirement and disability insurance. The government's reform for the pay-as-you-go system solves these problems by introducing a multi-layer system with privately managed pension funds and creating a strong and independent supervisory agency for pensions.

In 1999, the new pension system became effective and replaced the old, defined benefits, pay-as-you-go system with one linking the future pension more closely to the contributions paid. The basic concept of the system is security through diversity achieved by basing the system on three independent options - two of which are mandatory and one is voluntary. These options are:

1. The first option is operated by the Polish Social Security Institute and is predominately a national defined contribution pay-as-you-go system with the pension amount related to the amount of contributions made. As a result, the later a person retires, the larger the pension paid. Employees born prior to 1949 must remain with this old system.
2. The second option is a defined contribution program where an employee can select a fund of his choice (only one fund) from the ones registered. All employees born

in 1969 or later must join the second option. However, those born after 1949 and before 1969 have a choice - whether to remain in the old system or join the new one. This decision once made is irreversible.

3. The third option is voluntary and allows diverse organizational principles and forms of participation, which means that it can be adjusted to individual preferences. In this option, contributions are paid into life assurance, pension and investment funds and employee funds with after tax income but the benefits tax-free.

The new pension system was necessary because the old system would have gone bankrupt within a few years. With the new system employees' savings when placed in the financial markets are working on their owners' behalf and at the same providing finance which stimulates economic growth.

TRADITION OF THE CUSTOMS SERVICE

The history of the Customs Service in Poland goes back almost a thousand years. In the 9th Century, King Boleslaw Smialy gave orders to his officers to collect Customs duties on the Bug River. In 1136, the Gniezno Bull mentioned a Customs system in Poland whereby many monasteries and abbeys collected tributes in customhouses. However, the first Polish Customs Tariffs originated in the 12th Century - the Kolobrzeg Tariff in 1159.

The Polish Customs Administration was reorganized in the 14th Century. They issued many Customs privileges and set up customhouses. At this time, the gentry were exempted from Customs duties. In 1367, the world "CLA (Customs duty)" began to appear in documents.

In 1477, the Sejm passed two statutes concerning the collection of Customs duties. These statutes abolished the former privileges and gave the right to determine Customs duty rates exclusively to the King. The Sejm established a general Customs duty in 1764 and introduced a uniform Customs due for everyone.

During the Partition of Poland, a Customs Administration was established in the Duchy of Warsaw. According to records, numerous Customs notices and instructions were issued and the duty of 2% of the value of goods was collected.

After regaining its independence in 1918, the Customs Administration was reestablished in Poland. In 1919, the first Customs Tariff of the Second Republic was issued and the Department of Customs in the Ministry of Treasury was created in 1920. By 1938, the Customs Administration employed about 3,500 people. After World War II, the Ministry of Treasury and Department of Customs were created by decree in 1945. The Customs Law Act in 1961 established the Principal Office of Customs (Central Board of Customs in English).

Poland is not a newcomer to international cooperation and its customs policy is set to a large degree by international trade treaties signed. Poland also joined the World Trade Organization (WTO) and adjusted its foreign trade policy to the requirements of WTO membership. The Customs Code of 1997 provided the Council of Ministers with the ability to regulate customs duties and tariffs to stimulate economic development in line with the country's policy. The new Customs Tariff provides for the following types of rates:

1. Autonomous - applied to commodities originating from countries other than WTO members and not covered by the most favored nation clause and to which preferential rates do not apply.
2. Conventional - applied to commodities coming from WTO countries and regions as well as countries to which Poland granted the most favored nation clause within bilateral trade agreements.

All customs duties are determined based on the goods value inclusive of all costs. In all cases, certificates of origin complying with the World Trade Organization (WTO) standards must be submitted. Polish customs law provides for extra anti-dumping duties on goods imported to Poland at dumping prices. After receiving a certified request from a domestic company that has been affected, the Ministry of Economy initiates anti-dumping proceedings that can lead to imposition of an anti-dumping duty.

During recent years, Poland has adjusted its customs policy and tariffs to European Union standards including a further reduction in customs duties on agricultural and industrial goods in 2001. The Central Customs Office ceased to exist in 2002 and its duties were assigned to 17 regional Customs Chambers and the Ministry of Finance, however, the customs clearing procedures remained unchanged.

EDUCATION - A Historic Tradition

Education is important in Poland and always has been. The education of Polish society was a goal of rulers as early as the 12th Century when monks were brought in to teach agricultural methods to Polish peasants.

Krakow University, founded by Kazimierz the Great in 1364, is the second-oldest university in central Europe. Bishop Stanislaw Karnkowski created the Theological Seminary in Wloclawek in 1569 -- the first school of this kind in Poland and the third in the world. Jesuit College was founded in 1573 and existed until 1773, following the annulment of the Jesuit Order. University of Wroclaw was founded in 1702 (rebuilt in 1945) and the University of Warsaw was founded in 1818. The University of Social Work was founded in 1995 in Wloclawek.

In 1773 King Stanislaus August established the Commission on National Education, the world's first state ministry of education. The Commission set up a uniform national education system emphasizing mathematics, natural sciences and language study. It also stressed standardizing elementary education, integrating trade and agricultural skills into the elementary school program and improving textbooks at all levels.

Education suffered during eras of partition when Russia, Prussia and Austria occupied Poland. For over 123 years the Polish educational system was shaped by the policies of these countries which sought to destroy the Polish national identity. During this period, pockets of resistance continued teaching and publishing in Polish and some innovations such as vocational training school appeared. In the Russian zone, the University of Warsaw and all schools were closed, use of the Polish language was forbidden and even the Catholic Church was prosecuted. In the Prussian zone the goal was to eliminate the Polish language and culture. German was compulsory in all schools and it was a crime to speak Polish. In the Austrian region, conditions were very different. The Poles had a degree of self-rule, Polish was kept as the official language and the universities remained open. As a result, the Polish culture flourished.

During the period of 1890-1914, while Poland was part of the Russian Empire, an underground educational organization known as the Flying Universities held seminars in private apartments. The "Flying Universities" were so named because teachers and students moved from one location to another to avoid detection. The same secret seminar teaching became part of the underground educational system during the German occupation in World War II. In addition, all kinds of publications came into being in the 1890-1914 period and even more so under the German occupation of 1939-1945.

Between 1918 and 1939, the newly independent Poland faced the task of reconstructing a national education system from the three separate systems imposed during partition. Although national secondary education was established in the 1920s, the economic crisis of the 1930s drastically decreased school attendance. Educational achievements during this time included establishment of state universities, numerous specialized secondary schools and the Polish Academy of Learning.

During World War II, the Nazi occupation sought to destroy the national Polish culture once again. All secondary and higher schools were closed to Poles and the elementary school curriculum was stripped of all national content. In response, an extensive underground teaching movement developed under the leadership of the Polish Teachers' Association and the Committee for Public Education. It is estimated that 100,000 secondary students attended classes in the underground system during the Nazi occupation.

By the end of World War II, it was estimated that about 3 million poles were illiterate. Rapid development of the Polish educational system greatly increased access to education to large social groups such as factory workers and farmers. Positive legacies of communism pertaining to education include:

- Reduction of literacy.
- Equal right to education for both sexes.
- Lack of financial barriers to acquire education.

Despite these positive changes, educational level disparity dating back to the partitions continued and is still responsible for unequal access to education today.

The socialist system almost entirely eliminated any private ownership in the educational system and existing private schools were nationalized in the 1940s. The strong position of the Catholic Church in society meant that Catholic schools, founded and managed by monastic orders and religions organizations continued to function although they were very few in number. Pre-school education in communist Poland was not developed to the degree it was in other countries in the eastern bloc.

Poland's education system, built for the needs of rapid industrialization after World War II, has remained practically unchanged over the years. Many disparities in access to education were inherited from socialism. Since 1989, these differences have increased and are based on:

- Rural & small town origins – young people from rural areas have more difficult access to education at all levels.
- Regions – the best access to education is in large urban centers.
- Social groups – upward social mobility in Poland is low and children match the educational achievements of their parents.
- Disability – people with disabilities have less access to

education than other people.

- Nationality – access to education for national and ethnic minorities improved during the transition.

The state's role in the education system is undergoing major changes, both under the influence of political changes and transition to a market economy. It remains responsible for the conditions of implementation of the general nature and accessibility of education through:

- Making laws and rules for operation of schools thus leveling out opportunities for education;
- Developing and monitoring standards of education, especially standards of teachers;
- Ensuring basic funds for the functioning of education.

A serious disadvantage of the Polish educational system regarding disabled children lies in its allowing segregated classes. The most common form of disability in Poland is mental disability and educational opportunities for mentally disabled children in Poland are severely restricted. Children with physical disabilities are mainly accepted into integrated classes. The need to meet the educational needs of disabled children and include them in the general education system is a major challenge facing Poland's education system.

Belonging to a national minority does not limit one's access to education in Poland. Although the teaching of the native languages of national and ethnic minorities in the post-war period was marginal and poorly regulated, national minority education is now regulated by the Education System Act of 1991. The revival of the sense of national and ethnic identity of various minorities over recent years has influenced Poland's education system and school instruction. Schools provide native language instruction for five nationalities and one ethnic group.

In Poland, children are not required to begin their education before the age of 7. The tradition of entrusting the care of young children to families still prevails in Poland today, especially in the country. Educational reforms increased the age of compulsory education in Poland to 18 years that reduced the number of people in Poland who only possess a primary school diploma. In 1999, Polish children started their primary education in a new system, as follows:

- Primary education (6 years). During the first 3 years, children will learn writing, reading, mathematics and basic technical and social skills. During the next 3 years, they will learn subject with broader topics such as nature, history, science and art.
- Junior high school (3 years). In junior high school, students will learn traditional subjects such as mathematics, chemistry, physics, biology and geography.
- Vocational schools (2 years). Vocational schools will offer a wide range of training in specific skills.

or

- High school (3 years). High schools leading to a diploma and then to a university education. High school diplomas will be granted nationwide by a state commission.
- Universities & Technical colleges (5 years). They will continue to offer 5-year masters degree programs. In addition, a new two-stage educational program will be introduced which will consist of a 3-year program leading to a bachelor's degree with the option of enrolling in a 2-year master's degree program.

The belief that higher education was strong under the communist regimen is a myth. In fact, university attendance was extremely low due to weak finances, poor management and terrible facilities. Higher education definitely needs a major change. Currently, private schools are opening up all over Poland to fill the demand for higher education. Although they can offer payment plans, flexible schedules and work-study programs, the private schools are criticized because the quality of education offered in the new schools is lower than in public schools.

Universities and colleges in Poland are currently undergoing a major transformation to meet the objectives of higher education, which are to:

- Increase the number of students.
- Restructure vocational education along the lines of academic education.
- Offer greater possibilities for transferring among the various study programs in what is becoming a multi-level higher education system while reducing the number of overly narrow fields of study.
- Make Polish higher education compatible with the foreign higher education systems.
- Integrate the academic community through the merging of universities and other institutions located in the same locations.

Poland's approaching integration with the EU is creating strong pressure for a change in the approach to education. Equal access to education must be one of the priorities of educational reform and must include:

- Improved access to kindergartens and similar standards of primary schools;
- Increased availability of training opportunities for disabled people;
- Equalization of opportunities to access high-standard education;
- Attainment of the highest possible level of education by the largest possible segment of society;
- Continuation of education by adults and the acquisition of qualifications throughout one's life.

In 1989, Natelin College was created basically as part of the College of Europe but especially to serve the needs of the countries in Central Europe. The school teaches the law, economics and administrative systems of the EU. One of its goals is to prepare students to understand and thereby serve their countries in the EU.

Since the 1999 education reform, new types of schools were introduced, i.e. 6-year primary school, 3-year gymnasium (middle school) and 3-4 year secondary education. Both schools systems will co-exist during the transitional period but 2004 will be the last time maturity certificates will be awarded based on the pre-reform system. The total number of primary and secondary education is 12-13 and, at the completion of secondary education, students take the maturity examination (a standard national secondary school achievement examination) and receive the maturity certificate.

To qualify for higher education, the applicant must have the maturity certificate and comply with the rules of admission of the college or university they wish to attend. Each institution of higher learning establishes its own rules of admission. Some schools organize competitive entrance examinations, others rank applicants based on the final grades listed in the maturity certificate and others admit everyone who applies.

Poland's entry into the European Union will guarantee Polish University graduates comparable beginning conditions in their careers to their peers in EU countries provided that the university degrees are equivalent. Integration with the EU will promote the creation of conditions for taking courses in Poland with standards similar to those offered by tertiary schools in Western Europe.

POLAND's UNIVERSITIES

Poland, a country approximately the size of New Mexico, has 13 universities, numerous technology schools as well as specialty schools. The following is brief historical information about several of these schools.

UNIVERSITIES:

- **Jagiellonian University** (formerly Krakow University)In 1364, King Kazimierz the Great received permission from Pope Urban V to establish a Studium Generale in Krakow - the second university to be founded in Central Europe. After King Kazimierz's premature death in 1370, the total lack of interest in the University led to its gradual collapse. In 1400, the University was restored and modernized due to the endeavors of Queen-Saint Jadwiga. By the mid-15th Century Krakow University became Europe's leading academic center of mathematics, astronomy, astrology, geography and legal studies.

  The third and final Partition of Poland posed a serious threat to the very existence of the University but it gradually became a self-governing body and regained the right to teach in Polish. In 1817, the University was renamed Jagiellonian University and once again became a major academic center. In addition to numerous scientific achievements, Krakow historians made Poles aware of their own history and the Law Faculty played an important role in developing legal procedures. In 1897, the first female students were admitted to study pharmacy and were gradually accepted by other faculties. The Jagiellonian University was dramatically affected by the German occupation in Poland during World War II. The University was closed, its property dismantled, destroyed, looted or sent to German and 183 professors were sent to a concentration camp or killed at Katyn and Kharkov. Yet the remaining staff resolved to persevere and taught in a clandestine way - flaunting the Nazi ban on all but the most basic education.

In 1964, the Jagiellonian University celebrated its 600th anniversary and students at the University were actively involved in political protests in 1968, which resulted in repressive measures. Due to the University authorities that firmly defended the fundamental principles of academic ethics and cooperation, these repressive measures were considerably limited. In later periods, the University also took actions to defend academic freedom, human rights and its academic standards. In 1981, the Senate commission prepared a draft bill that was the basis for the democratic and liberal University Act of 1982.

The old Jagiellonian University, with its centuries-old tradition, is also a young and innovative school. With 13 faculties, the organizational structure of the University is unique in Poland. The Jagiellonian University Museum has an excellent collection of old scientific instruments and University treasures as well as a gallery of professors' portraits. It bears witness to the fact that the University is the oldest Polish institution that has continued in spite of all the political calamities suffered by Poland in the past.

- **University of Warsaw** was established in 1816 when the partitions of Poland separated the central region of Poland from the older academic center in Krakow. Many of its students entered the Polish social elite and contributed to the development of the country and kept national consciousness alive during the most difficult period of oppression until the beginning of the 20th Century. During World War I, the German occupation granted permission to establish a Polish university in Warsaw, which made the University of Warsaw one of the first Polish institutions to operate legally.

From 1918-1939 during Poland's Independence, the university was able to develop without restrictions and its method of instruction reached a European level. By the beginning of the 1930s, the University of Warsaw was the largest Polish University. At this time, the salary of a professor was 200% higher than the average white-collar worker and 400% higher than the coal miner's wage. Under Nazi occupying forces, the University was closed and its collections and laboratory equipment were taken to Germany. During World War II many professors, acting against orders and risking death as punishment, continued teaching students in private homes. Gradually, a secret framework of instruction was established which became part of the Polish resistance.

In 1945, classes resumed and the first few years the communist authorities were relatively liberal. The final years of the 1940s saw the elimination of the freedom of instruction, the use of ideological criteria in the selection of professors and the isolation from the world threatened the very existence of the university as a real institution of higher education. By the latter half of the 1950s, an identifiable academic life was revived and the majority of disciplines managed to rebuild free instruction and research on a European level. The university became a center of independent thought from which emerged many leaders of the anti-Communist opposition as well as reformers in the governing camp.

- **University of Bialystok** - created in 1997, it is the thirteenth university in Poland. It has become the biggest academic center in northeastern Poland and provides the region with highly qualified and educated personnel. In addition, the university fosters research concerned with the subject matter of the region and adjusts its fields of training to meet the needs and potential of the region.

TECHNOLOGY SCHOOLS:

- **<u>The Technical University of Lodz</u>** - created over 60 years ago, it is the biggest in Poland. Originally located in an old factory building, today it has over 70 separate buildings. The main research fields correspond to the teaching specialties and pure research projects are conducted with M.Sc. and Ph.D. theses closely connected to current research. Its faculties include:
  - <u>Institute of Turbomachinery</u> was established in 1970. The main fields of research conducted by the Institute include metrology of thermodynamic properties of the flow and measurement process automation, theoretical and experimental investigations to improve turbomachines and flow installations, energy conversion and automatics.
  - <u>Faculty of Textile Engineering</u> offers programs in the field of Mechanical Engineering of Textiles, Chemical Engineering of Textiles, Textile Architecture Clothing and Textile Engineering. The main areas of fundamental and applied research include bioactive fibers, chemistry and technology of synthetic fibers and chemical finishing of textiles and textile care.
  - <u>Faculty of Civil Engineering, Architecture & Environment Engineering</u> - The main areas of fundamental and applied research in Civil Engineering include stability of steel beams and columns, structural dynamics, computer methods in building engineering and civil engineering geodesy. Research in Architecture and Urban Planning includes history of architecture of European Early Middle Ages period, problems of composition in urban planning, the study and typology of small towns and methods of regional planning. The main research topics in Environmental Engineering include mathematical modeling of water supply systems, cartography of the environment,

environmental technology, wastewater and storm water treatment and development of new water and wastewater purification systems.

- <u>The Faculty of Electrical & Electronic Engineering</u> offers programs in the field of Electrical Engineering, Automatic Control & Robotics as well as Electronics and Telecommunications. The main areas of fundamental and applied research include electrical circuits and fields, electrical metrology, theory of control, material science and electro-technology, power plants and power systems, electrical machines and transformers, electronics and telecommunications, electric traction and electro-heat.

- **<u>The Technical University of Wroclaw</u>** - was founded in 1945 when a group of Polish academic teachers arrived in Wroclaw while the city was still burning from the last siege of World War II. The first class was on November 15, 1945 and this day is celebrated as University Day. It is the second largest school of engineering in Poland and has a significant commitment to research in many fields of engineering as well as in physics, mathematics and chemistry.

SPECIALIZED SCHOOLS:

- **<u>Pomeranian Academy of Medicine</u>** - Founded in 1948, it is the sole school of higher learning in Szczecin with full academic powers to hold doctoral and habilitated doctor studies and grants doctoral degrees. Since 1948, 8060 physicians and 3314 dentists have graduated from the Academy. A Faculty of Pharmacy shall be established in the near future and new, unconventional forms of teaching have been adopted in 1996 including:
  1. Extramural studies in nursing leading to title of Master.
  2. Studies for English-speaking students from Scandinavia.

3. Evening full-pay studies in medicine.

- **Wroclaw University of Economics** - The University of Economics began its activities in 1947 as a private, one-faculty College of Commercial Education. In 1950 it was nationalized and transformed into the College of Economics. The official English name of the school is Wroclaw University of Economics. The University has four faculties: National Economy, Management and Computer Science, Engineering and Economics and Regional Economy and Tourism. The University of Economics conducts research in several fields of science and its Publishing House publishes the results of research. The academic staff also plays an advisory role in the process of restructuring banks and other financial institutions. They also act as consultants sit on Boards of Directors of companies and cooperate with governmental bodies such as the Institute for Development and Strategic Studies, banks, insurance companies in Poland and the Stock Exchange.
- **The Higher Police Training School (Wyzsza Szkota Policji)** It is the only school in Poland training future senior officers for the Police, Border Guard and other law enforcement agencies. In addition to teaching, the academy carries out scientific work and research within branches related to fighting crime, forensic science, criminology, penal law and tactics of police work.
  - Institute of Criminal Police Formerly the Institute of Forensic Technique, it was transformed into the Institute of Criminal Police in 1997. The Institute carries out classes covering tactics of combating crime, forensic technique, investigation tactics as well as criminology, victimology and social pathology.
  - Institute of Law & Social Science Among the law subjects taught are: history of state and law, history of political and legal doctrines; jurisprudence; civil, constitutional, international and economic

laws as well as human rights protection. Social science subjects include police ethics, sociology, logistics and police statistics. The students may choose one of the following languages: English, French, German or Russian. The latest publication published by the Department of Foreign Languages is *Polish-English-German-Russian Dictionary of Police and Legal Terms*, edited by G. Ojcewicz and G. Peplowska-Sostek.

HEALTHCARE

The health of Poland's people improved in the two decades after World War II, as antibiotics became available and the standard of living rose in most areas. In the 1970s and 1980s alarming trends appeared in mortality rates. Experts listed the major contributing factors as:

- High levels of air and water pollution,
- Unsatisfactory working conditions and overcrowded housing,
- Psychological depression because of deteriorating economic conditions,
- Poorly balanced diets, and alcoholism.

The Health Care System that Poland inherited from the Soviet bloc era was owned and run by the state, financed by the national budget and governed by the Ministry of Health. The system was over-centralized, over-specialized, costly and poorly managed. Over the years, it had become full of inequalities, shortages, low efficiency and bribery.

In 1999 health care funding was decentralized through the establishment of regional Health Maintenance Agencies ("Kasa Chorych"). Each voievodship (province) has one of these institutions with an additional one for members of the Police, the Military and The State Rail. These institutions receive their funding through payroll taxes from the workforce in their region and are responsible for contracting all health care within that region. This radical shift to a decentralized, insurance-based system should provide a strong stimulus to the reform process despite initial financing problems.

The Polish health care system is characterized by an oversupply of medical personnel, over-aged medical hospitals and tight budgets. These circumstances put heavy pressure on health care and the necessary investments in equipment and facilities are disregarded. In addition, the situation is being driven by the strict budget requirements imposed on Poland in order to qualify for membership in the European Union.

The changes in the Polish health insurance system are more sweeping than anywhere else in Europe. Among other changes are plans to allow private individuals to choose between public health insurance and completely private insurance. It is estimated that nearly 40% of both the financing and provision of care will take place through private companies within a 5-year period.

POPULATION & The Central Statistical Office

In terms of population, Poland is 30th largest country in the world and 8th in Europe in terms of population. The population growth in Poland has been stable at 0.1% since 1995, a figure that has been on the decline. Population density in Poland is 124 persons per square kilometer.

The Sejm ordered the first nationwide census of the population in 1789. In 1810, the first statistical office was established to count the results of the census of population in the Grand Duchy of Warsaw. It was one of the first statistical offices in Europe. In 1897 a general census of population was performed in the Kingdom of Poland - the only census that was carried in that part of Poland until World War I. Results of the census showed demographic, professional, language and religious structure of the population in the Kingdom.

Several noteworthy statistical publications include:

- "About Statistics in Poland" published by Stanislaw Staszic in 1807. The report estimated the number of citizens of Polish lands in the 2nd half of the 18th Century.
- "Statistical Atlas of Poland and neighboring lands" was published in 1827. It was one of the first publications of this kind in Europe.
- "Geographical and statistical picture of the Kingdom of Poland" by Franciszek Rodecki was published in 1830. It contained statistical tables and text information on population, industry, agriculture and crafts.
- "The Principles of Probability Theory" by Wladyslaw Gosiewski was published in 1906. It was the first Polish manual in this field.

In 1912 the Polish Statistical Association was established in Krakow - the first professional organization of Polish statisticans. It published the first Polish statistical and historical yearbook in 1915. This book is a valuable source of number data on the past of Polish land.

The Polish Regency Office established the Central Statistical Office in 1918, which remains a permanent institution in the country. It carried the First General Census of the Population In 1921 and in 1929 organized the XVIII Plenary Session of the International Statistical Institute in Warsaw. Mechanical data stamps with fishplates were used for promoting the population census in 1931. It stopped its activity after the start of World War II. The population of Poland was reduced from about 35 million to about 24 million as a result of World War II. Poland did not come close to its pre-war population level until the 1970s.

In 1967 the bill of the Economic Commission of the Cabinet established the Management of Mechanization and Automation of the Statistical Data, a separate unit of the Central Statistical Office which manages the information in statistics. Also in 1967, the first computer was installed in the Central Statistical Office. The Central Statistical Office signed cooperation agreements in 1990 with Eurostat and the World Bank.

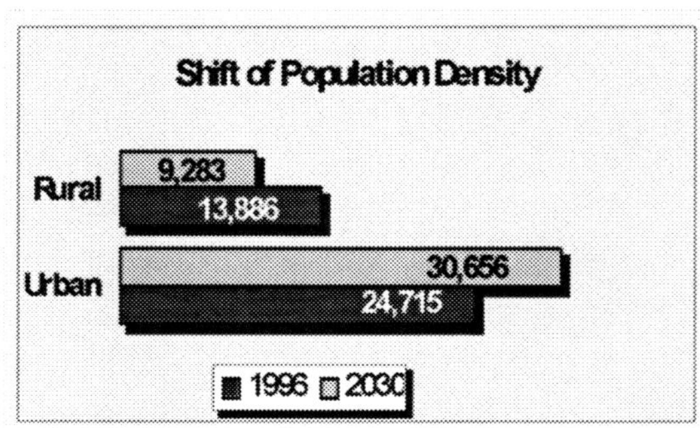

Population growth and migration from country to country are the two main factors having an impact on the population of a given country. Structural changes have been accompanied by a demographic trend of lower external and domestic migration. Migration from rural areas to the cities has particularly slowed primarily because of high housing prices and rents.

In recent years, the number of marriages has increased but the number of divorces has remained stable. The divorce rate in towns and cities is about three times higher than in the country. The number of births has been declining over the past 20 years and life expectancy is increasing. The most frequently recorded causes of death are cancer and circulatory system diseases. People of working age make up 59.5% of the population.

The decisive factor for population potential is the population growth rate, determined by the difference between the number of births and deaths. Poland's economic transformation has influenced the reproduction-related decisions of young women. Declining birth rates and high emigration have led to a demographic depression in the 1990's. It is caused by desire of young people to finish their education and stabilize their economic situation before creating families and having children. Over the past several years, Polish women have not only delayed their decision to marry and have children but have also had fewer children. The former model of a family with many children has changed to a model with one or two children.

Ethnicity

In terms of ethnicity, Poland is a homogenous country, with Poles making up more than 97% of the population. National minorities in Poland are guaranteed equal rights by the Polish constitution, including the right to develop their own culture and learn their native languages in elementary and secondary schools.

Women

Polish women are discriminated against in the job market and poorly protected in the courts. Poland was still lacking good laws in 2000 that would guarantee women basic rights. The regulations protecting women against discrimination were too general and did not encourage victims to go to court. But the law will have to be adjusted to European Union regulations.

At that time, women found it harder to find good jobs, earned about 30% less than men in the same position even though better educated, were less frequently promoted and seldom became directors. Since women's work is an important source of family income, Polish women who have already started to work delay or even rule out a decision to have children for fear of losing their jobs.

Half the medical doctors and most judges and dentists in Poland are women. Almost 1 million Polish women have their own business. Their decision to become independent was based on their desire to fulfil their ambitions and reduce exposure to discrimination in the workplace.

STATE ARCHIVES

Diocesans and monasteries, towns and provincial rules kept the first archives dating back to the 13th Century. Archiwum Koronne (the Crown Archive) was established in the middle of the 14th Century while Archiwum Metryki Koronnej (Archive of the Crown Register) which subsequently became the central archive of the Commonwealth, was founded towards the end of the 14th Century. The 2nd half of the 18th Century saw the emergence of the Archive of Stanislaw August Poniatowski, the last King of Poland.

During the partitions, the fate of Polish archives varied depending on the policies of the individual partitioning power. In the Russian zone, 10 provincial archives were established to collect court records. The Archive of Historical Records and the Treasury Archive were founded in 1867. In the Prussian zone, 2 state archives existed: in Poznan founded in 1869 and in Gdansk founded in 1878. In the Austrian zone, the Archive of Town and County Records existed in Lvov from 1784 and in Krakow from 1877. In 1808 the General National Archive was established in the Duchy of Warsaw. It was Poland's first modern archive and was subsequently transformed into the General Archive of Historical Records.

After regaining independence in 1919, the state archives of the Republic of Poland was established in 1919 and was charged with the gathering, custody, research and provision of access to the national archival collection. The State Archives Department of the Ministry of Religious Affairs and Public Education supervised its operation.

During World War II, the archival collections came under the administration of Nazi occupying authorities and suffered heavy losses. The worst affected were the Warsaw archives that were 95% destroyed. The archives in Poznan suffered wanton destruction and numerous other collections were extensively damaged. After World War II, efforts were made to reconstruct the network of archives whenever possible. The State Archive Head Office was established in 1951 to be in charge of archive collections and introduced the concept of state archival resources.

In addition to the state archives, Poland has many church archives, municipal archives, educational archives and family archives. One of the oldest is the Jagiellonian University Archive.

Jagiellonian University Archives:

The Archives date back to the 14th Century and include paper and parchment documents relating to privileges and endowments given to the university, diplomas, special books containing information on charters, resolutions and conclusions of general assembly meetings, university certificates as well as sentences of the Rector's Court. An important art of these materials is a unique collection of records concerning bokarnas - the first scholarship system in Europe.

A list of accumulated records was made in the 16th Century and the first inventory of documents was prepared. In 1796 the archive material was recorded in 8 volumes of summation books and 8 volumes of repertories for approximately 25,000 paper and parchment documents. In addition, alphabetical indices were introduced in 267 hand-written books.

During the long period under Austrian rule, the university never lost its special position in Polish culture. Between 1833-1836, all archival material was integrated into one collection. Towards the end of the 19th Century, historians became interested in documents pertaining to the oldest Polish university and the archive holdings were used for research works and studies connected with the history of the university.

World War II interrupted the period of dynamic development of the Archives and they incurred heavy losses. The losses included two documents concerning the university construction dating from 1364 and 1400; some of the foundation documents and scholarship records as well as many documents from 1930s were lost. After the war, records of student organizations, private papers of professors and materials concerning the occupation period came flooding in. Inventory work is ongoing and between 1963-1994, a team of Archives workers started their work on the biographical dictionary of the Jagiellonian University scholars from the 15th to 20th Century.

The Archdiocesan Archive in Poznan:

The main Archive for Poznan Archdiocese was founded in 1925 as an independent diocesan institution - the first institution of that kind in Poland. The Archive is divided into three parts:

- Old Records Archive (also called Old Polish Archives - preserves documents produced prior to the 14th Century and contains 1084 parchment documents. It contains over 500 manuscripts and books, which refer to central diocesan institutions. The oldest one is from 1231 - a diploma drawn up by Prince Wladyslaw Laskonogi.
- Modern Records Archive - which contains archival material from 14th to 20th Centuries.
- Special Collections - contains archival material which are most popular among searchers, i.e. birth, marriage and death records.

State Archives in Gdansk:

It was originally established in 1898 as the State Archive for the West Prussia Province of the German Empire in Gdansk. The Archive contains valuable information of the history of Pomerania as well as economic, social and political relations between Baltic state cities, Poland and Europe and historical records of Gdansk dating from the 14th Century. Without this information it would be impossible to write about the history of Gdansk, 16th to 18th Century Sejm, Royal Prussia, Hanseatic

League and commerce and shipping trade in Northern Europe.

Prior to the establishment of the Free City of Gdansk by the Treaty of Versailles, many precious holdings were taken to Berlin, some of which have never been returned to Gdansk. After the outbreak of World War II and the annexation of Gdansk by Germany in 1940, the Archive became the Reichsarchiv Danzig. The Germans added to the Archives with records of closed down Polish institutions and the institutions of the Free City of Gdansk. At the end of the war, the Archive evacuated a large part of its most valuable holdings and only the records evacuated were saved after the fighting in Gdansk in 1945. All other records were lost.

Today, the State Archive in Gdansk is one of the archives educating future archivists and introducing computer network-based methods of cataloguing the its holdings.

Pomerelian Archive of the Home Army:

The Pomerelian Archive of the Home Army was established in 1990. Its main purpose is to collect all materials concerning the history of underground resistance movement in Pomerelia during World War II, the history of Polish Women War Service of that time and the history of the Department of Foreign Communications of the Home Army main headquarters. Other functions include activities to increase the knowledge of events that occurred under German occupation and to remind current generations about the patriotic attitude of their ancestors.

SCIENCE in POLAND

There have been many scientists throughout Poland's history -- the one best known around the world is Nicholas Copernicus. More information about Poland's contribution to the development of world sciences can be found in Appendix A - Notable Poles.

Today, the strategic objective of science in Poland is:

a) Acquisition of original and important achievements in the most attractive research currents on the world,
b) Acquisition of original and important technologies and their utilization in technological collaboration in Poland and between Poland and the rest of the world.

There are a few key government offices that are engaged in the attaining the above goals. However, the executive power belongs to the State Committee for Scientific Research (SCSR), the Ministry of National Education (MNE) and the Polish Academy of Sciences (PAS).

<u>State Committee for Scientific Research (SCSR)</u> is the leading authority on state policy in the field of science and technology and the only central government source of funds for research. The SCSR also maintains the database - Data Exchange on Research Projects, which contains descriptions of some current research projects.

<u>Ministry of National Education (MNE)</u> supervises the activities of the higher education institutions. It is the policy of the MNE to provide equal opportunity to all persons seeking or having access to its institutions, services, activities and free from any restrictions.

<u>Polish Academy of Science (PAS)</u>, established in 1952, is the foremost scientific institution in Poland. It is a self-governing

corporation of eminent scientists and scholars from all disciplines and performs:

- The national tasks of research management and coordination;
- Peer reviews projects and programs;
- Pursues the mission of promoting science and furthering the beneficial influence of science on national life;
- Advises the public authorities on scientific matters; and
- Represents the scientific community in the international forum.

In Poland, there are about 150 colleges and universities, 264 research units, 126 museums, 6 scientific publishers, 39 state archives and 1200 scientific libraries that include:

- Jagiellonian Library (founded in 1363)
- Biblioteka Narodowa Ossolineum (founded in 1817)
- Centraina Biblioteka Statystyczna (founded in 1918)
- National Library (founded in 1928)

Poland also has 32 general and regional scientific societies, over 140 scientific societies, 50 professional medical societies, 30 professional scientific-engineering associations and 37 scientific foundations that include:

- Foundation for Polish Science
- The Polish Foundation for Science Advancement
- Stefan Batory Foundation
- The Polish-US Fulbright Commission

Finally, the Interministerial Consultation and Coordination Group for the Cosmos has begun work to oversee Poland's space policy and act as Poland's space agency. The association's Space Bureau will be responsible for promoting research activities concerned with outer space and facilitating cooperation with space agencies from other countries. Its first task was to conclude an agreement on scientific and industrial cooperation with European Space Agency (ESA).

After being granted special candidate country status by ESA, Poland will be involved in the Space Strategy for Europe program. The program includes plans for a network of navigation satellites, a network of satellites for monitoring the Earth and sending interplanetary probes to explore Mars, Mercury and Venus. For Polish companies, scientific cooperation with the ESA will open the doors to the European space industry and allow the companies to bid for contracts to build parts and components of these satellites.

INSURANCE INDUSTRY IN POLAND

For over 40 years PZU (State Insurance Company) held a monopoly on the domestic market while Warta S.A. monopolized the foreign trade insurance as well as the insurance of people going abroad. In 1990 the passage by the Sejm of a new Insurance Law was the beginning of necessary changes in the insurance industry in Poland in recent years. This law was extensively amended in 1995 to bring Poland's insurance sector in agreement with existing provisions in the European Union. The Pension Fund Supervisory Office (KNUFE) created in 2002 supervises the insurance industry in Poland. In addition, all insurance companies registered in Poland are members of the Polish Chamber of Insurance that was established in 1990.

Prior to providing Insurance and reinsurance services, companies must obtain approval of the Minister of Finance who grants a license and has the power to revoke it. According to KNUFE, by 2001 there were 72 insurance companies (70 domestic and 2 main branch offices of foreign companies) licensed by the Minister of Finance to operate in Poland.

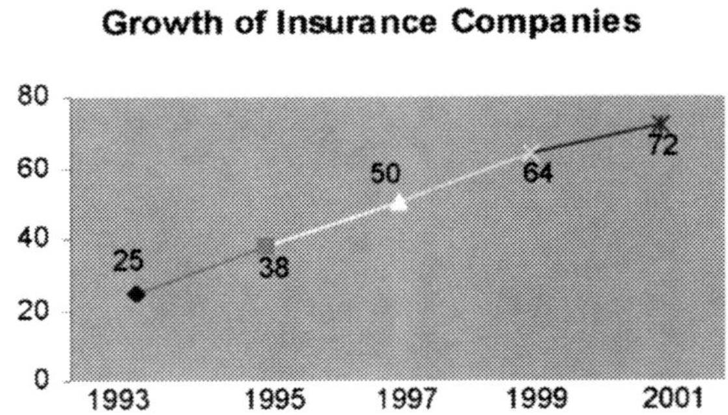

Individuals and/or companies required to carry civil liability insurance include:

a. Car owners
b. Farmers
c. Health care providers

d. Tax advisors
e. Organizers of public events

Since 1991, the Export Credit Insurance Corporation (KUKE), a Polish export credit insurance agency, has been insuring Polish companies against commercial risk as well as offering solutions that combine export and domestic contract insurance with credit information and credit portfolio management. It is available to all exporters regardless of the scale of their operations and provides the opportunity to insure export receivables from over 180 countries around the world.

ENERGY INDUSTRY

New guidelines for establishing reforms in the energy sector were approved in 1996. The goal is to attract the required investment for industrial modernization and environmental protection and to create a competitive energy market through the privatization of the energy industry. At this time, Poland meets its energy as follows:

Fuel Type	Percentage of Total
Hydroelectric	0.2
Natural Gas	8.8
Oil	16.6
Coal	69.5

In 1997, Poland passed a new Energy Act which required the government to pass "Guidelines on Poland's Energy Policy through 2020". The document sets forth energy forecasts and action plans. The key objectives include:

- Increased security of energy supplies requiring diversification of sources.
- Increased competitiveness for Polish energy sources in domestic and international markets.
- Environmental protection.
- Improving energy efficiency and reducing energy related emissions.

Oil

Poland has minor oil resources. The oil and gas exploration sector licensed for exploration in 1996 2 million acres in northern Poland and 1.8 million acres in central Poland. Nafta Polska, the holding company of Poland's oil industry, consists of two major refineries are located at Gdansk and Plock, 5 smaller refineries located in southern Poland and a Central Distribution Company (CPN). In 1996,CPN divided into 3 companies:

1. CPN S.A. - the gas station company.
2. DEC Ltd. - the railway tank company.
3. Naftobazy Ltd. - the oil storage company.

Investment needs in Poland's oil industry include refinery modernization and a new refinery in southern Poland.

Poland attempted to diversify its oil sources and to reduce its dependence on Russian oil but inexpensive prices and economic factors have resulted in Poland actually increasing its imports of Russian oil. Poland imports non-Russian crude oil on tankers unloading at Gdansk on the Baltic Sea. In 1999, Poland and Ukraine reached an agreement to jointly complete a pipeline for Caspian Sea oil. The pipeline will allow Poland and its neighbors to import sweet Caspian crude that will make it easier to meet the EU's new motor fuel specifications. There are expectations that this network will be expanded to northwestern Europe via export terminals at Gdansk, Poland and Rostock, Germany.

Natural Gas

Poland's natural gas resources are also minor. Although Poland has large coalbed methane reserves, production costs are relatively high and no determination of its economic potential has been made. The Polish Oil & Gas Company (POGA) is one of the last fully integrated hydrocarbon monopolies in Europe. It is responsible for the entire natural gas sector from exploration and production, to transmission, storage and distribution. Depleted natural gas reservoirs in southeast Poland are used to store Poland's natural gas. All 4 underground storage facilities are designed to respond to seasonal demand variations rather than meet strategic needs.

Poland has integrated its natural gas transmission system with Germany and plans larger imports of Russian natural gas via the Yamal-Europe Transit Gas Pipeline, which is currently under construction across Poland and Western Europe. In addition, to offset the country's reliance on Russian imports to meet the increased demand for natural gas, Poland plans to build additional natural gas storage facilities and is considering importing liquefied natural gas from Qatar, Nigeria, Norway and Algeria. In 2000, Poland and Norway signed a declaration to begin Norwegian gas exports to Poland and to build a new pipeline under the Baltic Sea connecting Scandinavia to Poland. Construction to be completed by 2004. Norwegian gas also helps Poland in their goal to diversify energy sources.

Coal

Although Poland has significant coal resources of high quality coal, it is one of the most coal dependent countries in the world. Similar to other former communist countries, Poland depends heavily on coal to meet its energy needs. All coal comes from approximately 70 underground mines. Despite industry reforms in the early 1990's, production costs at many coalmines remain high and the industry is expected to remain unprofitable without aggressive cost-reduction measures. In order to maintain production capacity, investments in new mines and continued development of existing mines are needed.

In 1998 Poland received $1 billion in loans from the World Bank to finance a comprehensive restructuring program for the coal industry which included capital investments for coal preparation plants, modernization and environmental protection.

Electricity

Poland's power generation sector is the largest in Central and Eastern Europe and as a result Poland produces more electricity than it consumes and exports the excess to nearby countries. The Polish electrical grid is part of the CENTREL system that links the Czech Republic, Slovakia and Hungary. The system was connected with Western Europe's system in 1995. Also, Poland has connections with Ukraine and Belarus. Both north-south and east-west connections are being expanded as part of the EU's Trans-European Energy Network.

The electricity industry in Poland needs modernization and refurbishment in order to create an economically efficient industry capable of meeting demand requirements. Investment opportunities exist in all sub-sectors of the power industry in Poland and they continue to emerge along with its privatization. It has been reorganized into three layers of companies dedicated to the generation, transmission and distribution subsections:

- **Generation** - Generation capacity construction in Poland has been inconsistent over the past 30 years resulting in an aging system with more than half of the current capacity built in the 1970s. Also, Poland's power plant technologies lagged behind more recent developments including environmental control. Priorities include the rehabilitation and retrofitting of aging coal-fired generating equipment to improve availability, efficiency and environmental control and reduce losses in transmission and distribution.
- **Transmission** - Poland's power distribution system is fully integrated into the Western European UCPTE system and maintains links with the distribution systems in the Ukraine and Belorussia. These links provide Poland with an exchange potential with Western Europe and these former Soviet Union states.
- **Distribution** - Representing about 40% of all Polish electricity sector assets, the distribution sector consists of 33 distribution companies, all of which are joint stock companies. A 1997 energy law provides for third-party access to the power grid and vests authority in an independent Energy Regulatory Office.

Currently, the electrical energy market can be divided into the wholesale market and retail market. The wholesale market includes energy exports and imports and its providers sell energy on a competitive basis. Energy trade is organized through direct contracts between the market participants, however, it is anticipated that in the future most of this trade will take place on the already established Electrical Energy Exchange.

The retail market consists of two sections which are:

- The competitive section - where distribution companies provide transfer services to customers while producers and electrical trade companies sell the energy to those customers who have acquired the right to transfer services.
- The regulated section - where distribution companies sell the energy to the "tariff" customers at prices approved by the President of the Energy Regulatory Office.

At present, the right to select an energy provider is given to those customers who consume more than 10 GW/h per year. As the market develops, additional customer groups will be eligible to purchase energy in the competitive section of the retail market. By 2005, all electric energy consumers in Poland will have the right to select their electrical energy provider.

In 1998, Poland committed to adapting its electricity market regulations to EU standards by 2002. The electrical voltage in Poland is 220 and the current frequency is 50 Hz. All power cables and plugs in Poland meet these standards.

TRANSPORTATION

During the 1970s, the transportation system began breaking down. About 50% of the railway cars, buses and trucks were down for repair that took a long time because of shortages of spare parts. There was also continual under-investment in roads and railway lines.

Currently, Poland has a well-developed transport infrastructure including approximately 250 thousand kilometers of hard surface roads and an extensive railway network that links all the major cities and towns. In 2001, motor transport was used to transport 60.3% of the goods in Poland.

Public Transportation:

Local transportation in local cities is well developed. The most popular means of transportation is the bus. Ticket prices are quite low but you need to purchase an extra ticket if you have luggage. Bus and train stations are usually located next to each other. There are tram/light rail networks in 13 cities and, in 1995, a 12 km metro opened in Warsaw.

Taxi drivers tend to overprice their services. Do not take taxis from Warsaw International Airport or the Warsaw Central Railway Station. Order taxis by telephone and settle the price first. If you feel cheated, always demand a bill (rachunek) with driven distance and taxi number on it.

Cars:

Drivers in Poland need valid driver's license, automobile registration documents, and accident insurance card. Traffic regulations include:

- Headlights must be on all day during November-March.
- Everyone must wear seatbelts, if available.
- Drivers must give right of way to pedestrians.
- Children under the age of 10 are forbidden to ride in the

front seat of the car.

- Parking on sidewalks is generally allowed although you must leave room for pedestrians.

Generally all signs correspond to European standards.

Kolelny	Deep ruts on road, caused by heavy trucks
Objazd	Detour
Kontrola radarowa	Speed control - watch out for Police!
Dotyczy rownlez chodnika	No parking (on sidewalk)

Highways:

The increasing road traffic in Poland is causing more problems with the quality of existing roads. Only 21% of national roads are in good condition; 37% of the roads in Poland require immediate repair or modernization.

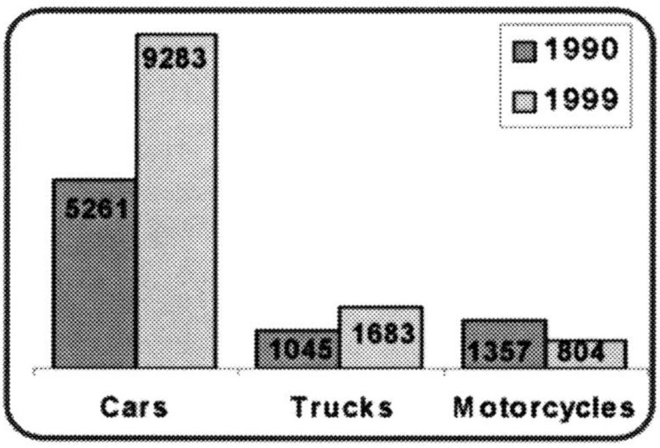

Since 1991, it is estimated that traffic volume has increased by 42% and the number of vehicles on Polish roads has increased by 50% since 1988.

The program of building a network of highways in Poland was adopted by Decree of the Council of Ministers in 1993 and is regarded as one of the most ambitious undertakings in the post-war history of Central Europe. The Highway Construction Program in Poland anticipates the construction of a network of four highways - two running from east to west and two from north to south.

To upgrade the existing roads to European Union standards, Poland would need to spend approximately PLN 90 billion on the construction of toll ways and expressways plus modernization of existing roads. According to the law on financing of the roads in Poland, 30% of the revenues from the excise tax on fuel sales is to be spent on construction and modernization of existing roads. The project for construction of a system of toll ways in Poland has seen big delays due to the problem with financing – the traffic studies showed lower traffic density than expected. In 2002, the government prepared a new program for road construction and modernization with the aim of adapting the Polish road transportation system to EU standards.

Railways:

The Polish State Railways (PKP) is one of the larger railway systems of central or Western Europe. Although the first tracks under its control dates to 1845, PKP was established in 1918 after Poland's independence following World War I. With different styles of locomotives, signaling and operating practices, PKP set out to establish a national system. By 1921, Polish-built locomotives were being made and electrification was begun in 1936 when the cross-city system in Warsaw was wired.

World War II brought massive destruction to Poland's railways as the system was subjected to extensive bombing. In 1945, the PKP started rebuilding under Soviet occupation.

Steam locomotives were the key source of motive power and were used extensively until the late 1980s.

During the 1970s and 1980s, continued electrification brought higher speeds and reliable service. Improved traveling conditions were provided by new generations of equipment. The PKP played an important part in the national transportation system.

When democracy came to Poland in 1989, the PKP was forced to operate with declining government subsidies, declining ridership (due to increased private automobile ownership) and declining freight traffic. At the same time, PKP has forged new links and cooperation with the railways of Western Europe, which have led to the introduction of inner city and Euro-City trains and improvements in tracks and signaling. With the road system still being developed, and the traffic and parking problems that many cities are experiencing, travel by rail is comfortable and convenient.

Some Polish trains feature sleeping cars or food service cars. These cars which are run by the Wars (Przedsiebiorstwo Wagonow Sypialnych i Restauracyjnych) an independent company separate from PKP.

Wars Sleeping Car

There are 4 types of trains in Poland:

1. <u>Express</u> - these trains reach only the larger cities and often make 3 stops before reaching its destination. The trip from Krakow to Warsaw takes 3 hours.
2. <u>Inter-City</u> - similar to Express trains, but require prior reservations. They usually include a small meal in the price of the ticket.

3. Fast - these trains stop in larger towns and are as fast as express trains. However, since no seat reservations are required, you may have to stand the entire trip.
4. Local - these trains stop at every station. Seats are very uncomfortable but the tickets are very cheap. For short distances, this may be the way to go.

Airlines/Airports:

In 1930, LOT Polish Airlines was accepted into the International Association of Air Transportation and the "crane" was acknowledged as its emblem. By the late 1930s, LOT Polish Airlines network covers the major part of the European continent with plans to launch flights over the Atlantic in 1940. During World War II, all hangers and airport buildings were destroyed.

LOT introduced the first turboprop aircraft in 1961 and began the jet aircraft era in Polish civil aviation in 1968. With its decision to purchase American aircraft in 1988, LOT became the first airline in Central and Eastern Europe to use American planes. By 1994, LOT Polish Airlines has the newest fleet of all airlines worldwide and a code-share agreement is signed with American Airlines. In 1999, LOT purchased 6 Embraer ERJ-145 jets, the first airline in Central and Eastern Europe to use this type of plane. This fast, small jet makes it possible to operate more flights daily and to connect more frequently with passenger travel centers in Europe.

By 1998, it is estimated that Poland had 74 airports with paved runways, 18 airports with unpaved runways and 3 heliports.. Although Warsaw International Airport is new, it is already too small to deal with the rising number of travelers.

Inland Waterways:

The middle course of the main river in Poland, the Vistula, contains many navigational hazards. As a result the major waterway is the smaller Oder, which is linked by the modern

Gilwice Canal to the Upper Silesian industrial region and carries coal to the port of Szczecin. Bydogoszcz Canal also lines the Oder basin to the lower Vistula. In 1995 there was 3,980 km of navigable inland waterways, which carried freight including coastal traffic. However, less than 1% of Polish freight is carried on rivers and canals.

COMMUNICATION

Telephones

In 1989, Poland had the poorest telephone network in Europe except for Albania. The telephone service had an unacceptable level of quality as well as excessive long wait to obtain telephone service. Realizing that fast network development was a prerequisite for dynamic economic goals, the Polish government reconstructed the sector and increased its efficiency through massive investment programs and fast network development.

The Telecommunication Law of 1990 provided for deregulation of the telecommunications sector. This law was later modified to meet European standards contained in the Association Agreement with the European Union. In 1995, a new automatic telephone exchange was installed in Klodzko capable of serving 15,000 numbers and providing automatic access to domestic and foreign telephone connections.

Although the number of telephone lines has almost doubled, Poland is still far behind other European countries. Since 1991 the telecommunication network has grown 14%. Poland now has a modern long distance and back bone network as well as almost exclusively digital switching equipment (92%) but the ability to provide lines to end users is still weak. By 1999, Poland had microwave radio relay and 3 cellular networks. Its international satellite earth

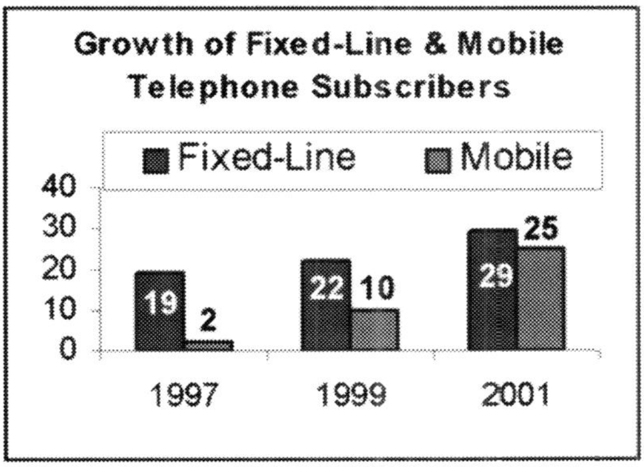

stations include 2 Intelsat, NA Eutelsat, 2 Inmarsat (Atlantic and Indian Ocean regions) and 1 Intersputnik (Atlantic Ocean region). By 2001, the average telephone density measured by the number of main lines per 100 inhabitants was up to 29.4 and the average mobile phone density rose to 24.9. It is expected that the number of cell phones in Poland may exceed the number of fixed lines by the end of 2002.

Mobile Communications

Mobile communications is the fastest growing segment of the telecommunication market in Poland. There is one countrywide paging system and the number of cellular phone users doubled in the last six months. The weakness of traditional fixed telecommunications infrastructure at a local level adds to the tremendous success of mobile telephones. For many individual and business representatives, mobile phones are still their only opportunity to obtain a telephone.

Internet

Poland joined the Internet in 1991 and has outpaced countries such as Russia, Hungary, the Czech Republic and Ireland. When it comes to number of connections, it is in 15th place in Europe. In 1996, NASK, the research and academic network which maintains all Polish Internet connections to servers abroad, started operating WARMAN, a state-of-the-art metropolitan area telecommunications network in Warsaw. The largest Internet service provider in Poland, NASK links 600 institutions, 40,000 companies and 400,000 users.

Companies mostly use the Internet for faster communication via e-mail. The possibilities of sending vast amounts of information over the net in a few seconds make e-mail the most efficient mode of communication and very appealing to companies. The Web's commercial opportunities remain largely under-utilized in Poland although companies are increasingly using the Web for advertising and promotion.

The Internet has the potential to become a vibrant and important new technology if it could only reach more people. The natural development of the Internet is being curtailed because the prices are too high to allow a large market to develop thereby restricting its growth. Polish companies are unable to learn fast enough about the new technology and utilize it, which in time will be reflected in the state of the economy.

One of EU's priorities is the development of an information society symbolized by the Internet. To take advantage of these new technological opportunities, it is essential that Poland to quickly adapt legal regulations and requirements for e-business and to liberalize the telecommunications market.

Broadcasting

The public Polski Radio I Telewizja broadcasts 3 radio programs and 2 TV programs. There are also 4 commercial TV channels. Independent radio and TV broadcasting were introduced in 1992 under the aegis of the National Council of Broadcasting and Television. A direct-to-home satellite pay television was launched in 1998.

Polish authorities formally approved issuing a license to a Belarusian-language radio in 1990. Radio Racja will broadcast on shortwave and ultra-shortwave bands in Belarusian to the Belarusian minority in Poland. The shortwave signal will also reach Minsk, the capital of neighboring Belarus. Radio Racja will be a cultural-informative radio station managed by a company bearing the same name. In 1999, Poland had 7 national radio stations and 181 regional and city stations. At this time, there were 3 national television stations and 40 regional and city stations.

Newspapers/Books

In 1996, there were 87 newspapers in Poland. The two most popular newspapers are "Gazeta Wyborcza" and

"Rzeczpospolita", plus the tabloid "Super Express". In addition, the Warsaw Voice is available online in English. Poland has more than 9000 libraries and in 1996 there were over 14,000 books published. The national library, Biblioteka Narodowa, is located in Warsaw.

Postal Service

During the 15th Century, the excellent postal service of Polish cities greatly stimulated the development of Polish commerce. In 1583, Sebastian Monteupi organized regular postal exchange with foreign countries. During his administration the larger cities in Poland received mail weekly and the rates charged were uniform and moderate in accordance with a schedule based on distance zones.

The fist postage stamps to appear on Polish Lands were issued in 1850 under the occupation by Austria and Prussia. Used for internal use in Poland and Russia, the first Polish Postage Stamp bearing the Coat of Arms of Polish Kingdom was withdrawn in 1865 and replaced by Russian stamp. The first Polish Postage Stamp of the Royal Polish Post office was issued in 1860 and replaced the Russian stamps. The first Polish Philatelic club under the name "Polski Klub Filatelistów" was founded on 6th January 1893.

1860 stamp

Poczta Polska, the Polish Postal Service, is a state public utility enterprise and holds a monopoly for the provision of postal services and issues stamps for the territory of Poland. The scope of postal service includes acceptance, conveyance and delivery of ordinary letter-post items, registered letter-post items, insured letter-post items, postal parcels and postal money orders. The last year operation deficits were covered by government subsidy was 1996. The Polish Post broke even in 1997 and made a profit in the following years.

The Polish Post took part in the Postal Service Regulation, Quality of Service Measurement and Management for Postal Services Projects. Guidelines provided helped draft the new Postal Law which takes into account recommendations of the European Parliament on common rules for the development of the internal market of community postal services. The experience facilitated conformity of the postal sector with European Union criteria as well as integration into Europe.

ECONOMY

ECONOMIC TRANSFORMATION

Poland has accomplished an economic transformation of historic significance motivated by the desire to safeguard human and economic rights of the individual and the collective and long-term interest of the country. As a result of the changes started at the end of the 1980s, the Polish economy has regained its capacity for rapid development.

Prior to World War II, Poland was predominately an agricultural country. After the war and the establishment of Communist control, attempts were made to form socialist-style cooperative farms. Most were disbanded after 1956 due to strong resistance from the peasants. Since World War II, the Poles have built a fishing industry in the Baltic Sea and on the Atlantic Ocean.

Industrial priority is given to the production of iron, steel, chemicals and electricity. Poland ranks 4th in the world in coal production and exports large amounts. The chemical industry is significant and the largest nitrogen-fertilizer plant in Europe is located south of Warsaw. The Polish engineering industry produces a variety of items including ships, transport equipment, agricultural machinery, machine tools and equipment for various industries. Finally, textile production, located in Lodz, is a traditional branch of Polish industry and exports both linen and cotton textiles. For more information on Polish industries and companies, see chapter on "Poland's Economic Diversity".

Poland stands out as one of the most successful and open transition economies. The privatization of small and medium state-owned companies and a liberal law establishing new firms marked the rapid development of a private sector. Further progress on public finance depends mainly on comprehensive reform of the social welfare system and privatization of Poland's remaining state sector. With the completion of its transition to a free market economy, Poland not only has an energetic economy but also has been determinedly progressing towards EU membership.

In 1990, Poland's coalition government began an ambitious, fast track agenda towards market reform following 20 years of a general economic slump which featured mounting inflation and the growth of a large external debt. Widespread restructuring also caused the Gross Domestic Product (GDP) to fall and unemployment rose to double digits. Since 1994, Poland's economy has been recovering with annual GDP growth averaging 6%, gradually declining inflation and unemployment. By 2001, Poland ranked 7th of the 15 EU member countries in total GDP. Trade continues to shift to the EU and Russia has fallen from 1st place to 4th place of Poland's trade partners.

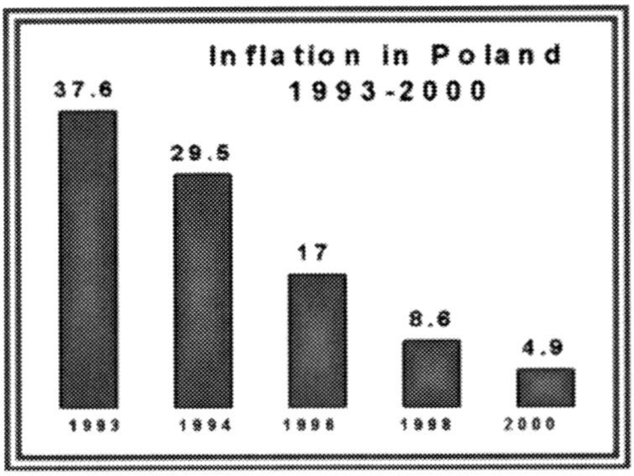

In 1996, Poland became a member of the Organization for Economic Cooperation and Development (OECD) and is also part of the Central European Free Trade Area (CEFTA).

Privatization

The privatization of former state-owned enterprises is one of the central elements of the transformation process to a market economy. Foreign capital is crucial to the privatization process and privatization's involving foreign investors were able to bring greater resources and expertise and have been more successful than those companies privatized under local management. The success of the Mass Privatization Program (MPP) introduced in 1995 will depend on the quality of western capital and management expertise and their ability to bring about successful restructuring plans.

In 1999, progress was achieved in privatization in banking, insurance, pharmaceuticals, energy and the air transportation sectors. Reorganization and privatization of Poland's steel-making operations are scheduled for 2001.

Unemployment

The restructuring and privatization of the steel and coal industries will undoubtedly add to the unemployment. In addition, it is anticipated that large numbers of the "hidden unemployed" will be released on the labor market following the structural reform of agriculture. Further reduction of Poland's high income tax and wage burden rates are critical to the government's high priority objective of creating jobs.

Cooperation with International Organizations

The assistance of international economic organizations has been a significant factor in the successful transition of Poland to a market economy. In 1986 Poland rejoined the World Bank which beginning in 1990 provided three main types of loans to support Poland's economic development and reform programs:

1. Fast disbursing program assistance to help offset some of the costs of economic reforms.
2. Lending for specific investments, i.e. equipment for infrastructure rehabilitation and modernization financing.
3. Expansion projects by state enterprises through credit lines managed by Polish banks.

When the challenging stabilization program was launched in Poland during 1989-1990, the International Monetary Fund arranged a standby loan to support the Polish currency that was never used for the original purpose.

The goals of the International Finance Corporation (IFC) are to foster economic growth in the developing world and promote sustainable private sector investment in developing countries. Since Poland joined in 1987, the IFC has invested in a wide range of sectors including manufacturing, agribusiness, telecommunications, urban development, health-care, banking and private equity funds. In addition, the IFC has undertaken many technical and advisory assignments in Poland. Currently, the IFC will focus its investment and advice in areas such as:

- Promoting public-private partnerships in health and education.
- Supporting further institutional development in the financial sector.
- Promoting renewable energy sources and energy efficiency.
- Advising the Warsaw Stock Exchange on strengthening corporate regulation measures.
- Selective financing of domestic manufacturing companies.

The European Bank for Reconstruction and Development (EBRD), one of the largest investors in Poland, was established in 1991 to finance development projects in Eastern and Central European countries which were transitioning to a market economy. Over the years, EBRD has developed substantial and valuable investment and experience in Poland, which it uses to help the government to accelerate the transition process. Its strategy for the 2002-2003 period is to target investments in the following sectors:

- <u>Infrastructure and Environment</u> - Due to the significant investment Poland has to make to ensure continued economic growth while modernizing its infrastructure to meet the EU accession requirements, EBRD will focus on financing infrastructure investment at national as well as at local levels.
- <u>Financial Sector</u> - EBRD will seek to increase the variety and availability of financing to support the expansion

and growth of the non-bank financial sector, support the completion of the modernization of the banking/ insurance sector and promote the availability of a wider variety of more sophisticated financial products and services.

- Enterprise Sector - EBRD will seek to support the restructuring, modernization and privatization of the remaining large-scale industrial enterprises whose effectiveness and competitiveness must be strengthened.
- Agriculture/Agribusiness - Pending the introduction of appropriate structural policies by the Government, EBRD is prepared to assist in financing the agricultural sector to improve competitiveness, to improve the quality and sanitary standards of domestic food products and to achieve the necessary consolidation.

The United Nations Industrial Development Organization (UNIDO) was established in 1967 to reduce the traditional gap between industrialized countries, developing countries and economies in transition. Its activities focus on promotion of investments and related technologies and assurance of clean and sustainable industrial development. When it opened an office in Warsaw in 1983, UNIDO became one of the first international organizations to establish close relations with Poland and has been very active in attracting foreign investors to Poland. In the late 1980s, the UNIDO office in Warsaw organized International Investor's Forums, which enabled the international business and financial community to get acquainted with the investment environment and opportunities in Poland. This office provides:

- Assistance to individual potential foreign investors.
- Promotion of industrial investments and technologies in Poland and other transition economies.
- Support to Poland's industry through managerial training.

The Investment and Technology Promotion Office (ITPO) was set up as part of the UNIDO investment and technology promotion network in 1983. ITPO supports the development process of Polish industry through:

- Identification of potential cooperation partners and strategic investors.
- Various management training courses.
- Editing and disseminating business manuals and related publications.

In addition, ITPO opens up new opportunities for investors and technology suppliers from Poland to find potential partners in countries in transition.

MONETARY SYSTEM - 1000 Years of Coins

Coins have been issued in Poland for over 1000 years. The earliest Polish coin was the DENAR of Mieszko I issued before 992 AD which was a small crude silver coin without any Polish symbols on it. Denars issued under Mieszko's son, Boleslaw Chrobry began to show Polish identity and show the first use of the Eagle on a Polish coin. During the political turmoil of the 11th Century, these coins lost value and were replaced in the latter half of the Century by coins called brakteat which were issued by Kings, Princes, the Church and others for a few hundred years. The value and thickness of the coins diminished until they were so thin at the end of the 13th Century that only one side die was used. During the 12th and 13th Centuries, copies of Byzantine type coins were used in Poland.

1400 AD

Kazimierz the Great did the next recoinage in the 14th Century with the new system based on a European one. Several factors caused havoc to trade at this time including:

- Use of gold coinage of Hungary in valuable transactions,
- Different systems used in parts of the country, and
- Different coinage of both Prussia and Lithuania.

The significant changes in the monetary system made by Kazimierz the Great included introduction of the GROSZ. The Grosz, Half Grosz as well as Denars were issued by many subsequent Polish Rulers. These coins usually had a Crown on one side and a Polish Eagle on the other. Under Queen Jadwiga, a small thin silver coin known as SZELAG started to be used in these Northern areas (becoming a copper Shilling much later. During the Jagiellonian period, coins were issued for Gdansk, Torun, Elblag, and other areas under Polish rule. The new zloty system was implemented in Poland in 1528, in Prussia in 1538 and in Lithuania in 1569. The system was stable until the beginning of the 17th Century. Later, under the Reign of Zygmunt I Stary, several new coin types were produced based on the ZLOTY system introduced in 1526. Some credit for these monetary reforms belongs to Kopernicus, who was as much an Economist as he was an Astronomer.

Many low value coins were struck during the reign of Jan Kazimierz, especially copper Szelags. Silver coins were also produced that had a lower percentage of pure silver in them (debased). After the war with Sweden, low value zlotys were issued called chich that contained half of the silver in the regal coinage and were given an obligatory value over intrinsic one. There were 500 different coin variations struck under Zygmunt III Wasa from several different mints. This situation continued until the end of reign of Saxon elector kings in Poland in 1763. During the 7-year war (1756-1763), Prussia obtained the genuine dies and produced fakes of very low intrinsic value.

In 1766, a new coinage was introduced. The first "paper money" of Poland is considered to the Treasury Notes issued by Stanislaw August (1764-1795) during the Kosciuszko Uprising in 1794. They were only in circulation during the period of insurrection.

Coins during the period of the Russian Occupation, which started in 1815, are identifiable by the presence of a Russian 2-headed Eagle. After several uprisings against the Russians, these coins were discontinued. During the last partition of Poland, Russian rubles were put in circulation in 1842 in

Russia Poland and remained until the end of World War I. In the remaining part of Poland under Prussian or Austrian control, the coinage of the respective countries were used. All three countries introduced gold coin in the later half of the 19th Century.

The Germans issued paper money for use in occupied Poland during World War I and local use of these notes continued for a while after the war. In late 1918, Poland adopted the Polish mark in areas formerly occupied by Germany and Koruna in the areas formerly occupied by Austria. Due to the uncertainty of the monetary system, many cities also issued money. The Polish mark soon became the standard and hyperinflation was overcome with re-introduction of new zloty system in 1924. The Polish zloty had been stabilized before World War II, but the war ruined the system again.

Polish banknotes were issued in 1945 and coins in 1949 under the name of Republic of Poland (see example at right). The monetary system of socialistic Poland suffered from inflation and the government attempts to fight it on several occasions.

In 1976, Poland issued its latest coin -- the Zloty. (There should be a line through the **l** to make it sound like a **w**.) Zloty is the adjective form of the word “gold”. The symbol of the eagle is on all the coins. The last change was in 1995 when new banknotes and coins were put into circulation. The new reform brought coins back to life since they were non-existent in transactions due to their very small value.

Prior to 1990, internal monetary operations were conducted in inconvertible local currency while external operations were conducted either in foreign currency or, for the Soviet block, in special units of account such as convertible rubles. In 1990, as part of a government program to move the Polish economy toward a free market system, the exchange rate of the zloty, Poland's currency was set freely on the international currency markets.

Polish State Mint

The Convocational Diet of 1764 after electing Poland's last King, Stanislaw August Poniatowski, gave him with the responsibility of re-establishing the Warsaw mint because the local mints had been closed for 80 years and there was not any good local currency in the circulation. In 1766, the new Mint was organized and coined gold, silver and copper pieces. the mintmark was introduced in 1791 and became the trademark of the mint. Closed in 1796, after the 3rd partition of Poland, the Mint received the new statutes in 1810 and restarted its activity for a short period for the needs of the Grand Duchy of Warsaw.

In 1816, the Mint started coinage under the stamp and for the account of Congress of Poland (for territories annexed by the Russians). Since 1824 the Mint has also been sued for the production of state seals and stamps, it coined pieces with the national emblem during 1831 and for a short time became an arms factory. The Mint in Warsaw was closed down in 1868 and the mint machinery, archives and numismatic collections taken away to Petersburg. Authorities tore down the Mint's building in 1905.

After the revival of independent Poland, it was necessary to rebuild the Mint. The Mint of Warsaw reopened in 1924, production of state seals started in 1925 and the division of precious metals was organized in 1926. Even though the Mint's buildings were damaged in 1939 and occupied by the German authorities during World War II, the Mint continued to operate under the control of the German authorities throughout the war until it was blown up by retreating German troops in 1944.

Between 1944-1952, the Mint restarted without coin production but developed its activity in the field of precious metal processing and the production of badges and decorations. On the occasion of its 200th anniversary, the State Mint was decorated with the Class Order of the Banner of Labour in 1966. Lech Walesa, the contemporary President of the Republic of Poland, opened the new Mint's building in 1994. The State Mint was transformed into a public Company in 1994 and since 1998 is quoted on the stock market.

Today's Mint is a modern production plant engaged in:

- Minting production (coins, medals, seals, and decorations),
- Precious metal processing for the needs of optics,
- Production of gold and platinum paints for glass and porcelain decoration,
- Production of products for jeweler's trade and laboratory equipment, and
- Production of precious metals for electronic industry.

POLISH CENTRAL BANKING

In 1828, Tsar Nicholas I of Russia established the Bank of Poland by royal decree. The bank was given responsibility for the Mint and issued the first banknotes in 1830. In 1870, the **Bank of Poland** was deprived of rights of issue and was transformed into an office of the Russian State Bank in 1885.

After World War I, the Kingdom of Poland was under German and Austrian occupation. In 1916, the German governor created the **Polish National Credit Bank** and the currency it issued was the Polish mark, which became bona fide legal tender. The currencies of the partitioning powers were exchanged for marks.

In 1924, parliament enacted a bill entitled "The renewal of the Treasury and reform of the currency". It made provision for the institution of a new monetary system based on gold standard and the creation of the **Bank of Poland SA** by special charter as a joint-stock bank with central government equity involvement. The bank's management was evacuated to Romania in 1939 and eventually London. Exile in London lasted until 1946 when the Bank's management together with its assets returned to Poland.

During World War II, the German and Soviet occupying forces introduced their own currencies in annexed Polish territories. In German-occupied Poland, a **Bank of Issue in Poland** began operations in 1940 bringing into circulation what was known as the "Krakow zloty" which was intended to replace Bank of Poland notes. In addition to issuing currency, this bank also conducted normal banking business.

The Polish Provisional Government, based in Lublin, issued a decree in 1945 which established the **National Bank of Poland** (NBP) as a state bank vested with monopoly rights to issue new currency, the zloty. The NBP played a major part in economic reconstruction and reintegration of the western regions of Poland, regained from Germany after several centuries. The Bank's initial objective was to regulate the issue of currency and provide a supply of credit for economic reconstruction. In 1946, the Bank began direct lending to industry in accordance with state economic and financial plans being adopted. The change in the economic system in 1948 caused the Bank's role to change into a bank providing financial services to a centrally planned economy. It continued in this function for almost 40 years.

In 1989, Poland began to lay the foundations for the process of economic transition to a market economy. The role of money and the banking system in an economy of this kind is radically different from that under a centrally planned economy. A two-tier banking system was developed in Poland – a system comprised of the central bank on one hand and commercial banks on the other.

Functions of the Central Bank:

The central bank plays a crucial role in a modern market economy. Its functions are macroeconomic and systemic in nature and are:

1. Bank to the government. The NBP provides banking services to central government and operates bank accounts for the Government and other agencies.
2. Bank of issue. The Bank has the exclusive right to issue notes and coin that is legal tender in Poland. It also determines the volume of issue and controls the liquidity of the money supply.
3. Bankers' bank. The NBP organizes the settlement system, conducts daily inter-bank settlements and is actively involved on the inter-bank money market. It supervises the operations of the commercial banks and monitors their compliance with the provisions of the

Banking Act. The Bank is responsible for the safety and soundness of the entire banking system.

Most banks in Poland operate as multipurpose institutions and offer a wide range of commercial and personal banking services. By the end of 2001, the Polish banking system was comprised of the National Bank of Poland, 69 commercial banks, and 642 co-operative banks. Since the establishment of Bankowy Fundusz Gwarancyjny (The Bank Guarantee Fund) in 1994, depositors at banks established and operating pursuant to Polish law are protected by a deposit insurance fund.

During these 13 years, Polish banks have had to invest heavily in their network as well as in automation and information technology to meet the challenges of competition. The modernization of banks has progressed rapidly but the huge investments incurred to do so has increased the costs of their operation. These investments include introduction of cash dispensers and electronic sales outlets for credit card payments. The bankcard market is one of the fastest growing segments of new services in Poland.

WARSAW STOCK EXCHANGE

The first stock exchange opened in Warsaw in 1817. In the 19th Century mostly bonds and other debt instruments were traded; equities trading developed in the second half of the 20th Century. Before World War II, seven stock exchanges operated in Poland. There were 130 securities traded on the Warsaw Exchange in 1938: municipal, corporate and government bonds as well as shares. Capital markets could not be recreated after World War II because of the change of political and economic systems.

In 1989, the new government began creating a capital market structure. Both the structure and the legal regulations of the Polish capital market were designed after the most modern and efficient systems used in the world that were applicable to Poland's situation. The Act on Public Trading in Securities and Trust Fund was adopted in 1991 and the State Treasury established the Warsaw Stock Exchange. At the same time, the Polish Securities Commission was created. The Warsaw Stock Exchange, the only securities exchange in Poland, is a self-regulatory organization.

The future privatization of the largest Polish companies will result in an increase of exchange capitalization. Future developments on the Exchange include:

- The National Investment Funds Program is an important element in the future development of the Polish capital market.
- In 1998, the new Securities Act further facilitates the development of the Polish capital markets. Among the changes are: further reconciliation of the Act with regulations of OECD and European Union, definition of rules of underwriting and introduction of securities lending and borrowing mechanisms.
- The Act of Investment Funds adopted in 1998 makes the creation of new investment vehicles possible. The

pension reform will result in establishment of pension funds.

Polish banks are facing a squeeze in their core corporate business where profits have been hit by a combination of falling interest rates, rising costs, slowing economic growth and the Russian crisis. On the other hand, a vast new market is opening in retail financial services (ATMs and credit/charge cards) which require rapid development of new skills and heavy capital investment. At the same time, continuing privatization is creating new threats and opportunities.

Bankers say the pressures will accelerate mergers and takeovers. In addition, the banks claim that their competitive position is particularly difficult because Polish regulatory requirements are stricter than those in Western Europe are, primarily for the compulsory reserves they must deposit at the central bank.

AGRICULTURE - A Difficult Transition

An agrarian state prior to World War II, the agricultural sector of Poland remains handicapped by structural problems, surplus labor, inefficient small farms and lack of investment. It provides less than 10% of the GDP, utilizes 26% of the labor force and does not adequately meet domestic requirements. Polish agriculture was unique in the Soviet bloc in that private farms accounted for the greater part of total output. Most of those private farms continue to be small than 5 hectares (12 acres).

The only noticeable change to affect the Polish countryside as a result of the economic transformations of the last decade has been the liquidation of state-owned farms. Meanwhile, lower production, higher costs and lower food prices have contributed to deterioration in the financial situation of farms. The lack of change in the Polish countryside is also a result of the weakness of the agricultural lobby in parliament.

Polish agriculture is very fragmented and many farms produce only enough to meet their own needs with nothing for sale. With the rise of fuel prices, along with prices for farm machines and equipment, mineral fertilizers and services, farmers had to sell far more produce than in preceding years to buy the means of production. It is also backward compared to other countries and 90% of Poland's farms are unable to carry out any adaptation processes, such as land concentration, specialization, or modernization and only 6% are able to accumulate capital. Many farmers don't think about what will happen after the country joins the EU because they don't make long-range plans. An unstable agricultural policy, fluctuating economic conditions and prices favor this outlook. Nevertheless, Poland remains one of the world's leading producers of rye and potatoes.

The fears of the Polish farmers about the purchase of Polish land by foreigners are groundless. According to experts, the mass purchase of land by foreigners is out of the question since nobody will buy land if they are not sure that production will be profitable.

Agricultural reform is one of the most divisive issues to separate Poland and its future EU partners. Agriculture has remained inefficient and resistant to structural change. The government has been very cautious in implementation of any decisive reforms in this sector due to the social and political importance of the rural community. Doubts have been expressed about whether full direct payments for the Polish farmers are the most appropriate instrument in a period of rapid structural change. Consolidation of many tiny farms, followed by specialization and modernization will be necessary to compete in the EU structural reform of agriculture.

Poland stated that it would introduce EU agricultural law to the Polish legal code and implement it by the end of 2002. At the same time, Poland is demanding equal treatment for its agricultural sector under the EU's Common Agriculture Policy (CAP). Two of the most contentious issues between Poland and the EU are:

(1) Pre-accession aid for Polish farmers.
(2) Liberalization of agricultural trade.

In addition, the EU will probably insist on the need for full implementation by Poland from the day of accession of EU quality standards for products such as fruit, vegetables, the buttermilk content of milk and registration of slaughter animals.

POLAND's INDUSTRIAL DIVERSITY

The following pages will provide a brief look at the current industries in Poland as well as some of the larger Polish companies. The diversity is surprising.

Agricultural Machines

Fryderyk Kuring founded Kuznia Jawor SA founded in 1890 for the production of axles, bolts and nuts, with production items covered by his patent. After 1918, the plant was converted into a company dealing with production of agricultural machines for the cultivation of plants (weeding and plowing) and machines for farming (breakers, agitators). The machines are available in various sizes and can be matched with farms of any size.

Kuznia is a leading producer of forgings, which are used throughout all branches of the machine building industry and pipe flanges for pressure pipe connections, which are sold throughout Poland as well as Europe.

Aluminum

Listed on the Warsaw Stock Exchange since 1996, Zaklady Metali Lekkich Kety is the only company in Poland to have its casting alloys brands listed on the London Metals Exchange. The company enjoys a home market share of about 50% in frames, bars, and aluminum tubing, nearly 25% share in flexible packaging and 45% share in casting alloys.

Apparel Industry

The total number of companies in the Polish apparel industry is estimated to be 44,000. The main reason for the existence of such great numbers of apparel enterprises is the low outlays to start the production. The most dynamic growth was recorded in the production of sports and tourist outfits. Jeans are produced by nearly 30 firms in Poland and sales of jeans have grown by several percent annually.

The main problem of the apparel industry in Poland is the high costs of developing distribution networks and promotional costs. The industry is highly fragmented and most companies find it difficult to cover such costs. The good condition of the Polish clothing industry is determined by exports which represent a high share of production and is dominated by apparels produced for foreign firms located both in Poland and abroad.

The men's apparel market in Poland is increasingly influenced by international fashion trends. New fashion trends do not take Poland by storm, as the average Polish man generally prefers traditional or classic styles. Men in the growing Polish middle class, the largest group that regularly wears suits, seek Polish brand names that keep pace with international fashion trends. Manufacturers serving this market dress bankers, politicians, businessmen, officials and traditionalists.

Garment companies were among the first Polish enterprises to take advantage of the country's political changes in the early 1990's. Their EU partners provided patterns, materials and new machines and tools vital for the survival, profitability and expansion of many companies. The production processes used, an accessible location and established trade with Western and Eastern markets, all make Poland Europe's second largest textile and garment center after Italy.

Auto Industry

In 1918, soon after World War I, Poland attempted to produce a "native" automobile. The following cars were made in Poland prior to World War II:

- SKAF – The first documented initiative to a Polish car was the robust SKAF minicar for 2 people in 1921. The vehicle was manufactured by Fabryka Malych Samochodow SKAF in Warsaw but didn't attract public attention and only 3 prototypes were made.
- POLONIA – In 1924, Mikolaj Karpowski presented

a prototype of a relatively big open car named the Polonia. His approach was focused on simplifying the repair and service activities, which is why his automobile incorporated some interesting, unparalleled features. Unfortunately, he was unable to attract sponsors to support mass production of the Polonia.

- RALF-STETYSZ – Count Stefan Tyszkiewicz constructed a chassis of a passenger car with relatively high ground clearance, especially designed for use on the bad roads common in Poland in 1924. The off-road driving capabilities of the car, named Ralf-Stetysz, were extended by the switchable differential gear. In 1928 the factory burnt down with all its equipment and a number of ready-made cars.
- AS – Towarzystwo Budowy Samochodow AS began manufacturing the AS cars in 1927. These vehicles were purely utilitarian and most of them were bodied as taxicabs and delivery vans. Taxis of this brand were seen in Warsaw until World War II.
- CWS – In 1927, the dream of making Polish automobiles became a reality when Centralne Warsztaty Samochodowe (CWS) produced a small number of Model T1s. Full-scale production began in 1928. The T1s were very well made, solid and reliable vehicles with better than average off-road capabilities. But by 1931 CWS was no longer making T1s, the original Polish automobiles.

The high cost of CWS cars, lack of mass-production capabilities and expense of changing production methods caused the parent company to abandon production in favor of producing cheaper ones under license of foreign automakers. This practice continues today.

In 1996, parts producers were doing better than car manufacturers. If international automakers have their way, Poland will become one of Europe's largest producers of automobile spare parts. The future of Polish car parts will be determined by how well Polish companies improve product quality. The companies will have to change its entire production scope, including introduction of new technology as well as changing production and supply organization.

Krotoszyn, one of the top companies in this sector, exports half of its products with 90% of the exports going to EU countries. Magneti Marelli Poland in Sosnowiec makes dashboards, heaters, headlights, plastic components and meter sets. Recent investments in its plant include installing 50 new injection molding machines, automated headlight and car meter spooling lines. Gestind Poland makes steering wheels, headrests, hubcaps and gear shifts. Roltra Morse Poland produces door locks, window rolling mechanisms, wrapping connectors and body parts for Fiats and Daewoos. More Polish parts are used in delivery truck and bus assembly. Apart from frames and stainless steel sheets, all parts for Scania buses are made in Poland.

Aviation Industry

Founded in 1928, PZL-Warsazawa-Okecie SA is the oldest Polish aircraft manufacturer. The company has manufactured over 3000 airplanes of different types so far which were sold to more than 30 countries. In 1995, the company was transformed into a stock company owned by the Ministry of Industry and Trade. Their products include:

- PZL-104 "Wilga" - a highly successful 4-seat, all metal monoplane that is excellent for "bush" flying, glider towing, parachuting, and traffic control.
- PZL-110 "Koliber" - light 4-seat multipurpose all metal

monoplane of STOL class that is a remarkable aircraft for training, cross-country pleasure and business flights.

- PZL-106 "Kruk" - a reliable, very safe, robust agricultural aircraft and competitive fire fighter with instant bomb disposal.
- PZL-130 "Orlik" - a 2-seat turboprop, fully acrobatic trainer combing jet like handing with turboprop efficiency. This aircraft was delivered to the Polish Air Force Academy in Debin.

In 1955, the company started production of the FIS speedway motorcycle. That very successful motorcycle, designed in the company, was very popular throughout Europe.

PZL-Swidnik S. A., established in 1951, manufactured control surfaces and wings for jet fighters and continued the aviation tradition of the Lublin region. In 1954 the company began manufacturing helicopters. The latest helicopter manufactured, PZL-Sokol, was granted certificates issued by the Polish, Russian, American and German Aviation Authorities. Development of production and technologies allowed the company to enter into cooperation with the world-biggest companies. PZL-Swidnik S.A. also manufactures the PW-5 Smyk, a world class glider made entirely of composites. The company developed a new single-engine helicopter designed to transport 4-5 people for which production began in 1999.

Polish aircraft are relatively well known on the Turkish market especially the An-2 model and the popular M-18 Dromader crop-dusting and fire-fighting planes manufactured by Polskie Zaklady Lotnicze Mielec. Prior to World War II, the Turkish air force purchased Polish-made P-24 fighter planes that had excellent ratings for their modern design at the time. The company wants to actively promote the flagship product -- the passenger-cargo M-28 Skytruck plane, which requires short runway space for takeoff and landing. PZL Mielec continues to work with Boeing in the production of plane doors and has also been cooperating with BAE Systems for which it makes airframe components for the Hawk jet trainer.

ETC-PZL Aerospace Industries Sp. is the only producer of simulators and advanced training devices including systems for pilots, locomotive-drivers, armored vehicles and weapon system operators in Poland. Such devices are currently an irreplaceable element in the process of training worldwide. Another product is a research simulator, the only such device in Poland, which is equipped with specialized medical equipment and is used by the Warsaw Military Institute of Aviation Medicine to perform specialist research programs.

Bar-Code Scanners

Systemy Kodow Kreskowych, a Krakow-based company, was created to distribute bar code solutions in 1992. By 1993, scanners were sold to electricity companies throughout the country and counter scanners were installed in the Polish supermarket chain, Wavel Markets. Since then, the company has been pursuing its development plan, broadening the product mix and improving the quality of its customer service. The company has won the "Solidny Partner 97" for integrity, honesty and punctuality in business and the gold medal at the "Tarpak 2000" trade fair.

Book Publishing

The Polish book market is developing fast. There are some 8,400 publishers registered in Poland but over 80% of the book trade are accounted for by about 30 publishing houses. The top publishers include:

- *WydawnictwaSzkolneIPedogogiczne* and *Wydawnictwo Naukowe* are Poland's leading publishers. The two publishers virtually monopolize the market for school and academic textbooks, encyclopedia and scientific literature.
- The publishing house of *Swiat Ksiazki* is a mail order specialist. It is estimated that every 4th parcel currently

mailed in Poland comes from Swiat Ksiazki.

- The situation of *Polskie Przedsiebiorstwo Wydawnictw Kartograficznych* is determined by development of tourism in Poland to bring higher demand for all kinds of maps, guidebooks, etc. The company's growth will be slow unless it allocates part of its resources to publications beyond its specialization.
- *Egmont* is a clear leader among publishers specializing in books for children.

Carpet Industry

Carpets are manufactured in Poland by more than 100 entities. The industry is highly concentrated and is dominated by three companies which share 75% of the local carpet production. Due to investment of leading manufacturers and increased production capacity, the production of carpets is estimated to grow. In 1997, Polish firms exported 2,036 tons of carpets to Great Britain and other countries.

Chemical Industry

The Alwernia SA Chemical Company was established in 1923 to create foundations for the Polish chemical industry. Products made are used in washing powder production, pharmaceutical and food industry, tannery, galvanizing industry, paint and enamel coating production. At present, the company specializes in three production profiles: chromium compounds, phosphorous compounds and sodium and magnesium sulfate. The most important implemented objectives include:

- To eliminate side effects of the company's environmental impact by technological process improvement, application of waste-free technologies and material recovery.
- To ensure high quality products, adjustment of product quality to clients' requirements and improve production effectiveness.
- To implement new lines for the production of anhydrous sodium sulfate designed for detergent production,

magnesium sulfate heptahydrous fertilizer and "Alboz" gypsum.

Computers (Hardware & Software)

Equipment made or assembled in Poland dominates the PC segment of the market. The main buyers of computer equipment are financial, transportation, telecommunications, manufacturing, trade, administration, science and educational organizations. Individual users, small and medium-sized companies and the education sector significantly increased purchases of computer equipment in 1999.

The financial and industrial segments of the economy remain the main purchasers of software although small and medium-sized companies are substantially increasing information technology investments. The impressive growth in computer software sales is due in part to the growth of computer networking in many organizations and the upgrading of database management systems as a result of the ongoing privatization process that has improved the competitiveness of Polish companies.

Cosmetics

Although foreign cosmetic companies are strong in the fragrance, make-up, nail and hair care segments of the cosmetic industry, Poland manufacturers continue to dominate the skin care cosmetic market. Domestic manufacturers have invested and modernized their facilities by developing modern laboratories and technologies for the past ten years with positive results. The Polish cosmetics market is considered the largest in Central and Eastern Europe with excellent prospects for further developments.

Dairy Industry

The dairy industry has been steadily growing since 1989 and is considered one of the most promising in Poland. The production of dairy-based beverages and deserts, ice cream in particular, has grown five-fold during the last 10 years. There continues to be growing demand for cheese, ice cream, milk drinks and butter. Quality and sanitary issues are at the forefront of Poland's negotiation with the European Union and its efforts to increase exports of dairy products.

E-Commerce in Poland

E-commerce in Poland is still in a preliminary stage of development. By number of computers, Poland is in 14th place in Europe. A recent poll conducted by Polish World shows that 52% of Internet users are interested in shopping through the Internet. The consumer market is limited by a number of key factors such as low percentage of households with Internet access, lack of a key-certification authority or fear about safety of payments with credit cards. Recognizing the importance of e-commerce, the Polish government created in 1999 a committee of experts to prepare legal regulations for e-commerce including the issue of electronic signature.

Electrical Industry

The production of electrical equipment in Poland is done by 1700 companies and includes cables and wires, high/low voltage switchgear, electric machines and transformers and fixtures. Poland is the 9th largest copper producer and an important producer of zinc, lead, silver, steel and aluminum. The electric machine manufacturers produce an entire range of products including asynchronous motors and small motors for household appliances. Poland is the 10th largest manufacturer of electric machines and the largest in Eastern Europe. Products are manufactured using the newest technologies and meet the requirements of international standards.

Transformer manufacturers produce a full range of main transformers up to 400KV, distribution and power transformers, high voltage switching equipment and static converters. Products meet the requirements of international standards. Poland is the largest producer of transformers in Central

Europe and is far ahead of countries like Sweden, Spain and Holland. The EU countries are Poland's main trading partners in the electrical industry.

Fish Processing Industry

The market for fish products is becoming increasingly attractive. There are currently 400 fish processing companies in Poland. The production of canned fish is one of the fastest developing sectors and employment in this sector grew by 9.2% in 1997. Local fishing firms supply only 30% of the fish processed in Poland.

Furniture Industry

Zamojskie Fabryki Mebli SA has been a rich furniture making tradition of the Zamojszczyzna region since it was established in 1910. The following generations of furniture makers contributed to the art of furniture making the company well known both on the Polish and international market. More than half the furniture made is exported. Modern equipment, well-developed facilities and advanced technology permit the company to offer foiled furniture in several colors, furniture in natural veneer and upholstered furniture.

Ostroszowicka Fabryka Mebli, established in 1946, was a state owned factory. It produced kitchen furniture and was a pioneer in this field in Poland. In 1968, the factory lost its independence and was incorporated into Strzelin Furniture Factories. When the Strzelin Furniture Factories went bankrupt, efforts were made to independently privatize the Ostroszowice Furniture Factory which was accomplished in 1993. The entire capital of the company is Polish and is held in the hands of its employees. At this time, the company is one of the leading producers of kitchen and office equipment in Poland.

Glass Industry

Alija, established in 1981, is a dynamically expanding glass works specializing in colored, laminated, cased glass entirely hand crafted. At first it produced lead glass but for many years it has produced sodium-lime glass which is friendly to the environment. The company is well known and a recognized exporter of its products to Europe, America and Asia.

Zabkowice Glass Factory has a tradition of over 100-years in glass manufacturing and specializes in production of glass articles which are used in households, hotels, and as decorative objects in modern architecture. As a result of its extensive experience, the company was able to develop its own technology of processing glass pulp into perfect glassware that is elegant and attractive. Its glass is completely ecological, processed with natural resources and broken glass is recycled.

Heating Equipment Industry

During the past ten years, the heating equipment industry in Poland has gone through a few ups and downs. Imports of furnaces, heaters and boilers continue to grow and the number of Polish firms assembling this equipment is also growing. Since the low quality of Polish communist production has made Polish buyers distrustful towards domestically produced equipment, some Polish firms have switched to assembling and fixing imported equipment. Polish firms continue to concentrate their exports towards Western markets.

Herbs & Spices

Kamis-Przyprawy was started in 1991 producing 20 spices from imported raw materials. Seven years later, the company produced 141 types of seasoning including a seasoning mix for the most important Polish dish - Bigos (see receipe for this dish in Appendix A). The company imports raw materials and produces its seasonings at a factory near Warsaw. Expansion outside Poland is one goal of the company with sales of Polish-made seasonings in Belarus, Russia, Ukraine and the Baltic states and eventually in southern Europe.

Household Appliance Industry

The 1998 foreign trade deficit showed that domestic manufacturers did not meet consumer demand for advanced energy efficient refrigerators, freezers and washing machines that accounted for 70% of overall imports of household appliances to Poland. In 1996, microwave ovens were not produced in Poland. Since then, domestic manufacturers have begun to better respond to market demands for more sophisticated equipment. As a result, the mix of Polish equipment now being produced includes new product lines, modern designs and good after-sales service.

Polish exports of household appliances have recently increased as a result of Polish and foreign investments: Daewoo Electronics in Pruszkow (microwave ovens), Bosh Siemens Hausgerate in Lodz (washing machines) and Polar in Poznan (gas cooker and washing machines). The largest domestic manufacturers of household appliances are: Polar, Amica and Wrozamet. *Polar Wroclaw* is the largest Polish manufacturer of automatic washers, refrigerators and dishwashers.

Amica Wronki manufactures high quality household appliances, heating equipment, washing machines and dishwashers. The company has modern manufacturing facilities, good development strategy and is known on the Polish market for its quality, design and competitive pricing. It is the biggest Polish exporter of household equipment to Germany, France, Great Britain, Russia, Norway, Sweden and Austria.

Wrozamet S.A. is a leading Polish manufacturer of gas, electric, gas-electric cookers, hoods and interior heaters. Its products hold internationally recognized CE, VDE and DVGW certificates. The company has focused its investment on the modernization of production lines.

Housing Industry

Poland still has a housing shortage of more than 1.5 million units. Housing is sold to private individuals, housing cooperatives and states/cities. Units sold to states/cities are generally rented to low-income individuals who cannot afford to buy their own homes. After 20 years of decline, the number of newly completed homes increased for the first time in 1997. Also, the tendency to build larger and better-equipped homes has been maintained. The rise in housing completion and the structure of investors mean that the system of legal incentives created for the housing industry and housing management finally worked.

A promising niche market is emerging for the development of luxury gate communities in the suburban areas of Poland's large cities. The target buyers are more affluent and can usually afford to pay cash thus bypassing limited mortgage arrangements in the Polish market. Small firms constructing 20 or less homes annually dominate the single family housing market. Tenants complete more than half of the apartments in social housing. This lowers the cost of the apartment and allows tenants to spread the finishing cost in time. There is a significant market for energy retrofitting of existing concrete high rise buildings in Poland as Polish energy prices rise to world levels. Poland is one of Central Europe's most lucrative markets for manufactured housing. Single-family housing is financially attractive but remains limited by inadequate land supply and difficulties in obtaining financing.

Liquor

Duchess Lubomirski founded the Lancut Distillery in 1784 and produced regular, anise flavored and sweetened vodkas. The distillery began to produce premium vodkas, liqueurs, creams and ratafias in addition to regular and anise flavored vodkas in 1823. After some of the buildings and equipment were destroyed during the World War I, a stock company was created in 1917 to solve these difficulties. The whole inter-war period was a time of sharp competition but Lancut Distillery managed to hold its own among the best in the country.

The plant survived World War II largely intact and in 1951 a state enterprise called Lancut Spirits Industries was created. By 1968, the bottling lines had been expanded, modernized and incorporated into a production complex with distillation rectification and blending units and was able to produce 15 kinds of unflavored and flavored vodka a day. The distillery became an autonomous state enterprise in 1991 while maintaining the previous product line of about 60 brands. Relying on tradition, an innovative quality conscious staff, a company culture of hard work and efficient and flexible management, the Lancut Distillery has added more than a dozen of its own products to the brand assortment. In 1996, production lines were commissioned for new premium, luxury and bison grass vodkas and, today, Lancut Distillery is one of the leading Polish producers of alcoholic beverages.

Locomotive Industry

BUMAR-FABLOK SA was established in 1919 in Chrzanow and delivered the first steam locomotive to Polish State Railways in 1924. Within the pre-war period, the factory manufactured several types of steam locomotives and narrow-gauge steam locomotives for passenger, express and freight trains. The company also produced electrical and diesel mining locomotives and mining cars. Building machinery was added to the production range in the 70s. Since the 90s, the company has manufactured road mobile cranes, transportable cranes, roadside assistance equipment, fabrications for the railway industry, locomotive and car axles, gears and toothed wheels, welded construction and all types of forgings.

Meat Processing Industry

Manufacturers of meat products constitute the 4th largest manufacturing group in Poland behind only the automotive, steel and oil refining industries. The Polish meat processing industry is dominated by domestic capital and is highly diversified and fragmented. Meat processing plants will have to pay attention to integration with agriculture especially quality improvements in such areas as the fattening of pigs and the reduction in the cost of raising broiler chickens. Meat processing companies sell more than 90% of their products on the domestic market and 30% of an average Polish household's food expenditures is spent on meat products.

Medical Equipment

Zaklady Elektroniki Medyczznej ASPEL SC was established in 1986 and specializes in producing medical electronic equipment particularly for the cardiology field. Among the most important products offered are electrocardiographs, spirometry attachments and ECG units. As a result of the high quality of its products, they were chosen to equip Polish hospitals.

Mining Industry

Surmin-Kaolin SA was established in 1947 and until 1956 it sold the raw material it mined as a raw product. The company began enriched kaolin production in 1963 and continued the development of the kaolin production for the following industries: ceramic, paper, paint and varnish, rubber and glass fiber. After privatization of the company, which was completed in 1998, the company started the investment process to use the most modern technologies of enriching the kaolins, doubling production and automation of the production process.

Motorcycles

The first Polish-designed motorcycles were built in the late 1920s. The Sokol, manufactured by Panstwowe Zaklady Inzynierii in Warsaw, was the most famous and comparable in quality and price to bikes of their class produced in other European countries at the time. In the 1960s and 1970s, Poland made the largest number of motorcycles of any country in Europe but could not satisfy the huge domestic demand for motorcycles.

After years in the doldrums, the motorcycle market began to develop again due to increase interest and growth of motorcycle enthusiasts. Also, motorcycles are beginning to be appreciated as a comfortable and convenient means of transportation in large cities. In addition, a growing number of motorcycles have been bought by courier firms and security agencies.

Petroleum Industry

The petroleum industry in Poland faces major problems including lack of capital, obsolete technology, poor energy efficiency and excessive use of raw materials, low utilization of existing capacities and burdens on the environment.

The largest Polish refinery *Petrochemia Plock* has invested in the construction of a new hydrocracking installation, which will allow the refinery to increase production of refined oil, gasoline production and diesel fuel. Also, the refinery ceased production of leaded fuel in 1999. The second largest Polish refinery *Rafineria Gdansk* has also undergone a tremendous modernization program. The construction of a hydrocracking facility and installation of sulfur-extraction technology has been undertaken to enhance the product's quality and energy efficiency and to increase production.

Pharmaceutical Industry

POLPHARMA SA, the leading pharmaceutical company in Poland, was established in 1935. The company produces a wide range of ready drugs and is the biggest producers of pharmaceutical substances. POLPHARMA is also investing in the next stage of development -- a new production facility Dry Forms II which will contain technological equipment for the production of non-sterile solid forms like tablets, pills and capsules. Lastly, in an effort to preserve the environment, the company monitors air quality, operates a biological purification plant which complies with waste products regulations and limits gas emissions to the atmosphere by use of sealed technological processes and modernization of its technology.

Polfa Kutna SA produces drugs made exclusively for pharmacies, both prescription and over-the-counter. In 1999, the company introduced 14 new products including 4 new brand names. It produces 75 types of drugs including drugs for nervous system diseases, anti-inflammatory drugs, cardiac drugs, diabetes medications, anti-osteoporosis drugs, gastroenterologic drugs, and multivitamins. The company plans to continue modernization investments until 2002 to upgrade individual production plants to meet Good Manufacturing Practice standards.

Radio Industry

Zaklady Radiowe RADMOR SA was started in 1947. In the beginning VHF/FM radiotelephones were developed and produced. It was later decided to expand towards the design and production of professional land and mobile communication equipment. The principal business lines include:

- Service of marine electronic equipment such as marine receivers, echo sounders, etc.
- Development and manufacture of land mobile radio equipment and electronic equipment for sea and water use.

In 1994, the factory transformed into a joint-stock company wholly held by the State Treasury.

Shipbuilding Industry

H. Cegielski-Poznan SA is the biggest Polish manufacturer of machines and equipment for the shipbuilding industry in Poland. After purchasing a license for building engines from Danish company Burmeister & Wain in 1958 and a license for building marine engines from Swiss company Sulzer-Brothers Ltd in 1965, the company is currently the main supplier of these products to Polish shipyards. The company was established in 1846 and initially manufactured agricultural tools and machines as well as tools for the agricultural-food industry. When Poland became an independent state in the Interwar Period, the company began manufacturing freight cars, passenger cars, steam locomotives and electric locomotives. In the late 1930s, the company began manufacturing trams.

Mostostal Gdask SA began in 1945 and currently specializes in the construction and assembly of industrial structures in ports, shipyards, oil refineries, chemical, pulp and paper industry. Since 1990, the company has successful entered the marine (shipbuilding) and offshore construction sectors. They have supplied customers with large-size steel structure-like parts of ships, components of offshore drilling rigs and flue gas ducts which were assembled in Polish ports and transported by sea to the place of destination.

Damen Shipyards Gdynia SA was founded in 1991 as one of the first private shipyards in Poland. The company specializes in building vessels under 300 tons designed to the client's individual desires and requirements.

Steel Industry

The existence of metallurgic and mining industries in Poland date back to the 14th Century. In 1896, two steelworks were built – one in Czestowchow and one in Zawiercie. At the start of Poland's economic transition, all steel mills were in state hands and the steel industry experienced dormancy because of a drop in domestic demand and the collapse of the Soviet Union.

In the early 20th Century Czestowchowa Steelworks had 2 blast furnaces, 5 open-hearth furnaces, a heavy steel mill, a medium section mill, a jobbing mill and a shape mill. Furnaces and other facilities were partly modernized during the inter-war period. During German occupation, the steelworks was made part of an arms manufacturing corporation. After World War II, the steelworks was included in the Central Polish Metallurgy Reconstruction Development Plan and erected a new steelmaking shop, a pipe mill, 2 blast furnaces, a power plant, a steel constructions department and a mechanical working workshop.

Batorex Sp. z o.o. manufactures knives for cutting steel, wood, paper, rubber, leather and textiles, hot and cold cutting applications and special purpose blades to customers' specifications. Huta Katowice S.A. makes cast billets and blooms, railway and tram rails, many types of section beams, channels, angles and sheet piles as well as heavy steel and pig iron castings. It is the largest exporter in Poland with over 50% of sales being made abroad.

Tires

Two companies have dominated the Polish tire market: T C Debica (passenger car tires) and Stomil Olsztyn (truck, light truck, van and agricultural vehicle tires). The situation changed dramatically after Michelin of France and Goodyear of the United States acquired a majority of shares in these companies in 1995. Both Polish companies will emphasize on exports and the demand for truck and passenger car tires in this part of Europe (including Russia and other ex-Soviet countries) will reach 57 million (for trucks) and 42 million (for passenger cars).

Water Treatment

AQVA-SYSTEM, established in 1980, initially designed and manufactured water supply and sewage system installations and designed equipment for water treatment. The company also consults in the field of water treatment, designs and constructs water treatment plants, and does water examination. AQVA-SYSTEM was the first firm in Poland that designed a reliable and simple filter for houses and small farms, which was affordable. It started production of the GA filters, which remove iron and other impurities from Polish water in 1989.

Woodworking Machines, Equipment & Tools

The rapid development of timber-related industries seems to guarantee good prospects for Polish producers of woodworking machine tools, equipment and instruments. Some 50 firms in Poland manufacture woodworking machine tools and other equipment used by the timber industry and the scope of products offered is very wide owing to the rapid pace of the restructuring process in this industry. The export volume and its growth are proof of the good quality of Polish machine tools and the reliability of suppliers who are punctual, meet shipment deadlines, supply spare parts and provide post-sale service.

INVESTING in POLAND's FUTURE

In addition to providing a favorable environment for foreign investors, Poland has been identified as one of the stronger and more consistent economies in Europe and plays a stabilizing role in the region. Since its return to democracy in 1989, Poland has become a politically stable country with no serious domestic conflicts. The country's long tradition of both religious and ethnic tolerance is also a significant factor.

Several important reasons for foreign companies to invest in Poland are:

- Market size - In addition to being the largest economy in Central Europe, Poland also has one of the most impressive growth rates in the world. A large middle class has emerged with the disposable income to afford a wide range of consumer goods and services.
- Location - Poland's location in the heart of Europe assures easy access of goods manufactured in Poland both to the EU and the Eastern market.
- Economics - Including:
  - Specific investment incentives.
  - Support and positive appraisal from international institutions such as the International Monetary Fund and the World Bank.
  - Success of foreign companies that have already invested in Poland since the 1990s.
- Work force - Poland has the largest working population in Central Europe and, with 35% of Poles under 25 years of age, is also one of the youngest countries on the continent.
- Education - The level of education of the Polish workforce is considerably high in both skilled and unskilled sectors because Poles realize that thorough education and hard work are determining factors of professional success.
- Public Opinion - In 2001, a report of the Public Opinion Research Center on "Foreign Investment in Poland"

reported as follows:

- 63% of Poles accept the presence of foreign capital in Poland.
- 55% of Poles are convinced that without foreign capital Poland's economy would not have developed up to its current level.
- 51% of Poles believe that activities of companies with foreign capital are profitable for Poland.

Poland's incentive policy creates a business friendly legal environment for foreign investment. The legal framework for foreign investors in Poland is determined by the Commercial Code (Kodeks Handlowy) of 1934 and the Law on Companies with Foreign Participation (Ustawa o spolkach z udzia em zagranicznym) of 1991. The Act on Public Help, which became effective in 2001, is the fundamental act regulating investment activity in Poland. It controls conditions, procedures, the amount and form of aid granted to investors and also presents new opportunities for foreign investors by authorizing competitive advantage for a company within the field of its activity. A rule of equal treatment of all entitles is in force that generally allows companies with foreign shareholding to run their business on the same principle as Polish firms.

Foreign investors can set up either a limited liability company (Spolka z organiczona odpowiedzialnoscia [Sp. z o.o.] or a joint stock company (Spolka akejna [S.A.] in order to carry out business activities in Poland. There are no restrictions on the foreign share of equity in such companies. Other legal entities such as civil partnership, registered partnership or professional partnership do have additional requirements for foreign investors. The foreign investor may:

- Form his wholly-owned company or a joint venture company with Polish or foreign partners; or
- Participate in the privatization process by purchasing shares of privatized enterprises on the Warsaw Stock Exchange or through private offerings.

Polish Agency for Foreign Investment (PAIZ) is a joint-stock company founded in 1992 to promote and assist foreign investors establish successful businesses in Poland. The Polish Government finances it and its services are free of charge. PAIZ offers potential investors:

- Reliable and customized information concerning economic and legal environment in Poland.
- Assistance in identifying the best locations for your business activities as well as potential partners.
- Professional advice in the initial stages of the investment process.
- Expert guidance through all the formal procedures and facilitation contacts with central administration authorities.

Its publication "*The List of Major Foreign Investors in Poland*" provides in-depth analyses of specific sectors in Poland's economy and is a valuable source of information about investing in Poland.

PAIZ estimates that between 1989-2001 a total of $56.8 billion was invested in Poland by foreign investors which means that Poland has retained its leading position as a very attractive target country for foreign investors in Central and Eastern Europe. According to PAIZ foreign investors' from countries in the European Union invested 68% in Poland by the end of 2001 while North American investors' invested over 15%.

The Polish economy has a high capacity for the absorption of foreign capital. Manufacturing is the most popular sector for investment accounting for over 41% of foreign investment. The next most popular sectors are financial services, transport, storage and telecommunications. Considering the size of investments needed to upgrade infrastructure, there are many potential and still untapped opportunities for foreign capital involvement. Foreign companies are important in Poland because not only do they create jobs but, through introducing modern technologies and management techniques, they also achieve much higher operational efficiency as proven by their labor productivity. Another important purpose for foreign investment in Poland is that once companies are well established in Poland, they usually reinvest most of the profits generated in the country to support and develop local operations.

To accelerate economic growth and facilitate new investments in Poland, the Sejm passed a new Law on Financial Assistance for Investments in 2002. According to this law, financial assistance can be granted to businesses in the following cases:

- The value of new investments is at least EUR 10 million.
- The value of new investment is at least EUR 500 thousand, the investment is related to development or modernization of an existing company and will maintain at least 100 jobs for at least 5 years.
- The new investment creates at least 20 jobs for at least 5 years
- The new investment has a favorable environmental impact in Poland.

In addition to meeting at least one of the above criteria, financial assistance can be granted to a business if the investment meets at least two of the following requirements:

- Favorable impact on regional economic development.
- Located in an Special Economic Zone.
- Introduces technological innovations.
- Contributes to the development of cooperation with the domestic scientific and research resources.
- Favorable impact on local labor market.

In order to purchase property in Poland, a foreign investor must be licensed to do business in Poland (all companies registered in Poland meet this condition) and justify his actual need for the acquisition of the property. Also, permission must be obtained from the Ministry of Internal Affairs and Administration to purchase land in Poland for industrial, commercial or agricultural use.

The US Government has identified Poland as one of 10 countries selected to participate in the "Big Emerging Markets Program" run by the US Department of Commerce. This designation gives Poland high visibility and enhanced access to a variety of trade and investment promotion programs. In 1994 a bilateral investment treaty was ratified between Poland and the US. It provides the principles of the treatment of American investment in Poland and Polish investment in the United States, the conduct of trade between the two countries, protection of intellectual property, exchange of information and settlement of investment disputes. The Treaty constitutes the acknowledgement of efforts made in Poland to bring the laws affecting the rights of foreigners to international standards and adds an additional safeguard to the guarantees provided under the national laws of both countries.

Poland also has access to financing and guarantees from the Overseas Private Investment Corporation (OPIC) and Export-Import Bank of the United States (EximBank). OPIC is a self-sustaining US government agency that assists in financing investments through direct loans and/or loan guarantees and has established five equity funds operating in Poland. EximBank provides direct loans to Polish public or private sector buyers of US products as well as guarantees for lenders to Polish buyers. Coverage by its Exporters Insurance Division is generally limited to irrevocable letters of credit issued by or guaranteed by one of the 15 Polish banks approved by EximBank. The function of the Polish-American Enterprise Fund, established by Congress in 1989, is to make possible loans, grants, feasibility studies, technical assistance, equity investments, insurance and guarantees to small and medium-sized Polish businesses and US-Polish joint ventures.

There are four Polish business and trade information centers located in New York, Chicago, Los Angeles and Washington, DC. Through these offices, information can be obtained on standards, tariffs, commercial laws and regulations in Poland, business exhibitions, marketing, banking, shipping, as well as Polish firms looking for trade cooperation and joint ventures and Poland's regional characteristics.

The US Department of Commerce maintains a Central and Eastern Europe Business Information Center (CEEBIC) and a US Foreign Commercial Center in Warsaw where information on potential Polish partners, distributors or clients can be obtained. The primary objective of the Polish-US Economic Council and the American Chamber of Commerce in Poland is the enhancement of mutual trade and investment between Poland and the United States while the Center for International Private Enterprise promotes the development of the private sector in Poland.

ACHIEVING EUROPEAN UNION MEMBERSHIP

The integration of Europe was proposed as early as the 14th Century but these ideas were not implemented until the period of economic, political and military reconstruction following World War II. Several treaties were entered into after the end of the war that merged in 1967 to become the European Community (EC). A summit meeting of the member countries in 1969 paved the way for the creation of a permanent financing arrangement for the EC, the development of a framework for foreign policy cooperation among member nations and the opening of membership negotiations with other countries.

The European Union (EU) was created in 1993 with the treaty on European Union ratified at Maastricht in the Netherlands by the heads of government of the 12 countries that formed the European Community. At present, the EU consists of 15 members but many other countries have applied for membership.

All member countries run the EU with each country taking turns every six months to hold the EU Chairmanship. Summit meetings and meetings of heads of state and of government are called the European Council. The citizens of the member countries directly elect members of the European Parliament. The Court of Justice is the final arbiter in all matters of EU law and is composed of 15 judges and 9 advocates who are appointed to 6-year terms with at least one from each country. The court deals with disputes between member governments and EU institutions.

Poland signed customs agreements with the European Union (EU) and Central European Free Trade Agreement (CEFTA) in 1996. As a result, products imported from the EU and CEFTA countries are not subject to customs duties. Poland submitted its application for acceptance into the European

Union to the European Commission in 1994. Poland joined NATO in 1999 and began negotiating its full membership in the European Union.

European citizenship was granted to citizens of each member country in the EU, therefore, citizens do not need to carry passports while visiting other member countries. People living in these 15 countries have freedom to live, work or study in any of the member countries. A goal of establishing a common European currency was set and in 2001 the Euro was introduced.

Criteria for membership of the EU includes:

- **Political**:
  1. Democracy and rule of law - Parliament and legislative powers, the Executive structure and the Judiciary structure.
  2. Human rights and the protection of minorities - Civil and political rights; economic, social and cultural rights and minority rights and the protection of minorities.

- **Economic**:
  1. Economic situation - Liberalization; stabilization of the economy; structural change; financial sector and economic and social development.
  2. Economy in the perspective of membership - The existence of a functioning market economy; the capacity to cope with competitive pressures and market forces and prospects and priorities.

- **Ability to assume the obligations of membership**:
  1. Internal market without frontiers - Free movement of goods; free movement of capital; free movement of services; free movement of persons and competition.
  2. Innovation - Information society; education, training

and youth; research and technological development; telecommunications and audio-visual.

3. Economic and fiscal affairs - EMU; taxation; direct taxation; indirect taxation; value added tax; excise; mutual assistance and statistics.
4. Sectoral policies - Industry; agriculture; fisheries; energy; transport; small and medium enterprises.
5. Economic and social cohesion - Employment and social affairs and regional policy and cohesion.
6. Quality of life and environment - Environment and consumer protection.
7. Justice and home affairs - General preconditions for JHA cooperation; asylum; immigration/border control; police cooperation, police, drugs and judicial cooperation.
8. External policies - Trade and international economic relations; development; customs; common foreign and security policy.
9. Financial questions - Financial control and budgetary implications.
10. Administration capacity to apply the acquis.

Agriculture

Contrary to most soviet bloc countries, 70% of all farmland in communist Poland remained in private hands. For older farmers it is very important that this land remain in Polish lands. The farmers fear Germans returning to their former property and buying up their family possessions leaving Poles with inadequate title to territories gained as a result of post-war settlements. With the average farm size in Poland far smaller than those in the EU (56% of all Polish farms are less than 5 hectares), the structure of farming in Poland is not up to western standards.

As a result, the right of non-Poles to buy agricultural real estate emerged as a potentially explosive issue in EU talks. There is a very large gap between the price of land in Western

Europe and Poland. Unfortunately, purchasing power among farmers is very low and if they have to compete, Polish farmers won't have a chance to buy better pieces of land. Poland has pushed for an 18-year interval before it will have to lift any barriers to farmland purchases presently in place. Hopefully, this transition period will give farmers an opportunity to gather funds to make their own land purchases and thereby enlarge their farms.

Progress Reports:

The 1999 EU Progress Report provided the following data regarding Poland's admission for membership:

- Once the health, education and social security system reforms are fully implemented they should facilitate Poland's integration into the European Union.
- While Poland fulfils the EU's political criteria, it is also noted that corruption continues to be an issue as does increasing the efficiency of the judiciary.
- Poland has not progressed sufficiently in the area of economic reform to ensure a smooth integration into EU structures. The greatest reservations are regarding industrial and agricultural policy and lack of environmental strategy. Economic reforms must continue and the process of privatization and restructuring must be accelerated.

The report concludes that Poland has made a "notable lack of progress regarding some long-standing issues."

In 2000, the European Commission report confirmed Poland's favorable status among candidates for membership in the European Union. Poland, Estonia and Hungary are in the second group of candidate states, which during the last 12 months have progressed the most in adjusting their national economies and law to European standards. The European Commission is:

- Pleased with Polish economic growth associated with restructuring and privatizing the most important sectors of the national economy such as armament and coal mining industries.

- Praising the progress made in telecommunications and information systems.
- Recognizing the progress of adjustment in areas of standardization especially the creation of the Committee of European Law in the Polish Sejm.
- Fearful of a too-high inflation index and growing unemployment.
- Concerned about a lasting paralysis of Polish courts, prison and customs services, brutality of the police and insufficient action against organized crime and corruption.

The report supports the theory that agriculture today is still the primary problem in Poland's integration with the EU. The objections concern the lack of structural changes, including delays in privatization and insufficient progress in legislative matters.

Poland was invited to join the EU after negotiations were concluded at the end of 2002. After approval by the European Parliament, the enlargement treaty was signed in April 2003. Experts estimate that the legislative process of ratifying enlargement treaties in all EU member states will last at least a year. As a result, Poland formally became a membership of the EU in May 2004 and participated in the election of the European Parliament in June 2004.

CULTURE

ANCIENT POLISH GODS & GODDESSES

The following is a partial list of ancient Polish Gods and Goddesses:

- **Bear** – Bears symbolize the Goddess in her aspect as Mother and Nurturer. They are the protectors of the weak and of the divine child.
- **Bee** - The Goddess of Regeneration, the Bee Goddess is the Mistress of Animals and the Lady of Wild Things. Honey produced by bees is sacred and is believed to ensure a long and healthy life and is a healing substance. The linden tree, which is the prime attractor of bees in Poland, is also sacred.
- **Boginki** – These "bank spirits" are snatchers of newborn babies, who leave behind their own offspring. These babies are called *Odmience*, changed ones.
- **Birds** – Birds are the sacred symbol of community – of tioka. It is the return each spring of the bocian that signals rebirth. Each type of bird has its own symbolism:
    - Sparrows – symbol of soul of man and community life.
    - Larks – protect fields
    - Nightingales – protect orchards
    - Ducks/Geese – protect lakes and rivers
    - Storks – protect villages
- **Bison** – The bison and its horns are symbols of the Year God in his mature and "feisty" aspect.
- **Butterfly** – Neolithic symbol of the Great Goddess in her guise, as Mother of Magic, the butterfly is the symbol of divine ambivalent transformation. She is a musician, possesses the secret of life and is the patroness of reincarnation.
- **Djabetek** – The djabetek is an imp – the player of practical jokes. Their families call little ones with too much energy who get into mischief djabetek.
- **Domowije** – The "Grandfather" or house spirit. He

is responsible for maintaining peace and order in the household and forewarns of threats and troubles. Before the death of family member, the *domowije* weeps.

- **Fish** – Ryba, the fish, is a sacred animal to the Poles, signifying regeneration.
- **Leszi** – Male woodland elves who protect wild animals and have a close relationship with the wolf.
- **Linden** – The linden, or lime blossom, is sacred to Poles. It protected against lightning and evil spirits and was a place to leave offerings and hold rituals.
- **Marzanna** – Death personified, the Marzanna appeared dressed in white, the traditional color of the Otherworld in Polish traditions.
- **Matka Ziemia** – She is the Mother of Plants and is honored at seedtime and at harvest.
- **Polewiki** – The spirits of the fields. In Polish, pole means fields and it was for that Poland was named.
- **Polundnica** – "Lady Midday" is the whirlwind. The *Polundnica* were most often seen in the middle of hot summer days as whirling dust clouds. In Polish tales, she appears when the day is the hottest and drives people out of their heads, weakens them or cuts off their heads with a sickle.
- **Rod/Rozanica** – These spirits stood for ancestors. *Rozanica* were female and stood for the stars and were spirits of birth and fate; *Rod* were male and represented the ancestors.
- **Snakes** – Waz, the snake, was a sacred animal to the Poles as the spirit of the hearth. They were connected not only to fire but also with birth and the bathhouse.
- **Sad** – Sad were spirits of judgment who also meted out fortune and destiny.
- **Triglav** – Triglav was a three-faced deity symbolizing dominion over the three realms – sky, earth, and places underground. He was shown blindfolded. Boleslaw Chroby, King of Poland during the Piast dynasty, commanded that a temple sacred to Triglav be built in Szezecin.

- **Weles** – Weles were the guardian spirit of domestic animals.
- **Wila** – The Wila were female spirits that lived in the woods, mountains and clouds and could shape-shift into swans, horses, falcons, or wolves. The are the incarnation of beauty and power, the benevolent friends of sufferers and geniuses of heroes. But they are implacable in their wrath to all who deceive them or who break a promise.
- **Wolf** – The wolf in Polish myths is not the feared hunter of humans that he is in many cultures. He is a double for the Lunar Goddess and symbolizes loyalty, family and wisdom. Wolves' teeth are used in pisanki designs.
- **Zadruga** – In the times of clans and tribes in Poland, Zadruga was the community, the clan, and the tribe.
- **Zwezda Dnieca** – Spirit of the Morning Star, she is patroness of horses, protection, exorcism and is associated with planet Venus. She was invoked to protect against death in battle.
- **Zwezda Wieczorniaia** – Spirit of the Evening Star, she is the mother and patroness of exorcism and protection.
- **Zwezda Poinoca** – The Night Star, she is patroness of death, rebirth and magic.

FOLKLORE & LEGENDS

Over the centuries, political boundaries changed, and with them the language and culture of the administrators. As a result, Poland evolved its own distinct folklore while absorbing the influences from neighboring areas leaving Poland with a rich and diverse folklore.

Box-Making

Box-making traditions arose in the Tatra Mountains located in southern Poland. During the long winters, farmers worked the wood and the whole family participated in the decoration. The oldest tradition preserved the white color of wood, ornamented with small-carved triangles, circles, lines, mountain flowers and rosettes. Surface preservation techniques such as waxing and oiling were developed. Wooden objects were traded between local families and carved wooden religious figures were used widely to protect fields, roads and houses.

Another popular product of this tradition was an ornamented dowry chest, which was decorated with the traditional symbols of love and prosperity. After marriage, a metal lock or secret opening mechanism was added and these chests were used to hold the families' most precious belongings.

During the late 19th Century, woodworking caught the attention of city dwellers that were disillusioned with the bleak life of early industrial cities. They not only studied folk culture of the countryside but also collected folk art and placed it in urban museums, which resulted in its detailed study and the documentation of folk art styles and techniques.

After World War II, the Polish communist government encouraged the box-making tradition as part of its program for the development of artistic talents and traditions of the common people. The government established local art co-operatives that arranged the production and marketing of tradition crafts.

Decoration was done by individual craftspeople working at home. Wood burning and brass inlay were added as decoration techniques and modern varnishes were applied to protect all decorated surfaces.

In 1989, when economic "shock therapy" was applied, the arts cooperatives lost their government subsides, forcing reorganization of the box-making industry and threatening its survival. The goal of Enchanted World of Boxes, established in Boston in 1990, is to preserve the traditional Polish box-making industry and, at the same time, infuse it with new life by introducing contemporary and international designs. Every year, new designs and models are introduced and the company has begun importing unfinished boxes for the use of hobbyists.

Folk Costumes

Prior to 1900, most peasants wore folk costumes daily. Rougher clothing was worn to work while the more elaborate dress was reserved for special occasions like church, festivals and weddings. Most clothing was produced from linen, cotton, wool, felt, leather and fur - whatever was available in the community. Folk costumes developed as fashions changed, new materials became available and new traditions arose.

Present-day Poland has 60 folkloric regions and each region has their own distinctive costumes. In some areas, the tradition of folk costumes is still alive while in other regions, costumes are still made but mostly for dance groups or choirs. The Polish traditional costumes are very colorful and diverse with variations that contain information about the town of origin, person's marital status and wealth. The most famous costume is that of Krakow, which is why it is seen as a national costume.

The White Eagle:

According to legend, an ancient tribe led by three brothers wandered across Europe. One day they entered a land of unsurpassed beauty. One brother saw an eagle in its nest as a good omen and wanted to settle there. The other brothers disagreed and the tribe split into three groups, each led by a brother.

Czech took his tribe west and settled in what latter became Czechoslvakia. Rus went east and settled what is today Russia. Lech went straight ahead. One day, Lech saw an eagle as it flew over their heads and landed on its nest. As the eagle left the nest and took to the sky, a ray of sunshine fell on the eagle's wings so they appeared tipped with gold while the rest of the eagle was pure white. Lech founded a city on the spot where he saw the eagle and called it Gniezno, eagle's nest.

They called themselves Polonians, which means "People of the Field" and Gniezno became the first historical capital of Poland. The white eagle became the official emblem of Poland during the reigns of Kings Wladyslaw Lokietek and Kazimierz the Great. It was set on a red banner, the white eagle having gold claws, beak and a crown on its head. Polish coins minted during the reigns of Boleslaw Chroby and Wladyslaw II depict the oldest known images of the eagle.

In 1295 King Przemysi II of Poland adopted it as a symbol of union within the dynasties. The eagle is on the majestic seal of Kazimir the Great and 14th Century coins and seals show an eagle with a slender silhouette, raised beak and wide outspread wings. In the 19th Century, after the partitioning powers had abolished autonomous Polish institutions, the use of the symbolic eagle became traditional in daily life. It was found on medallions, pendants, bracelets, brooches, postage stamps and emblems. In 1945, the Polish Government removed the crown but the emblem still remains the symbol of Poland today.

The Legend of Scolnus, the Polish Sailor Knight

Jan Scolnus, a Pole of Kolno near Gdansk, was bound to the service of the Danish King Christian. He was an adventurous man who wanted to learn more about the sea and the lands beyond. One day he begged the King for permission to sail west and discover the lands of which others speak. The King granted permission for the journey.

After sailing for weeks in his ship, the Swan, a huge iceberg suddenly appeared. The crew panicked and Scolnus' enemies seized the opportunity and encouraged a mutiny. But others who were faithful to Scolnus persuaded the sailor to return to their oars. After three months of sailing over uncharted sea, land was sighted. They had reached the land now called Labrador. This is how a Pole in the 15th Century discovered the North American continent.

Eve of St. Andrew's Day:

On the Eve of St. Andrew's Day (Nov. 29th), fortunes were told for young Polish girls who wish to find a husband. The results were taken seriously. Fortunes were told several ways:

- A girl counts to the 14th post on a fence to see what her future husband would be like. If the post is strong and fresh, she can expect a lean, strong young man; if fat, her chances of gaining an older not as desirable husband could be in her future.
- Another game to predict marriage involves placing a ribbon, kerchief and a rosary under three separate plates. Blindfolded, a girl turns around three times while other girls rearrange the plates. If the kerchief is

drawn, it denotes marriage; if the ribbon is drawn, she will remain single for another year. But if she pick the rosary, her choices were not considered good and she would either spend the rest of her life as an unmarried woman or enter a convent and become a nun.

Wycinanki

Wycinanki is an art form that had its origins in China many centuries ago. During the 19th Century, developments in the dye industry resulted in brightly colored shiny paper becoming readily available. With a tradition of decorating their cottages with hand-painted or stenciled motifs, the Polish peasants began using this paper to create colorful cutouts or wycinanki that would be affixed to the exposed ceiling beams or placed on doors.

After World War II, wycinanki was revived as a folk-art and often used to decorate official buildings. Because of their artistic and decorative beauty, it became fashionable to frame the wycinanki and use them as interior decorations. When tourism increased and created a demand for folk art including wycinanki, they were sold to tourists to earn hard currency. Today, while appreciated for its historical value, it is of no major relevance to modern Poland.

POLISH - A Difficult Language

The official language of Poland is Polish which is spoken by 99% of the population. The Polish language, a branch of the Slav dialect, is of Indo-Iranian origin. The earliest surviving manuscripts containing Polish words are some 12th Century Latin texts containing Polish proper names; there are no extant Polish writings of substantial length from before the 14th Century. The oldest documents written in Polish survive from the 14th Century. *Bogurodzica*, an ancient chant written in the 13th Century, was one of the earliest written documents of the Polish language. In the 16th Century as printed materials became available, Polish was more widely used in written documents.

In the Middle Ages, the Latin alphabet was used to write Polish. In order to transcribe the complex sounds of the language a few groups of consonants and diacritics were added. The result is intimidating to the eye of a stranger to Slavic languages. Modern Polish came into use in the 16th Century, developing as the sophisticated and expressive language of a great literature.

The Polish language has 10 vowels and 35 consonants. Polish is a very hard language to learn because of its complicated grammar where word endings vary according to number and gender and these rules are full of exceptions. Unlike English, Polish is pronounced phonetically. It is necessary to understand where to break the word and know that the second-to-last syllable is **always** stressed. A distinctive feature is the preservation in spoken Polish of the nasal vowels, which are no longer found in the other modern Slavic tongues. The nouns, pronouns, and adjectives have seven cases (nominative, genitive, dative, accusative, vocative, instrumental, and locative). The verb is inflected to indicate gender as well as person and number, and can do so without the use of the personal pronoun. There are three genders (masculine, feminine, and neuter) and two numbers (singular and plural). A large number of diminutive and augmentative forms are also characteristic. Polish numbers are hard to master and the number 2 is undoubtedly the most complex since it has all 13 different forms.

The language also contains a number of dialects, some of which are intermediate between Polish and German or Ukrainian. In addition the vocabulary of Polish is basically Slavic, but it has been enriched by borrowings from German in the Middle Ages, from Italian during the Renaissance, from French in the 17th and 18th centuries and also from English, White Russian, and Ukrainian.

By the 19th Century, Polish was the dominant language of common speech in Poland despite the efforts of the partitioning powers to Germanize or Russify the population. Just the opposite happened, and the Polish language became the main foundation of national identity.

Among foreign languages, English and German are the most readily spoken by the Polish population although knowledge of them is not universal. German is spoken mostly by the older generation in the southwestern regions. French was traditionally spoken by the aristocratic and elite society and is still considered a prestigious language. Until recently, Russian was compulsory at primary and secondary schools and most Poles have some knowledge or understanding of Russian.

In Polish only the first world in the title of a book or movie is capitalized and all-important words are capitalized in names of newspapers and organizations.

POLISH PROVERBS

A bad woman is worse than the devil in hell, he only tortures sinners, she the good as well.

A good painter need not give a name to his picture, a bad one must.

A guest sees more in an hour that the host in a year.

A hippo does not have a sting in its tail, but a wise man would still rather be sat on by a bee.

A poor dancer will be disturbed even by the hem of her skirt.

A sparrow in the hand is better than a pigeon on the roof.

Amidst cordial friends, the dogs ate the hare.

An old man with a young wife is like a bookbinder, he binds a book another man reads.

As long as a woman is desired, she does not get old.

As necessary as a hole in a bridge.

As the New Year, so the whole year.

Better no doctor at all than three.

Better to lose to a wise man than to win with a fool.

Beware of spring in January, for March is jealous.

Cold December, lots of snow, a fruitful year is in tow.

Do not push the river, it will flow by itself.

Don't listen with your ears, but with your feet.

Don't sit in other people's sleds.

Don't spit into the well, you may have to drink the water.

Even a clock that does not work is right twice a day.

Even the goats will jump on a slanted tree.

Every fool has his crest.

Fish, to taste good, must swim three times: in water, in butter and in wine.

For free, the throat hurts.

For cheap money, dogs eat meat.

Friends in need get to know each other.

From a big cloud, small rain.

Green March, poor harvest.

He is not the master who started, but he who finished.

Hunt the wolf with a brother-in-law, the bear with a brother.

I have neither body nor soul, but when I play on my flute everything starts to dance. What am I? - The Wind.

If everyone gives a thread, the naked one will have a shirt.

If in April bees don't fly, lingering cold they prophesy.

If October comes with snow, in the spring snow will lie long in the fields.

If you knew you'd fall, you'd place some straw there.

If you love him, don't lend him.

It is not the garment that makes the king.

Like mother, like daughter.

Lined with wind.

Love enters a man through his eyes, woman through her ears.

Love is when someone of the opposite sex shares the good opinion we have of ourselves.

Lucky is the oldster that lives through March.

Measure seven times, cut once.

Money is a good servant but a poor guide.

Morning rain, as maiden's tears, last not long.

Never disavow a jail or a beggar's purse.

No one sees a fly on a trotting horse.

On a thief, the hat's on fire.

One beggar does not hate another as much as one doctor hates another.

Other countries, other customs.

Overseas there is a cow that costs a penny.

Straightening roads homeward bound, ensures that home is never found.

The farther into the woods, the thicker the trees.

The first plums of the season, are usually filled with bugs.

The goat dies but once!

The greater love is a mother's; then comes a dog's; then a sweetheart's.

The heart is not a servant, it does not know a master; it will not let itself be chained by force.

The human soul is like a bee, extracts sweetness even from bitter herbs.

The hungry man thinks of bread.

The king reigns, but does not govern.

The miser loses twice.

The roots of learning are bitter, but the fruit is sweet.

The scythe hit a stone.

The word flies out a sparrow and comes back an ox.

To a wise head, two words are sufficient.

Those who invite a wolf for supper, will not be around for breakfast.

Under capitalism, man exploits man; under socialism, the reverse is true.

Useless and foolish to run and hide away from love, for how can one flee on foot from Cupid flying above?

What hurts most, teaches soonest.

What is to hang, will not drown.

What is written with a quill, can't be cut down with an ax.

What little Johnny has not learned, big John will not know.

What one thinks when sober, one says when drunk.

What was and is not should not be entered into the register.

Where cooks there are six, no meal will they fix.

Where the devil can't manage, he'll send a woman.

Where two fight, a third profits.

Who lacks armament should avoid argument.

Who walks barefoot hurts no one.

You will learn more wisdom from one wife than from a thousand mistresses.

Yule eve fair, the morrow bright, the barn will be too tight.

UNIQUE POLISH CUSTOMS

Although some Polish customs and beliefs are only known from descriptions, a lot of them are still observed today. Despite the passage of time and political turmoil in Poland, they are a part of contemporary Polish culture. Some of them are connected with religious beliefs; others from deep folk roots; and still others, combine both religious and folk elements.

Polish Months

In Poland, an agricultural society, the months are named as follows:

Month (English)	**Month** (Polish)	**Description**
January	Styczen	To meet - as in old year meeting the new year.
February	Luty	Bleak skies
March	Marzec	To freeze
April	Kwiecien	Blooming flowers
May	Maj	The may pole
June	Czerwiec	To ripen or redden
July	Lipiec	The linden tree
August	Sierpien	Sickle
September	Wrzesien	Heather
October	Pazdiernik	Flax
November	Listopad	Falling leaves
December	Grudzien	Hard ground

Babkas (Female Healers)

The term is used for the village or town Grandmother, the area Wise Woman, the healer/midwife or witch. One can still meet babkas, witches or shamans in Poland's easternmost region. Old women who still sit in their huts, muttering spells and Orthodox prayers, brewing mysterious potions and helping those who have given up on traditional medicine.

It is not known how many female healers there are in Poland and it's difficult to explain their popularity. Poverty in eastern Polish villages is one of the most important reasons as well as the shortcomings in the Polish health care system. The babkas are a part of Polish culture that is gradually becoming extinct.

Building a House

According to Polish customs and traditions, it is very important in Poland to consider where the house was built, what structure it took and the way it was used. After the location was chosen, a line was drawn around the future house and an animal (usually a hen or a rooster) was sacrificed and placed under the future doorway. Later, many things such as eggs, an ax or a horseshoe were substituted for the animal sacrifice.

It is still a tradition in Poland for people to place bread, wheat, herbs, salt and a holy image under the four corners of the house. The belief in a horseshoe bringing good luck has survived until modern times.

Coffee Traditions

Polish customs and history determine the manner of coffee consumption. Coffee in Poland is more than a beverage; it is an institution of social life. Drinking coffee has its rituals and traditions and its meaning are often symbolic. It has always been seen as a special kind of delicacy, to be savored slowly and lingered over.

In Poland, coffee has traditionally been drunk outside the home, so the history of its consumption is closely intertwined with the history of Polish cafes and pastry shops. Coffee came to Poland from Germany in the 17th Century but was not used as a morning drink. Coffee-drinkers were treated with reverence and respect: A man who finished his meal with a cup of coffee was excused from drinking toasts and women did not drink coffee in public at all.

The first café in Poland was opened in Warsaw around 1724 and rapidly gained popularity. Although coffee became more widely consumed during the Interwar period, it remained the center of social and cultural life. The Warsaw cafes remained open despite shortages during the German occupation. In 1950 under communism, all the cafes were nationalized; only take-out pastry shops were allowed to remain in private hands. During the food shortages during the 1980s, coffee was very scarce and became a popular bribe.

Despite the major role of coffee as a center of social life, Poles do not drink large amounts of it. Currently, advertising is changing not only the image of the product but also its consumption patterns. Still, a 1995 survey found that one-third of Poles drink coffee before breakfast; 16% drink it with breakfast; 59% like their coffee before dinner and 58% like it in the afternoon.

Dyngusy (Easter Monday)

Dyngusy is the tradition of the day following the Spring Equinox in Poland. On that day, boys search for girls to drench with water; girls of course must return the favor the next day. Any girl who isn't gotten wet will not be married that year. This custom of pouring water is an ancient spring rite of cleansing, purification and fertility. The pagan explanation of this traditional drenching, called "oblewanki" in Polish, is that Easter is a spring festival and that this Polish made downpour summons the rains for the spring sowing. Tradition also states that the first Polish ruler Prince Mieszko I along with his court was baptized on Easter Monday in 966.

Gromniczna

On Gromniczna, the bear either mends his lair or knocks it down. It is the bear, not the ground hog, which foretells the future on February 2nd in Polish culture. Attributes of the bear include guardian of the forest, bravery, wisdom, strength, endurance, reawakening, protection and the guardian of homeowners.

Candlemaking is the prime focus of this holiday. It is also believed that candles made at this time will protect against colds and illness in which the throat and lungs are affected. It is from this practice that the Catholic Church borrowed the festival of St. Blaise on February 3rd at which it is traditional to bless throats.

Odpusty:

Annual observances of patron feast days in each parish in old Poland were called odpusty. Odpust means indulgence - the remission of punishment after death for sins. Participation in the religious rites of odpust including a High Mass with a procession in the morning and Festal Vespers in the evening usually merited an indulgence. The remainder of the day was spent meeting friends and wandering through the maze of stalls and booths outside the church grounds, which featured a variety of devotional objects, food and crafts. Markets and fairs such as this were first and foremost economic events but also a time for social and family visits.

Imieniny - Naming Customs

Saints and their feast days are very important to the Polish people. Parents look for a saint whose feast day is on or near the birth or baptismal date of their child which is usually not more than three weeks after the birth or baptism. Poles do not celebrate their birthdays; they celebrate the feast day of the saint for whom they are named or the anniversary of their baptism. Some children are named after one of the godparents. The godfather is called a *kumoter* and the godmother is called a *kumoszka*.

Many immigrants from Poland may have given their baptismal date or feast day instead of their actual date of birth when providing a birth date for American records. See Appendix A for a brief list of common Polish first names and the corresponding Name Day. To this day, the custom of celebrating 'name days' instead of birthdays is practiced in Poland. The name day is celebrated on the canonization day of the saint whose name one bears. Originally the day was devoted to honoring one's patron saint, but today the emphasis is on celebrating and receiving gifts.

Name Origins (Surnames)

Surnames were a product of necessity. Various methods of identification were used:

- Birthplace: Their native village or birthplace identified peasants, gentry and royalty alike.
- -ski: During the 15th Century it became fashionable to adjectivalize place names. The -ak suffix is typical for Western Poland while -uk is chiefly found in the East. The gentry originally used surnames ending in –cki and –ski.
- Heraldic Names: The names of the heraldic crests of many noble families often became inherited surnames and the names of their ancestral seats.
- Clan names: The noble class originally used "clan" names, which later survived in the names of their coats of arms. Particular families within a clan often used a surname derived from the name of the village they owned.
- Patronymics: People were also distinguished on the basis of their father's given name.
- Nicknames: Their appearances, habits, quirks or other characteristics identified Kings and peasants alike. Adjectival nicknames were most common among nobility.
- Occupations: Names identifying someone's trade were typical of town dwellers. Derivatives meant the son or apprentice thereof.

Wedding (Wesele):

For centuries, most marriages in Poland took place in the beginning of September and continued through the fall and winter months. At the wedding celebration, the sharing of the bread, salt and wine is an old Polish tradition that has been passed down through the centuries. It symbolizes the union of the Bride and Groom and their families. The parents of the bride and groom greet the newly married couple at the wedding reception with bread that is lightly sprinkled with salt and a goblet of wine.

The bread symbolizes the hope that the couple will never be hungry or in need. With the salt, the parents are reminding the couple that their life may be difficult at times and that they must learn to cope with life's struggles. Finally, the wine symbolizes the hope that the couple will never thirst and have a life of good health, good cheer and share the couple of many good friends. Afterwards, the parents kiss the newly married couple as a sign of welcome, unity and love.

Also:

- Reception guests customarily buy a dance with the bride by pinning money to her veil or tucking bills into a special bridal purse to build a honeymoon fund.
- Luck comes to the bride who drinks a glass of wine at the celebration without spilling a drop.

At the end of the reception, the most important wedding custom takes place. The custom called "Oczepiny" (the capping ceremony) is when the Czepek - the cap of a married woman - is placed upon the bride's head and she is pronounced a member of the circle of women. This handcrafted and embroidered cap is held as special and reserved for wear to church, for special folk festivals and on her death, for burial. The marriage cap was usually a gift to the bride from her godmother. It was so essential and played such a vital roll in the wedding that where other customs have disappeared altogether, the Oczepiny has survived to this day.

Christening Customs:

In some sections of Poland, gold coins are still placed in the diaper of a baby about to be christened. It is believed that doing so will help ensure good luck and prosperity throughout the baby's lifetime.

Funeral Customs:

In addition to normal Latin requiem services of the Church, there are a number of traditional folk beliefs and practices that characterized Polish funeral traditions of the past. Because Polish peasants had a natural apprehension of the corpse and sprits of the dead, they tried to ease and expedite the process of dying so that the sprits of the dead would not linger. For this reason, pillows were removed from the dying, candles were lit to light the way for the departing soul and the dying person is sprinkled with holy waters and blessed herbs. After the person died, doors and windows were left open to allow the soul to depart, clocks were stopped and mirrors turned around so that the deceased would not see his own reflection in them. The departed was always dressed in a new suit of clothes so that he/she may stand unashamed at the Last Judgment.

The corpse always was, and still is, laid out at home with blazing candles surrounding the coffin. A vigil is kept over the body from the moment of death until the funeral. The night before the funeral a wake (pusta noc) is held characterized by the singing of both ecclesiastical and popular dirges. After two introductory prayers on the day of the funeral, the deceased is carried out feet first so that he/she would not return. On the way out, the coffin is banged three times against the doorstep in farewell to domestic spirits once thought to reside there. After church service, the funeral cortege is formed which usually stops at a wayside cross or shrine where the funeral oration is delivered. At this point, the relatives went home in order not to bring death home again from the cemetery.

A funeral feast called 'stypa' closes funeral rites. The stypa is a lavish banquet featuring the best possible foods. Ritual foods such as pecak (hulled barley) and lazanki (noodles with honey and poppy seed) are also served. The symbolism for the ritual foods is:

- Grain - life after death because it must die in the ground in order to be reborn.
- Honey - the sweetness of our future existence with God.
- Poppy seed - good sleep.

Catholic tradition:

The faith of Polish people greatly influences their daily lives:

- Children receive their religious education from parents or grandparents.
- Before cutting a loaf of bread for the first time, the sign of cross is made over it.

While new forms of religious organizations, new prayers, and new songs find their way into Polish society, the faith of Polish people is still very traditional. Especially at Christmas when religious carols are sung which have been passed from generation to generation for over 800 years.

HOLIDAY CELEBRATIONS

National Holidays

Constitution Day (May 3, 1791) - is Poland's most important civic holiday. The constitution recast Poland-Lithuania as a hereditary monarchy; provided a separation of powers among the legislative, executive and judicial branches of government and established "people's sovereignty". Although never fully implemented, it is an important part of Poland's political heritage.

Army Day (August 15, 1923) - was established by the Minister of Arms to celebrate the day when Poles crashed the Red Army attack on Warsaw in 1920. The Polish Army inherits army traditions of the Polish dynasties of Piasts and Jagiellons, the First Republic and Napoleon's era, national insurrections and the Second Republic and fights for freedom during World War I and II. The symbol of attachment to over 1,000 years arms tradition of the Polish Army is the Grave of the Unknown Soldier in Warsaw which honors thousands of Polish soldiers who lost their lives fighting for Poland.

In 1992, the solemn celebrations of the Polish Army Day were held for the first time since the end of World War II. It is a holiday that pays homage to soldiers of all units and to people of different political views who, in time of the independence threat, were linked by the common desire of defending their country. The day is particularly significant for soldiers as orders and distinctions are awarded as well as appointments to successive military ranks. Also, the formal sentry dispatch and laying of wreaths at the Tomb of the Unknown Soldier in Warsaw takes place with participation of the Polish Army Honorary Guard.

Independence Day (November 11, 1918) - is the day Poland recovered its statehood after 123 years under foreign rule.

Holidays

Easter (Polski Tradycje Wielkanocne) Traditional Easter celebrations are old and elaborate and actually begin on Ash Wednesday when willow twigs are cut and placed in water. When their buds open in a few days, it is regarded as a good omen for a fair and mild spring. In some regions, particularly in the country, many Poles prepare "palms" by decorating them with traditional patterns. These are later carried during a procession on Palm Sunday. It is believed that palms have similar properties to willow branches that have been regarded as the symbol of life. Also, many folk rituals are connected with Palm Sunday. For example, in southern regions of Poland, the palms are later dismantled and used for making aspergillums for blessing fields and small crosses for sticking in the ground to protect fields from hail and storms. In areas of northern Poland, fishermen tie bits of palms to nets to guarantee safe fishing.

Polish Easter customs have not changed much during the centuries. Years ago girls begin gathering eggs on Palm Sunday that became 'pisanki'. Still a major item at Easter, eggs are blessed and artistically painted in various lovely and intricate patterns with different sections of Poland noted for their special designs.

On Holy Thursday, the church bells fall silent and rattles and clappers take their place. There is a ceremonial washing of the feet of twelve impoverished old men at the church in memory of the Last Supper and as a reminder of the humility with which Christ washed the feet of his disciples. Years ago, Polish kings performed this rite; today, the bishops and priests do this. Also, the vestments are changed on the miraculous icon in the Pauline monastery at Jasna Gora in Czestochowa. Good Friday marks the start of the vigil at symbolic tombs of Christ. No animals could be slaughtered or bread baked and mirrors were covered over. A special kind of bread is prepared for Easter Sunday called “paska”, which is made of flour and yeast.

On Holy Saturday, services accompanied by processions are held to commemorate the Resurrection. Inside the churches, priest sprinkle holy water on small baskets of food brought by believers. In old Poland, this resurrection service was an opportunity to identify witches. Also on Holy Saturday, the blessing of fire ceremonies is performed in the churchyard, the reverence of which goes back to pagan times. The old fire in the house is extinguished and a large bonfire is made in the churchyard. After being blessed by the priest, each person takes a flaming piece of wood from the fire and hurriedly carries it home where a new fire is ignited to signify the renewal of faith and greeting of spring.

Sunday morning, sharing a boiled egg with one’s relatives is a national tradition. Each member of the household also received a piece of the consecrated bread which when spread with horseradish was supposed to give protection against throat diseases and illnesses.

St John’s Night (Sobotka) June 23rd - Celebrated at the time of summer solstice, it used to be held as a summer welcome festival, integrating the rites of fire (with ritual bonfires), water and great love and fertility celebrations. The St John’s night’s wreaths are woven of many kinds of herbs and flowers symbolizing virginity. Although the custom has been kept until present, today the tradition of Wreaths is celebrated by amateur and professional folklore group performances on a stage erected close to Wawel Castle, floating lit wreaths on the Vistula River and fireworks.

Harvest Holiday (Dozynki) August 15th - Harvest holiday was a great landowners' festival during the 16th to 18th Centuries and was a feast and dance given by the owners of the estate at the height of summer as a reward for the hard labor of their servants and farm workers. The symbol of holiday was a harvest wreath (Wieniec) made in the shape of dome-shaped crown of the most beautiful ears of grain, decorated with flowers, ribbons, hazelnuts and the fruit of the mountain ash tree, was blessed and presented to the landowner. After the presentation, the festivities, especially the dancing and refreshments, began. The wreath was cherished and hung in a prominent place as a symbol of prosperity.

The custom of celebrating the end of the harvest and other field works has been kept alive as an important feast of the whole agricultural state. Dozynki wreaths are exhibited from all over Poland and are a symbol of the crops and fruits of the earth that have been gathered. Today, they are still respectfully kept until the next year and the grain that shells off is later added to the spring sowing seed.

Feast of Greenery (Matki Boskiej Zielnej) - September 8th - During the Polish Feast of Greenery, the farm people brought to church bouquets of herbs, vegetables and corn interwoven with flowers from the fields and gardens, which were blessed by the priest. When there was sickness in the household, the herbs were brewed and used for medicinal purposes for both the people and the livestock.

All Saints - All Souls Day (Dzien Wszystkich Swietyck Dzien Zaduszny) - November 1st and 2nd - All Saints Day tradition has been associated in Polish legend with ghosts and wayward souls. Today, both days are celebrated by making pilgrimages to local cemeteries where the people decorate graves with chrysanthemums, asters and autumn flowers and place candles and votive lights on the graves. After decorating the graves and in the light of countless flickering flames casting shadows in the dusk, an outdoor service is held.

Sw. Mikolaj (Sw. Mikolaja) - December 6th -On the feast of St. Nicholas Sw. Mikolaj, a bishop of Poland, was known to visit the homes of people in the villages dressed in his bishop's robes. When he visited children and heard they were good, he would give them a small treat such as candy, cookies or fruit. One modern custom inspired by St. Nicholas' visits is the candy cane. It is a simple treat that symbolizes the shepherd's staff carried by the Bishop.

The celebration of the feast day of Sw. Mikolaj is one of the Christmas customs that has remained popular in Poland for centuries. Over the years there have been variations of how treats were given and received, but the custom of honoring this generous bishop of Poland in the season of giving remains a tradition enjoyed by Polish people all over the world.

Szopki - The building of "Szopki" (which are elaborate forms of the Nativity scene) is an old tradition which began in 13th Century in Krakow, Poland. It remains an annual tradition and major prizes are awarded for the most elaborately decorated and designed Szopki. The Krakowian crèches sometimes reach six feet in height. Their construction is based on elements of Krakow's historic architecture including Gothic spires, Renaissance facades and Baroquian-topped domes.

Christmas Eve (Wigilia) - December 24th - The ancient Polish custom of decoration was to hang from the ceiling in a central location the topmost part of spruce tree, upside down and to decorate doorways and wall with separate boughs of the same. These were called "podlaz". Within sight of the podlazy, reigned a total suspension of hostilities where one had to be civil and speak without anger to one's enemies. The Christmas tree came to Poland just a hundred years ago together with the custom of giving gifts on Christmas Eve.

However, the Christmas Eve magic is found in the sharing of the "oplatek" - an unconsecrated bread wafer. The oplatek is ceremoniously shared with each person breaking off a piece and wishing each other whatever the heart desires. Although frail and perishable, the oplatek has a mystical meaning for all Poles, which cannot be explained logically. The ceremony, one of the most enduring and meaningful Christmas Eve traditions, represents the most cherished sentiments of reconciliation and the coming together of all.

Christmas Day (Boze Narodzenia) - December 25th - Christmas Day is considered such an important holiday that menial work of any kind was not even thought of. Cooking included only the heating of previously prepared food. This day is spent in rest, prayer and visits to various members of the family. It is also the beginning of the twelve-day period of Christmas called "Gody". These days are observed very carefully, for it was believed that Christmas Day and each of the following eleven days foretold the weather for the equivalent month of the year.

St. Stephan's Day - December 26th - This is the traditional day of visiting and wishing everyone the joy of the holiday season. St. Stephan's Day also was the end of work contracts for the year and new bargains were made for the next year. It was also the official day for caroling to begin. The custom of caroling in Poland (Chodzenie Po Koledzie) began on St. Stephan's and lasted until the Feast of Purification on February 2nd, also known as Candlemas Day.

- The oldest known Polish Christmas carol "Come Again Angel King" dates back to 1424. Elements of Polish folklore appeared in Christmas carols. The Christmas carol is a religious song but during the partitions of Poland, it became a patriot song.

New Year's Eve - December 31st - In the city, New Year's Eve in Poland is celebrated at more or less formal balls that always begin with a polonaise. Some of these balls, such as the ball at the Warsaw Philharmonic Society or the sportsmen's ball have a long-standing tradition. In the country, New Year's Eve was an occasion for pranks of all kinds in the past, which were forgiven because they are believed to be ousting the old passing year.

Bread baking was an important characteristic of New Year's Day. Different animals were shaped from the dough and godparents often gave these bread animals with best wishes to godchildren as presents. In some areas of Poland, donuts were baked to assure wealth for the whole year. Bread in the shapes of a ring, cross or a child were hidden at the dinner table and used for fortune telling. If someone found a ring, marriage awaited; a cross, entry into clergy and a child, a child out of wedlock. Other traditions included:

- Those who wake up early on New Year's Day will wake up early for the rest of the year.
- Those who touched the floor with the right foot when getting up from bed could expect a lot of good luck the whole year.
- Those who wanted to get rich had to put change in a small bag and run through the fields shaking the bag and making a lot of noise.

Carnival (Karnawal) - In Poland, Carnival is a joyful time between the end of the Christmas holidays and the beginning of Lent. Years ago, it was a period of active socializing with all kinds of entertainment including hunting, weddings, balls and masquerades. Everyone enjoyed themselves during carnival; they not only ate, drank and danced but also sang songs sometimes with very frivolous lyrics. There were no special carnival delicacies.

RELIGION OF POLAND

ROMAN CATHOLIC CHURCH

Poland was Christianized in 966 when Prince Mieszko the First ruled Poland. The Church played an important role in the integration of the country and in its spiritual, economical, administrative and scientific development. Church institutions founded primary schools and universities and taught the peasants modern-day farming methods.

Rulers of Poland recognized the importance of Catholicism for spiritual and economical development of Poland. Deep-seated Catholicism in Poland protected the country from religious wars and religious intolerance. Polish bishops through the Trident Council in 1545 believed that the Christian faith can only be spread by peaceful means and not by military force. Two priests of that time are noteworthy:

- Jakub Wujek - the first translator of the whole Bible into Polish.
- Piotr Skarga - who engaged in improving the moral qualities of the politicians of that time.

The office of Primate of Poland, established in the 15th Century, has been the symbol of continuity of Polish State.

During the partition of Poland, the Holy See made the occupying powers angry by retaining the office of the Primate of Poland. Polish was retained as the language of prayers in churches and of religions teaching in partitioned Poland. The occupying powers considered Catholic Church as the main enemy and many priests and bishops were imprisoned and churches were closed or destroyed. Publication of religious books were hampered or forbidden. The Church was one of the major factors in reunification of Poland in 1918 after defeat of occupying powers in World War I.

The Catholic Church in Poland suffered much during World War II from the German Nazi State. More than 90% of all

Catholic priests were killed. The people found spiritual strength to survive psychologically during the war by attending Church services and by prayers. Poland gave the Church many saints including 108 blessed martyrs of World War II. (Appendix A contains a partial list of Polish saints.)

The importance of the Church for Polish identity grew in communist times. Countless priests and bishops were murdered or imprisoned. Publication of Catholic journals and newspapers were banned and Catholic organizations were dissolved. Catholics were not allowed to hold any of the high administrative positions in the military or in business.

Despite its long Catholic heritage, Poland has for centuries welcomed people of all faiths, making it one of the most tolerant countries in Europe. Currently, about 95% of Poland are Roman Catholic. Since 1993, the administrative structure of the Catholic Church in Poland consists of 13 archdioceses and 27 dioceses.

Cathedral, the Basilica of Sts Peter & Paul - Located in Poznan, most of this cathedral, Poland's oldest, was restored to its Gothic shape after wartime devastation. The archdiocesan museum has collections of paintings, sculptures and textile spanning the centuries from the Middle Ages to the present day. The museum was once Poland's oldest high school - the former Lubranski Academy built in 1516. Excavation of the crypt has uncovered foundations of the pre-Romanesque and Romanesque cathedrals that stood on the site as well as parts of the sarcophagi of the early Polish monarchs, Prince Mieszko I and King Boleslaw the Brave. Their current resting-place is the Golden Chapel behind the altar.

The Lichen Shrine - In Lichen, a small village near Konin, a giant church was erected – the largest in Poland and 7th largest in Europe. Upon completed in the year 2000, it will mark the 150th anniversary of the Lichen Madonna. No pilgrim will be denied the chance to see the likeness of the Sorrowful Madonna, with its purported miraculous powers.

The history of the shrine began when a humble shepherd Mikolaj Sikatko had a vision of the Madoona in 1850. The adoration of the Lichen Madonna is so widespread that the Madonna has been proclaimed the patroness of miners, steelworkers, power industry employees and transportation workers. The Lichen shrine, which has been looked after by Marian priests since 1949, is playing an ever-greater role in Polish religion rivaling other similar pilgrimage sites in the country.

The Paulite Monastery of Jasna Gora - located in Gzestochowa, it is the home of the miraculous icon, the Black Madonna. Jasna Gora is not only the religious center of the country, it has a very special place in the hearts of Polish people. The monastery draws people from all walks of life including Pope John Paul II, who was there five times after his election. More than one million pilgrims make the trek to see the Black Madonna in an average year.

Historically, Jasna Gora withstood a long-lasting seige during the Swedish invasion of 1655-56. When Poland was partitioned, the monastery served as both a religious site and one of the main centers of Polish patriotism. Over the centuries, it managed to survive the wars almost undamaged.

The monastery over time has acquired works of art, jewelry, musical instruments and antique religious artifacts. The Jasna Gora library contains more than 8000 volumes of old prints, illuminated manuscripts and unusual art objects from the royal collection of the Jagiellonian dynasty.

GREEK CATHOLIC CHURCH

In 1596, the Greek Catholic Church (or Uniate Church) was established by the Union of Brest-Litovsk and brought several million Eastern Orthodox Belorussians and Ukrainians under the authority of the Roman Catholic Church. Although they preserved Orthodox religious rites, members of the Orthodox Church were adamantly opposed Latinization and considered it a compromise of tradition. As a result, conflict between the Greek Catholic Church and both the Polish Catholic Church and the Orthodox Church erupted periodically into the early 1990s.

By 1989, the membership of the Greek Catholic Church in Poland was about 300,000. This included 85 centers of worship, 5 monasteries, 3 orders of nuns and 55 priests.

POLISH NATIONAL CATHOLIC CHURCH

The most interesting religious minority in Poland is the Polish National Catholic Church. This sect broke away from the Roman Catholic Church in 1897 in response to the church's poor record in Polish-American communities.

JEHOVAH's WITNESSES

The third largest denomination are the Swiadkowie Jehowy (Jehovah's Witnesses), who have several hundred thousand followers.

JEWS

Their prosecution in Western Europe caused the influx of Jews into Poland in 1098 where they found the protection and tolerance they sought in a country that was poorly developed and in need of merchants and craftsmen. The birth of towns and the development of commodity money relations further favored the settlement by Jews in Poland. Mieszko III employed Jews in his mint between 1138 and 1202 as engravers of dies and technical supervisors of all workers. From pure silver, they made coins called bracteates that were engraved with inscriptions in Hebrew.

However, Boleslaw Pobozny appreciated their talents and in 1246, his Charter of Kalisz guaranteed Jews protection of persons, protection of property and freedom in conducting religious rites. The turn of the 13th and 14th centuries saw the end of feudal disintegration in Poland and the rulers encouraged Jewish migration to Poland. By the middle of the 14th Century, Jews had occupied 35 Silesian towns although Jewish settlements in other parts of Poland grew much slower.

The expansion of the scope of economic activity of the Jews caused competition between them and their Christian counterparts. As a result, anti-Jewish riots broke out in Silesia in the 14th Century and in Wroclaw in 1454. In 1495, Jews were ordered out of the center of Krakow and allowed to settle in the "Jewish town" of Kazimierz.

The 16th and the first half of the 17th Century saw increased settlement and a relatively fast rate of natural population growth among the Polish Jews. By the middle of the 17th Century, there were 500,000 Jews living in Poland who practiced over 50 trades. During this time, Jews played an outstanding role in Poland's foreign trade. The Jews' trading activity also included credit operations and they pioneered centralized credit operations in Poland.

The legal position of the Jews was still regulated by royal and princely privileges and Sejm statutes and their legal status influenced by synodal resolutions and common law. All this resulted in a substantial disparity in the legal position of the Jewish population. A 1589 agreement between the Jews and the municipal authorities in Kamionka Strumilowa is noteworthy. In it the councilors agreed to accept the Jews into their own laws and freedoms while the Jews pledged themselves to help in keeping order and cleanliness in the town, hold guard and take part in anti-flood operations together with the Christians.

The wars against the Cossacks, Ukraine, Russia, Sweden, Turkey and the Tartars fought by Poland during 1648-1717 caused a permanent downfall of towns and agriculture and decimated the population. Jewish trade nearly came to a standstill. In the middle of the 17th Century, changes were made in the organization of credits and large banking houses disappeared. In the second half of the 17th and the 18th Century the Jewish population was poverty-stricken and disagreements between the people and the Jewish oligarchy deepened particularly on the issue of taxes.

The more educated members of Polish society investigated the problem of carrying out fundamental political reforms and solving both the peasant and the Jewish question. In the 1760s the Jewish question was the subject of Sejm debates. The only important concession for the Jews during these debates was contained in the 1792 law of police commission that guaranteed that all Jews had the right not to be imprisoned without a court verdict. In 1791, the Third of May Constitution was passed by the Four-Year Sejm which contained a provision that permitted all religions the right to exist provided they did not call for the overthrow of the monarchy.

The fate of the Jews during the period of Partitions depended largely on whether they were under Austrian, Russian or Prussian rule. After World War I, the official policy of anti-Semitism characteristic of Tsarist Russia had a harmful effect on the population of Poland. Since Polish Jews had a strong sense of their individual national identity, nationalistic conflicts between Poles and Jews were illustrative of the difficult problems that existed in the social and political life of the Polish nation. By the outbreak of World War II, Poland was tolerant of Jewish independence in religious, political and social life including education and cultural activities.

Jews in Poland developed a particular mode of Talmudic study and enriched Jewish culture with many new religious customs. They spoke Yiddish - a mixture of medieval German and Hebrew and their religious academies attracted students from all over the Jewish world. Over time, Poland became home to the largest concentration of Jews in Europe and the most potent hub for Jewish culture.

A unique Jewish culture flourished in pre-World War II Poland. Jewish entrepreneurs, bankers, industrialist and merchants played a major role in the industrialization of Poland. Jews were in the vanguard of modern banking, industry (including sugar refining, textile, paper and mechanical), commerce, export-import trade and transportation (construction of railway and river traffic on the Vistula). They also founded one of the first polytechnic colleges on Polish soil.

Jews actively participated in the national uprisings which took place on Polish soil including:

- Kosciuszko Insurrection – 1794
- November Insurrection – 1830
- January Insurrection – 1863
- Revolutionary Movement of 1905

During the period between the two World Wars, Jews accounted for 10% of Poland's population. Politicians and leaders with seats in the Sejm (the Senate) as well as in municipal councils represented their interests in Poland.

MUSLIMS

In northeast Poland, Bohoniki and Kruszyniany are home to a Muslim minority of Tartars. Their ancestors settled in Poland at the beginning of the 15th Century but it was not until the late 17th Century that King Jan III Sobieski granted them land in the area as a reward for their services.

The Polish Muslims are descended from Tartars and are of the Hanafi sect. They have built several mosques in Poland of which the Gdansk Mosque is the most celebrated. The mosque in Kruszyniany has an Islamic crescent hanging over the entrance but in all other ways resembles a typical Polish wooden church. Muslim clerics teach religious subjects and Shari'ah in these mosques and spiritual religion and beliefs have had large impacts on the art and culture of Poland.

The impact is evident in Poland's buildings, structures and the architectural styles and patterns adopted during their different historical dynasties. There are many temples in Poland, which are rich with ornamental objects and enchanting images displaying a world of beauty. The combination of the stones are a mixture of strength and delicacy. In temples special copper boxes have survived which have been fabricated by special tenderness and artistry that proves stone and metal prevailed in the Polish history during their domination of the eastern European nations.

ORTHODOX CHURCH

Poland's second largest religious denomination is the Polish Autocephalous Orthodox Church with an estimated 800,000 followers. The Orthodox Church has most of its followers along the country's eastern borderlands. The city of Bialystok is said to be about one-third Orthodox.

Grabarka, located in the Bialystok region near the town of Siemiatycze, has become a sacred place of worship for followers of the Orthodox Christian faith. Thousands of crosses surround a church and convent on a wooded hill. The hill has become a miraculous site and the tradition of pilgrims, seeking penance, putting crosses there goes back to 1710. Every August, believers make pilgrimages to this place on the day of the Transfiguration of the Savior.

PROTESTANTS

In 1515, Bernard of Lublin proclaimed the seminal principle of Protestantism in a work that was published in Krakow. About the same time, Protestant doctrines began to take root in other towns of Polish Prussia. Numerous books appeared at this time in Poland against Luther and his doctrines. In 1548, protestant truth was widely spread throughout the kingdom. In Polish Prussia, it was in its Lutheran form and in the rest of Poland it was embraced in its Calvinistic form. Many powerful nobles had abandoned Romanism but as yet there was no church.

From 1583-1596, SS Johns' Parish Church in Torun served as place of worship for Catholics and Protestants. The atmosphere of mutual respect among various denominations resulted in the Colloquium Charitativum in 1595. Although the conference did not achieve its intended goal, it is known as the 1st European attempt at ecumenicism.

The supreme authority in the Polish Protestant Church was the Grand Snyod of the nation, and in 1632 the Protestants were still powerful in Poland. After invasions by two armies who had exercised indiscriminate vengeance against both Protestants and papists, the monarch placed his kingdom under the special protection of the "Blessed Virgin". Religious equality was still the law of Poland.

The "Torun tumult" was caused by a street fight between the Jesuit College and the Protestant Grammar School and was a bloody finale to a long-lasting dispute over the right to manage Torun's main churches. In 1753, the king consented to the construction of a Protestant church that was a steeple-less edifice because that was the condition imposed by the Polish monarch. The present steeple was added in 1898.

WOMEN'S ISSUES

Emancipation:

Polish feminism dates back to the 1830s and the Entuzjastki (Female Enthusiasts) movement headed by Narcyza Zmichowska, the author of Poganka (1846). The work of Eliza Orzeskowa, whose book *Marta* (1873) belongs among the classics of European emancipationist prose. Even then, a dilemma arose that would confront women writers in Poland until 1989 - a patriotic country of men and women or the struggle for emancipation.

The emancipation of women in Poland occurred first through the joint fight with men for independence of the country. In Warsaw, women's groups centered on two journals - *Przeglad Naukowy* (Scientific Revue) and *Pierwiosnek* (Primrose). Women activists carried out semi-legal educational and information-oriented projects. In the Grand Duchy of Pozna, women played an important role in the Polish political life after the disastrous 1846 insurrection. Many women proved their adherence to the ideals of independence of Poland by helping to distribute illegal literature; hosting émigré emissaries in their homes and even participating in street riots in Krakow and Lviv.

Although women actively participated in the 1848-1849 revolution in Poland, they usually chose to do so in traditional feminine roles such as caring for the wounded and working in welfare organizations. Their energy allowed Polish troops during the armed conflict with the Prussian army to receive well-organized medical and sanitary assistance of the highest level.

The contribution of women to the 1848-1849 events in Poland has not attracted much attention of historians, due probably to the lack of women's studies in Poland. It was only the activity of women in the Russian partition at the time of the revolution that presented a unique phenomenon and proved how significant and influential a woman's conspiracy for independence can be.

Health:

Particularly alarming, is the increase in the prevalence of cancer and heart disease in women. The government has failed to consider the fact that women's health is impacted by their economic situation, their dependence on men, their low earnings (as compared to men), domestic violence and the limitation of birth control.

Women's right to health protection is seriously endangered because women's earnings and pensions are lower and they are more often faced with problems resulting from the growing costs and deficiencies of the health care system.

- The leading cause of death in Poland is illnesses of the circulatory system with the greatest number of deaths occurring in women. Heart attacks are a significant danger for every 2nd woman after menopause and cerebral hemorrhages for every 10th woman.
- Cancer-related illnesses are the second highest cause of death in Poland with breast cancer being the most common form of cancer for women. Apart from the low level of health education regarding self-breast exams and regular gynecological exams, there is also limited access to mammography facilities and a problem regarding the quality of these devices.
- The third cause of death among older women is osteoporosis. Limited accessibility to hormonal treatment for women during menopause that can allows this problem to exist.
- While all pregnant women have the right to receive periodic checkups and medical care, many women (particularly in villages) do not have access to this care. This lack of medical care equates with low education levels and lack of knowledge of birth control or prenatal care.

Reproductive Rights

Poland is one of the few countries where laws regarding sexual education, family planning, pre-natal tests and abortion have recently dramatically deteriorated.

Sexual Education - Although the basis for sexual education was introduced in Polish schools in the 1970s, it was never supported at an adequate level. The 1993 Law on Family Planning, Protection of Human Fetus and Conditions Permitting Pregnancy Terminations imposed an obligation on the Minister of Education to introduce the subject title "Knowledge of Human Sexual Life" into the school curriculum. The Catholic opponents of sexual education succeed in persuading the Sejm to repeal the section of the law pertaining to sexual education. As a result in 1998, the knowledge of sexual life was withdrawn from schools and replaced with "Education for Family Life" which is based on ultra-conservative and ultra-catholic ideology on sexual and family lives.

Family Planning - Laws and policies limiting access to information on family planning methods are particularly appalling in a country where the knowledge and use of contraception is at a very low level. Only about 12% of Polish women use modern contraceptives. Cultural barriers are the most significant reason for the lack of family planning, followed by lack of knowledge on the types available, their use, efficiency and possible side effects. The Catholic Church with its consistent policy, which prohibits all methods of contraception, has also profoundly affected attitudes towards family planning. Finally, anyone who performs an operation of sterilization is liable to penalty of 1 to 10 years in prison.

Pre-natal Tests - The 1993 Law on Family Planning, Protection of Human Fetus and Conditions Permitting

Pregnancy Terminations also regulates access to pre-natal exams. However, women have never been able to fully exercise this right:

+ They lack information,
+ They have received misleading information on the availability of pre-natal tests, or
+ They face difficulty in gaining access to them.

Even in Upper Silesia, a highly polluted region of Poland, pre-natal tests are not provided despite the high rates of fetuses that suffer genetic defect, presumably due to pollution. A new law on pre-natal tests has been drafted which would introduce a full ban on pre-natal tests. If enacted, this law would further infringe on a woman's right to protect the health of her unborn child.

<u>Abortion</u> - Legal abortion on social grounds was introduced in Poland in 1956. However the lack of sexual education, information and availability of contraceptives, together with the negative attitude of the Catholic Church towards birth control, resulted in a high percentage of terminated pregnancies. A draft of the Law on the Legal Protection for the Conceived Child was filed in 1989 which was intended to ban abortion irrespective of a woman's health, living and economic situation, or circumstances in which she got pregnant and also advocated punishment for abortion. The Code of Medical Ethics adopted in 1992, which is currently enforced, allows abortion to be performed in only three cases:

- When pregnancy endangers the mother's life or health;
- When pre-natal tests or other medical findings indicate a high risk that the fetus may be severely and irreversibly damaged, or to be suffering from an incurable disease dangerous to its life;
- When there are strong grounds for arguing that the pregnancy is a result of criminal activity.

Although the law in Poland does not provide men with the right to limit a woman's decision on abortion, the access to abortion has always been more difficult in practice than what the law has stated. With the banning of abortion on social grounds, Poland law has become the second most restrictive country in Europe.

Violence

Although major changes have been made, violence against women remains hidden and surrounded by taboos, powerful social myths and stereotypes as well as a strong tradition of shame and guilt in the case of disclosure, especially in small villages and towns. The Polish criminal justice system is neither effective nor responsive to victims' needs and there are serious legal and institutional deficiencies in the family violence intervention system.

Domestic Violence - Under the law domestic violence is publicly prosecuted in Poland and the police and prosecutor are legally obligated to investigate when domestic violence is committed. In actuality, both law enforcement officers and prosecutors rarely treat cases of domestic violence seriously. Women must request prosecution and often are required to produce well-documented complaints if they want to police to proceed. Meanwhile, she goes through an intimidating, unfamiliar and unfriendly procedure cannot obtain adequate legal protection and is exposed to the perpetrator's revenge. Polish laws do not provide for protection orders and very few shelters exist where victims can find refuge.

Rape - According to Polish law, rape is a crime against personal freedom and morality. However, in practice the police and courts commonly treat rape as an everyday incident that results from the provocative behavior of women. At trial, the court focuses its attention on the woman who must prove that nothing in her behavior could have provoked the rape and takes the victim's sexual life prior to the rape into account. Rape victims have problems finding specialized psychological assistance and counseling. Few rape crisis centers exist in Poland. In 1999, the Warsaw police started a training program for policewomen to prepare them for work with rape victims.

Prostitution - Prostitution is not a crime in Poland. In addition to the prostitution that occurs in the street and in hotels, there is a growing number of brothels or companionship agencies as they are commonly called in Poland. According to Interpol, as well as Polish police, wayside prostitution is widespread in Poland. The sex industry also markets pornographic magazines and films, which are widely distributed in Poland.

Sexual Harassment - Sexual harassment is a relatively new legal and social concept in Poland and the laws do not adequately address the issue. There is no definition of harassment and no provisions on the various forms of sexual harassment. This type of crime is only investigated if the victim reports it and there is hostility to the victims as well as a lack of procedures that grant safety for women who do testify. As a result, the lack of knowledge regarding the possibility of punishment for this type of crime, difficulties in proving it and unwillingness to speak about it for fear of losing their jobs, very few cases have been brought to court.

Education:

Poland has recently experienced a renaissance of ultra-conservative ideology advocated by the Catholic Church and its political allies. This ideology is supported by a large number of Polish men and women. The difference in the social roles of men and women is deeply rooted in Polish culture and form the basis for the stereotyped opinion about women's role in society.

Presently, two opposing forces influence education for women:

- The political and economic transformation caused by the breakdown of the communist system that resulted in major changes in the labor market, as well as in the mentality of the youth. Polish teenagers of the 1990s, are more practical, career oriented, understand the reality of the new system and the growing need for business professionals.
- The Catholic Church and the ultra-conservative parliamentary majority have challenged this general trend towards higher education. The church advocates the restoration of traditional gender roles and argues that women should seek personal fulfillment in the family. The Polish government has passed laws and pursued policies that reinforce stereotypes, support conservative family models and discriminate against women in all fields of social life, including education. Further, Polish authorities have recently introduced education reform, developed and applied a policy that strengthen the traditional views of gender roles and encourages women to relinquish educational aspirations for the sake of the family.

Employment:

Prior to 1989, women played an active and stable role in the workplace. Their high employment rate was the result of the ideological appreciation of women's emancipation and from a need for women's labor in the nation's accelerated industrialization process. Also, many families could not subsist on only one salary. Nevertheless, women were still primarily responsible for the family and were expected to play a traditional role at home.

By the end of 1988, women accounted for 37% of the employers and self-employed. A large number of these women-owned businesses engage in trade or provide services.

Surveys among these women indicate that the main incentive for self-employment is not only the need to increase the family's income, but also the need for independence, autonomy and utilization of skills.

Since Poland's political and economic transformation in 1989, the status of women has changed drastically and their position in the labor market has become weaker. Although better educated, women earn less, are promoted less frequently and are the first to be fired and the last to be hired. Factors that support this practice are:

1. Most employers are convinced that the free market system grants them the right to unlimited freedom in hiring his or her staff.
2. Employees are unaware they have the right to question or challenge the employer's decision.
3. A strongly held belief in Polish society that men should be granted priority over women in a shortage of jobs.
4. Women cope better when unemployed since lack of a job degrades men.

Poland's 19 million women play a relatively small role in public life. Women's organizations (there are more than 100 of them in Poland) are trying to fight stereotypes regarding the woman's role and status while combating discrimination and unemployment. The Nationwide Women's Promotion Center (OCPK) has set ambitious goals in its courses which primarily consist of helping women understand where the barriers are, to what extent gender plays a role and just how strong the stereotypes about women are. More and more organizations are working with organizations and foundations to help other women and to teach women the skills and attitudes they need to crack Poland's male-dominated employment market.

SOCIAL & BUSINESS ETIQUETTE

During its long history, Poland has developed its own individual forms of social and business etiquette. Poland is traditionally a formal culture and individuals are admired for their ability to do the right thing. A solid understanding of Poland's rich traditions can make your visit enjoyable and your business a success. As noted below, some etiquette is quite formal while in other situations, it is just different.

Babies

In Warsaw, baby boys are dressed in pink and baby girls in blue. However, in other parts of Poland just the opposite is done - girls are given pink outfits and boys get the blue ones.

Buses & Streetcars

Since the tickets required to use the bus and tram can only be purchased at street kiosks, tobacco shops or newsstands, it is wise to keep a supply of tickets on hand. Tickets are not collected but must be validated in the machines on the bus or tram. There is a fine for riding without a ticket and inspections are made. Customarily, it is expected that you give up your seat for pregnant women, mothers with young children, the elderly and the handicapped.

Business

Courtesy demands that foreign businesspeople make contact with the highest levels of Polish companies preferably with the person actually in charge. **It is considered it an insult to do otherwise**. The personal connection is an important part of business relations in Poland. While Poles are willing to assist on any level, while attempting to acquire management skills and gain experience in international business, they insist on trust and confidence in their prospective partners before they sign any agreement. The Polish spirit is composed of self-reliance and individualism. Most Poles are blunt, do not hesitate to say what they think and enter the decision making process fearless.

When doing business in Poland, any communication when planning meetings should be done by fax. Prior appointments are vital. The best times to schedule appointments are between 10:00 to 11:00 a.m. or 2:00 to 3:00 p.m. The best months for business travel are September through May as most business vacations are taken in late summer. Leave early and expect confusion with meetings. Patience in business dealings is essential as decisions can take some time to be completed. Most Polish officials have a good sense of humor and a lot of good will for foreigners. Also, be aware that Polish negotiators are always thoroughly prepared.

Enter the office quietly, close the door gently, say "Dzien dobry" (good day) and wait to be asked your business. It is the custom in Poland to shake hands when you meet, greet or take your leave. Men are particularly passionate hand shakers. Be wary of shaking hands over a threshold, for Poles consider that bad luck. But a foreign man should wait for a woman to extend her hand. If he wishes to show additional respect, he may make a short bow.

Exchanging business cards is a favorite pastime, so bring plenty and give them out freely. Business cards in both your language and Polish are exchanged with everyone in meetings. Include any advanced educational degrees and your full title on your business card. It is also invaluable to obtain letters of introduction. Patience is essential with Polish business people, as they are not always good timekeepers. If you are planning a social event or meeting, don't be concerned if no one turns up at the appointed time. Lateness of up to 15 minutes is thought to be acceptable.

Poles normally move fairly quickly to substantive issues in business discussions. It is not necessary for presentations to be elaborate as long as they are clear and easily understood. They can be in English, but backup documentation should be in Polish. Never offer an ultimatum or be condescending. Also, do not bargain, as it is not the Polish way. The Poles consider a contract to be serious and expect them to be clear, concise and written in both Polish and English.

The safest address is pan (sir) or pani (madam), accompanied by the person's job title or last name. Pani is preferred over pana (miss) for unmarried women. Titles carry prestige in Poland since historically, a title signified a person's nobility or status as a landowner. Today, it refers to educational attainment, profession or administrative position. Once you know a person's title, use it especially in work situations, formal occasions and any written communication. Dropping the Mr. or Ms. And using only such titles as Director, President of professions is considered impolite behavior. It is even worse to call someone by just their last name. Don't address your Polish business associate by first name unless you're invited to do so. The Poles have a ceremony that celebrates the passage to first name basis. It is called Bruderszaft (brotherhood in German) and involves lifting a shot glass of vodka, linking arms, drinking and then greeting each other by first names.

Conservative dress and conduct prevail, as Poles are conservative in dress and demeanor that translates into a business climate where humility and respect are favored over bravado and arrogance. They rarely blow their own horn and if you do, you will seem over-confident.

Although breakfast meetings are uncommon, business is often conducted at lunch and especially at dinners. Most entertaining is done in restaurants and invitations are serious business. In *Speaking Volumes about Poles*, author Laura Klos-Sokol writes, "Invitations from Poles are as serious as tax notices; if you don't respond appropriately, be prepared to pay a heavy price." You will be expected to eat and drink everything with gusto, be effusive in your appreciation and stay until the end of the festivities. It is rude in Poland to begin eating before everyone has been served but indulging to the "popping point" is proper etiquette. Beware, Poles are athletic consumers of vodka. Avoid drinking bouts unless you have a "mocna glowa" (strong head) and can remember what you promise under the influence.

A woman on a business call should not be surprised if a Polish man (particularly an older gentleman) kisses her hand in greeting. It's considered a sign of respect. Foreign businessmen aren't expected (or advised) to kiss hands, but if one is moved to try, he should bend at the waist and bow his head to her hand. The kiss is placed on the back of the hand, not the fingers.

While women are found at executive levels in most professions and industries and at the senior level in government, Poland is still a conservative society where rural and traditional Catholic moral values prevail. Appropriate business dress in Poland for women consists of understated dresses or suits. It is advised that women observe female behavior in Poland to learn what is appropriate and how best to blend in.

Even though sexual harassment is less likely, it may be easy to misinterpret specific social comments if you do not know the local norms. To avoid this situation, state your wishes clearly so that mixed signals do not become a problem. To repel harassment in public, ignore sexual advances, avoid eye contact and do not engage in any conversation. Polish women have a no-nonsense attitude toward most types of harassment.

Car Rental

Auto travel is the preferred mode of transport for many business people and rental cars are readily available. It is strongly recommended that you buy auto insurance. Traffic moves on the right as in the US and, while most main roads are adequate, country and secondary roads are narrow and sometimes in disrepair. Although there are fewer cars in Poland, the main routes are becoming increasingly congested due to the Poles' fascination with cars and the country's transit status. In addition, almost every lorry (truck) which crosses Europe passes through Poland and it is highly recommended that you do not race them. Traffic speeds are lower than average in the EU but drivers who break the speed limit are subject to heavy fines which can substantially raise the cost of visiting Poland.

Compliments

In Poland, don't forget to compliment friends and colleagues at work. If you don't, Poles will think you're a bore and distinctly lacking in culture.

Dignitaries

In Poland, when a dignitary arrives in the country, he/she is also greeted with bread and salt as a sign of welcome and hospitality similar to the American custom of presenting keys to the city to important people.

Dining & Entertainment

Poles prefer to use restaurants for business entertaining and tend to arrive promptly with their spouse, if the invitation includes them. Standards of hospitality are high and every attempt will be made to make you comfortable and accord you the honor due a guest. Your role as guest is to politely acknowledge and accept these gestures and be sure to compliment the host on the meal. It is appreciated if you express knowledge of Polish history and culture as your Polish host may have an educated interest in your culture and current affairs. Conversational topics to avoid include religion, politics, social and economic conditions in Poland unless your host introduces these subjects.

When dining, the knife remains in the right hand and the fork remains in the left hand. You are obligated by social custom to leave your coat in the checkroom when dining in restaurants as the attendants are usually people on disability pensions and the fees they collect are a source of supplementary income. A service charge of 10% is normally included in a restaurant bill but people often leave a little more.

Dress

On special occasions, i.e. invitation to a restaurant or a celebration, such as a name-day celebration (*imieniny*) or less often a birthday (*urodziny*), dress smartly with a shirt and tie unless told otherwise. Bundle up in the winter with woolens as the winters turn very cold and an umbrella may prove useful throughout the year.

Drinking

Alcohol consumption is falling and beer is enjoying more popularity than vodka although wine and cocktails are the in thing at parties. The first toast is usually raised by the host "to the guests' health" followed by guests drinking to the health of the host. Never try to out-drink a Pole. One method of breaking the ice at name-day parties involves toasting. Try not to empty the glass at each toast. Most Poles still prefer tea rather than coffee for breakfast. Coffee for many is a mid-afternoon cup of robust, aromatic espresso at a café.

Eating

Polish people have a heavy lunch (often with a nap) and light dinner. When invited to a Polish home, make a good impression by eating a lot especially if your Polish language skills are poor. Try small amounts of everything and learn how to say no and eat slowly. It is considered offensive if you don't eat a lot.

Elevators

When exiting an elevator, always say *dziekuje* (thanks). In reply to someone else saying it, say *dziekuje*. If there are two or more of you, say *dziekujemy* (we thank you). It is expected and courteous.

Hand Gestures

Hand gestures are normally limited. For example, flicking a few fingers against the neck is an invitation (usually between men) to join the person for a drink of vodka.

Invitations

If you keep refusing invitations to Polish homes for drinks, dinners or name-day parties, Poles will believe that you are boring, stiff and unfriendly. Flowers are the best choice for the hostess if you are visiting a Polish home. Bring them unwrapped, odd in number (for good luck) and avoid red roses (lovers' buds) and chrysanthemums (which are used at funerals). Chocolates or sweet liquor are also appropriate.

Gifts

Poles like to exchange inexpensive but thoughtful presents. On leaving his home, you might like to present your host with a small gift. If you bring a gift to your Polish associate, avoid bringing Russian vodka (or any vodka for that matter). Give other liquors, coffee, perfume or cigarettes.

Greetings

The Poles greet each other by shaking hands more than in other countries. Don't first extend your hand to older people, to women or to your boss. When greeting a close friend or relative, whether male or female, Poles will kiss at least once on each cheek and perhaps once more for luck! It is usual to shake hands whenever you meet someone, but not on the doorstep as this is considered bad luck.

Home Invitations

There are two well-known sayings in Polish, one is *"A guest in the house is God in the house"* and the other *"Pawn everything, but show your best"*. These two phrases give us an idea of just how hospitable the Poles are. Soon after a guest enters the house the tea, cakes, ham and other goodies are on the table. The guest would be well advised to partake of something to avoid offending the host.

Gatherings at home usually center around the dining room table set with food and associated with a bottle of vodka in the middle. Vodka is served undiluted in small glasses along with pickled dills and pickled wild mushrooms as an accompaniment. Traditionally you should say "Cheers" (*Na Zdrowie*) and drain your glass.

Poles don't usually go out dining in restaurants, they prefer to eat at home and go out for drinks, coffee or ice cream. Private gatherings at home are very much in favor. If you are invited to someone's home it is good manners to take along some flowers for the lady of the house. The host will always welcome a bottle of alcohol.

Kissing

A gentleman always kisses a lady's hand whether or not she is married. It is a sign of respect. If you wish to be gallant you may kiss a lady's hand, more mature ladies may raise their hand slightly as a signal for you to take it and plant a kiss.

Lunch

There is no lunch hour; therefore, you may be invited to eat at any time of the day.

Name Days

After taking part in the Bruderszaft fraternal toast, relations between people turn from official to personal. At this time, the most important obligation is to remember a person's name day – a person's saint's day rather than their birthday. In no other culture other than Poland is this anniversary so important or celebrated in such a special way. Even though the actual celebration is after hours at home, it is customary to offer a person "good wishes" when you see them. Small gifts such as flowers or a book are welcome but not necessary. If you don't see a person on their name day, a telephone call, text message or e-mail will suffice.

Numbers

When writing numerals, Poles use periods and commas in exactly the opposite way that Americas do. A comma in Poland serves as a decimal point (3,6%) and trios of digits are set off with periods (3.000.000).

Oaths

Only two fingers (the index and middle fingers) are extended whenever Poles take an oath. Poland is the only country in the world whose military, police officers and other uniformed services use a two-finger salute.

Polish Language

When visiting Poland, Polish should be spoken as much as possible since Poles know how difficult their language is. They also will become increasing friendly if a person tries to communicate in Polish.

Polish conversational language structure is very formal so if you don't know someone very well or they are older or of venerable stature you should call them Pan/Pani followed by their surname. Pan and Pani are the equivalent of Mr. and Mrs. When you are greeting someone that you know longer, you can call them Pan/Pani followed by their first name. If you are unfamiliar with a person you should greet them with *Dzien Dobry*, which means "Good Day"; there is no equivalent of "Good Morning". In the evening you should say *Dobry Wieczor* which means "Good Evening". It is best to stick to these formalities especially if dealing with people of the older generation or on business. To your friend or colleague you can say "Hello" with *Czesc.*

Rings

Polish women were their engagement ring and both spouses were their wedding band on the ring finger of the right hand.

Public Toilets

The appearances of Polish toilets are unusual. They have a shelf on which everything solid falls and the water is deep only in the very front. When you flush, the water sluices everything off the shelf into the deep end.

At public toilets pay the woman at the door the amount posted near her station. She keeps the place clean and is master of all toilet paper. Unless you are using some fancy place, there is no toilet paper in the toilet stall and it is advised that you bring your own.

Shoes & Socks

It is a Polish custom to take off your shoes when entering a home so don't forget to wear clean socks with no holes. You may then be given slippers to wear.

Taxis

Taxis are available at the airport but fix the price to the city center with the driver before commencing the journey as some drivers try to take advantage of unwary tourists. Cabs can be hailed on the street or found at taxi stands. Radio taxis are also available but the wait can be lengthy. It is customary to tip the driver by rounding up the fare on the meter. Since drivers often do not have change, try to have small notes on hand.

Toasting

Toasts are made over hard liquor, not wine or beer and are initiated by the host as an expression of hospitality, gratitude, friendship or good wishes. It is customary for the guest to return the compliment by making a toast of his own. The most frequent toast of al na zdrowie (to your health).

Toasting is also central to Polish hospitality in business situations as well. Although it is not unusual to be served vodka or brandy at an office at the end of a meeting, there will often be other things to drink as well such as soda water, fruit juice, tea or coffee. There is a traditional attitude that a person refusing to drink is afraid of something, cannot maintain self-control or has something to hide.

Acceptable reasons to refuse a drink include:

- You are the driver (since it is strictly forbidden to drive if you have had any alcohol).
- You are under doctor's orders not to drink, you are on *lekarstwo* (medication) or have an allergy to grain products.
- You are pregnant.

This will not necessarily close the subject and you may be asked more questions or receive sympathetic comments but it is much more effective than a simple "No, thank you". Women generally are not expected to drink as much as men.

Whistling

Whistling in a Polish theatre or stadium is an expression of an audience's displeasure and is the same as booing or jeering in America. To express their support and satisfaction for athletes or performers, Polish spectators applaud.

Women's Day

Men should be prepared to give flowers and chocolates on Women's Day. This was a communist invention to give women one day off a year from the drudgery of cooking, cleaning, and running the house while holding a full-time job.

DISTINCTIVE FOOD & DRINK

Food

Archaeologists have substantiated that rye has been grown in Poland since the 6th Century as a major food source. Among Poles' best-liked vegetables are cabbage, peas, carrots, parsley, beets and turnips. Seasonings such as onion, dill and garlic have prevailed for centuries.

The traditional Polish menu is derived from the peasant's diet of rye bread, noodles, pierogi dumplings, borscht, fried cabbage with potations, pork chops and tripe. In the 16th and 17th Centuries, Queen Bona Sforza, wife of King Zygmunt the Old, introduced cauliflower, celery, leeks, asparagus, lettuce and artichokes into cultivation. It was not until the first half of the 18th Century, however, that potatoes appeared on the Polish table. Although Poles like meat, it was rarely present on peasant tables. The aristocrats, nobles, and city dwellers, however, ate roasts, wild game and fish.

Polish food is hearty and filling with thick soups and sauces, abundant in potatoes and dumplings, rich in meat but not in vegetables. From the garden come beets and, the favorite, cabbage both of that are used in soups, salads, stews, etc. Also harvested from local forests are mushrooms that are picked during the long season that extends into late autumn.

Pork is the main meat in the cuisine of Poland. Their pigs are raised with care and are fed on grain, milk and potatoes. Pork is used extensively for sausage making and more than 90 kinds of sausage are made in Poland. Also, canned hams are prized all over the world and account for a large part of Poland's exports. Wild game, which is plentiful, is second. There are four daily meals in Poland:

- An early breakfast;
- A light snack for second breakfast;
- A substantial lunch eaten after work; and
- A small supper before bed.

The favorite breakfast in Poland is cheese and cold cuts usually in the form of an open-face sandwich on bread or rolls. Tea with lemon is the common breakfast beverage. Some sample recipes are included in Appendix "A".

Drink

- **Coffee** – Coffee consumption in Poland is continuously rising with current consumption 2½ times higher than in 1990. Better and more expensive coffees are replacing robust brands. Most coffee consumers (73%) buy pre-ground coffee, 19% buy instant coffee and 8% purchase coffee beans. The growth of coffee consumption has resulted in stable coffee prices.
- **Tea** – Although Poles do not consider themselves a typical tea drinking nation, the annual consumption puts Poland in 3rd place in Europe, just behind Great Britain and Russia. A few years ago, Poles preferred loose-leaf tea but today their preference is reversed with tea-bag sales more than 60%. The largest suppliers are introducing new brands of tea and trying to popularize fruit flavored tea and fruit ice tea but Polish consumers continue to prefer strong teas.
- **Beer** – Ancient Poles began drinking mead and beer prior to the early 18th Century. Today, 63% of adult Poles drink beer with 5% drinking beer every day and 21% drinking beer a couple times a week. Beer is more and more the drink of choice in Poland. The consumption of beer has increased substantially although the percentage of beer consumption has not change. Although men still drink twice as much as women, beer is no longer considered a man's drink. The most popular brands are EB Special Pils, Zywiec Full Light and Lech Premium.
- **Vodka** – In the early 18th Century, rye and potatoes became the basis of a beverage that made Poland famous -- vodka. It is a favorite alcoholic drink and is served neat and well chilled. There are many varieties; some flavored with honey, lemon, rowanberry and even pepper. The most famous, Zubrowka, is flavored with the grass that wild

bison feed on. A blade of the grass can be found floating in each bottle of Zubrowka.

ARCHITECTURE

Between the 8th and 12th Centuries, the Slav population of Poland lived in lowland areas in circular, planned settlements with simple log houses. With the introduction of Christianity in 966, stone buildings appeared. After the disasters of the 11th Century and the transfer of Poland's capital to Krakow, Romanesque architectures appeared during the reconstruction of Poland. At the end of the 12th Century, the Cistercian Order played an important role in the development of religious architecture. They introduced a standard design for their monasteries and a new type of basilica. The abbeys founded by Cistercians from England used more brick and combined stone detail with conservatism of structure.

The 13th Century brought social and economic changes that were reflected in Poland's settlement structure. Developments included planned towns and villages and the building of communal buildings such as town halls and new churches. At the same time, brick castles replaced the ancient wooden civic seats. In 1320, the unification of Poland stimulated the architecture of Krakow to independent development. The builder-king, Kazimierz built over 50 castles and town halls as well as numerous churches.

During the latter half of the 15th Century, the improved economic situation and development of towns, stimulated construction. Town-dwelling craftsmen replaced journeymen and builders' guilds were established. This stimulus to building resulted in the renewal of ties with European centers of art and the assimilation of fashionable detail into small-scale architecture. Late medieval castle, town hall or town house designs developed independently and included high-pitched roofs giving way to parapets. After 1550, Krakow craftsmen developed an individual, expressive style linked with the organized production of prefabricated sculptural and architectural units at sandstone quarries.

Marble, especially black marble, was a favorite material of Italian architects who built in the early Roman Baroque style. In palace architecture, Italian forms were united with the high-pitched roofs and towers of the north. Beginning in 1630, another Baroque variation was the construction of small-scale and ephemeral architecture such as tombs and other funerary decoration. The masons' guild from Lublin introduced vault decorations in their residential buildings. This period of diverse development in Polish architecture ended because of the disasters which overtook the country from the mid-17th Century. As a result, architecture for the middle class went from the use of brick to wood for the next 100 years.

The Northern War and plagues brought construction to a standstill until after 1710. A new period of construction began around 1730, which lasted until the end of the Century. During this period Warsaw grew from a provincial, Gothic-dominated town to a great Baroque capital.

After the Napoleonic Wars, building was primarily connected with industrialization -- settlements and cloth mills in the west and heavy industry in the south. During this period, the government regulated building within a legal framework, developed towns and constructed numerous public buildings. In the third quarter of the 19th Century, Poland underwent a widespread growth in industrialization and capital investment as well as an increase in associated urbanization.

While under conditions of oppression, developments in the history of art and preservation of monuments in Poland led architects back to national historic styles. Because of this need for a national style, architects returned to the traditional wooden architecture of the lower social classes. The mistaken attribution by folklorists of the origins of this 'folk construction' to the distant past only served to enhance its value as a symbol of national identity and as a source of inspiration to architects.

After the growth of patriotism during World War I, the building of new suburbs and public facilities included nationalist themes whenever possible after Poland regained her independence. With the exception of the rehabilitation and reconstruction of the historic centers of Warsaw and other larger towns destroyed during World War II, the second half of the 20th Century was not a favorable time for architecture in Poland. From the end of World War II until the 1980s, the communist government was the sole patron of architecture and concentrated on the building of industrial plants and housing estates consisting of prefabricated residential blocks of forms.

Interior Decoration:

Although archaeological excavations have provided some information about the layout of the first timber and stone buildings and the objects or textiles that were used, few have survived Poland's turbulent history. The main source of information about the evolution of Polish interiors remains iconographic and written evidence.

Interior decoration in the Middle Ages is portrayed in iconographic. The carving on the altar at St Mary in Krakow illustrate the modest beauty of Gothic interiors - bare walls of cut building stone, windows with mullioned tracery and small, round leaded panes, decorative framing of doors and fireplaces, patterned tile floors and simple furniture. The illuminated miniatures of Baltazar Behem, a Krakow notary c. 1508, provide a detailed record of contemporary interiors of various craftsmen's workshops in Krakow.

During the first half of the 16th Century, the royal residence set the pattern for Renaissance interiors that was followed by the nobility and, in a more humble way, by gentry and rich merchants throughout Poland. The interior decoration of the Baroque period reflects the Sarmatian culture of the Polish nobility, in which Western and Oriental influences were combined with strong local elements. The coat of arms was a universal decorative motif as it stressed the chivalrous origins and virtues of the Polish nobility.

In the 17th Century, the prevailing type of house was one or two story country manor built of timber. Although the homes had no standard plan, a hallway usually separated the house into two parts - one for the family, the other for servants and utility rooms. In the family part, the largest rooms were the dining room and reception room. Although Gdansk furniture was considered a luxury, lime wood benches and tables painted or covered with rugs were more common. The walls were painted or covered in painted fabrics. From the mid-17th Century ceilings were compartmentalized and painted with battle scenes. The rooms were lit with chandeliers of Venetian glass or gilded copper.

Black marble and reddish-brown marble were among the costly materials used in royal and noble residences for patterned floors, portals and monumental fireplaces. The Marble Room at the Royal Castle in Warsaw (built 1637, destroyed 1945 and reconstructed 1984) is an exceptional example of interiors with walls covered entirely with marble and of the early application of architectural divisions and principles of symmetry in Polish interior decoration.

In the 19th Century, the interior decoration styles were influenced by western European trends and Poland's political and economic condition as a partitioned country. World War II caused irreparable damage to all kinds of interiors and boxlike rooms in overcrowded flats became the most typical interiors of the post-war period and later.

FINE ARTS

LITERATURE

One of the major Polish cultural contributions to the world has been its literature. Long ago it developed into the main form of national expression and, together with religion, stands as the twin pillars of the country's heritage. It provides one of their most cherished links with Western civilization and one of the main safeguards of their national identity.

In the 1400s Jan Dlugosz wrote the 12-volume *Historia Polonica* (Chronicle of the Famous Kingdom of Poland) in Latin. Mikolaj Rej was the first Polish writer to forsake Latin in favor of Polish and is recognized as the Father of Polish literature. The literature of the 18th Century showed the influence of contact with Western Europe. In 1765 the National Theater in Warsaw was established which encouraged a number of dramatists. Aleksander Fredro (the "Polish Moliere") wrote popular comedies.

At the end of the 19th Century the novel "*Quo Vadis*?" by Henryk Sienkiewicz became internationally famous and he won the Nobel Prize for literature in 1905. Eliza Orzeszkowa wrote on feminist, peasant and Jewish topics and many of her novels were translated into English. Wladyslaw Reymont, a notable author of the early 20th Century achieved worldwide fame with his 4-volumne novel "*The Peasants*" and won a Nobel Prize in literature.

Political controls were imposed on writers during the Communist era after World War II. Some writers wrote pessimistic novels about Polish life while others went into exile rather than continue writing in Poland. Despite these restrictions, Jerzy Andrzejewski achieved recognition for his novel "*Ashes and Diamonds*". The liberalization that began in 1989 has seen the virtual end of censorship.

Women Writers

A complete overview of Polish women's literary output would include almost ten centuries of Polish literature. The first lady of Polish women's literary culture was Duchess Gertruda (1020-1108). In the exquisitely illustrated Psalter prepared for Archbishop Egbert of Treviso at the end of the 10th Century, she wrote the texts of over one hundred prayers in the spaces between the psalms and on bound-in pages.

The first noted woman writer of the 19th Century was Izabela Flemming Czartoryska (1746-1835). After Poland's loss of independence in 1795, she founded a center of sentimental patriotic culture. Her most interesting work was *Pielgrzym w Dobromilu* (Pilgrim in Dobromil) published in 1816. This booklet is a multi-layered work presenting the Sudetenland landscape, the legends associated with the Piast period of Silesian history and the traveler's own sentiments. Her output is a notable witness to the rise of patriotic sentimentality.

A celebrated figure on the Polish literary scene, Zofia Nalkowski (1884-1954) was intrigued by the world of women and their relations to reality, historical turmoil and social conditioning. Her first book was *Kobiety* (Women) published in 1906. The diary that she began keeping in 1899 was her greatest work especially the part dealing with the German occupation (1939-1945).

Polish National Library

The traditions of the Polish National Library go back to the beginning of the 18th Century. Andrzej Stanislaw Zaluski and Jozef Andrzej Zaluski were the founders of Poland's first large public/national library which, after their death, became known as the Zaluski Library of the Republic. The tragic fate of its collection became a symbol of the losses of Polish culture. However, the vision of a national book repository was kept alive by successive generations of Poles and became a reality in 1928, after Poland regained its independence, when the National Library of Warsaw was created.

The National Library is both the central library of the State and one of the most important cultural institutions in the country. Responsible for the safekeeping, maintenance and popularity of Polish heritage, the National Library shares a sense of obligation for the cultural continuity and national memory of the Polish nation.

ART

Painting:

The most impressive surviving example of Polish painting before the 16th Century is the early medieval wall paintings. One of the finest examples of wall painting from the first half of the 15th Century is the *Crucifixion* (1420) in the Church of the Holy Cross in Krakow.

Polish painters did not address the problems of realism until the 1460s. During this time, painters used tempura on panel painting, usually on a lime board. By the 1530s, painters in artistic centers used oil with tempera. During the first half of the 16th Century, artists applied gold leaf ornamentation and tracery overlays to gold backgrounds by carving deep floral and geometric patterns. During the Renaissance, Polish painters accurately represented the faces of models rather than the landscape. In general during the 16th Century Polish painters used prints as models far more frequently than in the 15th Century.

In 1621 the Counter-Reformation decrees of the Council of Bishops at Krakow virtually restricted artists to producing idealizing pictures featuring the Virgin and hagiographic themes. The stability of the period following the Swedish Wars together with the patronage of King Jan Sobrieski III led to an increase in painting commissions. Jerzey Eleuter Szymonowicz-Siemiginowski (1660-1711) received a scholarship from the

King to study in Rome and became well known for his frescoes and ceiling paintings. His paintings also popularized previously neglected mythological and allegorical subjects.

A characteristic feature of Polish Baroque painting is portraits that reflect Sarmatism, the ideology of Poland's nobility of the time, characterized by self-glorification, Catholicism, traditionalism and the cult of chivalrous rural life. This type of portrait, which endured until the 19th Century, expressively defines the model in linear, flat, decoratively colored forms, accurately depicting the splendid costume and facial lines. "Coffin" portraits painted on metal plates and shown at funerals in the 17th and 18th Centuries were following these principles.

The social and political decline of the 18th Century limited painting commissions to the Royal Court, several magnates and the Church. After the end of the Northern War in 1721, church mural painting flourished. The patronage of King Stanislaw August Poniatowski affected painting more than any other artistic discipline due to the painting center established at The Royal Castle. There was also the Malarnia (painting studio), a predecessor of the art school, which resulted in the prevalence in Polish painting during the 18th and 19th Century of the modern portrait in courtly, realistic or romantic versions.

The development of artistic life was restricted following Poland's loss of independence in 1795. An unusual exception was Piotr Michalowski who was fascinated by the Napoleonic epic adventure that liberated Poland, which he expressed in his pictures of cavalry charges or painters of riders. His portraits of peasants are equally impressive. Although Polish painters did indulge in the Romantic themes of the struggle against a superior force and the tragedy of those defeated by evil, they expressed them in artistically traditional forms. Several generations of painters portrayed themes from ancient and modern history, enriching the Romantic iconography of the oppressed nation in conflict with the enemy. Stimulated by the demand for cheap representations of national, historic and genre subjects, lithographic establishments began to flourish in the 1820s.

The democratic ideas generated by the revolution of 1848 prompted artists to depart from history painting to other patriotic tasks, such as the portrayal and recording of Polish life, the countryside and the vitality of nature. The 1863 insurrection shaped the attitudes of the realists until they felt it was their patriotic task to represent actual events in modern history.

Symbolism was a vibrant tendency in Polish painting and graphic arts at the end of the 19th Century and the beginning of the 20th Century. Stanislaw Wyspialski became a reformer of decorative arts and book design and created mystic visions of the past, nostalgic landscapes and lyrical portraits. In his stained glass window designs and landscapes he often distorted the natural shapes and colors to intensify the expression of the subject.

In the 1950s, the Polish school of poster art emerged that provided the only permitted medium for metaphor, the distortion of form and the free use of color. During the next thirty years, Polish artists progressively emerged from the isolation that had been forced upon them and experienced the same problems as their fellow artists in Western Europe.

Sculpture:

Stone idols from the 8th and 9th Centuries include carved images of women or men with drinking horns, swords, sticks or scepters and are found as a relief on the front of a stone. Monumental stone carving began in Poland in the 10th Century. The largest collection is in Sobotka in Silesia. These carvings include human figures, animal figures and more abstract form - all of which have a diagonal solar sign.

In the 11th Century, Romanesque forms of sculpture appeared in architectural decoration in the form of animal and floral motifs mostly of a symbolic character. The bronze doors of the cathedral in Gniezno, built in 1180, are one of the most notable Romanesque artifacts. It is signed *Petrus Luitinius* and portrays the *Life of St Adalbert*. The border surrounding the narrative scenes provides commentary in the form of mythological and astrological symbols and allegories. The door harmoniously combines tradition values with realistic observation.

From 1300-1370, Silesia focused their local artistic centers on the development of stone architectural sculpture with rich iconographic programs and also some political content. Traditonal courtly idealism dominates tomb sculpture at the beginning of the 14th Century. The sides of the tomb of Prince Henry IV are decorated with weepers and served as a model for the kings' tombs in Wawel Cathedral. The morning procession depicted on the sides of the tomb was usually of political significance.

The burial vault was the main subject of Renaissance sculpture. It served the contemporary need for reaffirmation of the glory of the subject and his family and revealed the aspirations of the nobility and gentry who were beginning to gain political status. In the 1540s, a unique Polish form of tomb was developed: the two-tiered monument with two figures - a father and son, two brothers, or a husband and wife -- were placed in niches one above the other. In the second half of the 16th Century, the portrait bust developed and became popular especially among the nobility and intelligentsia.

The extensive production of wooden altars was one consequence of the Counter-Reformation in the beginning of the 17th Century. At this time a form of tomb with a kneeling subject in a gesture of perpetual adoration became popular. Baroque sculpture in Poland began to dominate in ornamentation and in figure sculpture in the middle of the 17th Century. After a period of stagnation caused by war, the sculpture of the last quarter of the 17th Century showed a marked unity. The most popular form of tombstone in Poland in the 18th Century was the epitaph in the form of a bas-relief, or painting, of the deceased set in an architectural, carved frame with mythical figures.

The social and political situation of Poland after the Partitions resulted in a decline in the demand for sculpture and limited its subject matter to religious themes, some tombs and a few portrait busts. Lyricism and the impressionistic breaking down of forms and the exploitation of texture identified Polish modernism in sculpture. Figurative art with an emotional approach to reality and a tendency towards monumentalism defined the parameters of Polish sculpture after World War II. The most interesting architectural-sculptural compositions are the monuments commemorating the *Victims of Treblinka* (1964) and the monument to the *Silesian Insurgents* (1967). In the early 1980s, the political situation brought about the creation of monuments and the manifestation of patriotic and religious themes in church art.

Gold & Silver:

During the early Christian and migration periods, a wide variety of gold and silver ornaments, particularly kaptorgas (small caskets for relics, talismans or perfume) were produced. From the 11th to 13th Centuries, silver chalices were made in the region of Gniezno. The Polish Coronation Swords (1240) is one of the finest pieces from this period.

The turn of the 16th Century brought about a second period of prominence for Polish gold and silver work. A distinct form of Polish gold and silver work distinguished by lavish but restrained ornament appeared during this period. Provincial silversmiths also produced fine silver work including the ostulatory (reliquary in the form of a glass pipe in which there is a bone of a saint) and the sword of King Zygmunt I (with engravings on the hilt and scabbard).

During the 1st half of the 17th Century, the development of gold and silver work was stimulated by the period of prosperity under the reign of King Zygmunt III, a connoisseur and amateur goldsmith. Krakow and Gdansk continued to be the main centers of production and local features began to emerge especially shell-like motifs that remained popular until the 1680s. Goldsmiths in Gdansk created mainly non-religious works including nautilus and windmill cups, tankards and spoons with inscriptions.

During the latter half of the 17th Century and the beginning of the 17th Century, gold and silversmiths in Gdansk produced both ecclesiastical and non-religious items -- dishes, cups, table services and high quality tankards. Because medal engraving was also practiced in Gdansk, products decorated with coins and medals became a local specialty. Products decorated with enamels, especially those from Krakow, and cameos set with coral were also popular in Poland at this time.

During the early 18th Century, there was a tendency to decorate interiors, especially those of churches, with silver ornaments. Jews were admitted to metalwork guilds in the late 18th Century and, using filigree techniques, created exquisite small pieces that can be seen in museums in Poland and elsewhere. Adam and Ludwik Norblin developed the production of plated silver on an industrial scale in the first half of the 19th Century and large-scale production of silverware continued in the late 19th Century and 20th Century.

Metalwork:

Archaeological discoveries of Bronze dishes and ornaments as well as iron weapons prove that they were imported via trade routes into Poland during prehistoric times. During the early Christian period, copper and silver crosses and coins were produced. The door to a side chapel of Gniezno Cathedral is the most outstanding example of Polish metalwork from the 12th Century.

In the 15th and 16th Centuries, founders specialized in casting of bells, candlesticks and decorated baptismal cups. During this period, Lublin became a major center of bronze production, Gdansk became the leading center of gunsmithing and pewter wares particularly tankards were produced in Gdansk and Krakow. Large-scale production of clocks began in Poland during the 16th Century.

Two types of armor were produced in Poland. Armor for the cavalry (husaria) had been made since the 16th Century and in the 17th Century, wings were fitted to the back-plates. While the armor making craft declined in Western Europe in the second half of the 17th Century, an original type of karacena (scale armor consisting of steel scales knitted to leather with brass ornaments) was developed in Poland.

Many 17th Century metal coffins survived. Located in Wawel Cathedral in Krakow are the coffin of King Zygmunt III which is decorated with skillfully designed battle scenes and the coffins of King Wladyslaw IV and Queen Cecilia which are decorated with sheet-copper panels representing political events, coats of arms and ornaments. The production of metalwork declined during the 18th Century and by the end of the Century, the newly established steelworks produced cast-iron objects.

Textiles:

Textiles were in demand in Poland for both practical and purely decorative use by the Middle Ages. The art of weaving was already well developed by the 10th Century and able to satisfy the demand from castles, churches and monasteries for fine clothing and decorative textiles. Local wool was woven into striped or checked fabrics and, when finely spun, into light cloth dyed red with madder.

The importation of wool from the Low Countries and silk from Byzantium greatly influenced the development of Polish textiles and culture in general. Italian silks were introduced in the 14th Century to make religious vestments and robes for the nobility. Although no tapestries or rugs have survived from in the 16th Century, it is probable that they were produced in local manufactories located on magnates' estates. The oldest preserved tapestry date from the 17th Century and is characterized by a severity of style, linear treatment of design and monotonous sandy-brown colors with occasional patches of blue and pink.

Knotted rugs woven in black and white wool were made locally as early as the 15th Century. Pile carpets with patterns based on Ushak medallion carpets were woven in Poland during the 17th Century. Polish-made carpets of the 18th Century featured homely motifs as baskets of flowers or fruit, birds, and cornucopias and executed in bright, well-harmonized colors. There was also a flourishing production of kilims made of wool, woven in broad stripes with geometric motifs and floral designs which served as wall hangings, bedspreads and bench and table covers.

From the early 15th Century, embroidery worked with freshwater pearls was used extensively on garments and furnishings of the church and nobility and was a technique reserved for men embroiders. Linen and silk embroideries were usually the work of women, both professionals and amateurs. The elaborate cross orphrey given to Wawel Cathedral is decorated with scenes from the life of St Stanislas, patron saint of Poland. An example of early-embroidered church investments, it was worked in silk and metal thread in high relief. This form of raised embroidery survived in Poland well into the 17th Century.

In the 15th Century the soft turban and waist sashes became an inseparable element of the national costume. The soft, pliable sashes were produced locally and were some of the finest textiles produced in Poland. They were made of thick colorful silk thread, often in red or black, and decorated with geometric patterns or motifs as well as bands of gold thread woven in at either end. The first workshops in Poland were established in the 1740s on the estates of magnate families and were equipped with mangles or rolling presses, which gave luster to the silk woven with gold or silver thread. A typical Polish sash is several meters long and up to 450mm wide. It has a narrow ornamental border pattern with the ends decorated with more elaborate design and a fringe.

Although most of the magnate manufactories ceased to operate after the partitions of Poland at the end of the 18th Century, the production of sashes continued far into following Century. The system of production changed in the 19th Century as factories organized for large-scale production and high profits for their owners gradually replaced local manufactories. The Society of Polish Applied Art (1901) and the Society of Krakow Workshops (1913) attempted to revive local factories to weave kilims and tapestries and to combat the degeneration of mass production. Textile artists investigated vegetable dyes and the inherent qualities of natural materials as well as exploring ways of adapting designs to the technical possibilities and limitations of the loom. Much of this experimentation was focused on the revived art of kilim weaving.

Although World War I halted the development of these societies, it did not destroy their philosophy, which was to provide a conceptual foundation for a Polish school of textile artists. In the 1920s folk-weaving techniques were revived. During the Nazi Occupation in World War II, weaving was prohibited and the activities of art schools were curtailed. Polish artists during the 1950s began to enrich the textures of their fabrics by using materials of different thickness and by inventing new weaves and contributed to the development of FIBRE ART.

MUSIC

Poland cherishes its musical heritage, enriched and sustained over the past thousand years. Although the history of Polish music began with the acceptance of Christianity by the Slavic nation in the 10th Century, Poland has an oral music tradition of pre-Christian Slavs that survives in the treasury of Polish folklore that has inspired numerous composers. Even though travelers in Poland wrote about musicians playing pipes and primitive fiddles, nothing is known about professional music makers and players in Poland until the mid-13th Century. Polish music history began with the liturgical chants of the Latin Church that reached Poland from Rome.

The talents of Polish composers reveal Poland's heritage of religious music while being enriched from the lively cultural contacts between Poland and other European countries. In 1422, the first professional orchestra was formed at the royal court in Wawel castle and the Rorantian Band was established at Wawel Cathedral in 1543. Various forms of worldly and religious music thrived during the 16th and 17th centuries -- the Golden Age of Polish culture. Polish art music appeared and flourished with its form of choral music, dances for the court and various types of songs for one and many voices. The country's musical life suffered and regressed during the 18th Century due to wars and internal instability which resulted in the partition of the country between Austria, Russia and Prussia.

The greatest Polish composer, Fryderyk Chopin became a national symbol of resistance and a source of cultural identity during the 19th Century. His works became part of the standard repertoire of all pianists and provided models for successive generations of musicians. Polish composers of the 19th Century included those who created music for home and homeland

and those who wrote music of great technical difficulty and brilliance.

Between 1918 and 1939, Polish music prospered due to close cultural contacts with other European countries as well as with North America. During 1949 to 1956 the official ideology of the state stylistic requirements in music meant folk-orient, simple, neo-romantic with more advanced creative efforts banned. From 1956 when the first Warsaw Autumn International Festival of Contemporary Music took place until the fall of the socialist government in 1989 composers were free to do as they pleased as long as the subject matter and titles of their works avoided political controversy. The cultural policies of the communist government left a universal system of musical education and the wide publication of information on composers, performers and their achievements.

Poland holds a leading position in world music, and has been the birthplace of many of the outstanding composers of the second half of the 20th Century including Lutosawski, Górecki, and Kilar. Today, music is thriving in Poland and composers have the status of celebrities. There are innumerable festivals, concerts and competitions throughout the year in both large cities and small towns and villages. All branches of classical music are well represented in Poland and several orchestras and choirs appear regularly on the international circuit. Polish jazz has earned a reputation for experimentation and excellence.

Opera

Royal Prince Wladyslaw IV Waza brought opera to Poland in 1628, only 20 years after it first appeared in Florence. When he became King in 1632, he had a theatre built in his castle where regular opera performances were produced.

Starting in 1774, opera, theatre and ballet performances were held in the Radziweill Mansion (today the Polish "White

House"). In 1778, a company of Polish artists produced the first Polish opera "Poverty Made Happy". This was the beginning of Polish National Opera. For over 200 years, Teatr Wielki (the Grand Theatre), today called the Grand Theatre - National Opera, has been Poland's grandest opera and ballet institution and produces works by Polish composers as well as world classics.

Wroclaw's opera traditions began in the mid-18th Century. The municipal theater was created in 1797 and the most important operas of Mozart were staged there. The new large classicist building was opened in 1841 and had a very modern stage at the time. The Wroclaw Opera Theater operated regularly until 1944 and was rated among the top opera houses.

Stanislaw Moniuszko (1818-1872) wrote *Halka*, the first national opera that was a triumphal success on the stage of the Wielki Theatre in Warsaw in 1858. His creative adaptation of folk melodies lifted Polish morale during the period of partition. He composed over 300 songs and was the author of vaudevilles and operettas. His best opera completed in 1864, *Straszny Dwor* (The Haunted Manor) combines national implications and comic features. The real pearls of his talents are two one-act operas:

- *Verbum Nobile* which derided in a friendly manner the customs and habits of the gentry.
- *The Raftsman* which was a middle-class idyll situated on the Vistula river bank.

The post-World War II history of the Wroclaw Opera began in 1945. Since then around 260 premiers have taken place and it was rated among the best opera theaters in Poland. It takes special interest in a Polish repertoire and many world premieres of operas and ballets by Polish composers took place on its stage.

National Anthem

Bogurodzica, a religious hymn served Poland as it's earliest "state anthem" and was called the song of the homeland. During the partitions of the 19th Century, *Bojurodzica* was usually printed in patriotic-religious hymnals as the first, most ancient and revered song. Composer Andrzej Panufnik was so impressed with its solemn grandeur that in 1963 he wrote a symphony based on and dedicated to *Bogurodzica* entitled *Sinfonia Sacra*. To this day, it is sung in Polish churches.

Another religious song that became a patriotic anthem associated with the historical traditions of Poland was *Graude Mater Poloniae*. Because of the fact that this anthem was distributed with its text in Latin prevented it from becoming a true symbol of the country.

In 1774 the patriotic poet-bishop Ignacy Krasicki wrote a hymn "Holy Love of the Beloved Homeland" which is sung to this day at the military academy Szkola Rycerska. It is fittingly so, since the hymn calls for ultimate sacrifices for the sake of the country including the offerings of poverty and death.

The current Polish national anthem *Dabrowski's Mazurka*, was written in 1797 when Poles gathered to fight for their country's independence. The first line of the text states that "Poland is not dead, as long as we live" and Poles sang these words throughout the 19th Century while struggling for their country's reemergence. The *Dabrowski's Mazurka* was declared the official anthem of the country in 1926 after Jozef Pilsudski took control of the country. After World War II, *Dabrowski's Mazurka* continued to serve as the official anthem of Poland, reminding Poles of the duty to be active for the sake of their homeland.

The Solidarity movement chose another song for its unofficial hymn *Zeby Polska byla Polska* (Let Poland be Poland) written by Jan Pietrzak in 1976. The song meditates on the past wars fought by generations of Poles to Make Poland, Poland.

DANCE

Polish folk music and dance is among the most distinctive in Europe. Chopin popularized the mazurka and polonaise of central Poland. The polonaise is more stately and ceremonial and the mazurka is livelier. However, both Poland and the Czech Republic claim the polka.

Poland has five national dances and they are:

1. Polonaise - By the end of the 16th Century, the Polish folk dances that are ancestors of the polonaise were adopted by the lower ranks of the nobility. The polonaise is a stately Polish processional dance that has been used on formal occasions and during public ceremonies. The greatest composer of polonaises in classical music was Fryderyk Chopin whose works made this dance the musical symbol of Poland and Polishness. The political symbolism of this dance and its association with national causes made it the primary national dance of Poland.
2. Oberek - It originated in the villages of central Poland and is danced by couples to instrumental music in triple time. The oberek is a national dance not only because it is common all over Poland but because it is also danced by all the social classes. Different regions still retain their local style, variations and their specific music. It has also become a recreational dance growing in popularity and providing competition to the Polish American polka. The oberek does not occur among the titles of Polish dances composed in 19th Century America.
3. Mazur - The dance was known as early as the 16th Century and originated in the plains around Warsaw. During the 17th Century the dance spread over Poland and into neighboring countries. Following Poland's loss of independence, the dance became fashionable in

higher social circles in Western Europe and served as a sign of solidarity with the oppressed Polish nation. The folk dance is impromptu in character and as an "exhibition dance" is regarded as the most exciting and intricate of the five national dances of Poland. In the United States, the mazurka appeared in the 1840s and is associated with Poland and its celebrated loss of independence.

4. Kujawiak - The dance originated from the region in central Poland. It was originally danced with a calm dignity and simplicity and this style was passed on from generation to generation. The nobility admired the beauty of the kujawiak, polished it and incorporated it at elegant parties and fancy balls. Thus, the kujawiak exists in two forms: as a regional folk dance including many varieties nd as the unified national dance.
5. Krakowiak - Krakowiak is a Polish dance from the region of Krakow that dates back to the 16th and 17th Centuries. Originally, it was connected with courtship rituals. In the mid-19th Century, the krakowiak became a popular ballroom dance in Austria and France and was regarded as the national dance of Poland. The krakowiak is the exhibition dance of choice of the Polish-American dance companies.

Another interesting Polish folk dance is the zbojnicki, which is an energetic men's dance from the rocky foothills of the Tatra Mountains. The name is an adjective created from the noun *zbojnik* meaning a brigand or robber. Between the 12th and 18th Century, the most famous leader of the robbers' bands that thrived in the Tatra Mountains was Juraj Janosik. Acts from his life were mixed with folk legends and stories about the "good robber". According to the legend, he had a generous heart and, like Robin Hood, robbed the rich but protected and shared his wealth with the poor.

Poland's first professional contemporary dance company, Silesian Dance Theatre, was established in 1991 and has developed a new dance form and style based on the rich cultural traditions of Poland. The elements that shape the movement and motion are drawn from the exploration of the typical factors of Polish folklore such as tempo rubato, impulses from unusual music structures plus many other elements. Each of the regions has some specific features that are distinctive to folk tradition in that area. For example, the music, dance and singing from Podhale show diverse and very complex rhythms while open throat singing reveals power and invincibility. Meanwhile, the Kurpie brings a lot or original forms of music that has remained unchanged for centuries -- not only tempo rubato but also irregular structure of musical form.

THEATRE

The Polish National theatre dates from the end of the 18th Century and was founded by Wojciech Boguslawski - an actor, director and playwright. Political conditions during the period of partition (1772-1914) inhibited theatrical development although Krakow, in Austrian Galicia, became a center of lively theatre at the turn of the Century. During the Interwar Period, Juliusz Osterwa in Warsaw and Leon Schiller in Lodz launched the experimental tradition. During the 1960s the Laboratory Theatre of Jerzy Grotowski (whose theories and methods emphasizing the nonverbal aspects of theatre had a broad impact, especially in the United States) gained international recognition.

The Ludwik Solski Academy for the Dramatic Arts in Krakow began in 1946. Initially the college offered a three-year training program for prospective actors. Between 1954-1964 and after 1972, the academy provided a course for dramatic artists specializing in the puppetry and the Puppet Theater. The third course of study is theater directing. The academy's history was created and influenced over the years by outstanding teachers and trainers for the actors' and directors' professions as well as by famous theoreticians of the dramatic arts. Since 1946, over a thousand students have graduated from the academy and work on the theater stages in Poland and in many other European countries.

MOVIES

Although Polish cinema originated in 1909, it was not until the late 1950s that its products began attracting international attention. Undoubtedly, the leader is Andrzej Wajda, whose films and theatre productions set precedents for independence and quality in exploring the conflicts in Polish society. Historical epics have been very popular.

In the business of movie making, any Academy Award nomination is in itself a great recognition. In 1963, *Knife in the Water*, became the first Polish-made film to be nominated for an Oscar. It was written by Roman Polanski and had a fantastic musical score by Krzysztof Komeda. Jerzy Kawalerowicz's *Pharaoh*, an epic tale of politics in the times of ancient Egypt, based on the classic novel by Boleslaw Prus was nominated in 1966. In 1975 the next Polish nomination was *The Deluge*, a film adaptation of the popular historical novel by Nobel laureate Henryk Sienkiewicz. This film was the most costly production in the history of Polish cinema.

Polish cinema has survived the most difficult period of economic transition and today 25-30 feature films are made in Poland each year. Eastern-Central Europe's only national film festival continues to be held in Gdynia.

MUSEUMS - Home of Historic Memories

Because of colossal wartime destruction and the long periods of being subject to official controls, the need to preserve and cherish the records and artifacts of the past is felt with special urgency. Archives and museums of art, ethnography, archaeology and natural history can be found in many Polish cities. There are more than 30 museums in Poland today and examples of these museums include:

1. **The National Ossolinski Institute** was founded in 1817 by Count Jozef Maksymilian Ossolinski when he gave the Polish nation his valuable collection of books, manuscripts and museum pieces. The Institute consists of a Library, Publishing House and the Lubomirski Museum. Revenues from the founder's landed estates funded its upkeep and its mission was to save the cultural heritage of the nation. The post of literary curator, the Institute's highest authority, became a hereditary function of the Lubomirski family. During the years of partition, the Institute published *Monumenta Poloniae Historica*, *Dictionary of the Polish Language* and numerous other books in the fields of history, history of Poland, literary sciences and history of culture. During World War II, many private collections were stored at the Institute for safety. For almost 200 years, the Institute's collection of 19th and 20th Century books and periodicals, old books, manuscripts, prints, maps and numismatic objects has grown. The Ossolinski Institute is one of the largest scientific libraries in Poland and its focus on Polish and Slavonic history, culture and literature is unique not only in Poland but also worldwide.
2. **The Tatra Museum in Zakopane** originated in the second half of the 19th Century and is one of the oldest regional museums in Poland. Its beginnings occurred when the Tatra Mountains and the region of Podhale played a prominent role in Polish culture. The Tatra

Museum is multi-departmental and includes three collections of natural science, ethnography and art. The 'spatial museum', a display of architectural relics in natural settings, resulted from the combination of basic museum activities and restoration endeavors. Among its educational activities, the Museum popularizes the region through lectures, talks, films and excursions. It is also the publisher of *Rocznik Polhalanski* (Podhale Yearly) as well as scholarly sessions and guidebooks.

3. **National Museum in Warsaw**, formerly the Museum of Fine Arts created in 1862 by Law on Public Education in the Kingdom of Poland, was renamed in 1916. Credit for the rank of the National Museum, preserved in spite of the dramatic war years and the vicissitudes of recent history, goes to its first two directors. Today, the collection includes 780,000 items displayed in permanent galleries. The museum's collection contains the largest Polish scholarly library of art catalogues, art history books, books on cultures from all over the world as well as old maps and prints.
4. **Wawel Royal Castle (Museum)** established in 1930 is one of the most majestic monuments of Renaissance architecture in Europe and was the residence of Polish rules from mid-11th to the early 17th Century. From 1795-1905, the castle was converted into Austrian army barracks. During World War II, Wawel was the seat of the German occupation authorities. A collection of Flemish tapestries, that once belonged to King Augustus (1548-1572), were returned to Wawel in 1961 to be hung in the royal chambers. In 1992, large-scale repairs and conservation work was done in the Royal Castle and the nearby Cathedral.
5. **Historical Museum of Warsaw** (Old Warsaw Museum) was founded in 1936 and was completely destroyed during fighting in the Warsaw Uprising in 1944. After World War II, the Museum of Warsaw was created and established in 11 tenement houses

reconstructed according to old plans and drawings. It has preserved the beauty of the Renaissance facades, vaults, staircases and interiors. Today's exhibition called "Seven Centuries of Warsaw" presents history of the town from its foundation, its development through the centuries, its extermination in 1944 and then its return to life. Clothes, furniture, utensils, gold crafts and reconstructed interiors of houses fully illustrate life in Warsaw in the old times. Much attention is paid to Warsaw's part in the history of Poland and the heroic struggle of Warsaw's people.

6. **Tarnow Diocesan Museum**, founded in 1888, is the oldest diocesan museum in Poland. It is currently located near the Cathedral Basilica in tenement houses dating back to the XVI Century. The major part of the collection are the monuments of guild art which are very important in recognizing the level and history of Polish and Medieval culture. The second part includes church fabrics (vestments, covers, etc.) from the Middle Ages until the XIX Century. There is also folk-art including folk paintings on glass, which were collected not only in Poland but also throughout Europe and other continents as well.
7. **Krakow Aviation Museum**, formed in 1964, is located on the grounds of the Rakowice-Czyzny airfield, one of the oldest military airfields in Europe. The museum preserves and exhibits aircraft, engines and other items of importance to the world's aviation heritage and forms a premier European collection. At the end of the 1800s, the airfield was home to a balloon detachment of Garrison Artillery 2nd Regiment of Krakow Fortress. After World War I, the airfield became one of the staging points for airmail services between Vienna and Kiev/Odessa, the first such scheduled service in Europe. In 1918, the authorities took command of the airfield, which made the airfield the first airfield of Poland, and the first Polish aviation unit, known as the

1st Combat Squadron, was formed there. During 1920, the 1st Lower School for Pilots, which trained airmen for the rapidly expanding Polish Air Force, was located on the airfield. The aviation repair workshop even started some limited manufacture of new aircraft. By the late 1920s, the airfield was the second largest Polish Air Force base.

8. **Lubuskie Military Museum** was founded in 1978 and is dedicated to educating people about Poland's military history. Its primary goal is to build a permanent collection of military aircraft and heavy military vehicles. Exhibits at the museum include: Polish Army 1914-1945, Polish Army since 1945, Old XVI-XIX Century weapons, Aircraft and Helicopters and Heavy Military Equipment.
9. **Auschwitz-Birkenau State Museum** was created by an act of the Sejm in 1947 and includes the grounds of two parts of the Auschwitz I and Auschwitz II-Birkenau concentration camps. On the museum grounds stand several hundred camp buildings and ruins, including the ruins of the gas chambers and crematoria at Birkenau. The first exhibition in 1947 was opened in several camp blocks at the Auschwitz I site, which presented the history of extermination, and the conditions in which the prisoners lived. After 1960, "national exhibitions" were created at some of the camp blocks that mainly portray the fate of the citizens of those countries who were deported by the Nazis to Auschwitz concentration camp. Since the site of the Birkenau camp is essentially a cemetery, no exhibits have been situated there with the exception of the International Monument to the Victims of the Camp, unveiled in 1967. The site of Auschwitz-Birkenau concentration camp was entered on the UNESCO international list of world heritage sites in 1979.
10. **Cracow Salt Works Museum**, one of the most important mining museums in Europe, is located in the original

underground excavation of the 700-year old salt mine in Wieliczka, which was placed on the first UNESCO World Cultural and National Heritage list in 1978. The museum was created in 1981 by the Minister of Mining Industry and contains objects from various scientific disciplines connected with the Cracow Salt Works and the history of the mining cities of Wieliczka and Bochnia. At present the museum has 30,000 exhibits contained in three separate departments:

- Department of Coal Mining History & Engineering - includes mining tools and equipment, miner's lamps, unique 18th Century water pump, flags, minerals, plant moulds and 4,000 technical drawings from 18th & 19th centuries.
- Department of Mechanical Processing of Coal - includes devices used for enrichment, briquetting, coking and chemical processing of coal.
- Department of Miner's Culture - includes objects connected with the tradition of miner's profession, customs, beliefs, manners, cultural activity and everyday life. It contains miner's uniforms from 19th & 20th centuries, miner's insignia, hammers, swords, pickaxes, musical instruments from miner's bands and beer mugs.

11. **Central Museum of Textiles**, originally Department of Textiles at Muzeum Sztuki in Lodz, was established in 1975. "The White Factory" is the seat of the museum and was built by Ludwik Geyer in 1835-1839. It is one of the most beautiful examples of industrial architecture and was the first "multi-departmental" mill in Lodz that housed the first Polish mechanical cotton spinning and weaving room with the first Polish steam machine. The museum is interested in all aspects of textile production and, since 1981, has been the sole organizer of the International Triennial of Tapestry in Lodz. Currently, the Lodz Triennial is the world's oldest and largest international exhibition promoting contemporary tapestry.

The museum includes the following departments:

- Department of Tapestry is divided into three separate collections: antique tapestries that include textiles from the 5th Century to the first half of the 20th Century that illustrates the variety of types, techniques and styles of West European, oriental and Polish weaving. Its contemporary textiles that reflects the most recent history of Polish tapestry since 1945 and documentation which includes several thousand designs and cartoons of rugs and wall hangings.
- Department of Industrial Textiles contains the largest collection in Poland and one of the most important world collections of industrial textiles which date back to the beginnings of the 19th Century. The items in the collection document the production and design achievements of all outstanding textile mills in the Lodz region.
- Department of Fashion collects garment pieces and accessories from the beginning of the 19th Century to the present and currently has a varied and large collection of garments from 1900-1939. The department is also engaged in collecting contemporary garment design, ranging from "the street fashion" to collections produced on commission for leading Polish fashion houses and unique creations produced by artists. Since 1986, the department has collected contemporary art jewelry.
- Department of the History of Textile Techniques has a collection of textile tools, machines and appliances linked with the past decades of textile production in the Lodz area especially objects illustrating cotton processing techniques in the 19th & 20th Century. Also, the department has various types of knitting machines, numerous sewing machines and rare appliances for textile metrology.
- Department of the History of Textiles Production has a collection of items and is engaged in scientific work

concerning the history of the development of the textile industry in Poland - both in guilds and mills. Documentation includes government regulations which date back to the beginnings of the textile industry in the Polish Kingdom, mill plans, company reports, production books, factory bills and guild certificates. Especially interesting is the large collection of shares and obligations of Polish textile companies, guild and factory flags, medals and company prints.

SPORTS

Archery

When the first international women's archery competition was held in 1931, Janina Spychajowa-Kurkowska of Poland won the women's singles title. She won six more world titles in archery, more than any other man or woman in history.

Basketball

The popularity of basketball is growing among Polish youths and gaining on soccer. There are around 100,000 people playing basketball and as many as 800 amateur sports clubs. Poland's 7th place in the 1997 European Championship and the success of the Polish players worldwide are helping to facilitate further interest in this relatively peaceful sport.

In 1998, Adam Wojcik of the Zepter Slask Wroclaw team that won the 7th game of the Polish basketball league final and Dominik Tomczyk of the Pekaaes Pruszkow team were awarded the most valuable player title for their performance in the finals. It was the first time the MVP award was given in Poland.

Boxing

Professional boxing is well on the way to becoming one of the most popular and profitable sports in Poland. It is very likely that professional boxing will continue to gain popularity and recognition in Poland especially since Polish soccer is on the decline. The three big names associated with Polish boxing are Andrzej Golota, Przemyslaw Saleta and Dariusz Michalczewski.

- Andrzej Golota is Poland's most famous boxer who also earns the biggest purses. He is one of the world's best paid heavyweight boxers without a champion's title. Many people believe he could make it to the top except for his lack of control over his emotions.
- Przemyslaw Saleta had several years of extraordinary

success. In 1999 he won the IBO intercontinental title but later lost a defending match with Fred Westgeest of Holland. Saleta, who already works as a sports commentator, likes his future with the media and would like to take up other types of journalism such as writing about extreme sports.

- Dariusz Michalczewski was born in Gdansk and won Poland's championship title in 1987. He is the only Polish boxer with a world title. His popularity is limited to Germany, Poland and possibly Britain.

Canoeing

The Polish Canoe Federation was founded in 1928 in Warsaw and was officially accepted as the beginning of organized sport and touring canoeing in Poland. The greatest success in pre-war canoeing was the silver medal of Czeslaw Sobierag, won during the World Championships in Vaxholm, Sweden.

Canoeing is one of the most popular sports in Poland and has had many successes. Polish canoeists have won 11 Olympic medals, 92 World Championship and 19 European Championship medals.

Cycling

Cycling is gaining popularity in Poland for both ecological and health reasons. The demand for mountain bikes may have been what saved the largest bicycle factory in Poland from bankruptcy. In addition, the market for accessories, including standard helmets and water bottles to cycling clothes and shoes, is also expanding. Although the law in Poland does not require helmets, they are increasingly required by fashion.

On the negative side, cyclists' carelessness is a cause of frequent accidents as they often ride without the required lights and have no knowledge of traffic rules. In Poland, a biking permit is required to ride on public roads although police estimate that about 60% of cyclists do not have permits. Also, the number of reported bike thefts is a rapidly growing item in police statistics.

Biking tourism is gaining popularity. Thanks to the efforts of the Polish Ecological Society and the Poznan Biking Society, the longest bike route in Poland was built in 1994 through the picturesque territory along the Cybina River from Poznan to Pobiedziska. In Bydgoszcz, the uncrowned center of Polish biking, an abandoned railway line from Snin to Szubin was developed for biking which is an extension of the international bike route which starts in Rotterdam.

Figure Skating

In 1995, Zuzanna Szwed won Poland's Women's Figure Skating Champion and became Poland's First Lady of Ice. Dorota Zagorska and Mariusz Siudek, Polish pairs figure skaters, came in 4th at the 1998 European championship in Milan and 10th at the Winter Olympics in Ngano. Figure skating is popular primarily as TV entertainment in Poland.

Football

Football Club Legia was founded in 1916 during World War I and is one of the largest clubs in Poland. The team plays in First Division of Poland and won both the Cup of Poland and Poland's Championship in the years 1955, 1956, 1994, 1995. Legia has participated in 20 games of European Champion Club's Cup, 10 games of UEFA Champions League, 36 games of European Cup Winner's Cup and 32 games of UEFA Cup. In 1974, Poland won silver medal in the World Cup in West Germany.

Golf

In 1996, Poland's first Professional Golf Association tournament was held at the Amber Baltic Hotel and Golf Club in Miedzyzdroje on the Baltic coast -- the first PGA tournament in Poland. The championship was a step in promoting the development of golf in Poland. At that time, the country had only five courses. Recruiting several hundred youngsters nationwide to play will be among the most important ways of developing the game in Poland especially if they see it as both entertaining recreation and a potential career opportunity.

Ice Hockey

As a result of new interest in ice hockey, Poland may soon have its very own professional league. Much of the popularity of ice hockey is attributed to Mariusz Czerkawski, the first Polish player in the NHL (North America's professional league). The future of ice hockey in Poland requires overcoming three major difficulties:

1. Lose of top players - To overcome this, the Polish Ice Hockey Union has begun youth training and established three sports schools for gifted youngsters.
2. Lack of sponsors - Because of the high financial costs which include rink maintenance, equipment, player's salaries, and transportation costs, those who are interested in hockey will do so only if it's shown on TV.
3. Lack of media coverage - Lobbying for biweekly game broadcasts are being negotiated with Polsat, Wisla and local stations.

If these goals are achieved, it is probable that Polsat or Wisla broadcasts will result in an ice hockey boom in Poland and Poland anticipates being represented in the EuroLeague (the European equivalent of NHL) in a few years.

Kick-boxing

Iwona Guzowska was Poland's champion in kick-boxing and in 1995, she earned her first world championship in full-contact kick-boxing. As a kick-boxing ace, she fought 60 times with only 3 losses.

Martial Arts

The popularity of martial arts in Poland increases every year as new clubs are formed and Polish representatives succeed in international arenas. Also, training doesn't require much money, expensive equipment or special facilities.

- Karate - The Polish Karate Union has 150 clubs from all over Poland and the Lodz Federation of Traditional Karate has several dozen clubs. It is estimated that 40,000 people take karate in Poland.
- Judo - According to the Polish Judo Union there are 140 judo clubs in Poland. Almost 15,000 people take judo in Poland. Pawel Nastula of Poland, a world and Olympic champion, is the best judoka in the world with excellent technique, extraordinary mental strength and a strong personality. He has become the idol of many young Poles who dream about a judo career.
- Taikowndo - Mariusz Golian of the Polish Taekwondo Union says that 2,000 people study this art in Poland and that the interest is growing.
- Kung fu - About 10,000 people study kung fu, the most elite of the martial arts, in Poland. The kung fu practiced in Poland meets very high standards, with international victories and medals won at all competitions.

Olympics

With the exception of the 1984 Summer Olympics in Los Angeles, Poland has participated in both Summer and Winter Olympics since 1924.

At the 2000 Summer Olympics in Australia, Polish athletes won 14 medals: 6 gold, 5 silver and 3 bronze. Olympic gold medal winners included: Robert Korzeniowski won 2 gold medals in men's 20 km and 50 km race walk, Renata Mauer won gold in women's 50 m rifle shooting, Kamila Skolimowska won gold in women's hammer throw and Szymon Ziolowski won gold in men's hammer throw. Szymon Koleck won silver in men's 94 kg weightlifting, Agata Wrobel won silver in women's over 75 kg weightlifting and Leszek Blanik won bronze in men's vault. Other medals were in men's lightweight double sculls, men's 500-m canoe doubles, men's canoe slalom doubles, women's fencing team, men's 1000-m kayak fours and women's 500 m kayak doubles.

At the 1996 Summer Olympics in Atlanta, Polish athletes won 17 medals: 7 gold, 5 silver and 5 bronze. Olympic Medalists included: Wlodzimierz Zawadzki won a gold medal in the 62-kg category in wrestling, Jacek Fafinski won a silver in the 90-kg category and Jozef Tracz won a bronze in the 74-kg category. Tracz is the first Polish wrestler to stand on the podium during three consecutive Olympics - he won a silver medal at the 1992 Barcelonia Olympics and a bronze medal at the 1988 Seoul Olympics.

In Men's Soccer, Poland won a gold medal in 1972 and silver medals in 1976 and 1992.

Polish Olympic medallists from prior Olympics included:

- **Egon Franke**, a foilsman from the Gliwice Sports Club, became an Olympic champion in Toyko in 1964.
- **Jerzy Pawlowski** - He won five Olympic medals for sabre fencing. including individual gold in 1968 and silver in 1956 and team silver in 1956, 1960 and bronze in 1964.
- **Zbigniew Pietrzykowski** - He won silver in 1960 and two bronze medals in 1956 and 1964 for boxing. In 1960, he lost to Cassius Clay (Mohammed Ali) in the final.
- **Józef Szmidt** - (b. 1935) Winner of two gold medals in track and field triple jump in 1960 and 1964, he was the first to triple jump over 17 meters with 17.03 in 1960, which remained unbeaten until the Olympics at Mexico City, when it was bettered five times.
- **Andrzej Wronski** - He won two gold medals in wrestling in the 100-kg category in 1988 and 1996.

- **Józef Zapedzki** - He won two gold medals for rapid-fire pistol shooting in 1968 and 1972.
- **Waldemar Baszanowski** - (b. 1935) He won two gold medals in weight lifting in the 67.5-kg category in 1964 and 1968.
- **Jerzy Kulej** - (b. 1940) He won two gold boxing medals in the 63.5-kg category in 1964 and 1968. In the beginning, he was interested in football and swimming, but at age 19, he represented Poland in the European boxing championships and later became European Champion.
- **Waldemar Legien** - (b. 1963) He won two gold medals in judo in the 78-kg in 1988 and in the 86-kg in 1992.
- **Kazimierz Lipien** - He received a bronze medal in wrestling, 62-kg category in 1972 and a gold medal in 1976.
- **Bronislaw Malinowski** - (b. 1951) He won a gold medal in track and field for the 3000 m steeplechase in 1980 and a silver in 1976. Kenya's boycott of the Moskva Games gave one of the best technicians of the steeplechase a gold medal.

Orienteering

Although orienteering began in 1897 in Norway, it became more popular after World War I. In 1961 the International Orienteering Federation was created and the first official European Championship was held in 1962 and World Championships are held every two years since then. Since 1970 Poland has participated in the World Championships. World Championships in ski orienteering have been organized since 1975.

Orienteering is running a course usually through the woods with control points indicated on a map given at the beginning of the competition in the shortest time. Since you can choose the route as long as you visit all the control points, the goal is to find the quickest speed (depending on the terrain) at which you can still navigate accurately.

Sailing

In 1919, Otto Weiland founded the Association of Sailing Friends, which was the beginning of sport yachting in Poland. In 1924, the Polish Yacht Association was formed and in the same year, the first Polish sailor, Edward Bryzemajster, participated in the Olympic games in Paris - he finished 12th. Since 1930, the frigate "Dar Pomorza" has been the national sailing boat. In 1980, Henryk Jaskula sailed around the world without coming into any harbors.

Soccer

Polonia Warszawa was established in 1912 and is one of the oldest and most meritorious polish soccer teams. During the 1920s and 1930s, the team became the most popular, strictly Warsaw-spirit team. Polonia Warszawa symbolizes all the best memories, the brightest ideals and objectives of sports rivalry.

In 1921 and 1926, the team won the Vice-championship of Poland. The biggest achievement was winning the 1946 title of Champion of Poland, which occurred when Warsaw was 80% destroyed due to warfare. That impressive victory gave all the citizens of ruined Warsaw a new hope to rebuild and revive their capital. Another big success was a victory in the 1952 Polish Cup competition. Since 1989, the club was totally reorganized and soon after won the Vice-championship of Poland, the third time in the club's history.

Tennis

The first Polish book on tennis, *A Guide to Playing Lawn Tennis* by A. Wodniakowski, was published in 1896 and the Polish Lawn Tennis Union was established in 1921. Although the sport has always been popular, why is Poland so obviously absent in the tennis world? Some contend that the sport as a whole has been hampered by the physical and psychological legacy of communism.

Beside Jadwiga Jedrzejowska, who was in the Wimbledon finals before World War II, the only other Pole to make a career in world tennis was Wojciech Fibak who won 15 singles tournaments and 48 doubles. His triumphs in international tournaments inspired the great revival in Polish tennis during the 1970s and 1980s. Today, tennis courts and centers are growing, there is no lack of equipment and training materials and there are even big professional tournaments organized in Poland.

Windsurfing

Thousands of people in Poland enjoy windsurfing and places offering training and equipment can be found all over the country. The best place for windsurfing is the Hel Peninsula, particularly the Pucka Bay region, because of a consistent wind from the same direction and shallow, clean water far from the coast. Most of the windsurfing schools are located here. The Leba region, on the middle coast, is the center for more advanced windsurfing.

In 1998 and 1999, Fun Wind received the title of the best windsurfing school in a survey performed by Deska magazine. Here one can get an international windsurfing license. The school has the newest equipment and its instructors have Polish and international licenses.

Bibliography

1. How to do Business in Poland by Ministry of Economy, Economic Promotion Department, 2002.
2. Nobility of the Polish Commonwealth by Polish Nobility Association Foundation.
3. Notable Personages of Polish Ancestry by W. Moore McLean, The Unique Press, Inc., 1938.
4. Poland, Nation in Transition by Steven Otfinoski, Facts on File, 1995.
5. Poland, A Country Study, edited by Glenn E. Curtis, Federal Research Divison, Library of Congress, 1994.
6. Michael Novak, "Don't Abandon Us?" Forbes, 1/17/94, p. 51.
7. 1999 CIA World Factbook, http://odci.gov/cia/publications/factbook/pl.html.
8. A Brief History of Poland, http://ampolinstitute.org/kings.html.
9. A Short History of Poland, (This is a Polish internet site), http://www.ipipan.waw.pl/~klopotek/pl/polnhist.htm
10. ABC Country Book of Poland, http://www.theodora.com/wfb/polandeconomy.html.
11. An Energy Overview of the Republic of Poland, http://www.fe.doe.gov/international/plndover.html.
12. Archives in Poland, http://www.archiwa.gov.pl/index.eng.html.
13. Archiwum Panstwowe w Gdansk (State Archives in Gdansk), http://www.gdanskk.ap.gov.pl/english/historia.php
14. Background Notes: Poland, http://www.state.gov/www/background_notes/poland_gn.html.
15. Biblioteka Narodowa Warszawi (National Library in Warsaw), http://www.bn.org.pl.
16. Catholic Encylclopedia, http://www.newadvent.org
17. Catholic Online Saints, http://saints.catholic.org/saints
18. Central Europe Review http://www.ce_review.org/00/polandnews.html.

19. Christmas in Poland and Polonia, http://www.wings.buffalo.edu/info-poland/classroom/xmas.html.
20. Coffee Market in Poland by Ewa Kostecka, 1997, http://www.mac.doc.gov/eebic/countryr/poland/market/coffee/htm
21. Corporate Information, http://www.corporationinformation.com/plsector
22. Country Study & Country Guide to Poland, http://www.1upinfo.com/country~guide~study/poland/poland.html.
23. CountryWatch.com - Poland Information, http://countrywatch.com
24. Criminal Justice Profile of Poland by Andrezej Adamski, 1997, (This is a Polish internet site), http://www.law.uni.torun.pl/pulbikacje/aadamski/raport/
25. Criteria for Membership of the EU, http://europa.eu.int/comm/enlargement/keys/details/c/criteria_membership.htm
26. Customs Service of the Republic of Poland, http://www.guc.gov.pl
27. CWS, Poland's First Series Produced Automobiles, http://www.clearlight.com/~brawicz/cws/.
28. Early Poland, http://www.monmouth.com/~fkobylarz/history/01earlypoland.htm.
29. Early Polish Cars by Dariusz Piecinski, 1997, http://www.team.net/ktud/polis.html.
30. Easter in Poland, http://www.polstore.com/polishester.html.
31. Eastern European Folklore & Customs, http://tccweb.org/eefolkoore.htm.
32. Education of Women by Joanna Woycicka and Andrzej Dominiczak, http://free.ngo/temida/edu.htm.
33. Education Reform in Poland, by Zofia Sobiepanek, 1998, http://www.mac/doc/gov/eebic/countryr/poland/market/edsys.htm
34. Embassy Information: A Guide for American Investors (Embassy of the Republic of Poland), http://www.

polishworld.com
35. End of Jagiellon Dynasty: Beginning of Era of Popular Election of Kings, http://freepages.history.rootsweb.com/~koby/.../09jagdynasty.htm.
36. Etiquette Guide: Poland by Dean Foster, http://workabroad.monster.com/articles/poland/
37. Famous Quotations Network, http://www.famous_quotations.com.
38. Famous Polish Discoverers, Travelers and Scientists (This is a Polish Internet site), http://hum.amu.edu.pl/~zbzw/ph/sci/distra.htm.
39. Geographical Location and Topographic Features by Ministerstwo Ochrony Srodowiska (This is a Polish Internet site), http://www.mos.gov.pl/soe/1a.htm.
40. Global Gourmet, http://www.globalgourmet.com/destinations/poland.html.
41. Health Care Reform in Poland, http://medicover.com/healthpoland.html.
42. Health Care Reform in Poland 1999 by Krysztof P. Jasiutowicz, http://republika.pl/kpjas/en/nhs_reform.html.
43. History and Today of Polish State Mint in Warsaw, http://www.mennica.com.pl/english/powstanie.html.
44. History of Box-Making in Poland, http://www.worldofboxes.com/craft/histfrm.htm.
45. History of the EU, http://www.salford.ac.uk/economics/euro2/history.htm.
46. History of the Aurochs in Poland by Mieczyslaw Rokoxz, http://www.aristotle.net/~swarmack/aurohist.html.
47. History of the City of Gliwice (This is a Polish internet site), http://www.gliwice.pl/historia/eindex.html
48. History of the Polish Eagle, http://ultranet.com/eaglehis.html.
49. History of Polish Armed Forces in WW2, http://wildsau.idv.uni-linz.ac.at/~k20011e9/paf_his1.htm.
50. History of Polish Central Banking by National Bank of Poland, 1998, http://www.nbp.pl/en/onbp/historia/html.
51. History of the Port Szczecin, (This is a Polish internet

site), http://www.port.szczecin.pl/history/history.htm.
52. Hussaria - Polish Winged Cavalry by Slawek K. Grzechnik, http://home.san.it.com/slawek/Tata/papers/Husaria.eng.html.
53. Inside Poland: Poland and NATO, 1998 (This is a Polish Internet site), http://www.insidepoland.com/html/polandandnato.html.
54. Institute of Forensic Research, (This is a Polish Internet site), http://www.ies.krakow.pl/history.htm.
55. Interactive Map of Poland, http://2poland.com/InteractiveMap/Places.
56. International Wildlife, Across a Divide, http://www.findarticles.com
57. Jagiellonian University Archives, http://www.archiwum.uj.edu.pl/eng/index.html.
58. Katyn History, http://www.polishcommunity.com/Katyn/KatynHistory.htm
59. Knocking on Heaven's Door: Polish Efforts to Win at the Oscars by Zbigniew J. Pasek, http://www.personal.engin.umich.edu/~zbigniew/Periphery/No2/pasek.html.
60. Liberal International: The Hall of Freedom, http://www.worldlib.org/other/freedombiogs.html
61. Lili's Polish Holiday Recipes, http://goeasteurope.about.com/library/texts/blrecipe1.htm.
62. LOT Travel, http://www.lot.com/about/history/main.html.
63. Mineral Resources of Poland, (This is a Polish internet site), http://www.pgi.waw.pl/midas/mineral_resources.
64. Ministry of the Environment, (This is a Polish internet site), http://www.mos.gov.pl/mos/podsekretarze/symonides2-eng.html.
65. Ministerstwo Ochrony Srodowiska...Polska (This is a Polish Internet site), http://www.mos.gov.pl/soe.htm.
66. Naming Customs Found in Poland, http://www.rootsweb.com/~polwgw/naming.html.
67. National Anthems of Poland by Maria Anna Harley, 1997, http://www.usc.edu/dept/polish_music/repertoi/anthems.html

68. National Human Development Report for Poland, 1998, http://www.undp.org.pl/pages/nhdr1998/foreword.htm.
69. Northern War: The Course of Hostilities, http://www.encyclopedia.com/articles/TheCourseofHostilities.html.
70. Okana's Web, http://www.okana.net
71. Orders & Decorations of Poland, http://www.geocities.com/Athens/Oracle/6585/pl4a.htm
72. Patron Saints Index, http://www.catholic-forum.com
73. Poland and Its History, http://www.geocities.com/Heartland/Estates/9538/
74. Poland and the Internet by Michael Zadara, 1996, http://informatics.sunysb.edu/apap/archives/1996/2215/html.
75. Poland's guide - cities & towns, http://www.explore-poland.pl/guide/3j.htm
76. Polish Agency for Foreign Investment (PAIZ), http://www.paiz.gov.pl/paiz1_1html.
77. Polish Armed Forces - Traditions, http://www.wp.mil.pl/_en_paf/e_4_10_n.htm.
78. Polish Artillery in the XVII Century by Rick Orli, 2001, http://www.kismeta.com/deGrasse/PolishArtillerySVII.htm.
79. Polish Coins (This is a Polish Internet site in Polish), http://www.pol.pl/staff/icw/num/caly/htm.
80. Polish Canoe Federation, http://www.hbz.com.pl/pzk/history.htm.
81. Polish Contributions to the Development of World's Sciences http://www.ampolinstitute.org/polish_scientists.html.
82. Polish Folklore, http://members.aol.com/jjnowicki/polfolk.htm.
83. Polish Genealogical Society of America, http://www.pgsa.org/traditions.htm.
84. Polish Jews in World War II, http://cyberroad.com/poland/jews_ww2.html
85. Polish Kings, http://artyzm.com/matejko/poczet/e_poczet.htm
86. Polish Music Center, http://www.usc.edu/dept/polish_

music/dance
87. Polish National Parks, http://hum.amu.edu.pl/~zbzw/ph/pnp/pnp.htm
88. Polish Naval Academy (This is a Polish Internet site in Polish), http://www.amw.gdynia.pl/bg.htm
89. Polish Nobility and Its Heraldry, http://www.szlachta.org/heraldry.htm
90. Polish Recipes, http://soar.berkeley.edu/recipes/ethnic/polish
91. Polish Society from 1989-1994 by Antoni Rajkiewicz, Warsaw, 1996 (This is a Polish Internet site), http://www.insidepoland.com/html/ethnicity.html.
92. Polish Suburban News, http://www.polishnews.com
93. Polish Train Travel by Jeffrey Dobek, http://www.polrail.com/pkptrav.html.
94. Polish Treasures - Polish Recipes - Archives, http://www.polishtreasures.com/oldrec.htm.
95. Pomerelian Archive and Museum of the Home Army and Polish Women War Service, http://www.um.torun.pl/~archak/english.html
96. Republic of Poland, Ministry of Defence, http://www.wp.mil.pl/_e_paf/e_4_10_n.htm
97. Roman Catholic Church in Poland by Mieczyslaw A. Klopotek, May 1st 2000, http://www.ipipan.waw.pl/~klopotek/church/rcc_in_p.htm.
98. SKK - Systemy Kodow Kreskowych, http://www.skk.com.pl/?skk=historia
99. Source: The Central Statistical Office, The 1998 Statistical Yearbook (This is a Polish Internet site), http://www.insidepoland.com/html/population.html.
100. Steel News on Steel Mill Site, http://www.steelmill.com/Steel%20News.htm
101. Stefan Grabinski: An Introduction, http://members.aol.com/eurosin/sgintro.htm
102. The American Institute of Polish Culture, http://www.ampolinstitute.org.
103. The Biographical Dictionary, http://www.s9.com/

biography.
104. The Central and Eastern Europe Business Information Center, http://www.mac.doc.gov/country/poland/
105. The Beer Market in Poland by Ewa Kostecka, 1998, http://www.mac.doc.gov/eebic/countryr/poland/market/beer/htm
106. The Grove Dictionary of Art, http://www.groveart.com
107. The History of Lancut Distillery, http://www.lancut distillery.polishvodka.com.pl/historyof/lancut.htm
108. The Home Army Intelligence Service by Andrzej Suchcitz, http://www.polishresistance-ak.org
109. The Polish Underground State and Home Army by Marek Ney-Krwawicz, http://www.polishresistance-ak.org
110. The State of the Environment in Poland by Zhigniew Kamienski at the State Inspectorate for Environmental Protection. (This is a Polish Internet site), http://nfp-pl.elonet.eu.int/SoE/wwwang/okno2.htm.
111. The Story of One Tragic September by Stan Biernacik, 1990, http://www.polamjournal.com/library/invaded.html.
112. The Tea Market in Poland by Ewa Kostecka, 1998, http://www.mac.doc.gov/eebic/countryr/poland/market/tea/htm.
113. The Washington Diplomat, http://washdiplomat.com
114. Travel (Public Transportation), http://www.newpoland.com/travel_public_transportation.htm
115. Urzad Miejski w Gdansku - Historia Miasta (This is a Polish Internet site), htt://www.gdansk.gda.pl/um_green/hg_historia_gdansk/hg_us_historia_gdanska.htm
116. Violence Against Women by Urszula Nowakowska, http://free.ngo.pl/temida/violence.htm.
117. Women's Health by Maja Korzeniewska and Urszula Nowakowska, http://free.ngo.pl/temida/health.htm.
118. Women in the Labor Market by Urszula Nowakowska and Anna Swedrowska, http://free.ngo.pl/temida/labor.htm.
119. Women's Reproductive Rights by Urszula Nowakowska, http://free.ngo.pl/temida/reproductive.htm.
120. WSE – History of the Polish capital market (This is a

Polish Internet site), http://www.wse.com.pl/gpw/historen.htm.

121. Zofia Stryjenska, Princess of Polish Painting by Danuta Batorska and published in Woman's Art Journal, Fall 1998, http://www.forum_polonia_houston.com/Art/Zstryj/zs.htm.

APPENDIX

MEMORABLE POLES

Throughout the history of Poland, many Poles made important contributions to education, science, medicine, music, etc. - both within Poland and around the world. The following is a partial list of some notable Poles:

1020

Duchess Gertruda (1020-1108)
In the exquisitely illustrated Psalter prepared for Archbishop Egbert of Treviso at the end of the 10th Century, she wrote the texts of over one hundred prayers in the spaces between the psalms and on bound-in pages. Her compositions showed a creative attitude to religion and prayers and made her the first lady of Polish women's literary culture.

1415

Jan Dlugosz (Johannes Longinus) (1415-1480)
Historian and diplomat of King Casimir Jagiellonczyk, he was the author of many historical works. His monumental 12-volume *Historia Polonica* (Chronicle of the Famous Kingdom of Poland) was written in Latin and took a quarter Century to prepare.

1473

Mikolaj Kopernik (Nicolaus Copernicus) (1473-1573)
A Polish astronomer, he developed the theory that the earth is a moving planet and is considered the founder of modern astronomy. His astronomical observations were made using simple wooden instruments without lenses. He wrote about his revolutionary heliocentric theory that the earth rotates on its axis and planets revolve in orbit around the sun in *De Revolutionibus Orbium Coelestium*, which was published in 1543. He attended the University of Krakow, served as a canon of the cathedral of Frauenburg, served as a physician and also worked on the principles of currency reform.

1488

Jan Tarnowski (1488-1561)

Known as the Father of Polish military science, he was Grand Royal Hetman (General) from 1527, led the Polish Army to many victories and developed the horse artillery. He elaborated the old tactic of forming a gigantic square, a mobile fortress which could save a small army caught out in the open field, and also developed the traditional features of Polish strategy, most of which were unique. Another peculiar feature was the tradition of the deep cavalry raid ahead of the main army. It was an elaborate maneuver of probing charges by light cavalry supported by artillery leading up to the final decisive charge by heavy cavalry deployed in a checkerboard pattern and not a single mass. In 1558, he published *Consilium Rationis Bellicae*.

1503

Andrzej Frycz Modrzewski (1503-1572)

Political writer and theorist, he wrote a lengthy socio-political treatise *Commentoariorum de Republica Emendanda* (On the Reform of the Republic) in 1551. In the treatise, he gave an incisive analysis of the state as a whole and presented an all-inclusive program of change, pioneer of the modern European science of state and law. He advocated equal citizenship for all Poles, the democratization of the state and the church and a centralized though not absolute monarchy.

1505

Mikolaj Rej (1505-1569)

Recognized as the Father of Polish literature, he was the first Polish writer to forsake Latin in favor of Polish. His satires criticized the faults of the society in a picturesque and terse language. He also wrote in verse and prose and one of his most famous pieces describes the life of a Polish country gentlemen. As a Protestant, he took an active part in the

Reformation movement and was a member of Parliament. Nicholas Rey, the US Ambassador to Poland from 1993-1997, is a direct descendant of the 16th Century writer.

1530

Jan Kochanowski (1530-1584)

The father of Polish poetry, his surviving lyrical poems and satires include 16,700 verses in Polish and 7000 in Latin. He assimilated the poetic traditions of Italy and France and created new rhythmic patterns, expressive phrases, and syntactic structures that were integrated into the Polish literary language. His philosophical, erotic, and patriotic lyrics lifted Polish literature out of its provincialism and brought it into the mainstream of the European Renaissance. His works include *Trifles* published in 1584, short poems on many subjects; *Laments* published in 1580, elegies upon the death of his daughter; an epic, *The Standard*; and a tragedy, *The Dismissal of the Greek Envoys* published in 1578, the first Polish Drama. Of special note is his Polish version of the Psalms. Much of his work is available in English translation.

1542

Jan Zamojski (1542-1605)

Polish statesman, general, and author, he championed the rights of the lesser nobility. After the extinction of the Jagiello dynasty in 1572, he used his influence to restrict the royal power with constitutional limitations, thus transforming Poland into a royal republic. A humanist, he supported art and learning and founded both the city and the University of Zamosc. In 1563 he wrote *De senatu Romano* which showed great admiration of ancient Rome, and he sought to apply constitutional principles of republican Rome to the Poland of his time. As a result of his reforms, Poland avoided the trend toward absolutism that characterized the other states of Europe. Appointed Commander-in- Chief in 1580, he distinguished himself against Russia, Sweden, the Crimean Tatars, and the hospodar [governor] of Moldavia.

1554

Magdalena Morteska (1554-1631)

She became abbess in a Benedictine monastery and started reforming the order. The changes consisted in reinforcing the sisters' spirituality through mediation and contemplation and in modifying an overly ascetic regime. Her two works of religious-mystical literature consist of *Nauki duchowne sluzace do postepu duchownego* (Spiritual Teachings Serving Spiritual Progess) that was a biblical documentary and *Rozmyslania o mece panskiej* (Mediations on the Passion of Christ) which reflects on Christ's sufferings in accordance to Benedictine rule.

1566

Michal Sedziwoj (1566-1636)

A famous Polish alchemist, he was the first man in history of chemistry to describe oxygen – "the food of life, which exists in the air". He advanced the theory of combustion and breathing.

1588

Jan Brozek (1588-1652)

Mathematician, physician and Rector of Jagiellonian University in Krakow, he contributed to a greater knowledge of Copernicus' theories. He was the most prominent Polish mathematician of the 17th Century.

1600

Kazimierz Siemlenowica (1600-1651)

Nobleman, military engineer and artillery specialist, he was sent by King Wladyslaw IV to serve in the army of Duke Frederick-Henry of Oran during the war with Spain. From 1648, he served as Second-in-Command of Polish Royal Artillery, as an expert in the field of artillery and rocketry. In 1650, he published his fundamental work *Great Art of Artillery, the*

First Part that was used in Europe as a basic artillery manual for almost 200 years. The book contains a large chapter on construction, production and properties of rockets including multi-stage rockets, batteries of rockets and rockets with delta-shaped stabilizers. The manuscript of the second part was lost, together with its author in obscure circumstances. His amazing ideas are considered a precursor of space flight

.

1603

Anna Maria Marchocka (1603-1652)

A member of the Discalced Carmelites, she made her name in Polish literature and spirituality as the author of a mystical autobiography that was the first text of its kind in Polish. It was modeled on the works of St Teresa of Avila in which the depth of religious feeling is conveyed by simple, matter-of-fact language. Her autobiography is a distinguished work comparable with the mystical masterpieces of Western Europe.

1611

Jan Heweliusz (1611-1687)

This famous astronomer constructed telescopes and other instruments including the pendulum clock and a micrometric screw. In 1640, he created the Astronomical Observatory of Gdansk and constructed the biggest telescope of the 17th Century. He founded modern selenography and was a member of the London Royal Society since 1664. His published work *Selenographia: sive, Lunae Descriptio* contained the most detailed maps of the Moon containing many new names of its surface objects. For more than 100 years, his maps were considered the best maps of the Moon. He discovered and observed many comets, observed sunspots, planets and their satellites and variable stars as well as compiled a large star atlas with seven new constellations. *Prodromus astronomiae*, the most complete catalog of the stars of his time was published posthumous in 1690.

1652

Anna Stanislawska (1652-1701)

After three marriages, she accepted widowhood for the rest of her life. In the history of literature, she was known as the author of *Transakcja albo opisanie calego zycia jednej sieroty, przez zalosne treny od tejze samej pisane rok 1685* (The Transaction, or a Description of the Whole Life of One Orphan through Doleful Laments Written by the Same in the Year 1685). An important part of the text was the notes in the margin, which explained in prose what is not clear enough in the verse. The poem is imperfect in literary terms but it is one of the first works written by a woman and a testimony to the situation of women in the Old Polish Republic.

1746

Izabela Flemming Czartoryska (1746-1835)

She was the first noted woman writer of the 19th Century. After Poland's loss of independence in 1795, she founded a center of sentimental patriotic culture. Her most interesting work was *Pielgrzym w Dobromilu* (Pilgrim in Dobromil) published in 1816. This booklet is a multi-layered work presenting the Sudetenland landscape, the legends associated with the Piast period of Silesian history and the traveler's own sentiments. Her output is a notable witness to the rise of patriotic sentimentality.

Thaddeus Kosciuszko (1746-1817)

One of Poland's greatest heroes and patriots, he fought for freedom with the American Revolutionary Army where he built and fortified West Point. He returned to Poland and led the Insurrection of 1794 where his indomitable devotion to the cause of freedom made him a symbol of the pursuit of freedom.

1747

Konstancja Benislawska of Ryki (1747-1806)

The mother of 22 children, she was also a gifted poet of unique religious poetry. Her verse can be compared to the great mystical work of St. Teresa and St. John of the Cross. In 1776, she published the collection *piesni sobie spiewane od Konstancji z Rykow Benislawskiej, stolnikowej ksiestwa inflanckiego, za naleganiem przyjaciol z cienia wieskiego na jasnie wydane* (Songs Sung to Herself, at the Instigation of Friends, Brought by Konstancja of Ryki Benislawska from Rural Shade to the Daylight of Publication). The songs consist of cycles of notable religious poetry.

Casimir Pulaski (1747-1779)

He fought courageously but unsuccessfully to save Poland from partition. In 1777, he came to America to fight in the war for independence and, as a cavalry general, won distinction in numerous campaigns. After his death, his cavalry unit became the nucleus for future squadrons and earned him the title of "Father of the American Cavalry".

1750

Hugo Kollatay (1750-1812)

Priest, statesman, scholar, and writer, he reformed the University of Krakow, guided the movement of national regeneration and inspired the Constitution of the Third of May. In 1794, he was co-author of the principle documents of the Kosciuszko Insurrection. His book *The Moral and Physical Order* (1810) created a system of social philosophy and ethics.

Jan Sniadecki (1756-1830)

The greatest Polish mathematician and astronomer at the turn of the 18th Century, he published many works including his observations on recently discovered planetoid. His observations on the possibilities of a theory of probability, contained in *O rachunku losow* (On the Calculation of Chances) published in 1817, were of a pioneer nature.

1768

Jedrzej Sniadecki (1768-1838)
Chemist and medical doctor, he was the pioneer of modern chemistry. In 1800, he wrote the first Polish chemical handbook in which he described scientifically the Polish chemical nomeclature.

Maria Czartoryska Wirtemberska (1768-1854)
Her services to Polish culture were huge. Although she founded many churches and cloisters and was an inspector of girls' schools, she was first and foremost a subtle and exceptional writer. Her greatest work, *Malwina, czyli Domyslnosc serca* (Malwina, or the Shrewdness of the Heart), published in 1816, was the first psychological love story in Polish.

1769

Abraham Stern (1769-1842)
He demonstrated the first calculating machine in the world that could perform the four basic arithmetical processes and extract roots, which he named the arithometre in 1817. He also built a harvester and thresher, as well as various measuring instruments of strikingly novel design.

1770

Prince Adam Czartoryski (1770-1861)
He helped in the reform of the government, served as Minister of Foreign Affairs and spoke for Poland at the Congress of Vienna in 1815. He later returned as President of the Polish provisional government. After the Polish Insurrection of 1830, he fled to Paris where his home became a center of political activities aimed at restoring Polish independence.

1775

Stanislaw Staszic (1775-1826)

Priest, philosopher; statesman, geologist, scholar; poet and writer, he graduated from the seminary in Poznan. One of the leaders of the Polish Enlightenment, he was a strong partisan of reforms and advocated the interests of the lower classes. As a director of the Department of Industry and Crafts, he evaluated opinions on the hydrographic conditions, described the area surrounding the city and evaluated the Lodz area as to its usability for the new form of textile production. Thanks to his positive opinion and favorable description, industry in Lodz and governmental projects were developed. He prepared an outline of educational programs for weekend polytechnic schools as centers for educating highly qualified workers, prepared for the changing profile of production, and developments in the technology and science. His works include *Warnings for Poland* and *The Human Race*. After the partitions, he organized mining schools, societies of learning, departments of industry and arts.

1778

Jan Siestrzynski (1788-1824)

A doctor and teacher working with deaf-mutes, he is considered the precursor of phoniatrics in Poland. He graduated from the Department of Medicine at the University of Vienna in 1813. In 1815 he founded the Institute for the Deaf and Dumb in Warsaw. Besides medicine he was also interested the education of deaf children and popularized the audible, articulated speech, introducing it in place of the sign language or mechanical sign and letter-form recognition methods. Around 1821 he finished "*Teoryja i mechanizm mowy*" (The Theory and the Mechanism of Speech) which consisted of two parts. The first part concerned the theory of speech and reading and the other includes the theory of human speech mechanism as well as remarks on deaf children education.

1798

Adam Mickiewicz (1798-1855)

While at the University of Vilna, he was arrested in 1823 for pan-Polish activities and deported to Russia. In the revolutionary upheavals of 1848 and again in the Crimean War he organized legions for Polish emancipation. A romantic poet and playwright, his poetry gave international stature to Polish literature and expressed a romantic view of the soul and the mysteries of life often employing Polish folk themes. His works include the fantastic drama *The Forefathers*, the philosophical poem *Konrad Wallenrod* and *The Books of the Polish Nation and of Polish Pilgrimage*. However, his masterpiece, the great epic *Pan Tadeusz* published in 1834 is a comprehensive and Homeric treatment of the life of the Polish gentry.

1804

Jozef Dietl (1804-1878),

A physician, who pioneered in balneology, he identified the kidney ailment known as "Dietl's Crisis." In 1858, at his insistence, the Balneological Commission of the Krakow Scientific Association conducted a physical and chemical analysis of the saline springs at Rabka: the springs were found to contain the best concentration of Iodine-bromine saline in Europe.

1810

Fryderyk Francois Chopin (1810-1849)

One of the masters of piano composition, he wrote chamber music, songs and pieces for piano and orchestra but his fame rests on his more than 200 compositions for the solo piano. A creator of melody, some of his pieces now seems as familiar as folk music. He also influenced the whole future of music by including Slavic folk harmonies and rhythms in his work. His music expresses Polish patriotism in the Polish harmonies and rhythms of his mazurkas and polonaises.

1812

Count Zygmunt Krasinski (1812-1859)

He is one of Poland's great romantic poets, dramatists and writers. In *Undivine Comedy* he portrays the tragedy of old-world aristocracy defeated by the new democracy and *Irydion* deals with the problem of the struggle of a subjugated nation against the oppressor. His works transcend nationalist themes in their philosophical concern with the plight of modern humanity.

1814

Oskar Kolberg (1814-1890)

Folklorist and ethnographer, he was the author of a monumental work *Lud. Jego zwyczaje, sposob zycia, mowa, podania, przyslowia, obrzedy, gusla, zabawy, piesni, muzyka I tance* (Nation. Its customs, way of life, spoken language, traditions, proverbs, ceremonies, witchcraft, rejoicing, songs, music and dance), that gave the richest description of the Polish folk culture.

1820

Tytus Chalubinski (1820-1889)

Physician and student of folklore, he was professor of the Medical-Surgical Academy and of the Principal School in Warsaw. He founded The School of the Philosophy and History of Medicine - a research field in which Poland was undoubtedly a leader. Above all he emphasized the importance for a doctor of serious training in logic and methodology, on the basis of which medical-semiotic investigation can be scientifically organized, and he viewed disease holistically as a perturbation of the overall functional structure of an organism. He also established systematic tuberculosis sanatorium in Zakopane in the Tatra Mountains.

1821
Adam Prazmowski (1821-1885)

First Polish astrophysicist, he pioneered astrophysical observations of the Sun and co-discovered the polarized emission from the solar corona. He also designed and constructed innovative astronomical instruments including the coelostat.

1822
Ignacy Lukasiewicz (1822-1882)

Pharmacist and inventor, he was the founder of the Polish oil industry. He was the first to drill and distill crude oil in Poland in 1854 and built the first refinery in Jaslo. He replaced hand mining with drilling machinery and steam power. In 1852, he developed a product called "nafta" kerosene and invented the kerosene lamp. In 1853 he used it for lighting General Hospital in Lvov.

1838
Jan Matejko (1838-1893)

His love for Poland's history and tradition gave Europe many vast narrative paintings. The Prussian Homage, The Battle of Grunwald and the Union of Lublin as well as portraits of Poland's Kings kept alive the memory of his nation's greatness and gave Poland insights into her past as well as a sense of the individuality of her culture. (A black & white copy of his portrait of Jadwiga, King of Poland, is on the cover.)

1841
Eliza Orzeskowa (1841-1910)

A highly popular novelist, she emphasized equality and justice in her novels that dissected small town life for such diverse people as Jews, fishermen and poor gentility. She wrote 11 books, 5 of which were on women's rights. In her emancipation program, she always emphasized that women should educate themselves in order to help their husbands in domestic management. In *A Few Words About Women*, she criticized the Polish custom of socializing women needing to be dependent and docile. Her best novel was *Nad Niemnem* (On the Banks of the Niemen) published in 1888, an epic poem showing the most significant aspects of national life at the end of the 19th Century. All of her works reflect her concern for and pride in her country and her novels have been translated into many languages including English.

1842

Maria Konopnicka (1842-1910)

Prolific poet, novelist, translator and essayist, she wrote many sensitive poetical works which project realism, freshness and spontaneity. She was a tireless worker for women's suffrage and their right to education and denounced the Catholic Church's rules about women, marriage, and the lower classes. In her writings, she touched upon many social issues besetting the society of her time and thus influenced the next generation of Polish poets and novelists. She expressed ideals of democracy and patriotism in her cycle of folk songs and in a poem about peasant emigrants, *Mr Balcer in Brasil.* She also wrote novels for children and was a co-organizer of the international protest against the persecution of Polish children.

1844

Stefan Drzewiecki (1844-1938)

Scientist, inventor mainly in aviation and shipbuilding and pioneer airplane constructor, he created designs of a series of submersibles, including one with an electric motor (1880). Between 1892 -1920, he was the first to rigorously examine and apply Blade Element Theory (BET) which is an analysis method that may be applied to a rotor, propeller, fan, and even a lightly loaded compressor. BET is the foundation for almost all analyses of helicopter aerodynamics because it deals with the detailed flow and loading of the blade. Working on calculations and designs of propellers, he developed theory of gliding flight, developed a method for manufacture of ship and plane propellers (1892), and presented a general theory for screw-propeller thrust (1920). His dissertation, *Theorie generale de l'helice* (1920), was honored by the French Academy of Science as a fundamental work in the development of modern propellers.

1845

Zygmunt Wroblewski (1845-1888)

A physicist, he researched the phenomena of gas diffusion in liquids and solids. Of special importance was his research in the field of low temperatures. In 1883, he liquefied and condensed oxygen and nitrogen, solidified carbon dioxide and alcohol and discovered a critical formula for stabilizing hydrogen molecules.

1846

Karol Olszewski (1846-1915)

Chemist, physicist and expert of low temperatures, he was the first scholar who liquefied nitrogen and oxygen. An alumnus of Jagiellonian University, he entered the University of Krakow, as an assistant to the chemistry professor in 1886 where he succeeded in liquefying and solidifying carbon dioxide. He also discovered a method of hydrogen liquefaction and constructed machinery for that purpose, which enabled him to reach the then-lowest world temperature, -225 C. His redesign of existing equipment allowed them to liquefy oxygen. On April 9, 1883 a report was sent to the Academy of Science in Paris and is recognized as the date of the liquefaction of oxygen.

Henryk Sienkiewicz (1846-1916)

He wrote about the most heroic and tragic episodes of Polish history. His best known work is *Quo Vadis?* Written in 1896 but his greatest work is the trilogy *With Fire and Sword*, *The Deluge* and *Pan Wolodyjowski* completed in 1888. In his day, Poland had ceased to exist politically and he was the Ambassador of Poland to the world through his historical writings. In 1905, he was the first Polish author to receive the Nobel Prize for literature.

1850

Samuel Dickstein (1851-1939)

Poland did not formally exist at the time of his birth and much of the pattern of his life was dominated by the aim of Poles to restore their country. Since there was no Polish university for him to attend, he obtained a Master's degree in mathematics in 1876 from the Russian University of Warsaw. With the education system controlled by the Russian rulers, he decided to do what he could to promote a Polish education and beginning in 1878 he directed his own private school in an effort to promote Polish education. In 1884, he co-wrote in Polish a series of mathematics and physics textbooks. A few years later he founded the journal *Mathematical and Physical Papers*, edited *Mathematical News* and continued publication of *Circle of Polish Mathematicians*. In 1903, he founded the Warsaw Scientific Society and was important in the development of the Polish Mathematical Society. His work was mostly in algebra and the history of mathematics. He died in the Nazi bombing of Warsaw in 1939 and his entire family died during the German occupation of Poland.

1852

Albert Abraham Michelson (1852-1931)

He invented an interferometer for measuring distances by means of the length of light waves; measured a meter on terms of the wave of cadmium light. This experiment showed that there is no absolute motion of the earth relative to an ether. In 1907, he was awarded the Nobel Prize in physics.

1854

Napoleon Cybulski (1854-1919)

Pioneer of the science of neurophsiology, he discovered a mysterious substance named adrenalin in 1897, which was secreted by the adrenal cortex and influence blood pressure. It was the first hormone to be discovered. He advanced the hypothesis that adrenalin affects nerve cells and also laid the foundations of electro-encephalography.

1855

Wladyslaw Oltuszewski (1855-1922)

He was the first physician who devoted all his activity to the pathophysiology of voice, hearing and speech. From 1896 to 1922, he ran the Therapeutic Institute for Speech Impairments and also conducted scientific research. He created the foundation for Polish phoniatric literature among them the handbook “On Speech and its Deviations” issued in the Warsaw Medical Library in 1905.

1857

Wladyslaw Bieganski (1857-1917)

He studied in Warsaw and is considered to be one of the founders of medical methodology. In his most important work, *The Logic of Medicine* [*Logika Medycyny*] (which was also translated into German), he outlined the first systematic theory of diagnosis. He identified various methods of diagnosis, using the classificatory method to capture the similarities and differences between pathological phenomena. Of equal importance was his classification of the errors of observation made by physicians, which was the first collection of diagnostic errors in medical methodological literature.

1860

Jan Kasprowicz (1860-1926)

Polish poet, his writings progressed from social revolt (e.g., *From a Peasant’s Field,* 1891) to poems of spiritual struggle and philosophical intensity. Among his later works are *To a Dying World* published in 1902, *Ballad of the Sunflower* published in 1908, and *The Book of the Poor* published in 1916. He was also renowned for his translations of English, French, German, and Italian classics.

Ignacy Paderewski (1860-1941)
Pianist, composer and statesman, he became a member of the Polish National Committee during World War I and appointed its representative to the United States where he urged President Wilson to support the cause of Polish independence. His international reputation and his efforts for his country during World War I caused him to chosen Prime Minister of the new independent Polish republic after the war.

1863
Maria Rodziewicz (1863-?)
She is best known for her masterpiece *Dewajtis*, which is symbolic of the border populations of Poland and their economic struggles and denationalization. She was considered a modern writer of democratic ideas who espoused hard work as a way to national strength. In her literary works, she blended the thread of today with the tradition of the past. She strongly believed that "*culture does not thrive on sand and it is not formed by one generation – it is the result of many previous generations, and therefore, we must not forget what we owe to those who were before us.*"

1864
Walther Hermann Nernst (1864-1941)
A physical chemist, he made many outstanding contributions to the diffusion, hydration and dissociation of electrolytes. His famous heat theorem known as the Third Law of Thermodynamics was developed in 1906 which was soon applied to industrial problems. He developed an electric lamp, called the Nernst lamp, which was more efficient than the

old carbonaric lamp. He also invented an electric piano. He received the Nobel Prize in Chemistry in 1920.

1865

Gabriel Narutowicz (1865-1922)

He graduated from the Technical University in Zurich but during his studies, he was affiliated to the Proletariat party, which made it impossible for him to return to Poland because the Russian authorities had issued a warrant of arrest for him. Due to his scientific publications and their implementations, he won international recognition as a waterpower engineer and was recognized as one of the most outstanding European waterpower plant constructors and a superb expert in geology. After the World War I, he participated in the Vistula riverbed control project. In 1920, he was nominated Minister for Public Works, became President of the Academy of Technical Sciences and Chairman of the National Reconstruction Council. He was appointed Minister of Foreign Affairs in 1922. Due to a demagogic action of the nationalists, he became the leader of the left side of the Sejm and was elected first President of the Republic of Poland in 1922. Five days later at the opening of an art exhibition, he was assassinated during a conversation with the British Envoy.

1866

Edmund Biernacki (1866-1911)

Physician, he was the first to notice a relationship between the rate of disappearance of red corpuscles in a human blood sample and the general condition of the individual. This method known as the Biernacki Reaction is universally practiced in all laboratories in the world and is a cornerstone of modern medicine.

1867

Ignacy Moscicki (1867-1946)

Scientist and President of Poland during 1926-1939, he was the inventor of nitrogen acid production from the atmosphere and also invented a new method of concentrating nitrogen acid and sulfuric acid. He established a big chemical plant to produce nitric acids from ammonia.

Wladyslaw Stanislaw Reymont (1867-1925)

Polish short-story writer and novelist, his poverty-stricken farm childhood and his early manhood as a touring actor and worker in the provinces provided rich material for his writings. His major works are *The Comedienne* published in 1896, a story of a wandering theatrical troupe; *The Promised Land* published in 1899, a novel attacking modern industrial society; and *The Peasants* published in 1909, the great prose epic of Polish village life. He was awarded the 1924 Nobel Prize in Literature.

Maria Curie-Sklodowska (1867-1934)

A famous physicist, she and her husband discovered radioactive polonium and radium in 1898 and in 1903 she was the first woman awarded the Nobel Prize for physics. After her husband's death in 1906, she was appointed to fill his vacant chair at the Sorbonne as the first woman in history to teach there and two years later, she received professorial rank - the first woman in France to do so. It was also a turning point in her career -- she focused all her energy on completing alone the scientific work on radioactive materials that she and her husband had undertaken. It resulted in her being awarded a second Nobel Prize in 1911, this time in the field of chemistry, for isolating radium and studying its nature and atomic make-up. During World War I, her campaign to send automobiles outfitted with X-Ray equipment nearer the front lines saved many lives. After the war, she became a world-renowned figure. In 1932, she helped to establish the Radium Institute in Warsaw - the second institution designed by her to make use of radioactivity in medical treatment. She also worked for international scientific co-operation on a committee of the League of Nations. She died at age 67, in 1934, of leukemia related to years of exposure to radioactivity.

1871

Eugeniusz Romer (1871-1954)

Geographer and creator of modern Polish cartography, he was an author of important synthesis relative to the climate of Poland. His geographical textbooks *include Geographical Atlas, Ice Epoch in Tatra Mountains* and *Climatic Regions in Poland.*

1872

Marian Smoluchowski (1872-1917)

A physicist and professor at Lvov and Krakow Universities, he established a correct hypothesis on the theory of Brownian movement in 1906. His studies on thermodynamic fluctuation confirmed the theory of the existence of atoms and particles, which were still in question at the time.

Jan Szczepanik (1872-1926)

Inventor, he is called the "Polish Edison". He patented many important inventions, which were of use in textile machinery, electric television, color photography and films and devised a method for the optical registration of sound.

1873

Wladyslaw Theodor Benda (1873-1948)

He studied at the Art Academy in Krakow and in Vienna, San Francisco, and New York City. In addition to decorative works and many illustrations for magazines and books, he created modern masks, used in the theater; they were first seen in *Greenwich Village Follies* in 1920. He wrote *Masks* in 1945.

1875

Kazimierz Proszynski (1875-1945)

Inventor, he built one of the first cinema cameras in the world in 1894. This pleograph, or apparatus for taking photographs and projecting pictures, was built before the Lumiere Brothers lodged their patent. He also made the first pocket film-camera and devised a method of synchronizing sound and film tracks. He died in the Nazi concentration camp of Mauthausen in 1945.

1878

Jan Lukasiewica (1878-1946)

He was a logician, professor and Rector of Warsaw University. As author of "Polish Notion", he became the founder of the 'new triple logics' and member of Lvov-Warsaw school of mathematical logic. He made a number of original contributions to its methodology and also dealt with the theory of probability.

Lady Dean Paul (pseudonym Poldowski) (1878-1932)

Her musical legacy consists mainly of 30 art songs. She also wrote pieces for piano (a cycle of 8 compositions), for violin and piano, and for clarinet and piano. The music critics of her time praised the beauty and originality of her music. Most of her orchestral works were destroyed during World War II.

1879

Wanda Louise Landowska (1879-1959)

She received worldwide acclaim as the high priestess of the harpsichord and was the recognized authority on keyboard instruments of the 17th and 18th Centuries. In 1925, she founded Ecole de Musique Ancienne for experienced musicians to learn old musical instruments and musical styles. She wrote many pieces for solo piano and harpsichord and also composed pieces for orchestra, choir and string ensemble. Her most significant piano composition is the set of variations for two pianos entitled *Polonia*.

1880

Ignace Jan Paderewski (1860-1941)

Polish pianist, composer, and statesman, he studied at the Warsaw Conservatory. Following debuts in Vienna (1887) and Paris (1888), his brilliant, sensitive playing won him worldwide popularity exceeding that of any performer since Franz Liszt. He amassed a large fortune, most of which he donated to the service of Poland and the benefit of needy musicians and Jewish refugees. In addition to the famous *Minuet in G* for piano, his works include some orchestral music, an opera, a cantata, a violin sonata, and piano pieces and songs. In 1900 he established the Paderewski Fund to forward musical composition in the United States. An ardent patriot, he played an important role in establishing free Poland after the World War I, in 1919 and as Prime Minister briefly headed Polish governments 1940-41 (the latter in exile).

1881

Marian Falski (1881-1974)

Educationist, she is famous for writing the elementary book, Nauka pisania i czytania (*Learning to Write and Read)*.

Wladyslaw Sikorski (1881-1943)

Polish general and politician, he fought in World War I and held various cabinet posts between 1922-25. After the German conquest of Poland in 1939, he became Premier of the Polish government in exile and Commander-in-Chief of the Polish forces that continued to fight alongside the Allies in World War II. In 1941, he restored diplomatic relations with the USSR, but after the International Red Cross investigation of the Katyn incident, relations were broken off in 1943.

Wojciech Swietoslawski (1881-1968)
Physico-chemist, he was the father of termochemistry and founder of ebullioscopy. He designed a microcalorimeter and various other types of calorimeters. Before World War II, he was a candidate for the Nobel Prize for his sensational work on the theory of liquid-steam balance systems and on problems of the distillation of carbon compounds.

1882

Tadeusz Banachiewicz (1882-1954)
Renowned astronomer, mathematician and geodesist, he was a long-time professor at Jagillonian University in Krakow and heat of its Astronomical Observatory. He worked on celestial mechanics, spherical astronomy and geodesy, observations of the Sun and eclipsing binary stars. In 1925, he developed a special kind of matrix algebra known as the Cracovian Calculus used in spherical astronomy, geodesy, celestial mechanics and calculation of the orbits of heavenly bodies,. Also in 1925, he founded the *Acta Astronomica Journal* and served as its Editor-in-Chief until 1954. In 1927, he also developed the chronokinematographical camera for recording eclipses of the Sun and one of the lunar craters is named after him. Pioneer of Polish radioastronomy, he wrote over 230 scientific works. From 1932-1938, he was Vice President of International Astronomical Union.

Jan Czekanowski (1882-1965),
A famous anthropologist, ethnologist, statistician and linguist, he developed several mathematical statistical methods which were applied in anthropological and ethnographic research and contributed to the filed of taxonomy while studying societies in Africa. The majority of anthropologists now use the methods of measurement and typology established by him. He was the author of the synthetic classification of Slavic enthogenesa.

Waclaw Sierpinski (1882-1969)

A mathematician, he was the father of the famous Polish School of Mathematics. His most important works are in the area of set theory, point set topology and number theory. He was also the founder of the world famous mathematical journals of that time: *Fundamenta Mathematicae* and *Acta Arithmetica* published in 1920.

Karol Szymanowski (1882-1937)

Polish composer, his early works show marked German, French, and Russian influences, but in his later compositions he developed a distinctive, national style. Yet his music was not readily accepted in Poland. He was a founder of Young Poland in Music, an association of composers. His works include *Love Songs of Hafiz* for voice and instruments; *Myths*, a set of three pieces for violin and piano which includes *The Fountain of Arethusa;* two operas, *Hagith* and *King Roger* and the ballet *Harnasie*. In addition, he wrote nine preludes for piano, three symphonies, orchestral and chamber music, songs, and liturgical music.

1884

Kazimierz Funk (1884-1967)

A Polish biochemist, he was the creator of word "vitamins" in 1912. He also created the hypothesis, that later became theory: undertaking the amount of vitamins can cause different diseases such as beriberi, pellagra. He also worked on sex hormones, and isolated tobacco acid. In 1933, he published his first report on the discovery of vitamins.

Ludwik Hirszfeld (1884-1954)

A professor of microbiology and immunology, he established the foundation of knowledge of human blood types. He introduced the new cholera vaccination while he worked in Serbia, began research into the pathology of pregnancy in Poland and discovered bacillus of paratyphoid fever C. His works include the first Polish medical periodical that dealt with experimental medicine. He co-organized the Maria Sklodowska-Curie University in Lublin after World War II.

Bronislaw Malinowski (1884-1942)
Founder of social anthropology, his contributions to sociology, ethnography, linguistics, psychology and the theory of culture made him one of the most important anthropologists of the 20th Century. He became known for his study of the culture and peoples of the Trobriand Islands in the southwest Pacific and for his contributions to theories on human culture. His books include *Argonauts of the Western Pacific, Crime and Custom in Savage Society* and *Sex and Repression in Savage Society.*

1885

Jan Czochralski (1885-1953)
In 1929 he became professor of metallurgy and metal research in Chemical Department of the Technical University in Warsaw and organized the Institute of Metallurgy and Metal Sciences of Technical University and Metallurgical Department of the Chemical Research Institute. Both research laboratories played a significant role in the progress of Polish industry and metal sciences. After the war, he returned to his hometown to run the small druggist`s firm BION, producing different types of cosmetics and household chemicals. Well-known for his many contributions in metallurgy, especially for this studies of the velocity of metal crystallization and for his method of monocrystalline growth, published in 1916. The Czochralski method of pulling crystal is still up-to-date and belongs today to the simplest and fundamental crystal growth methods in the semiconductor industry. Among his patents are the highly famous patent on a tin-free bearing alloy for railways, called metal B, patented in 1924 and bought by many countries all over the world, including USA, France and England. Between 1913-1923, he also pioneered investigations of the anisotropy of the hardness of single crystals that are of great importance for the plastic treatment of materials. He wrote two handbooks:

Lagermetale und ihre technologische Bewertung [Bearing metal and its technological evaluation (1920)] and *Moderne Metallkunde* in Theorie and Praxis [Modern metal science in theory and practice (1924)], which were later translated into several languages. Many of his works were military secrets and have never been published. He is one of the most famous Polish scientists and the Foundation for Materials Research Development in Poland established the Prof. Jan Czochralski Gold Medal for achievements in materials science

Jozef Teodor Konrad Korzeniowski (Joseph Conrad) (1857-1924)

He is regarded as one of the greatest English novelists, not only because of his genius as a writer of novels, short stories and essays but because of the variety of his experiences during his years at sea. He published his first novel in 1985 *Almayer's Folly* and it was as author of that novel that he adopted the name Joseph Conrad.

Jozef Kostrzewski (1885-1969)

Archeologist and investigator of the Pre-Slavs, he created the Neoautochtonic School. He propagated that if the forefathers of the Slavs were tribes of Lusatian culture, then peoples within the Oder and Vistula drainage basins were autochtons.

Zofia Nalkowska (1885-1954)

A celebrated figure on the Polish literary scene, she was intrigued by the world of women and their relations to reality, historical turmoil and social conditioning. Her first book was *Kobiety* (Women) published in 1906, which was later translated into English. She wrote from a feminist perspective and her work was noted for its technical simplicity. The diary that she began keeping in 1899 was her greatest work especially the part dealing with the German occupation (1939-1945).

1886

Stefan Bryla (1886-1943)

A construction engineer and welding pioneer, he was the author of *Basic Methods of Welding Steel Structures*. In 1927, he designed and built the first welded road bridge in the world on the Sludwia River and in 1932, he designed a high rise building called Prudential in Warsaw. The Nazis executed him in Warsaw in 1943.

Tadeusz Kotarbinski (1886-1981)

Philosopher, logician, praxiologist, he was the pioneer and co-creator of Polish praxiology. He also created the philosophical concept of regime and independent ethics. In the 1930s he actively participated in the cultural and political life of the city, in particular struggling against nationalism, clericalism and the anti-Semitic tendencies which were widespread at the time in Poland. Under the German occupation during World War II he took part in clandestine teaching activity and also narrowly escaped being sentenced to death by a right-wing clandestine faction who declared him to be an enemy of the Polish nation. After the War, he taught at the University of Lodz, helping to organize it in his capacity as Rector (1945-49). He was also President of the Polish Academy of Sciences (1957-1962), where he founded and directed the Laboratory of Praxiology.

Ludwik Marcin Skubiszewski (1886 - 1957)

In 1905 he was expelled from Russian gymnasium (secondary school) for the participation in a school strike. In 1914, he obtained a diploma of a doctor '"cum eximia laude" at the Medical Faculty of St. Wlodzimierz University. From 1913-1915, he worked in the area of anatomic pathology at the Jesus Infant Hospital in Warsaw while continuing his education in the Department of Anatomic Pathology. In 1921 the Medical Faculty of Warsaw University granted him a degree of a Doctor of Medicine on the basis of the theses: *Histogenesis of carotid body tumors*. In 1923 he obtained the post of a docent in anatomic pathology, and in 1924 he became an associated professor. His efforts were especially vital during the foundation and organization of Poznañ University. In very poor conditions he organized at the University the Department of Anatomic Pathology which placed itself among the best in the country. He left a valuable scientific output contained in 85 publications and papers concerning mainly the following problems: etiopathogenesis and diagnostics of tumors, pathophysiology and morphology of rheumatism, pathophysiology of the pituitary gland, and tubercular meningitis. Those studies were original and highly appreciated both in Poland and abroad. Ten of them were published in highly recognized foreign scientific journals.

1887

Stefan Grabinski (1887-1936)

Known as "The Polish Poe", he wrote a vast quantity of some of the most original and interesting fantastic and bizarre fiction of the 20th Century. Five collections of his stories were published between 1918 and 1922. All of his innovative tales were examples of a particular type of fantasy, which he called "psycho-fantasy". Nowhere in Polish literature has there been an author who excelled in supernatural fiction and who devoted himself to only that one genre as he did.

1888

Anna Maria Klechniowska (1888-1973)

Her most important compositions are piano works for young children and numerous vocal works. She also wrote three ballets and three orchestral pieces: *A Wedding Overture*, a symphonic poem about Wawel, The Royal Castle in Krakow; and a symphonic suite *The Seasons of the Year.*

1890

Kazimierz Ajdukiewicz (1890-1963)

He enrolled at University to read Philosophy, Mathematics and Physics and in 1912 he was awarded a Ph.D. degree in Philosophy on the basis of a thesis on Kant's philosophy of space. During World War I he joined the newly formed Polish army and in 1920 left with the rank of an artillery captain. He qualified as a university lecturer at Warsaw University after submitting a dissertation entitled *From the Methodology of Deductive Science* (Lvov, 1921), a pioneer work with a deep influence on the development of logic in Poland. It contained formal (syntactical) definitions of such meta-logical concepts as "proof", "theorem", "consequence", "logical theorem", "logical consequence", and introduced the structural method of defining these concepts in Poland. During World War II he was forced to earn his living as a clerk under German occupation but found time to teach in clandestine Polish schools. After the war ended he became Chair of the Methodology and Theory of Science (afterwards re-named the Chair of Logic) in the Faculty of Mathematical and Physical Sciences of the University of Poznan. In the years 1948-52 he was Rector of Poznan University. Towards the end of his life, he developed the outlines of a new research program in epistemology and in the philosophy of language (*The Problem of Empiricism and the Concept of Meaning*, 1964).

1891

Count Edward Raczynski (1891-1993)

An heir to historical tradition, politician and writer, he was awarded Ph.D. in Law in Kracow. He joined the Polish Foreign Service in 1919 and was a delegate to the 1932-34 disarmament conference in Geneva. As ambassador to the Court of St. James (1934-45), he signed the Anglo-Polish Pact that brought the United Kingdom into the war when Poland was invaded in 1939. A central figure in the Polish government-in-exile based in London during and after World War II, he served as foreign minister (1941-43) and President-in-exile (1979-86).

Zofia Stryjenska (1891-1974)

One of the most acclaimed artists in Poland during the period between the two world wars, she was called "Her Royal Highness, Princess of Polish Painting". A multifaceted artist, she was a painter, muralist, graphic artist, book illustrator as well as designer of kilims, toys, posters, stage sets and costumes. Her greatest accomplishment was when she painted six large panels for the Polish exhibit at the Exposition Internationale des Arts Decoratifs et Industriels Modernes in Paris. Each of the six panels depicted two months as they related to village life and seasonal change and portrayed Polish rites and old Slavic beliefs and customs.

1892

Stefan Banach (1892-1945)

Mathematician and professor at the University of Lvov, he developed the major concepts and theorems of modern functional analysis and made major contributions to the theory of topological vector spaces. He contributed to measure theory, integration and orthogonal series and was co-author of Banach's algebra and Banach's space.

Stanislaw Ostrowski (1892-1982)

In 1912, he joined the secret National Youth Organisation and was a member of the Gunners' Union where he completed non-commissioned officers' school and officers' college. During World War I, he joined the 1st Brigade of the Legions and later served in the Polish Army as a physician with Captain's rank until 1922. After the war, he was an Assistant Professor of the Jan Kazimierz University. As a soldier of the 2nd Corps of General Anders, he took part in the Italian Campaign. After World War II, he worked as a physician and professor of medicine. From 1972-1979, he served as President of Poland.

1893

Roman Ingarden, (1893 - 1970)

Polish phenomenologist with a realist leaning. His works, written in Polish and German, deal with various problems of aesthetics. *Das literarische Kunstwerk* (the best known of his works outside Poland) was published in 1931 and *The Controversy about the Existence of the World*, 2 volumes, was published 1947-1949, in Polish. He accepted the method of eidetic reduction but argued that a realist ontology may be built on a phenomenological basis which provides a method to classify various modalities of being, including specific existence forms of the objects of aesthetic perception. He was a consistent critic of positivism, nominalism, physicalism, and idealism.

1894

Tadeusz Sendzimir (1894-1989)

A Polish engineer and inventor of over 50 inventions in mining and metallurgy, his name has been given to revolutionary methods of processing steel and metals used in every industrialized nation of the world. Internationally renown, he was one of the greatest innovators in the steel industry since Henry Bessemer. The upheavals of the First World War and the Russian Revolution eventually displaced him to Shanghai, where he built the first factory in China to produce screws, nails and wire. Designing and making his own machines, he began experimenting with a new way to galvanize steel that would ultimately revolutionize the steel industry. Returning to Poland in 1930, he obtained support for the construction of the first industrial-scale-galvanizing unit and put into operation several cold strip mills. In 1974, he received the Brinell Gold Medal from the Royal Academy of Technical Sciences in Stockholm (the engineer's equivalent of the Nobel Prize). Among other awards, he has received are the Golden Cross of Merit presented by the President of Poland in 1938, and on the 100th anniversary of the Statue of Liberty, he was one of those prominent immigrants honored for their contributions to America. In 1990 a further tribute was paid to him by his native land when Poland's largest steel plant was renamed Tadeusz Sendzimir Steelworks in recognition of his unique contributions to the steel industry worldwide.

1896

Wiktor Dega (1896-1995)

Orthopedic surgeon, he pioneered in medical rehabilitation of motion organs and was the creator of original methods of healing. Also an initiator of Polish physiotherapy school, he started START (Sports Association of the Disabled) which is a non-profit organisation that uses sport as the most important factor in rehabilitation work. Its competitors represented Poland during all Paralympic Games, won hundreds of medals and for many times were Polish, European and World Champions.

Ludwik Fleck (1896-?)

He enrolled at the Jan Kazimierz University of Lvov, where he received his medical degree and became interested in the problems of microbiological research. From 1923-1935 he worked only in the private bacteriological laboratory which he had founded. During World War II he was appointed teacher and director of the Microbiological Department at the Ukrainian Medical Institute. His work in producing typhus serum became known to the German authorities and he and his family were arrested in 1942 and deported first to the "Laokoon" pharmaceutical factory and subsequently to the Auschwitz concentration camp. Between 1945-1952 he served as the head of the Institute of Microbiology of the School of Medicine of Maria Sklodowska-Curie University of Lublin. In 1954 he was elected a member of the Polish Academy of Sciences. He was awarded the National Prize for Scientific Achievements, second degree in 1951 and he was distinguished with the Officer's Cross of the Order of the Renaissance of Poland in 1955.

Kazimierz Kuratowski (1896-1980)

Known as the father of topology, he specialized in topology, set theory and logic, as well as other branches of mathematics like analysis, differential equations and geometry. In 1917 he wrote his first paper - *On the definitions in mathematics*. He was awarded his doctorate in 1921 and was appointed as a professor at the Technical University of Lvov in 1927. After the German invasion of Poland in 1939, the Poles organized an underground university in Warsaw and he risked his life to teach in this illegal educational establishment through the war. At the end of World War II the whole educational system was destroyed and he took on the role of leader in its rebuilding process. In 1949 he was appointed the Director of the Mathematical Institute of the Polish Academy of Sciences and held this position for 19 years. He also played a major role in the publishing of mathematics in general and Polish mathematics in particular. He was the author of *Topologie,* referred to above, which was the crowning achievement of the Warsaw School in point set topology. The first volume of this work was the major source on metric spaces for several decades.

1898

Janusz Groszkowski (1898-1984)

President of the Polish Academy of Sciences (1962-1972), he discovered a new method of high-vacuum measurements and invented the JG vacuometer. He developed leading research into certain fields of electronics and radio engineering and also devised a method of analyzing non-linear electric oscillations, known as the "Groszkowski method of harmonious oscillations" and developed the most important research in electronics and radio engineering. Before World War II, he published the first summary of the problems connected with cathode tubes.

Aleksander Jablonski (1898-1980)

One of the pioneers of molecular photophysics, he created the concept of the "luminescent centre" and his own theories of quantum-mechanical pressure broadening and concentrational quenching and depolarization of photo luminescence. He studied physics at Krakow University and, after World War I, receiving his Ph.D. in 1930. His early studies on fluorescence in the 1930s lead him to propose the scheme for the energetic transitions in fluorescing molecules, which is now known as the 'Jablonski diagram'. This experimental achievement was later fully confirmed and developed by quantum mechanics.

Henryk Lowmianski (1898-1984)
Historian, he investigated the ancient history of Poland, Slavs and Lithuania and wrote *The Beginnings of Poland*.

1899

Witold Jan Doroszewski (1899-1976)
Linguist, he was a specialist in Polish philology, dialectology, word-formation, and semantics and was the editor of the 11-volumne Polish Language Dictionary.

1900

Helena Syrkus (1900 – 1982)
Professor at Warsaw Polytechnic School, Faculty of Architecture, she was inducted into the Golden Book of the Warsaw Polytechnic School as an outstanding academic teacher in 1979. She is also a partner in the creation of the Polish School of Architecture. She worked for the underground during World War II and afterwards was head of the committee devoted to the rebuilding of Warsaw.

1902

Alfred Tarski (1902-1983)
Mathematician and logician, he introduced the distinction between language and metalanguage. *The Concept of Truth in Formalized Languages* which recognized the paradoxes detected within the foundations of set theory, made numerous contributions to decision theory and model theory and pioneered the application of algebra to the study of formal systems.

1903

Jerzy Konorski (1903-1973)
He introduced a new direction of research, established new theories concerning the physiology of the brain and explained

the mechanism of acquired reflexes, known as secondary conditioned reflexes. His research included the physiological and experiential nature of the learning of voluntary behavior, with special attention to instrumental conditioning of autonomic responses. His books, *Conditioned Reflexes and Neuron Organization* (1948) and *Integrative Activity of the Brain: An Interdisciplinary Approach* (1967) reflects his life's work. The Institute of Psychiatry and Neurology was established as an institution for psychiatric and neurological research by a decision of the Cabinet in 1951. An outstanding neuro-physiologist, he conceived the idea of the Institute as a national center for promotion of basic and clinical research on mental and neurological disorders.

1906

Grazyna Bacewicz (1906-1969)

Composer and accomplished violinist and pianist, she received her musical education in Lodz and in Warsaw. She was a prolific composer and as early as 1933 received the First Prize in Paris for her Brass Quintet. During World War II, she composed two symphonies and a number of chamber works - altogether she has composed over 200 works. She also wrote many outstanding works for piano and for teaching purposes. In Poland, she was honored by the City of Warsaw in 1949, 1950 and 1952; received the Ministry of Culture and Art Award in 1955 and 1962; and was honored by the Association of Polish Composers in 1960. The Polish Government bestowed its higher honor upon her with the Order of Polonia Restituta.

Maria Goeppert-Mayer (1906-1972)

A physicist, she independently developed theory of structure of atomic nuclei. Her works include *Statistical Mechanics* and *Elementary Theory of Nuclear Shell Structure*. In 1963, she won the Nobel Prize for Physics for studies on nuclear shell structure.

1909

Marian Danysz (1909 -)

Physicist, he helped in the development of nuclear technique research in Krakow. From 1950-1952, he participated in research with nuclear emulsion techniques. He co-discovered a new kind of matter - an atom nucleus, which alongside a proton and neutron contains a third particle, the lambda hyperon. In 1962, he obtained hyper-nuclei in excited state and the following year a hyper-nucleus with two lambda hyperons.

Maria Dziewulska (1909 -)

Professor of Music Theory at the Academy of Music in Warsaw, she later studied special effects for radio, film and recording. In 1959, she composed *Inventions* for use in music schools at the first and second levels with the purpose of introducing young students to contemporary music.

Stanislaw Marcin Ulam (1909-1984)

He received his Ph.D. from the University of Lvov and worked on the Manhattan Project where he solved the problem of how to initiate fusion in the hydrogen bomb. He developed the Monte-Carlo Method, which is used to search for solutions to mathematical problems using a statistical sampling method with random numbers. This method is widely used in formulating mathematical software. He proposed the Orion plan for nuclear propulsion of space vehicles.

1910

Tadeusz Krwawicz (1910 -)

Ophthalmologist, he was the inventor of tool for the removal of cataract. He also discovered new methods of eye cryosurgery and cryotherapy. His method consists of the rapid freezing of the tissue to be operated on.

1912

Jadwiga Szajina-Lewandowska (1912-1994)

She has composed 5 compositions for orchestra and piano, 2 children's ballets (*Pinnochio* and *Abduction in Tiutiurlistan*) and a 3-act ballet, *Tais*. In addition, she has written a total of 50 pieces of stage music for puppet and drama theaters and received state awards for several of her compositions.

1913

Jan Nowak-Jezioralski (1913-)

During World War II, he was a courier for the Polish resistance movement. After the war, he became editor of the European service of BBC Radio in London and, later, Director of the Radio Free Europe Polish Service. From 1979-1992, he was a consultant to the U.S. National Security Council and the National Director of the Polish-American Congress. He has written a number of books and articles for magazines, periodicals and newspapers including *Kurier z Warszawy* [A Courier from Warsaw], *Wojna w eterze* [War on the Airways], and *Polska z oddali* [Poland from Afar].

1915

Elisabeth Schwartzkopf (1915 -)

Made her debut as operatic soprano at Berlin Stadtische Oper in *Parsifal*. After WWII, she sang in Vienna State Opera, Covent Gardens in London, LaScala in Milan, the Bayreuth Festival and Salzburg Festival. Her first specialty was in coloratura roles but she later changed to lyric soprano especially in recitals of lieder.

1916

Louise Dobrzynska-Rybicka

She organized pre-elections for the purpose of collaborating in the formation of the necessary elite to support the national movement under the German regime in Poznan. In 1916 she took an active part in the movement of independence in

German-Poland and secretly taught the Polish language under the Russian government.

1917

Janusz Groniowski (1917 - 1989)

He worked at Poznañ University of Medical Sciences for 12 years and during this period his efforts resulted in the construction of a new building of the Department of Anatomic Pathology, which he furnished with the modern equipment. Under his direction, 16 pathologists obtained a doctor's degree and 4 obtained a position of assistant professor. He also initiated the development of a new discipline, which he called ultrastructural anatomy. The application of ultrastructural analyses accompanied by biochemical studies made his scientific achievements recognized all over the world. The rest of his scientific output concerns the first in the country ultrastructural biopsies of kidneys, liver, and lungs as well as pathology of the development period and molecular aspects of colagenogenesis. In 1983 his book entitled *Pathology* was recognized as the best of all textbooks. Another pioneering book in Poland should be recognized is his *Atlas patologii mikroskopowej* (Atlas of microscopic pathology", 1983), which for many years had been the only textbook in the country for practical usage of electron microscopy achievements in pathology. He participated in establishing the Polish Society of Anatomic Pathologists, participated in founding the European Society of Pathologists, and worked in boards and committees of the Polish Academy of Sciences.

Helena Rasiowa (1917-1994)

A mathematician, her main research was in algebraic logic and the mathematical foundations of computer science. In 1984, she introduced an important concept of inference, which led to approximate reasoning and approximate logic, which are now central to the study of artificial intelligence. She helped set up the journal *Fundamenta Informaticae* in 1977 and, from 1986, was an associate editor of the *Journal of Approximate*

Reasoning. A member of the Polish Mathematical Society, she also played a major role in the mathematical life of Poland.

1918

Edmund Nowak (1918 -)

Mechanical design engineer and inventor, he made numerous inventions in designing machinery for processing mechanically and thermally metals and plastics.

Florian Witold Znaniecki

He graduated in philosophy in Jagiellonian University in Krakow and after, in 1910, he received a Ph.D. on the basis of the dissertation entitled *The problem of Values in Philosophy.* In Warsaw he was director of the Polish Emigrants' Protective Association and worked on a study of Polish emigrants, which came out in five volumes in 1918-1920 under the title *The Polish Peasant in Europe and America*, today the classic work in sociology. In 1920 he was chair of sociology at the University of Poznan and founded the Polish Sociological Institute and the first Polish sociological journal -"Polski Przeglad Socjologiczny". In this way Poznan University became the center of sociology as an academic discipline in Poland. He was a visiting professor at Columbia University in New York at the outbreak of the II World War, which kept him from returning to Poland. After II World War he refused to return home to Poland because he did not accept the communist regime. His life and work spanned two cultures: Polish and American. Now, in his homeland, he is considered not only as an eminent figure of Polish sociology but also as a philosopher.

1919

Ryszard Kaczorowski (1919-)

As the last emigre President of the Republic of Poland, he handed over the insignia of the presidential power of the 2nd Republic to President Lech Walesa. His military background included serving in General Anders' Army and, after its evacuation, joined the 3rd Division of Carpathian Gunners, where he completed division secondary school. In England he completed a foreign trade college and until 1986, worked in business as an accountant. During 1955-1967, he was the Chief of Scouts, and, subsequently, President of the emigre Polish Scouting Union (ZHP).

1920

Leslaw Bartelski (1920-)

He was co-editor of Nowiny Literackie (1947-48), Nowa Kultura (1953-63) and Kultura (1963-72). Author of numerous books, he was a member of Union Fighters for Freedom and Democracy (1969-79) and vice president of Warsaw City Council (1973-80). Among his honors are Commanders Cross Polonia Restituta Order, Order of the Banner of Labour, Order of Cyril and Methodius of Bulgaria, Cross of Valour, and Warsaw Insurgent Cross.

Maria Reymanowna (1920-1997)

An outstanding specialist in Mesozoic floras in Poland, she completed her botanical studies at the Jagiellonian University in 1948. From 1947-1953, she worked as an assistant at the Forestry Research Institute. She obtained her doctor's degree in natural sciences in 1960 and her doctoral thesis was entitled *A Cycadeoidean stem from the Western Carpathians*. The paper *The Jurassic flora from Grojec near Krakow in Poland, Caytoniales and anatomy of Caytonia* (1973) describes the new species of *Caytonia*, which she found and was her dissertation for the degree of docent, which she obtained in 1974. In her scientific career she was interested particularly in fossil plant remains with a well-preserved anatomical structure and she published more than 60 scientific papers that were a significant contribution to the progress of world paleobotany. She was concerned not only with plant anatomy and taxonomy but also plant geography, geology, pollination biology, palynology, ecology, paleoclimatology and botanical nomenclature.

Karol Jozef Wojtyla [Pope John Paul II] (1920-2005)

In 1938, he enrolled at Jagiellonian University where he balanced studies with an interest in acting and religiously inspired poetry. After the Nazi occupation forces closed the university in 1939, he worked in a quarry (1940-1944) and then in the Solvay chemical factory to earn his living and to avoid being deported to Germany. In 1942, he began courses in the clandestine seminary of Krakow run by Cardinal Adam Stefan Sapieha, Archbishop of Krakow. He was ordained in 1946 in Krakow and spent much of the next few years studying – he earned two masters degrees and a doctorate. From 1948-1951, he served as a parish priest in the Krakow diocese and then returned to study philosophy at Jagiellonian University. He taught social ethics at the Krakow Seminary from 1952-1958 and in 1956 became a professor at the University of Lublin. In 1958, he was appointed titular bishop of Ombi and auxiliary bishop of Krakow by Pope Pius CII – the youngest bishop in Poland's history. Besides taking part in Vatican Council II (1962-1965) where he made an important contribution to drafting the landmark document *Gaudium et Spes* (The Church in the Modern World), he participated in all the assemblies of the Synod of Bishops. He was appointed Archbishop of Krakow in 1964 by Pope Paul VI, who made him a Cardinal in 1967. He wrote a treatise in 1960 called *"Love and Responsibility"* that laid out the foundation for a modern Catholic sexual ethic. In 1969, the Polish Theological Society published his "The Acting Person," a dense philosophical tract on phenomenology. When elected Pope in 1978, he was the first non-Italian pope in 455 years and the youngest pope in 132 years. Not only was he the most traveled pope in history; he spoke eight languages and was quick to use the media and technology to his advantage. Pope John Paul II is almost universally praised for attempting to build greater understanding between Judaism, Islam and Christianity, as well as for visiting more than 120 countries during his 26-year papacy, nearly every country in the would that would receive him and promoting non-violent revolution against oppressive regimes, especially communism in whose collapse he is sometimes given a personal and vital role. In 1979, his first visit to his homeland of Poland as Pope was a major catalyst for the collapse of communism in Poland and his support for the Solidarity movement in Poland was a key to the downfall of communism in Poland. His successor, the Holy Father Benedict XVI announced that the normal five-year waiting period before beginning the cause of beatification and canonization would be waived for John Paul II and the cause was officially opened by Cardinal Camillo Ruini, vicar general for the diocese of Rome on June 28, 2005.

1923

Wojciech Jaruzelski (1923-)

During the Second World War, he was deported to Siberia and, after the formation of the Polish Army in the Soviet Union, he completed the Polish Army officers' school. He was commander of the reconnaissance platoon, and later chief of reconnaissance of a regiment in the Henryk Dabrowski 2nd Infantry Division. This division took part in the fighting on the Vistula, at the Magnuszew Bridgehead and fought for the liberation of Warsaw, at the Baltic Sea, the Oder and the Elbe rivers as well as working with the armed underground. After graduating with honors from the Infantry College and the Academy of General Staff, he lectured in tactics and staff service and was chief of board of military academies and officers' colleges. Promoted to the post of Chief of Central Political Board, appointed Deputy Minister of National Defense, and, in 1968 - Minister of National Defense. In 1981, he assumed the office of the Chairman of the Council of Ministers (Prime Minister), and declared imposition of the martial law as head of the Military Council for National Salvation. As the only candidate, the National Assembly elected him President of the Republic of Poland with an absolute minimum majority of votes in 1989.

Wislawa Szymborska (1923-)

An accomplished translator, literary critic, and essayist, she was highly acclaimed in her homeland, but unknown in the West until she won the Nobel Prize for Literature in 1996. She wrote *Dlatego zjemy* [that's why we are alive] published in 1952 and *Pytania zadawane sobie* [questions put to myself] published in 1954 under Stalinist pressure and has since repudiated them. Turning to philosophical observation, she wrote in *Wolanie do Yeti* [calling to the yeti] in 1957, and *Sól* [salt] in 1962 and *Sto pociech* [a barrel of laughs] in 1967 in which she explored human isolation and celebrated poetic creation. She often emphasizes the uniqueness of the individual and her verse is deceptively simple; her language colloquial, precise, and contained; and her tone detached and dryly sardonic. Collections of her poetry in English translation include *Sounds, Feelings, Thoughts: Seventy Poems* in 1981, *View with a Grain of Sand* in 1995, and *Poems New and Collected, 1957-1997* published in 1998.

Jan Wladyslaw Wegrzyn (1923-)

Welding metallurgy consultant and researcher, he graduated with BS from the Academy of Mining in 1949 and Dr Habilation in 1964. He was manager of welding metallurgy department of Polish Welding Institute (1949-1981), professional manager of welding department of Silesian Technical University (1981-1993) and consultant to metallurgy plant Huta Baildon (1993-1997). In addition to contributing over 200 articles on welding physics and metallurgy, welding techniques and materials to professional journals, he is author or co-author of 8 books and has numerous patents on welding and filler materials.

1925

Maria Dabrowska (1889-1965)

Polish sociologist, novelist and journalist, she worked as a militant publicist to further social and economic reform in Poland. In 1925, she wrote her epic novel, *Noce I Dnie*, a saga of a family through several generations, which examined the conditions of Polish peasants and calls for land reform. It is deemed to be one of the best works in Polish. Her last novel *Przygody Czlowieka Myslacego* examined life under Hitler's conquering army.

Sylwester Kaliski (1925-1978)
Engineer and specialist in applied physics, he developed the theory of continuous amplification of ultra and hyper sounds in semi-conductive crystals. He also developed the theory of connected magneto-thermo-mechanic fields obtained using laser impulse plasma temperature of tens of millions of degrees Centigrade, i.e. a temperature at which thermonuclear microsynthesis occurs with the isolation of the neutrons of the synthesis. This result brought Polish science into the mainstream of world research as regards new, cheap sources of energy for the future.

Mariusz Machiej Zydowo (1925-)
Biochemistry educator, he graduated from Medical University of Gdansk with MD in 1950 and Ph.D. in 1951. Since 1951, he taught at Medical University of Gdansk. In 1976, he wrote *Biochemia*. His achievements include discovery of a different enzyme regulation in homeothermic and poikilothermic animals and discovery of heart enzyme (ampdeaminase) regulation by lipid membranes. He is a member of Polish Biochemists Society, Gdansk Science Society and Polish Academy of Science.

1927

Marian Kucala (1927-)
Linguistics educator, he graduated from Jagiellonian University with MA (1952), PhD (1962) and Doctor Habilitation (1967). He was director of Institute of Polish Language History (1982-1998). His books include *Grammatical Gender in the History of the Polish Language* (1975), *History of the Polish Language* (1978). He was co-author of *Encyclopedia of the Polish Language* (1978) and *Old Polish Dictionary* (1953-1999). Also,

he was editor-in-chief of Dictionary of Jan Kochanowski's Language since 1994 and editor-in-chief of Jezyk Polski (Polish language) magazine.

1928

Dorota Simonides (1928-)

After studying Polish philology and ethnography at Jagellonian University (1953), she obtained a MA and Ph.D. in Humanities (1970) from the Faculty of Humanities at Wroclaw University (1962) and Doctor Habilitated from Poznan University (1977). She specializes in Silesian folklore and in theory of folklore and has published over 300 scientific work - many in foreign languages. From 1980-1985, she was Deputy to the 8th term of the Sejm. She has been Senator to the 1st, 2nd, 3rd and 4th term of the Senate of the Republic of Poland and has served as Chair of the Senate Emigration and Poles Abroad Committee.

1929

Zdzislaw Beksinski (1929 -)

Creator of striking and mysterious world of dreams and the best artist Poland has produced, he attended university in Kracow where he studied architecture and worked several years as a construction site supervisor. In 1958, he began to gain critical praise for his photography, and later went on to drawing. His highly detailed drawings are often quite large, and very intricate. He soon became the leading figure in contemporary Polish art and has had many exhibitions throughout his native Poland and Europe.

Janusz Zbigniew Brozyna (1929-)

Cybernetician, he received an engineering degree from Polytech University in 1952, M of Cybernetics in 1954 and DS in 1969. He worked as researcher at Radar Institute (1951-54-); director of research and development (1961-64); director Department Ministry (1966-76) and research vytvorology (1977-78). His achievements include patents on new displays for marine radar, inventor of the new system of anti-collision and navigation radar, of a computer expert system and general math theory of civilization.

Olga Teresa Krzyzanowska (1929-)
During the Nazi occupation, she belonged to the scouting resistance movement and is the recipient of the Cross of Courage in Combat. In 1952, she graduated from the Medical Academy in Gdansk as specialist in internal and occupational diseases. Between 1952-1962, she worked at the District Hospital in Puck, Provincial Hospital in Gdansk and Medical Academy in Gdansk. From 1962-1989, she was head of the Provincial Occupational OutPatient Clinic in Gdansk. Since 1989, she has been Deputy to the 10th, 1st, 2nd and 3rd Sejm of the Republic of Poland. She has chaired the Rules and Deputies Affairs Committee, the Deputies Ethics Committee and was Deputy chair of the Foreign Affairs Committee.

Wladyslaw Radzikowski (1929-)
Econometrician and researcher, he was forced to work as a metal worker at age 14 for various German firms during World War II. After receiving his masters in Industrial Economic in 1955, he began his research career. As Deputy Director of Research at the Institute of Industrial Economics and Organization in Warsaw, he was in charge of developing and implementing mathematical methods in machine building, metallurgy, fiber and other industries. He became Head Director at the Institute of Machine-Building Industry in 1957. His books include *Project Management* (1979*), Informatics Systems in Organization and Management* (1981) and *Operations Research in Management* (1985). He is a member of the Polish Society for Operations and Systems Research.

1930

Bogdan Wojciech Burxzyk (1930-)
Chemist, he obtained M.Sc in Chemistry from Wroclaw University of Technology in 1955, Ph.D. in 1962 and DS in 1971. From 1955-74 he was assistant adjunct docent at Faculty

of Chemistry, Wroclaw University of Technology and professor of chemistry since 1976, head chemistry division at Institute of Organic and Polymer Technology (1972-96), deputy director (1972-81) and director (1991-96). He has contributed articles to professional journals and is a patentee in field.

Tomasz Strzembosz (1930-)
Historian, professor at the Catholic University of Lublin and the Institute of Political Studies at the Polish Academy of Sciences. Author of *Military Actions of the Underground in Warsaw, 1939-1945, The Rescue and Freeing of Prisoners in Warsaw, 1939-1944,* and *The Underground Republic of Poland.* He also writes about the history of the Polish resistance movement in northeastern Polish territories under the Soviet occupation between 1939 and 1941.

1931

Halina Bortnowska (1931-)
Catholic activist and commentator, She was a member of the editorial staff of *Znak* from 1960-1983. She participated actively in the work of the World Council of Churches (1967-1982). From 1991-1997, she was a member of the International Council of *Pax Christi* and co-founder of *Otwarta Rzeczpospolita* [Open Republic] Association against Anti-Semitism and Xenophobia.

Jerzy Gazdzicki (1931-)
Geodesist, he was department head at the Institute of Geodesy and Cartography (1962-1974), research director of Gedetic and Cartographic Information Center (1974-1981) and director of Institute of Technology at Warsaw University (1981-1987). His books include Information in *Geodesy & Cartography* (1975), *Spatial Information Systems* (1990) and *Cadastral Systems* (1995). He is a member of European Cooperation Network for Education and Research in Land Information Systems and Polish Association for Spatial Information.

1932

Roma Rokicka-Milewska (1932-)

Pediatrician, hematologist and oncologist, she received her MD from the Medical School of Warsaw in 1955 and Ph.D. in 1974. From 1970-1983 she was head of Hematology Ward and head of Department of Pediatrics, Hematology/Oncology since 1984. She was editor and co-author of *Pediatric Hematology* (1982), *Pediatrics for Dentistry* (1986), *Hemophilia in Children* (1992) and *Correction of Genetic Diseases by Transplantation* (1996). Since 1989, she is President of the Foundation for Support of Children with Blood Cancer.

1933

Janina Brzostowska (1907-1986)

She published her first novel *Bezrobatni Warszawy* in 1933, which was withdrawn from publication by censorship. It was a cry of protest of the unemployed from the depth of their physical and moral misery. Her second novel described a woman coming of age. She spent the years of German occupation working in the Polish underground.

Marian Czarnowski (1933-)

Plant physiologist and researcher, he has an MS from Jagiellonian University (1952), D in Natural Sciences (1962) and D.Sc. in 1973. He has taught at the Polish Academy of Sciences for many years and is head of the Department of Plant Physiology since 1998. In 1973, he published a book *Methods for Estimation of Photosynthetic Production* and has contributed articles to professional journals. He is also a recipient of Polonia Restituta-Knight's Cross.

Krystyna Orzechowska-Juzwenko (1933-)

Physician, clinical pharmacologist and researcher, she was assistant professor of pharmacology at Wroclaw Medical University (1957-1979) and physician at Clinic Internal Diseases (1957-1979). Her books include *Clinical Pharmacology* (1986),

Cancer Chemotherapy (1990), *Angiotensin Converting Enzyme Inhibitors* (1992) and *Pharmacology* (1995). She was decorated with Order of Golden Cross of Merit in 1981 and Order Cross Polonia Restituta in 1996. Also, she is a member of Polish Academy of Science, Polish Pharmacology Society and International Society of Therapeutic Drug Monitoring.

1934

Marian Elbanowski (1934-)

Chemist, educator and researcher, he received is MS from Adam Mickiewicz University (1955), D.Sc. (1959) and Ph.D. from Warsaw Technical University (1962). Since 1979, he has been associate professor and head of the Department of Rare Earth, Faculty of Chemistry at Adam Mickiewicz University. He has contributed numerous articles to professional journals and is a patentee in field. From 1992-1994, he was Vice President of Polish Chemical Society and is a member of Inter-American Photo-chemistry Society and European Rare Earth and Actinide Society.

Kazimierz Wincenty Siudzinski (1934-)

Biologist, oceanographer and zoologist, he graduated with MS from Adam Mickiewicz University (1957) and D Natural Sciences from Academy of Agriculture (1969). He worked at the Sea Fisheries Institute as planktologist (1957-1968), head of oceanography department (1968-1979) and head of the Center of Hydrobiology (1979-1990). Since 1990, he is director of Oceanographic Museum and Marine Aquarium. He was editor of Works of Sea Fisheries Institute and is author of textbook, *Oceanographic Research Technologies* (1962). His interests are history of oceanographic-biologic research of Poland and other countries of the Baltic Sea.

1935

Eugeniusz Adamczak (1935-)

He obtained an MS from the University of Wroclaw in 1958 and has been director of the branch office of Romer Polish

Cartographical Publishing House since 1997. From 1986-1990 he was chairman of Panorama Raclawicka Council and vice-president of the Polish Publishers Association (1979-1980). His honors include decorated Knight of Polonia Restituta Order (1977), Commander of Polonia Restituta Order (1985) and Golden Medal of Merit (1987).

Konstanty Kalinowski (1935-)
Art historian, he graduated with MA (1957) and Ph.D. (1963) from Adam Micklewicz University. He work as assistant at the National Museum of Poznan (1957-1961) and, since 1971 has taught at the Institute of Art History at Adam Micklewicz University. His books include *Glorification of a Ruler and Dynasty in the 17th and 18th Century* (1973), *Baroque Architecture in Silesia* (1986) and *Baroque Art in Silesia* (1990). He received the Golden Cross of Merit (1973), Order of Polonia Restitute (1982) and Knight Commander Constantinian of Order of St. George.

1936

Krystyna Chojnowska-Liskiewicy (1936 -)
Yachtswoman, she was educated at the Polytechnical University in Gdansk where she has been a shipbuilding engineer since 1960. In March 1976 she set out to circumnavigate the globe in her single-handed yacht *Mazurek*, completing her voyage exactly two years later, in March 1978. The feat won her many decorations in Poland and abroad, and she described her adventure in *Pierwsza dook ola Swiata* (The first one round the world (1979)).

Stanislaw Kostka Flieger (1936-)
Veterinarian and specialist in automatic nervous system, he has been head of the Institute of Animal Anatomy, Lublin Agricultural Academy since 1995. His books include *Splanchnology of Domestic Animals* (1995) and *Peripheral Nervous Systems in Domestic Animals* (1995). He is also a member of the Polish

Society of Veterinary Sciences and European Anatomical Society.

Jan Pirozynski (1936-)
Historian, librarian and educator, he graduated from Jagiellonian University with an MA in 1957, D in History in 1968 and Habilitation in 1987. He was an archivist at the State Archives in Krakow from 1958-1959 and worked at Jagiellonian University in Krakow from 1959-1988. Since 1988, he has taught modern history, librarianship and information science at Jagiellonian University. His books include *Warsaw Sjem 1570* and *Cracow Printing of the 15th -16th Century.*

1937

Roald Hoffmann (1937-)
The Nobel Prize winner in 1981 for the "application of molecular orbital theory to chemical reactions." He co-formulated the Woodward-Hoffman Rules of Orbital Symestry. In 1962 he received his doctorate from Harvard University and worked on the electronic structure of stable and unstable molecules. He developed the extended Huckel method, "a molecular orbital scheme which allowed the calculation of the approximate electronic structure of molecules." His second major contribution was "a two-pronged exploration of the electronic structure of transition sites and intermediates in organic reactions."

1938

Zdzislaw Bubnicki (1938-)
Computer science and engineering educator, he was associate professor of Control and Systems Engineering at Wroclaw University of Technology (1960-73), and director Institute Control and Systems Engineering since 1981. He is editor-in-chief since 1975 of Systems Science, an international journal. His books include *Introduction to Expert Systems* (1990) and *Foundations of Management Information Systems* (1993). He received an award for Outstanding Scientific Achievements from the Ministry of Research and Higher Education in 1992

and silver medal from the International Federation of Information Processing in 1998.

Aleksandra Bujakiewicz (1938-)
A photogrammetry and mapping educator, she received M.Sc from Warsaw University of Science and Technology in 1961, Ph.D. in 1971 and DS in 1980. From 1962-63, she worked as photogrammetist at Cartographic Enterprise and from 1964-81, went from junior lecturer to associate professor and since 1999 full professor at the Warsaw University of Science and Technology. She has contributed articles to professional journals and is co-author of *Geographic Information* (1994).

Zbigniew Religa (1938 -)
Cardiologist, he is a pioneer of heart transplantation in Poland and has grafted an artificial valve created from materials taken from human corpses in 1995. He is head of the Foundation for Heart Surgery Development created in 1992. It is the only non-state medical research institute in Central and Eastern Europe. The foundation designed the a new pneumatic artificial heart that is three times smaller than similar models; is working to introduce a unique type of heart valve and monitors for artificial heart function.

1939

Kazimierz Flaga (1939)
Civil engineer and educator, he was associate professor Krakow University of Technology (1984-1992), head of bridge and tunnels since 1979, and director of the Institute of Building Materials and Structures (1992-1996). He is author of *Energetic Bases of the Increase of Concrete Strength Subjected to Thermal Treatment* (1971) and co-author of *Concrete Building*, Vol. 5 (1973). He is a member of the Polish Academy of Science (chairman of the Concrete Construction section 1990-1996) and a member of the Committee of Science and Research (chairman of section of Construction Buildings Materials 1993-1996). His honors include the Silver Cross of Merit Polish

Authority (1976) and Companion's Cross Order of Revival of Poland (1984).

1940

Jerzy Buzek (1940-)

In the 1960s, he obtained his Ph.D. in engineering and his academic work focused on chemical engineering and environmental protection. In 1980 he joined the Solidarity trade union and became one of its advisers. During the period of martial law, he was a representative of his region in the underground national structures and was active in the underground publishing activities. He was Four times, at various points of his career, he was chosen chairman of the National Convention of "Solidarity". He worked for ideals of the Solidarity trade union movement: the restoration of Poland's sovereignty; the reconstruction of the country after half a Century of the ruinous communist regime; the assurance of safety and development of his homeland through the adoption of a clear pro-Western approach. From 1997-2001 he was Prime Minister of the Polish government at a time when Poland was going through another stage of transformation. The government took up the challenge and started - against a very strong resistance of the leftist opposition - a program of four reforms, i.e. the administration, insurance, education and healthcare system reforms. It was also this government that brought Poland into the NATO structures and made a great progress in its integration with the European Union. Currently he is engaged in the creation of Poland's pro-European policy and supports the preparation of his country to the presence in the European structures and teaching students in the area of international relations, including the European integration.

Tomasz Szarota (1940-)

Historian, professor at the Historical Institute at the Polish Academy of Sciences and a prominent expert on the history of World War II and the Nazi occupation. The author of a number of books including *Everyday Life In Warsaw Under the*

Occupation, (published in Polish and German with an English translation forthcoming) and *Ordinary Life In European Capitals Under the Occupation*. In 2000 he published *On the Threshold of Destruction: Anti-Jewish Riots and Pogroms in Occupied Europe* about anti-Jewish actions in European cities occupied by the Nazis.

1941

Miroslaw Hermaszewski (1941 -)

Airforce Pilot, Brigadier General and Commander of Deblin Air Force School, he joined the Polish Air Force after graduating from High Aviation School in 1965. In 1971, he graduated from the Karol Sverchevski Military Academy. Before he became a cosmonaut, he was a fighter pilot. He was accepted into the Soviet cosmonaut unit in 1976 and underwent the full general space preparation course under the Intercosmos program for co-operation with socialist countries. In 1978 he became the first citizen of Poland to make a space flight when he flew aboard Soyuz 30 and spent eight days aboard the Salyut space station. After 1978, he continued service in the Polish Air Force. From 1981-1982 he was a member of Poland's Military Council for National Salvation. In 1982 he graduated from the Voroshilov Military Academy and served as the Chief of the Shkola Orlyat High Aviation School (1982 - 1985). Afterwards, he served in the Defense Office of Poland (1985-1989).

Alicja Julia Grzeskowiak (1941-)

Lawyer and politician, she graduated from Nicholas Copernicus University with a MA in 1963, LLD in 1971 and D Habilitation in 1978. She worked as credit inspector at National Bank of Poland in 1963 and was admitted to the bar in 1969. Since 1991, she is a member of the administrative council of John Paul II Foundation and counselor of Pontifical Council Family since 1993. She was elected to the Senate of the Republic of Poland in 1989, was deputy speaker (1991-1993) and speaker (1997). Her books include *Death Penalty in the Polish Penal Law* (1978), *Issues of the Legal Protection of the Conceived*

Child in the Work of Sejm and Senate of the Republic of Poland in the Years 1990-1991 (1994), and *The Name of God in the Constitution* (1996). In 1992, she was member and founder of the Polish Federation Life Protection Movement. She is recipient of Pro Ecclesia et Pontifice, The Holy See in 1991 and Dame of the Order of Holy Sepulchre in Jerusalem in 1996.

1942

Janina Gudzio Orlowska (1942-)

Gastrointestinal pathologist, she graduated with an MB from Warsaw Medical Academy in 1967 with a specialty in pathology. Since 1994, she is head of Pathology Department at Central Railway Hospital. In addition to contributing articles to scientific journals, she is author of manual *Pathology of the Esophagus, Stomach and Intestines* published in 1979. A member of the European Society of Pathology, she is a member of the Polish Society of Pathology and board director since 1995.

Marek Maria Sozanski (1942-)

Environmental engineering consultant, he graduated with MS in Sanitary Appliances from Wroclaw University of Technology (1966), Ph.D. (1975) and D.Sc. (1990). He has participated in numerous conferences on environmental protection engineering, municipal and rural water supply and water quality. Since 1994, he is an expert with the Ministry of Environmental Protection and Natural Resources. His achievements include many research works on modeling and optimization of selected water treatment processes, theology of alum sludges and sewage sludges, non-Newtonian flow of sludges in pipes and characteristics of wastewater sludge.

1943

Joanna Bruzdowicz (1943 -)

She studied at the Warsaw Lyceum of Music and earned her MA in 1966. Her doctoral thesis was *Mathematics and Logic in Contemporary Music* at the Sorbonne. In addition to composing two operas, orchestral, chamber, keyboard, vocal and electronic music, she has written incidental music to several films and TV shows. She also works as a journalist, critic and lecturer on contemporary electroacoustic and Polish music. In 2001, she received the Order of Polonia Restituta, the highest distinction from the Polish government, for her contribution to Polish culture.

Stanislaw Burzynski (1943 -)
His main scientific accomplishments include discovery of antineoplastons and formulation of the theory of biochemical defense system against cancer and his inventions of new treatment for cancer, AIDS, viral infection, autoimmune diseases, neurofibromatosis and Parkinson's Disease. He obtained approval of 49 patents and is author and co-author of 169 scientific publications.

Juliusz Cezary Chojnacki (1943-)
Hydrobiologist and oceanographer, he obtained his BS in Marine Fisheries from the Agricultural University of Szczecin (1968) and Ph.D. in Oceanography (1984). From 1990-1996, he was associate professor of the International Center of Ecology and head of investigations in artificial reefs at Polish Foundation of Sciences. In 1997, he became a member of the science board of Wolin National Park and in 1999, professor at the Maritime University of Szczecin. He is co-author of *What Happened to the Baltic Sea* (1992) and author of *Outline of Water Ecology* (1996) and *Basic in Water Ecology* (1998). In addition, he is a fellow of World Association of Copepodologists and a member of Polish Academy of Science, European Union Coastal Conservation and European Artificial Reefs Research Network.

Jacek Kurczewski (1943-)
Sociologist, professor at the University of Warsaw, he holds the Chair of Sociology of Customs and Law at the Institute of Applied Social Sciences. From 1991-1993, he was the deputy speaker of the Polish *Sejm* [parliament], member of the

Polish Television Program Council, and member of the Mass Media Ethics Council. His is author of a number of books on sociology and the sociology of law, including (in English): *The Resurrection of Rights in Poland* and *Family Law and Family Policy in the New Europe.*

Marta Ptaszynska (1943 -)
As a percussionist, she specializes in the performance of avant-garde works. She is a prolific composer and has written 10 orchestral works, 11 vocal-instrumental pieces, 4 stage works and the largest number of works for chamber groups. Her opera *Oscar from Alva* received the Polish Television Award in 1986. The same year, another of her compositions *Opowiesc Zimowa* (Winter's Tale) was honored with second prize at the International Rostrum of Composers organized by UNESCO in Paris. In 1995, she received the Cross of Merit from president Lech Walesa and in 1996 was the recipient of the prestigious Jurzkowski Foundation Award in music.

Elzieta Zawacka
Prior to World War II, she was an instructor of Polish Women Military Training Organization and, after the German invasion, she was a courier and emissary of the Home Army Main Headquater to the Commander of the Polish Army in London. She was the only woman paratrooper, called 'nightmares', trained in Britain and dropped from British planes over Poland in 1943. After the war, she worked as a mathematician, teacher and humanist.

1944

Elzbieta Sikora (1944 -)
A professor of electronic music at the Music Conservatory in Angouleme, she studied sound recording at the Music Academy in Warsaw before shifting to composition. In 1971, she made her debut as a composer with *Intervention* - a musical parable for two percussionists, baritone tuba and symphony orchestra

on tape. Her must recent commission was a cantata celebrating the millennium of her native city of Gdansk.

Ewa Symonides (1944-)

She graduated from the Faculty of Biology and Earth Science (1972), obtained doctor's degree in Natural Sciences (1978) from Nicolaus Copernicus University. After graduation she taught at the University of Warsaw and, currently, is Under Secretary of State and Chief Nature Conservator at the Ministry of the Environment. She has served on the editorial board of numerous publications including *Journal of Vegetation Science, Ecological News, Polish Ecology*, etc. Member of numerous professional organizations, she is author of more than 160 publications and 20 expert opinions in the field of nature conservation. In 1996, she was awarded a Golden Medal for merits for environmental protection and water management and in 2000, received the Hunting Knife of the Polish Hunter for special merits for forestry.

Stanislaw Zelichowski (1944-)

In 1967, he graduated from the Faculty of Forestry, The Main College of Rural Management. He was employed in the Ciechanow Forest Inspectorate as lecturer (1969-1974), forest inspector in Dwukoly Forest Inspectorate (1974-1987) and member of the National Forestry Council (1987-1989). While a Member of Parliament during the 9th, 10th, 1st, 2nd and 3rd terms, he served as Deputy Chairman of the Commission for Agriculture, Food, Economy and Forestry, Chairman of the Team for Forestry and Nature Conservation, Chairman of Commission for Environmental Protection Natural Resources and Forestry. From 1993-1997, he was Minister of Environmental Protection Natural Resources and Forestry.

1945

Brigadier-General Tadeusz Balachowicz (1945-)

His education includes graduation from the Officers School of Radio Technology (1967), Master of Law from University of Warsaw (1977) and Center for Post-graduate Studies of Legislative Issues at the University of Warsaw (1984). From 1967-1977, he served in the National Air Defense as Commander of the Radio Localization Station and from 1977-1994 he served as Chief of the Organization and Legal Department within the Secretariat of the National Defense Committee. Since 1996, he worked at the National Security Bureau as Deputy Director of the Defense Preparedness Department. He was appointed Deputy Head of the National Security Bureau.

Teresa Liszcz (1945-)
After graduating from the Faculty of Law and Administration (1968) and Doctor of Legal Sciences in labor law (1970) from Marie Curie-Sklodowska University, she obtained the degree of Doctor Habilitated in legal sciences (labor law) from Lodz University (1988). Since 1992, she has been assistant professor at Marie Curie-Sklodowska University and head of the Labor Law Institute. She is author of approximately 150 scientific works on labor law and social insurance including 10 books. In 1991, she was Secretary of State for Socio-Economic and Rural Affairs at the Presidential Chancellery and, from 1994-1997, she was adviser to the Chairman of the Supreme Chamber of Control and member of the College of the Chamber. She has been Deputy to the 10th, 1st and 3rd term Sejm of the Republic of Poland. During the 1st term Sejm, she chaired the Legislation Committee and represented the 3rd term Sejm as member of the National Council of the Judiciary.

1946

Marek Borowski (1946-)
He studied in the Foreign Trade Faculty of the Warsaw School of Economics with a specialization in international economic relations. From 1968-1982, he worked in the Centrum Department Stores finishing as its chief economic specialist. Subsequently, he worked in the Economic Department of the Domestic Market Ministry where he represented the Ministry in a panel of economic experts mandated with preparing economic

reform guidelines. From 1989-1991, he was Deputy Minister of the Domestic Market involved in the process of privatization of trade and the tourist sector and the implementation of economic reforms. He was a Member of Parliament since 1991 and served as a member of the Economic Policy, Budget and Finance Committee of the Sejm. From 1993-1994, he was Deputy Prime Minister and Minister of Finance, Head of the Council of Ministers Office (1995-1996), Vice-marshal of the Sejm (1996-2001) and Marshal of the Sejm of the 4th Term since 2001.

Zbigniew Wladyslaw Porada (1946-)
Electronics educator, he graduated with MS from the Mining & Metallurgical Academy (1970), Ph.D. (1978) and D.Sc. from the Institute of Electron Technology (1996). He has worked as Assistant Professor (1979-1996) at Kracow University of Technology and is currently head of the Electronics Division. His books include *Automotive Sensory System* and *Road Vehicle Automation* both published in 1993.

Irena Kirszenstein-Szewinska (1946 -)
One of the greatest women track and field athletes of all time, she won three Olympic gold medals, plus two silvers and two bronzes; as well as five European gold medal championships (and five other medals). This is a feat never accomplished before by any runner, male or female and a record unequaled in the history of women's track and field. She was Poland's Athlete of the Year in l965 and was elected to the International Women's Sports Hall of Fame in 1992.

Aleksander Wolszczan (1946-)
Contemporary Polish radioastronomer and astrophysicist, he is one of the foremost researchers of pulsars. He graduated from Nicolaus Copernicus University in 1969, then earned a Ph.D. degree in physics there in 1975. His Ph.D. thesis concerned spectra of pulsars. Throughout his career he collaborated with Polish and American research centers. Since

1992 he lectured at Nicolaus Copernicus University. Between 1991-1994, he discovered the first extraterrestrial planetary system (comprising at least three planets) orbiting pulsar *PSR B1257+12'* in the constellation Virgin [Virgo]. This is one of the most important astronomical discoveries of the last decade and is "*the greatest discovery Polish astronomers made since Copernicus.*" The discovery has aroused a worldwide interest and triggered extensive hunt for other extraterrestrial planetary systems, leading to discoveries of many other such systems.

1947

Grazyna Bacewicz (1947 -)
Musicologist and lecturer at the Wroclaw Academy of Music, she has written compositions for orchestra, chamber groups, choir, piano and voice and other instruments. She received honors at the All-Polish Competition for Composers in 1968 and 1973, in 1975 at the International Competition for Women Composers in Mannheim and in 1987 at the UNESCO international Composers Rostrum in Paris.

Leszek Balcerowicz (1947-)
He graduated with distinction from Foreign Trade faculty in 1970 and received his Ph.D. in economics in 1975 from the Central School of Planning and Statistics (now Warsaw School of Economics). Since 1992, he has been a professor at the Warsaw School of Economics and since 1993 he was director of Chair of International Comparative Studies at Warsaw School of Economics. He has lectured worldwide and has written numerous publications on economic issues in Poland and abroad. From 1989-1991 and 1997-2000, he was Deputy Prime Minister, Minister of Finance and President of the Economic Committee of the Council of Ministers. As Poland's financial minister in the 1990s, he supervised a program of economic reform that ensured Poland's successful transition to a market economy. In 2001, the Sejm of the Republic of Poland appointed him President of the National Bank of Poland.

1948

Stanislaw Flejterski (1948-)

Economist, educator and banker, he was assistant lecturer at Economic Institute, Technical University (1970-1985) and senior lecturer (1985-1989). From 1989-1993, he was senior lecturer in International Economic and Business at Agricultural Academy and since 1992 has been professor of Finance and Banking at University of Szczecin. He has been on the Board of Directors of the Pekao Bank, Szczecin branch (1991-1992) and director of Bank BIG S.A., Szczecin branch. Since 1991, he is co-editor of *Polish Studies on Asia, Africa and Latin American Affairs* and has received two prizes from the Ministry of Education.

Boguslaw Liberadzki (1948-)

After graduating with MS in Economy (1970) and DS in Economy (1975), he was Director of the Research Institute for Transport Economy from 1986-1989. He was undersecretary of state at the Ministry of Transport and Maritime Economy (1989-1993), vice minister (1993-1997) and a deputy to Sejm Parliament since 1997. Between 1993-1994, he was chairman of the Polish Transport Adjustment Program to the European Union and is chairman of the supervisory board of LOT Polish Airlines. He was decorated with the Silver and Golden Cross of Merit.

1950

Wlodzimierz Cimoszewicz (1950-)

Farmer, international jurist and politician, he graduated from the Law Faculty of Warsaw University with a doctor's degree in international law. A member of the Sejm since 1989, he served on the Sejm Foreign Affairs Committee. From he was Deputy Prime Minister and Minister of Justice (1993-1995), Deputy Marshall of the Sejm and deputy chairman of the Constitutional Commission (1995-1996), Prime Minister (1996-1997) and Minister of Foreign Affairs since 2001. His awards include Cavalier of the Order of Merit of the French Republic and Cavalier of the Order of Merit of the Republic of Greece.

Przemyslaw Grudzinski (1950-)
Educator and political activist, he received his Ph.D. from the Institute of History, Polish Academy of Sciences in 1977. From 1976-1996, he was professor of history at the Polish Academy of Sciences. During the 1980s, he was involved in independent publishing activities as a member of Solidarity, which contributed to the fall of Poland's communist government. He was advisor the Deputy Minister of National Defense (1990), Director of the Bureau of Research for the Polish Parliament (1991) and Deputy Minister of National Defense (1992-1993). In 2000, he became Ambassador of Poland to the United States.

Anna Walentynowicz
In 1950, she began working in the Lenin Shipyard in Gdansk, Poland. She joined the communist party but soon became disillusioned as she saw that workers were not allowed to organize or speak out. As a crane operator, she began to speak for workers and challenged the shipyard management and eventually became a leader in the labor strikes. In August of 1980, she was fired for standing up for herself and other workers. After she was fired, Polish workers were incited to strike in her defense that eventually resulted in the right for all Polish workers to form independent unions.

1951

Jan Krzysztof Bielecki (1951-)
Active in political and economic affairs of Poland for over two decades, he started his career as an economic lecturer at Gdansk University in 1973-1981. An advisor to key Solidarity figures in the early 1980s, he organized economic publications and was involved in the historic strike at Gdansk shipyard in 1981. During the first half of the 1980s, he continued to play an active role in the then illegal 'Solidarity' - publishing underground political materials, contacting foreign supporters

contributed to the formation of Solidarity's economic policy by developing a market-based approach as an alternative to Poland's communist state planning. From 1985-1990 he was the Chief Executive Officer of 'Doradca' - a consulting co-operative in Gdansk, Poland. (As a means to both earn a living outside of state enterprises and provide support for Solidarity resistance activities against communist regime , members of Solidarity founded 'Doradca' in 1985.) President Walesa and the Parliament confirmed him as Prime Minister on January 5, 1991. His cabinet successfully negotiated foreign debt reduction and the EC Association Agreement. He was a member of the Foreign Relations Committee in the Sejm (Polish Parliament) and the Chief Delegate of the Polish Parliament to the European Parliament. From 1992-1993 he served as a Minister for European Integration in the new coalition government of Poland. In 1993 the Governor for Poland appointed him to the Board of Directors at the European Bank for Reconstruction and Development. He has published numerous articles for both foreign and Polish specialist papers and magazines and is also a co-author of the book *Histoire de l'Europe* (1997).

1952

Stanislaw Jerzy Czuczwar (1952-)

Pharmacologist, he was professor of pharmacology at Lublin Medical School (1975-1987) and since 1997, he is head of the isotope lab at the Lublin Institute of Rural Medicine. He has contributed numerous articles to professional journals and has been the recipient of seven 1st degree awards from the Ministry of Health. His achievements include new strategies for treatment of epilepsy.

August Dehnel

In 1952, he founded the Mammal Research Institute (MRI) which since 1960 has been scientifically supervising the program of European bison restitution conducted by the Bialowieski National Park. It has also been involved in the long-term research on bison including the problems of physiology, morphology, disease, ecology and behavior in the free-living populations in Bialowieski Primeval Forest. He founded an international journal of mammalogy in 1954 that covers all aspects of mammalian biology.

Apolonia Klepacz (1952-)
In 1975, she graduated from the Faculty of Machine Production Technology at Silesian Technical University and in 1990, obtained her doctorate of Technical Sciences from Wroclaw Technical University. She has worked as an academic teacher at the Higher School of Engineering in Opole and then in the Faculty of Natural Science Technology at Opole University. Since 1998, she was Deputy Chair of the Management Board of LOBBE Opole - a waste management and road construction company.

1954

Aleksander Kwasniewski (1954-)
Polish politician, he studied transport economics (foreign trade) at the University of Gdansk, and was an organizer of the Socialist Union of Polish Students during the late 1970s. He was the editor of *ITD* (1981-84) and of *Sztandar Mlodych* (1984-85), both youth-oriented party newspapers, where he earned a reputation as a moderate reformist thinker. He was also founder of the *Bajtek*, the first Polish computer magazine for young readers. From 1988 to 1991, he was Chairman of the Polish Olympic Committee. In 1991, after the collapse of the Communist party, he founded the Democratic Left Alliance (SLD), a social democratic party and became a Member of Parliament. He became president of Poland in 1995, promising to ease the problems caused by Poland's abrupt shift to a free-market economy. He worked intensely for Poland's entrance to NATO (1999) and the European Union (2004).

Zbigniew Maczka (1954-)

He graduated with M.Sc. in Electrical Engineering from the Mining and Metallurgic Academy in Krakow in 1978. Between 1989-1993, he was the leading avionics constructor at the Research and Development Center in Mielec and was responsible for the supervision of avionics construction of a patrol plane designed for the Navy and a passenger aircraft Skytruck. He also participated in the development of projects leading to the restructuring of Mielec Airworks. In 1993, he became a Member of Parliament and served on the National Defense Committee, the Aviation Working Group and the Committee for Economic and Industrial System. While a member of these committees, he participated in the development of acts leading to the restructuring of the defense industry. In 1997, he was appointed General Inspector of Civil Aviation.

1955

Marek M. Siwiec (1955-)

He graduated with J.Sc. from the Academy of Mining and Metallurgy specializing in the physics of solid bodies (1980) and completed Post-graduate Journalist Studies at the University of Warsaw (1988). From 1984-1991, he worked as Editor-in-Chief at magazines and newspaper in Warsaw. Between 1991-1997, he was a member of the Sejm and served as member of the Foreign Affairs Committee, Culture and Media Committee and member of Poland-Columbia and Poland-South Korea parliamentary bilateral group. Between 1993-1996, he was member of the National Broadcasting Council and the Parliamentary Assembly of the Council of Europe. He was Secretary of State 1996-2004 and National Security Adviser to the President and Head of the National Security Bureau from 2000-2004.

Janusz Stanczyk (1955-)

From 1978-1992, he was a scholar at the Historical and Legal Institute of the Jagiellonian University and the Institute of Legal Sciences of the Polish Academy of Sciences. He received a

Ph.D. in legal sciences form the Institute of Legal Sciences of the Polish Academy of Sciences in 1985 based on his dissertation *Common Heritage of Mankind as a Concept of International Law*. From 1992-1996 and 1998-2000, he was a member of Poland's delegation to the UN General Assembly. In 2000, he was appointed the Permanent Representative of Poland to the United Nations. Prior to this appointment, he was Under-Secretary of State responsible for legal and economic affairs, Poland's relations with international organizations and the Foreign Ministry's contact with the Sejm. He has also participated in the negotiations of many multilateral and bilateral treaties.

1957

Agnieszka Magdziak-Miszewska (1957-)

She was counselor-minister at the Polish embassy in Moscow (1991-1995), adviser to Prime Minister Jerzy Buzek on Polish-Jewish affairs) from 1995 to 1997 and director of the independent Center for International Relations (2000-2001). She was Polish Consul General in New York from 2001-2005.

1958

Wieslaw Kaczmarek (1958-)

In 1981, he graduated from the Warsaw Technical University with a M.Sc. in Industrial Automation at the Precision Engineering Department. From 1984-1989, he was senior assistant at the Mechanics and Technology Department of the Warasaw Technical University, Deputy Director of the Industrial & Commercial Chamber of Foreign Investors (1989-1991) and branch manager of Pierwszy Komercyjny Bank SA (1991-1993). He has been a Member of Parliament since 1989 and has served as Minister of Privatization (1993-1996), Minister of Economy (1997) and Minister of the Treasury since 2001.

Malgorzata Ostrowska (1958-)
She obtained an MA in Political Studies at the University of Gdansk and taught Polish literature from 1982-1988. From 1987-1992, she was the commander of a scout troop in the Polish Scouts Association. Since 1993, she has been a Member of Parliament and in 2002, she was appointed Secretary of State at the Ministry of the Treasury.

1959

Stanislaw Lojasiewicz
At the end of the fifties, he solved the problem of distribution division by analytical functions. Its solution opened the road to important results in the new theory of partial differential equations. The method established by him led to the advancement of the theory of semi-analytical sets, which opened an important chapter inn modern analysis.

1960

Magdalena Abakanowicz (1930 -)
A world-renowned artist, she studied at the Warsaw Academy of Fine arts and sought to escape from conventional art forms through weaving. In 1960 she achieved international recognition with her monumental abstract woven fibre installations called "Abakans". Her works in bronze including "Hand-Like Tree", which was on exhibit in Central Park, are simple in form but redolent with the power of suggestion and emotional impact.

Tadeusz Bak (1960-)
A materials scientist, he received his B. Ph.D. from University Mining and Metallurgy in 1992 and was a research associate lecturer from 1992-1995. He has contributed articles to Solid State Ionics, Journal of European Ceramics Society, Ceramika and Bulletin of Polish Academy of Science. In 1997, he published a book *Electrical Properties of Oxide Materials* (1997).

Wladislaw Tatarkiewicz

Philosopher, historian and aesthetician, he was a great figure in the Polish humanities. In his monumental *History of Aesthetics* (which appeared in the years 1960-67, in three volumes) he introduced a pair of very important concepts: *implicite* and *explicite* aesthetics that became very famous and internationally recognized. The first embraces all views implied in works of art, while the latter refers to systematic theories.

1962

Slawomir Chlon (1962-)

Software company executive, he graduated with M of Engineering from the Technical University of Warsaw and is a certified vehicle mechanic. From 1986-1987, he worked as Public Relations Specialist at International Computer Ltd. and since 1999, he is vice president and managing director for Computer Systems Business International.

1969

Irena Malinowska

In 1969, she received a patent for a method of disinfecting refrigerator rooms that allowed the room to be disinfected without warming since the freezing point of her disinfectant was below -20°C.

Andrzej Towpik

He obtained his doctor in law degree from the Jagiellonian University in 1969 and was a research fellow in the Polish Institute of International Affairs from 1962-1975. Since 1975, he has been in the Ministry of Foreign Affairs. He has served as 1st Secretary of the Embassy of Poland in Madrid (1977-1981), Deputy Director of the Policy Planning Department (1981-1986), Counselor-Minister of the Polish Mission to UN (1986-1990) and Political Director of the Ministry of Foreign Affairs (1994). From 1997-2002, he was Ambassador, Head of the Polish Mission to NATO and WEU.

1976
Wojciech Kosinski

In 1976 he received his Ph.D. from the Architectural Technology Department at the University of Krakow. Author of many publications on scientific subjects, urban planning and architecture, he has given numerous guest lectures in Europe, has his own Studio Company on planning and urban architecture, and is currently Assistant Professor at the Architectural Technology Department, University of Krakow.

1989
Stanislaw Radwan

He completed his doctorate at the University Marie Curie Sklodowska and commenced his professional career at the Academy of Agriculture in Lublin, Poland, where he has been full Professor since 1989. He has specialized in the ecology of water animals, especially invertebrates, and the human impact on the protection of inland waters, about which he has published 60 original scientific papers and 35 scientific articles. Also, he has been participated in many international, limnological conferences and has organized national hydro-biological meetings, conferences and seminars.

1990
Tomasz Michalak

He graduated from Warsaw University with an MA in Political Studies specializing in International Relations. From 1990-1996 he was Deputy Director of the International Relations Office of the Central Board of Customs where he was responsible for European Integration and Customs Policy and worked on drafting the Customs Code, transit procedures and computerization. He was appointed Under-Secretary of State in Ministry of Finance and Chief of the Customs Service.

1991

Irena Borowik

She is a sociologist of religion at the Institute for the Study of Religion, Jagiellonian University. Since 1991, she is Director of NOMOS Publishing House and has published and edited many works on the study of religion including *The Future of Religion: East-West and New Religious Phenomena in Central and Eastern Europe.*

1993

Hanna Suchocka (1946-)

After receiving a Master of Law degree (1968) and Doctor of Law degree (1975), she became Prime Minister of the Republic of Poland in 1993 - the first female Prime Minister in post-communist Eastern Europe. Since she lost power, she has become one of the most active politicians in Poland. From 1982-1985, she was a member of the Parliament of Poland and a member of the Parliamentary Committee for Foreign Affairs and the Constitutional Committee of the National Assembly (1991-1997). She was a member of the Polish Delegation for the Parliamentary Assembly of the Council of Europe from 1991-1992 and 1994-1997. Since 1990, she has been a member of the Venice Commission "Democracy through Law" and since 1997, she is Minister of Justice, Attorney General.

1996

Wislawa Szymborska (1923 -)

She received Nobel Prize for Literature in 1996 for poetry that allows the historically and biological context to emerge in fragments of human reality. She has been described as the Mozart of poetry. During 1945-1948 she studied Polish Literature and Sociology at the Jagiellonian University and made her poetry début in March 1945 with a poem "Szukam slowa" (*I am Looking for a Word*) in the daily "Dziennik Polski". From 1953-1981 she worked as poetry editor and columnist in the Kraków literary weekly "Zycie Literackie". In 1995, she received a degree of Honorary Doctor of Letters of Poznan University. Her poetry has been translated (and published in book form) in English, German, Swedish, Italian, Danish, Hebrew, Hungarian, Czech, Slovakian, Serbo-Croatian, Romanian, Bulgarian as well as in Arabic, Hebrew, Japanese and Chinese.

1997

Jerzy Chmiel

He is Professor of Biblical Hermeneutics and Judaism at the Pontifical Academy of Theology in Krakow where he has been Vice-Rector since 1997. A Catholic Priest, he is a Member of the Studiorum Novi Testamenti Societas and the International Organization for the Study of the Old Testament. He is also editor-in-chief of the quarterly *Ruch Biblijny I Liturgiczny.*

2000

Roman Madejewski

In 2000, he created a new variety of pea which is characterized by the fact that leaves have been replaced by runners. This makes the plant easier to harvest. The Piast pea variety is a commercial success and the first Polish species to be registered in the UK.

Czeslaw Mietek

He co-developed a new variety of regenerative materials, namely epoxide-metallic composites and was named Champion of Technology in 2000. The material he developed is like plastic metal or plastic rubber and is used in industry for regenerating pumps and machines.

POLISH RECIPES

APPETIZERS:

Paluszki
(Little Fingers)

½ cup butter
½ cup cooked potato, mashed
½ cup flour
1 egg, beaten
1 tbs caraway seed
Dash of salt

Combine butter, potato and flour to make a dough. Place on a well-floured board and knead. Refrigerate for 15 minutes, then roll out very thinly. Cut into narrow strips. Place on a well-greased baking tray and brush with beaten egg. Sprinkle with salt and caraway seeds.

Preheat oven to 475F. Bake for approx. 10 minutes, until golden. Serves 4.

Sledzie w Smietanie
(Herring with Sour Cream)

Herring is a traditional Polish appetizer. There is an abundance of herring in Poland as it is fished in large quantities in the Baltic Sea. This is a favorite recipe.

12 salted herring fillets
4 oz onion, diced
4 hard-boiled eggs
1 cup sour cream

Rinse the herrings and set aside. Peel and dice onions. Mix onions with sour cream in bowl. Add herrings and chill.

When ready to serve, decorate with sliced hard-boiled eggs. Serves 4.

SALAD:

Mizeria
(Cucumber Salad)

1 large cucumber ¼ pint sour cream 1 tsp salt juice of ½ a lemon 2 tbs freshly chopped dill	Peel and slice cucumber. Place in colander, sprinkle with salt and leave drain for 30 minutes. Rinse and pat dry. Arrange cucumber in dish. Make dressing from sour cream and lemon juice. Pour over cucumber, sprinkle with dill and serve.

SOUPS:

Zupa Ogorkowa
(Sour Cucumber Soup)

1 qt chicken stock 2 medium potatoes 2 medium cucumbers, pickled in brine 2 tbs butter ½ cup sour cream 1 tsp flour salt & pepper	Heat the stock. Peel and dice potatoes and boil in stock until soft. Peel the cucumbers and grate coarsely. Melt butter and add grated cucumber until soft. Add to stock and potatoes. Mix sour cream with flour and stir into soup. Season with salt and pepper. Serve immediately without bringing to boil. Serves 4.

Zupa Grzybowa (Mushroom Soup)

This is a simple but filling soup dating from the Middle Ages.

1 lb mushrooms 2 large onions juice of ½ lemon vegetable stock ⅓ pint sour cream croutons parsley	Slice and fry the mushrooms and onions, place in a dish. Make 2½ pints of vegetable stock in a large saucepan and add juice of ½ lemon. When stock comes to boil, add fried mushrooms and onions. (Soup can be cooled and stored for later use.) When ready to serve, bring soup to boil, add sour cream stirring briskly at full heat until the creamed surface of the soup flares upwards. Serve with croutons and garnish with parsley. Serves 6.

VEGETABLES:

Kalafior po Polsku (Cauliflower a al Polonaise)

1 large cauliflower salt 3 tbs butter 4 tbs breadcrumbs	Wash the cauliflower and divide into florets. Cook in lightly salted boiling water until tender. Drain. Melt butter and fry breadcrumbs until golden. Pour over cauliflower just before serving. Serves 6.

Placki Kartoflane
(Potato Pancakes)

3 large potatoes
1 small onion
1¼ cup sour cream
salt and pepper
oil (for frying)

Peel potatoes and onion, grate coarsely. Mix well and squeeze out as much excess liquid as possible. Season with salt and pepper.

When pan is hot, put large spoonfuls of potato mixture and immediately flatten until quite thin. When bottom is brown, turn over. Serve with sour cream. Serves 4.

Grzyby Duszone w S'mietanie
(Creamed Mushrooms)

1½ lb fresh mushrooms, sliced
2 medium onions, minced
4 tbs butter
1 tbs dill, chopped
¾ cup sour cream
1 tbs flour

Gently wash mushrooms. In large skillet, simmer onions and butter until tender. Add mushrooms and 1 cup water. Simmer for 30 minutes or until tender. Season with salt and pepper and add the dill. Blend the sour cream and flour separately; and add to mushrooms.

Polish Cabbages with Apple

- 1 medium head cabbage
- 1 tbs Salt
- 3 or 4 green apples
- 2 tomatoes (optional)
- 1 tsp sugar
- 1 tbs butter
- 3 slices crisp bacon
- 2 sliced onions

Shred cabbage. Cover cabbage and onion with boiling water. Let stand 10 minutes.

Place butter and bacon in bottom of kettle. Remove seeds from tomatoes. Add drained cabbage with onion, apples and tomatoes. Add sugar and simmer until tender, about 20 minutes.

FISH:

Fladra z Grzybami
(Flounder with Mushrooms)

- 2 lbs flounder
- 1½ cups milk
- ½ cup flour
- ½ tsp salt
- 1 cup water
- 2½ cups mushrooms
- ⅓ cup butter

Place founder in pan, add 1 cup water and ½ tsp salt. Simmer until flounder is tender. Drain off and place water on side allowing fish to cool.

After cool, slice flounder into large pieces. Place back in pan and add chopped mushrooms. Fry in butter until brown. Mix remaining flounder stock with flour and milk, stir constantly and bring to boil. Simmer until thick and serve.

MEAT:

Polish Pierogi

Dough

4 cups flour
2 eggs
½ cup sour cream
1 tsp salt
¾ cup warm water

Mix flour, eggs, sour cream, and salt. Add water, a little at a time. Knead dough until firm and elastic. Cover and let rest 10 minutes.

Divide dough into 3 parts. On floured surface, roll dough about ⅛-inch thick, cut into 3-inch rounds. Place a spoonful of filling in center of each round, fold and press edges together firmly to seal.

Drop the pierogi in simmering chicken bouillon with 1 tsp of oil. Do not crowd. Simmer for 15 minutes, stirring gently to prevent sticking. Remove with slotted spoon and drain well.

Potato Filling

3 medium potatos
½ medium onion
¼ cup butter
salt and pepper

Cook, drain and mash potatoes. Dice onion and sauté in butter until golden. Mix potatoes and onion, add salt and pepper to taste.

Cheese Filling

1 lb dry cottage cheese
2 eggs
½ tsp salt
¼ cup butter

Beat eggs and melt butter. Combine cottage cheese, beaten eggs, salt and butter, mix.

Beef Filling

- 1 large onion, sliced
- 2 tbs margarine
- 1¾ cups ground beef
- ¾ cup cooked rice
- 2 tsp beef bouillon
- 3 tbs hot water
- 1 tbs chopped parsley

Sauté onion in margarine. Stir in meat and rice. Dissolve bouillon in hot water. Add to meat mixture with parsley. Salt and pepper to taste.

Sauerkraut & Mushroom Filling

- 2½ cups sauerkraut
- ½ cup chopped onion
- 4 oz mushrooms, sliced
- ¼ tsp pepper
- 1 hard-boiled egg, chopped
- 2 tbs sour cream

Cook sauerkraut about 20 minutes in saucepan. In frying pan, saute onion and mushrooms in butter. Stir in sauerkraut and pepper. Fry until sauerkraut is golden. Add chopped egg and sour cream. Mix.

Fruit Filling

2 cups pitted cherries, blueberries or apples ¾ cup water ½ cup sugar - optional ½ tsp cinnamon 1 tsp lemon juice 3 tbs dry bread crumbs	Combine fruit, water and sugar in saucepan. Bring to boil and simmer until fruit is tender and water is almost gone. Remove from heat and mash slightly with potato masher. Add cinnamon and lemon juice. Cook and stir over low heat until thick. Stir in enough bread crumbs to further thicken.

Bigos
(Hunter's Stew)

Poland's national dish and every family has its own recipe for Bigos. The ingredients vary - some use mushrooms and juniper berries while others contain apples, venison, lamb or beef. It is best-prepared two days in advance and reheated on low heat before serving which enhances the flavor.

¼ cup butter 2 onions, peeled & chopped 1 can sauerkraut 1 can tomatoes, peeled 1 small white cabbage 1¼ cup beef stock ½ lb smoked Polish sausage 5 to 6 pork ribs salt and pepper	Melt butter in saucepan and fry onions until golden. Rinse sauerkraut in cold water, drain thoroughly and mix with the onions. Add tomatoes. Chop the cabbage finely and mix in. Add the stock, stirring well and then the pork ribs. Slice the sausage and add to the stew. Simmer on low heat for one hour. Season to taste. Remove from heat and leave covered for 24 hours. Refrigerate and reheat before serving. Serves 8.

Golabki
(Stuffed Cabbage Rolls)

- 1 head cabbage
- 1 lb ground beef
- ½ lb ground pork or veal (optional)
- 1 can tomato soup
- 2 cups cooked rice
- 2 eggs
- 1 onion finely chopped
- 2 tbs margarine
- salt and pepper

Remove core from cabbage and put in boiling water. Remove leaves as they soften.

Saute onions in margarine until golden. In bowl, mix onions, meat, rice, and eggs. Add salt and pepper to taste.

Place portion of meat mixture on cabbage leaf, fold in sides and then roll leaf. Put rolled cabbage next to each other in pot. Pour tomato soup over rolls and simmer over low heat for 2 hours. Serve.

Kapusta Duzona
(Stewed Cabbage and Meat)

1 lb boneless pork, cubed
1 large onion, diced
1 small cabbage
2-5 tsps vinegar
1 tsp caraway seeds
1 tbs chopped dill
1 tbs sour cream

Roll pork in flour and brown in few tbs of cooking oil in skillet. Add diced onion, reduce heat, add a little water and simmer the mixture covered until tender.

Shred cabbage, place in pot and scald with boiling water to cover. Bring cabbage to boil and simmer until soft and translucent. Drain cabbage.

Combine cabbage with pork and simmer together in skillet a few minutes. Season to taste with salt, pepper, vinegar, caraway and dill. Mix in the sour cream. Serves 4.

DESERTS:

Paczki
(Doughnuts)

Doughnuts are very popular in Poland and traditionally eaten on Shrove Tuesday, at midnight on St. Sylvester's Day (New Year's Eve) and also at Epiphany (January 6th) when a coin is normally hidden in one of them.

- 4 cups flour
- 2 cups warm water
- 2 pkgs yeast
- ¾ cup sunflower oil
- 2 oz rum
- salt
- powdered sugar

Mix half the flour with 1 cup warm water and yeast. Leave to rise in warm place for 20 minutes. Mix the remaining flour, water, sunflower oil and rum. Sprinkle a little salt on the dough and knead until it becomes moist. Sprinkle lightly with flour and leave to rise in warm place about 30 minutes. When you press dough with your finger and it springs back immediately, it is ready to fry.

Pull off pieces of dough and shape into doughnuts. Set aside. Heat oil in deep frying pan until very hot and drop doughnuts into it. Fry until brown on all sides. When cooked, they should feel light when pricked with a toothpick.

Drain on paper towels and sprinkle with powdered sugar. Makes about 16.

Jablka Smazone w Ciescie
(Apple Fritters)

2 eggs, separated
3 tbs sugar
5 tbs cream
½ cup flour
1 tbs cornstarch
1 lb cooking apples
½ cup oil
powdered sugar

To make batter, beat egg yolks with sugar and cream. Whisk egg whites until very stiff and fold in. Sift flour and cornstarch and mix in lightly.

Peel, core and cut apples into rings. Spike the apple rings and turn in the batter. Heat oil in frying pan and drop the apple rings in it. Fry on both sides until golden and nicely puffed up. Sprinkle with powdered sugar. Serves 2-4.

Piernik
(Honey Cake)

1 cup honey
1 cup strong coffee
1 cup vegetable oil
1 tsp ground cinnamon
1 tsp ground cloves
1 tsp ground nutmeg

3 large eggs
1 cup brown sugar
3 tsp baking powder
4 cups flour

Mix together the honey, coffee, oil, cinnamon, cloves and nutmeg, bring to boil. Then set aside and allow to cool to warm temperature.

In mixing bowl, beat eggs, brown sugar and baking powder. Slowly add the above liquid to the beaten eggs, beating at slow speed. Add flour and mix thoroughly.

Preheat oven to 350F and grease 3 loaf pans. Pour final mixture into the loaf pans and bake for 45-55 minutes, until an inserted toothpick comes out clean. Remove pans from oven and cool for 15 minutes.

<u>Frosting</u>:
2½ oz semi-sweet chocolate
3 oz sweet butter
⅓ cup water
½ tsp vanilla extract
1 cup confectionery sugar

Stir chocolate, butter, vanilla and water together, gradually adding sugar. Bring it slowly to boil, stirring constantly. Let it boil for 5 minutes. Cool until it becomes a think mass, easily spreadable with a knife.

Place cakes upside down and spread chocolate frosting evenly on top and sides. Cool in refrigerator until frosting is hard. Wrap in aluminum foil, then in plastic. Store in refrigerator or cold place for 4 weeks before serving.

Chrusiki
(Polish Bows)

9 egg yolks
3 tbs sour cream
1 tbs rum
1 tsp vanilla
3 cups flour, sifted
½ tsp baking powder
½ tsp salt
3 tbs sugar
confectioners sugar
oil (for deep frying)

Beat egg yolks with sugar until well combined. Add sour cream, rum and vanilla and mix until smooth. Sift flour, baking powder and salt and add to egg yolk mixture, slowly. On a heavily floured surface, knead dough vigorously, punching and squeezing as much flour into it as it will take until the dough is no longer sticky.

Separate dough into several portions and roll very thin. Dough should look like parchment paper. Cut dough into strips about 1½-inches wide x 4 inches long. Make a slit closer to one end and bring the longer end through slit.

Heat oil to 375F and fry quickly (only a few seconds) until golden - not brown. Turn only once. Drain on paper towels. Dust with confectioners sugar. Makes 8 dozen.

Ciazteczka z Makiem
(Poppyseed Cookies)

¼ lb butter
⅔ cup confectioners sugar
2 egg yolks
3 tbs sour cream
2¾ cup flour
2 tsp baking powder
1 egg
3 tbs poppyseeds

Combine all ingredients and mix well. Knead dough for few minutes and refrigerate for 15 minutes.

Roll out dough ⅛-inch. Using cookie cutters, cut dough and place on greased cookie sheet. Bake for 10 minutes at 375F.

Polish Saints

Saint Florian (3rd Century)

Martyr. 3rd Century Roman officer, military administrator of the town of Noricum, and a closet Christian. Said to have stopped a town from burning by throwing a single bucket of water on the blaze, and thus his association with firefighters and those who protect us from fire, including chimney sweeps. When ordered to execute a group of Christians during the persecutions of Diocletian, he refused, and professed his own faith. When he made his faith known, his final torture was to be skinned alive before being drowned in the River Enns with a millstone secured about his neck. Part of his relics were given to King Casimir of Poland and the bishop of Krakow by Pope Lucius III, which led to Florian's patronage of Poland

Saint Wojciech (956-997)

Bishop and martyr. He lived as a Benedictine monk in Rome and in 982 was consecrated Bishop of Prague and founded the Abbey of Brevnov. He twice left his diocese to protest against heathen practices. In 996, after the murder of his family by the Vrsovecs, he returned to Poland and Boleslaus I, duke of Poland, invited him to evangelize the Prussians of Pomerania. He was murdered by pagan Prussians in 997 with six spears piercing his body on suspicion of being a Polish spy. Duke Boleslaw, the Bold, had him buried in Gniezno Cathedral where he had been ordained. Adalbert lived as a Benedictine monk in Rome.

Saint Brunon Bonifacy (974-1009)

Priest and Second Apostle of the Prussians and martyr from Kwerfurt. He joined the monastery of Pereum and in 1004 he was consecrated and given property for the founding of a monastery. In 1008 he went to found a mission among the Prussians but was not successful. He traveled toward the borders of Russian and was attached by the heathen and murdered.

Saint Stanislaus Szczepanowski (1030-1079)

Polish nobility. Stanislas studied canon law and theology in Gniezno in 1030 . On the death of his parents, Stanislas gave away his ample fortune, to the poor. He was ordained at Gnesen, a parish priest in Czembocz and in 1072 was named Bishop of Krakow. He gained a reputation for his charity and his work as a reformer and preacher. When he excommunicated King Boleslaus for cruelties and injustices and stopped services at the Cathedral when the King entered. Boleslaus killed him while the Bishop was saying Mass in a chapel. Saint Stanislaus has long been a symbol of Polish nationhood and is the principle patron of Krakow. Pope Innocent IV canonized him in 1253.

Saint Otto (1060-1139)

Bishop and missionary of Pomerania. He was consecrated Bishop of Bamberg in 1106 where he devoted himself to his diocese. He founded over 20 monasteries, reformed others and was known as of "Father of the Monks".. However, his greatest service was his missionary work among the Pomeranians. Between 1120-1125 he established 11 churches and baptized over 22,000 people

Saint Izaak - 10th century

Hermit, martyr Benedictine monk. Missionary with Saint Adalbert of Prague to the Slavs. He was martyred in 1005 by robbers near Gnesen

St Hedwig (1174-1243)

Educated in the Benedictine Convent, she married Henryk I Brodatega, Duke of Greater Poland. She had a great zeal for religion and she lived like a hermit within the court of her husband and eventually donated her entire fortune to the church and the poor. After her husband died in 1238, she entered the Cisterian convent of Trebnitz, which she helped found. St. Hedwig was the patron saint of Silesia, Wroclaw and Krakow.

Saint Hyacinth (1185-1257)
Priest, known as Apostle to Poland. A Doctor of Sacred Studies and a priest, he worked to reform convents in Poland, evangelized throughout the country and also brought the Dominican Order to Poland. In 1219, entered the Dominican Order in Poland. By 1228, Hyacinth was enrolled with the Dominicans in Krakow in the Holy Trinity Church. He was the founder of a number of houses, such as Krakow Dominican Order in 1222 and Gdansk in 1227. During an attack on a monastery, Hyacinth managed to save a crucifix and statue of Mary, though the statue weighed far more than he could normally have lifted.

Saint Kunegunda [nickname Kinga] (1234-1292)
Princess of Poland, she was married to Prince Boleslas the Chaste but by mutual consent, the marriage was not consummated. During the 40 years of marriage, they shared the many sufferings that the Tartar invasion subjected them. She spent her time in prayer, mortification and daily attendance on the poor in the hospitals. After Boleslas's death in 1279, she took the veil in the Sandecz Abbey, which she had built for the Poor Clare nuns. In the course of her lifetime, she had built churches and hospitals, paid the expenses of chapters of the Friars Minor, and ransomed Christians from the Turks. Her last years were marked by many miracles and supernatural manifestations.

Saint Jadwiga (1374-1399)
Crowned King of Poland in 1382 and later co-ruled with her husband. She is known for her charity to all but especially the sick and poor and for a revision of the laws to help the poor.

Saint Jan Kanty (1390-1473)
Priest, Though he left the Academy of Krakow for a time after his graduation, he soon returned there as professor of Sacrae Scripturae, a position he held until his death in 1473.Cantius

was noted throughout his life for his good humor and humility. He would subsist only on what was strictly necessary to sustain his life, giving the rest of his salary away to the poor. He made four pilgrimages to Rome and was declared patron of Poland and Lithuania in 1737 by Pope Clement XII, 30 years before his final canonization.

Saint John of Dukla (1414-1484)

Hermit, Franciscan Priest, In 1463 he joined part of the Observant Franciscans, who observed their Rule very strictly. Helped repel a Tartar attack on Lvív in 1474. His life was characterized by poverty, obedience, asceticism, and devotion to Our Lady. Sought to reconcile schismatics to the Church. Blind at age 70, he continued his ministry as preacher and confessor

Saint Kazimierz (1461-1484)

As Prince of Poland, his life was scheduled to cement his father's authority and increase Poland's power but Kazimierz was committed to God from childhood, showed his devotion to God in his love for the poor, and he gave away all his worldly goods. When his father, furius at being deterred from his plans, banished Kazimierz to a castle in Dobzki, Kazimierz's commitment to what he believed was right only grew stronger in his exile. Because of his love for the hymn "Daily, Daily Sing to Mary", it is know as the Hymn of St. Kazimierz even though he didn't write it.

Saint Stanislaus Kostka (1550-1568)

Jesuit friar, he is the patron saint of youth. Known for his amiability, cheerfulness, and spirit of devotion, He entered the Society of Jesus in 1567 and died 10 months later. One of the popular saints of Poland, he was chosen as the protector of noviatiates by many religious institutions.

Saint Jan Sarkander (1576-1620)

Priest, martyr of the confessional. Ordained in 1607. When Polish forces moved into the Hollenshau area during the Thirty Years War, he visited the field commander and no battles were fought there. He was subsequently branded a spy by the Protestant forces, arrested and tortured for a confession and to get him to break the seal of the confessional.

Saint Jozofat Kuncewicz (1580-1623)

Bishop. He was the first leader of the Ruthenian Catholics. In 1604 he entered the monastery of the Holy Trinity at Vilna and was admitted to the Basilican Order. He became abbot at Vilna in 1614 and visited a community of 200 monks at the Caves at Kiev. In 1620, he became Bishop of Vitebsk and turned the Ruthenians back to the Orthodox. As archbishop he restored the churches, issued a catechism to the clergy with instructions that he should be learned by heart and composed rules for the priestly life. He was murdered by Orthodox fanatics in 1623.

Saint Melchior Grodziecki (1582-1619)

Priest, martyr. Born into the Polish aristocracy in Silesia, he joined the Jesuits in 1603. During the 30-Years' War, he arrived in Kosice, Hungary to help the few Catholics who lived in the city and its outlying district who had been without a priest for some time. The Calvinist Minister arrested, brutually burned, dismembered, and beheaded him.

Saint Andrzej Bobalo (1591-1657)

A Jesuit missionary and martyr, he was known as "an Apostle of Pinszczyzna" and "a hunter of souls". Ordained in 1622, he taught the elements of Christian doctrine at Vilna. By public sermons, private instruction, the fervor of his exceptional holiness and the zeal of his apostate in the countries to the East, he freed the wavering faith of a multitude of Christians, brought them back to sound principles, and invited all he could to return to Jesus Christ. In 1657 he was captured by the Cossacks of Chmielnicki, subjected to incredible slow and diabolical tortures and killed. In 1701 his body was found completely undecomposed, which was widely recognized as a proof of holiness. Since May 16, 2002 Andrew Bobola is a patron saint of Poland. He is a patron saint of the Warsaw archdiocese too.

Saint Rafal' Kalinowski (1835-1907)
A Polish Discalced Carmelite friar. In 1877 Kalinowski joined the Carmel of Linz, and took the name "Brother Raphael of St. Joseph. Kalinowski was ordained as priest at Czerna in 1882 by Bishop Albin Dunajewski, and in 1883 became prior of the convent at Czerna. He founded multiple Catholic organizations around Poland and the Ukraine, most prominent of which was a monastery in Wadowice, Poland. From 1892-1907 he worked to document the life and work of Mother Theresa Marchocka, a 17th Century Discalced Carmelite, to assist with her beatification.

Saint Joseph Sebastian Pelczar (1842-1924)
Doctor of theology and a canon lawyer. Professor at the seminary at Przemysl from 1869 to 1877, and at the *University of Krakow* from 1877 to 1899, he was known as a great educator who was always available to students. Dean of the Theology Department. Rector of the *University of Krakow* from 1882 to 1883. All the while he was teaching Joseph was still involved at the parish level. He worked with the *Saint Vincent de Paul Society* and was president of the *Society for the Education of the People* for 16 years. He started hundreds of libraries, delivered free lectures, published over a thousand books, wrote several books of history, theology and canon law himself, and started a school for servants. He founded the *Fraternity of Our Lady, Queen of the Polish Crown* in 1891; the *Fraternity* cared for the poor, orphans, apprentices, servants, the sick and unemployed. Founded the *Congregation of Sister Servants of the Most Sacred Heart of Jesus* on 15 April 1894 in Krakow to work with the sick and spread devotion to the Sacred Heart of Jesus. He made frequent visits to the parishes, supported

the religious orders, conducted three synods, and worked for the education and religious formation of his priests. He encouraged devotion to the Blessed Sacrament, Eucharistic devotions, the Sacred Heart of Jesus, and the Virgin Mary. He built and restored churches, built nurseries, kitchens, homeless shelters, schools for the poor, and gave tuition assistance to poor seminarians.

Saint Albert Chmielowski (1845-1916)

Friar. In 1863, he took part in the failed uprisings against the Russian occupation and was imprisoned where his left leg was amputated. After 10 years as an artist, he joined the Jesuits. After a nervous breakdown, he left and began a life of working with and for the poorest of Krakow. In 1887 he founded the *Brothers of the Third Order of Saint Francis, Servants of the Poor*, known as the *Albertines* (named for him) or the *Gray Brothers* (after their rough gray habits). In 1891 he founded the women's congregation of the Order (*Gray Sisters*). The Albertines organized food and shelter for the poor and homeless.

Saint Zygmunt Gorazdowski (1845-1920)

Priest, he was Ordained in 1871. Organized The Affordable Public House and The House for Workers, shelters for the poor, hungry, and homeless. Built a dormitory for poor students of a teacher's college so they could concentrate on study. Founded The House of the Child Jesus, a shelter for abandoned children and single mothers and their children. Founded a convent for the Sister of Mercy of Saint Joseph in 1884 so the sisters could help with these organizations; their mission was to work in boarding schools, and to care for the aged and sick Wrote catechisms and other educational works.

Saint Józef Bilczewski (1860-1923)

Catholic archbishop of the city of Lwów, a professor of theology at the Lwów University and a rector of that school. Bilczewski started an extensive work on construction of new churches and initiated the construction of more than 330 churches in the arch-diocese of Lwów alone, including the monumental St. Elisabeth's Church. Guided his flock during World War I (1914-1918), the Polish-Ukrainian War (1918-1919), the Bolshevik invasion (1919-1920), and the anti-Catholic terror started by the Communists; from 1918-1921 his archdiocese lost about 120 priests. During the World War I he was one of the people to create committees of relief for the workers of Galicia, severely touched by the war and shortages of food. During the Polish-Ukrainian War of 1918 and the Siege of Lwów, he was responsible for organization of food convoys for the besieged city. His help for the poor and the homeless was awarded by the homeless themselves with the title of *honorary patron of louts* in 1917.

Saint Maria Karlowska (1865- 1935)

The daughter of pious parents, was taught her devotions to God. and had a great devotion to the Sacred Heart of Jesus. She wanted to use this devotion to send Jesus' mission to the world. She cared for the sick young women in her region of Poland. St. Karlowska was the founder of the Good Shepherd Sisters in Poland.

Saint Bernardina Maria Jablonska (1878-1940)

Co-foundress of the *Sisters of the Third Order of Saint Francis Servants of the Poor* (*Albertine Sisters*). Known as a mystic with a great concern for those who are suffering. As superior of the *Sisters* she founded hospices for the sick and poor.

Saint Teresa Benedicta of the Cross (1891-1942)

Polish Saint, philosopher, a Carmelite nun, and martyr who died at Auschwitz. She entered the Carmelite convent at Cologne in 1934 and took the name Teresa Benedicta of the Cross. There she wrote her metaphysical book *Endliches und ewiges Sein* which tries to combine the philosophies of Aquinas and Husserl. To avoid the growing Nazi threat, her order transferred her to the Carmelite convent in the Netherlands. There she wrote *Studie über Joannes a Cruce: Kreuzeswissenschaft* ("The Science of the Cross: Studies on John of the Cross").

Saint Maksymilian Kolbe (1894-1941)
Priest, friar and martyr. He joined the Franciscan Order in 1910 and founded the Knights of the Immaculata in 1917. In 1919, father Maksymilian returned to the newly independent Poland, where he was very active in promoting the veneration of the Immaculate Virgin Mary, founding and supervising the monastery of Niepokalanów near Warsaw, a seminary, a radio station, and several other organizations and publications. Between 1930 and 1936, he took a series of missions to Japan, where he founded a monastery at the outskirts of Nagasaki, a Japanese paper, and a seminary.During the Second World War, in the Niepokalanów friary, he provided shelter to refugees from Greater Poland, including 2,000 Jews. In 1941, he was arrested by the Germans and later transferred to Auschwitz. Although ill, he continued to hear confessions, say prayers and sacrificed his life for that of the family of Francis Gajowniczek.

Saint Faustyna Kowalska (1905-1938)
Polish nun and mystic. She joined the Sisters of Our Lady of Mercy in Warsaw and took her vows as a nun in 1928. Her diary was later published under the title *Divine Mercy in My Soul: The Diary of St. Faustina*.The Chaplet of the Divine Mercey is based on the remarkable prayer she recalled from a vision in 1935. She never was able to found the religious order which Jesus had asked for, but she had left clear rules for the life of the prospective community, and at last in 1941, the order, now known as the Institute of Divine Mercy, was founded.

Common Polish First Names

The following is a brief list of some common first names in Poland together with the corresponding Name Day. These names are based on the saints and feast days as found in the old-style Proper of the Saints of the Roman Calendar. There are also many first names that are celebrated on more than one saint's name and feast day, which are not included. Is your name on this list?

English Name	Polish Name	Date	Comment
Albert, George	Wojciech, Jerzy	Apr 23	
Adam	Adam	Dec 24	
Agatha	Agata	Feb 5	
Albert	Albert	Nov 15	Albert the Great
Alexander	Aleksander	May 5	
Anna	Anna	July 26	mother of Mary
Barbara	Barbara	Dec 4	
Basil	Bazyli	June 14	Basil the Great
Benedict	Benedykt	Apr 23	

English Name	Polish Name	Date	Comments
Bernice, Bertha	Bronislawa	Sept 3	
Camille	Kamilia	July 18	
Casimir	Kazimierz	Mar 4	patron of Poland & Lithuania
Caspar	Kasper	Jan 8	Caspar, one of the Magi
Catherine	Katarczyna	Apr 30	
Cecelia	Cecylia	Nov 22	
Chester	Czeslaw	July 17	
Christopher	Krzysztof	July 25	
Clara, Clare	Klara	Aug 12	
Conrad	Konrad	Mar 11	Constantine, King of Cornwall (first martyr of Scotland)
Dolores	Doloreta	Sept 15	Seven Sorrows of the Blessed Virgin Mary
Dominic	Dominik	Aug 4	
Edmund	Edmund	Nov 20	
Eva	Ewa	Dec 24	Christmas Eve

English Name	Polish Name	Date	Comment
Felicity, Phyllis	Felicia	Mar 6	
Florian	Florjan	May 4	patron of Poland and Upper Austria
Frances	Franciszka	Mar 9	
Frederick	Fryderyk	July 18	
Gabriel	Gabriel	Mar 24	Archangel
Genevieve	Genowefa	Jan 3	
Gertrude	Giertruda	Nov 16	
Hattie	Jadwiga	Feb 28	Saint Jadwiga, Queen of Poland
Helen	Halina	Aug 18	
Hyacinth	Hiacynt, Jacek	Aug 17	Hyacinth, patron of Poland
Irene	Irina	Apr 3	
January	Januariusz	Sept 19	
John	Jan	July 10	John of Dukla, patron of Poland & Lithuania
Joseph	Jozef	Mar 19	Joseph, father of Jesus
Julia	Julia	May 22	
Justin	Justyn	Apr 14	
Karl, Charles	Karol	Jan 28	

English Name	Polish Name	Date	Comments
Laura	Leokadia	Dec 9	
Leonard	Leonard	Nov 6	
Louis	Ludwik	Aug 25	Louis IX, King of France
Louise	Ludwika	Mar 15	
Lucas, Luke	Lukasz	Oct 18	Luke the Evangelist
Lydia	Lidia	Aug 3	
Madeline	Magdalena	July 22	Mary Magdalene
Mark	Marek	Apr 25	Mark the Archangel
Martha	Marta	Jan 19	martyr
Matthew	Maciej	Sept 21	Apostle & Evangelist
Maximillan	Maksymillan	Aug 14	Maksymillan Kolbe
Cyril	Metody, Cyryl	July 7	Cyril & Methodius, Apostles of the Slavs
Michael	Mieczyslaw	Sept 29	Michael the Archangel
Michalina	Michalina	June 20	
Miecislaus	Mieczyslaw	Jan 1	Mieczyslaw I (King of Poland who accepted Christianity on behalf of all Poland)

English Name	Polish Name	Date	Comments
Monica, Mona	Monika	May 4	mother of St. Ausgustine
Olga, Sandra	Olga	July 11	
Paul	Pawel	Jan 15	Paul the Hermit
Pauline	Apolonia	Feb 9	
Peter	Piotr	June 29	Peter the Apostle
Petronilla	Petrolela	May 31	
Raphael	Rafal	Oct 24	Archangel
Regina	Regina	Sept 7	
Richard	Ryszard	Feb 7	
Rose	Roza	Aug 30	
Salome, Sarah	Salomeja	Nov 6	Blessed Salome
Sebastian	Sebastian	Jan 20	
Sigmund	Zygmunt	Oct 31	Zytmunt III Wasa, King of Poland
Simon	Szymon	July 30	Simon of Lipnica
Sophie	Zofia	Sept 30	
Stanley	Stanislawa	May 7	Stanislaus, Bishop of Krakow
Stanley	Stanislawa	Nov 13	Stanislaus Kostka, patron of Poland

English Name	Polish Name	Date	Comments
Stephen, Steven	Szczepan, Stefan	Dec 26	Stephen, the First Martyr
Thaddeus, Ted	Tadeusz	Oct 28	Jude Thaddeus the Apostle
Theresa	Teresa, Czeslawa	Oct 15	
Thomas	Tomasz	Mar 7	
Timothy	Timoteusz	Jan 24	
Ursula	Urzula	Oct 21	
Valentina	Walentyna	July 25	
Valentine	Walenty	Feb 14	Bishop/martyr
Valery	Walery	Apr 14	
Veronica	Weronika	July 12	
Vincent	Wicenty	Oct 11	Blessed Wincenty Kadlubek, bishop of Krakow
Viviana	Biblana	Dec 2	
Walter	Wladyslaw	May 11	Blessed Ladislaus of Gielnow, patron of Poland, Galicia and Lithuania
Walter	Waclaw	Sep 28	
William	Wilhelm	June 25	

English Name	Polish Name	Date	Comments
Yolanda	Jolanta	June 12	Blessed Jolenta (Helen of Poland)
Zachery	Zachariasz	Nov 5	Zachery, father of John the Baptist

Lightning Source UK Ltd.
Milton Keynes UK
UKOW052024040112

184746UK00003B/12/A

9 781425 918392